TRANSPORT GEOGRAPHY OF INDIA

ISBN 81-7022-089-0 (HB)

First Published 1986
Reprinted 1999

Published and Printed by
Ashok Kumar Mittal
Concept Publishing Company
A/15-16, Commercial Block, Mohan Garden,
NEW DELHI-110059 (India)

Phones : 25351460, 25351794
Fax : 091-11-25357103
***E-mail* : publishing@conceptpub.com**

TRANSPORT GEOGRAPHY OF INDIA

Commodity Flows and the Regional Structure of the Indian Economy

MOONIS RAZA

YASH AGGARWAL

CONCEPT PUBLISHING COMPANY, NEW DELHI

ACKNOWLEDGEMENTS

This volume is the end product of a research project entitled, "Commodity Flows and the Regional Structure of the Indian Economy" sponsored by the University Grants Commission, located at the Centre for the Study of Regional Development of the Jawaharlal Nehru University and directed by Professor Moonis Raza.

The contribution of the following to the present study is gratefully acknowledged:

* The University Grants Commission for sponsoring and funding the project:
* The Centre for the Study of Regional Development of the Jawaharlal Nehru University wherein the research project was located and its faculty members—particularly Professor G.S. Bhalla, Professor A. Mathur and Professor A. Kundu—for their advice and suggestions;
* Shri P.N. Tyagi for providing the necessary cartographic assistance;
* Staff members of the Computer Centre of the Jawaharlal Nehru University—particularly Shri Ajay Roy—for providing assistance in data processing;
* The following researchers who worked in the project for various durations and/or worked for their M. Phil/Ph.D. theses under the supervision of Professor Moonis Raza:

Name	Research Associate	Research Assistant	M.Phil	Ph.D.
Dr. Yash Aggarwal	*		*	*
Dr. H. Ramachandran	*			
Dr. N. Ramachandran				*
Dr. Ajay Kumar		*	*	*
Ms. Mondira Dutta		*	*	
Ms. Indu Khurana		*	*	
Saifur Rehman		*		

The list of Ph.D./M. Phil dissertations based on the work in the above mentioned project and carried out under the supervision of Professor Moonia Raza at the Centre for the Study of Regional Development of the Jawaharlal Nehru University is given below:

Ph.D. Theses

Aggarwal, Yash (1982): Railway Freight Flows, Transport Costs and the Regional Structure of the Indian Economy.

Kumar, Ajay (1979): Commodity Flows and the Spatial Organisation of the Indian Economy: An Analysis of Rural-Urban Interactions.

Ramachandran, Nira (1979): Commodity Flows and the Regional Organisation of the Indian Economy.

M.Phil Dissertations

Aggarwal, Yash (1979): Patterns of Railway Freight in India: A Regional Analysis.

Dutta, Mondira (1979): Metropolis and the Hinterland: A Spatial Analysis of Commodity Flows in India.

Khurana, Indu (1979): Economic Base and Freight Characteristics: A Study of the Indian Urban System.

*The list of research papers based on the work in the above mentioned project, jointly authored by Professor Moonis Raza and/or Dr. Y.P. Aggarwal and published in various journals is given below:

Research Papers Published

Moonis Raza & Aggarwal, Y.P. (1981): "Commodity Flows and the Levels of Development in India: A Districtwise Analysis", in L.R. Singh, *New Perspective in Geography*, Thinkers Library, Allahabad.

Aggarwal, Y.P. & Raza, Moonis (1981): "Railway Freight Flows and the Regional Structure of the Indian Economy", *The Geographer*, Aligarh.

Raza, Moonis & Aggarwal, Y.P. (1980): "Distance Decay and Railway Freight Flows in India: A Preliminary Enquiry", *Indian Journal of Regional Science*, Vol. XII, No. II.

Raza, Moonis, Aggarwal Y.P. & Khurana, Indu (1980): "Economic Base and Commodity Flows: A Case Study of the Indian Urban System". *The National Geographical Journal of India*, Vol. 26.

Raza, Moonis, Aggarwal, Y.P. & Dutta, Mondira (1980): "A Spatial Analysis of Metropolitan Freight Flows in India", *Geographical Review of India*, Vol. 42.

Some major findings of the various dissertations/theses and research publications mentioned above have been assimilated in the present volume. The contributions of the research team is gratefully acknowledged. However, the undersigned take the full responsibility for the errors and inadequacies of the present volume.

YASH AGGARWAL
National Institute of
Educational Planning and Administration
Aurobindo Marg, New Delhi
December 11, 1985

MOONIS RAZA
Vice-Chancellor
University of Delhi
Delhi

CONTENTS

LIST OF FIGURES

LIST OF TABLES

PART ONE

DATA BASE, METHODOLOGY AND THE FRAMEWORK OF ANALYSIS

1

BACKGROUND OF THE STUDY

THE ANALYTICAL FRAME

STATED in the simplest of terms, inter-regional trade may be considered to be the consequence of the immobility of some factors of production which are not spread evenly across space. If all the factors of production—land, labour and capital—were mobile in all aspects, exchange of goods would have been rendered unnecessary since they could be produced anywhere in response to demand. In real world, however, the inter-regional mobility of labour and capital is only partial. In view of the fact that the socio-economic development of different regions is larely determined by the complex of fuctional relationships between inter-regional trade, on the one hand, and the mobility of labour as well as capital, on the other; it may be quite in order to treat inter-regional trade as a short-term result of regional variations and factor mobility as the long-term response to trade imbalances.

The space economy thus responds to the requirements of intra and inter-sectoral relationships through bi-lateral and multi-lateral commodity flows, occuring over a range of varying distances from a discrete node to another in the network of an interactive system and not along spatial continuum as is the case of surface flows in a stream. The spatial elasticity of demand and the critical range of these flows is greatly influenced by two factors; namely, the dynamic requirements of the development process as reflected in the structure and pattern of the inter-sectoral linkages, that are usually articulated through input-output matrices; and through the resource availability and the location of economic activities over space.

In view of the diversity of resource availability over space, it is expected that various regions would specialise in different production processes. As regional specialisation proceeds with development, the economies of scale, agglomeration and urbanisation emerge on the scene as important determinants of location of production processes at different levels of the settlement hierarchy. Each region, thus, specialises in the production of a commodity or commodities in which it has a production advantage compared to other regions. However, it may be noted that comparative advantage by itself is not a sufficient condition for inter-regional trade. The absolute differences between the prices in different regions must also be considered in relation to transport costs.

The fact that large volume of traffic terminates over short distances testifies to the operation of the 'friction of distance' and to the consequent realization of the economies of scale at several locations. In view of this, there is a tendency of the various regions of the economic system to concentrate their trade with a few regions rather than with all the regions of the system. Viewed like this, the system of inter-settlement interactions gets enmeshed into the system of inter-regional trade. The inter-meshing of these two operates within the national space economy, which is bound by tariff barriers, a common currency and an integrated transport network. It is through these processes that a loosely knit and weakly connected system of settlements gets transformed into a highly differentiated and well integrated field of a unified home market in national space. Thus, the interdependencies of various sectors of the economy forms the basis of spatial interaction and result in commercial exchange within the regions, which in its turn contribute to the development of a sense of nationhood (Smith, 1970)

The reorganisation of space is based, firstly on the transformation of a surface of settlements into the multilayered surfaces comprising anticlines and synclines; and secondly, on the strengthening of the interactive mechanisms operating both horizontally among settlements at the same level and vertically among settlements at different levels. The latter mechanisms are crucial, particularly in the developing economies, as they articulate the interactions between the large sub-stratum of the rural hinterland and the upper crust of urban settlements.

The increasing intensity of such interactions, which accompanies the development process, leads to redistribution of productive forces in space through diverse mixes of the complimentary tendencies of concentration and dispersion. As a consequence, certain nodal locations and some crucial links acquire relatively greater importance than others and hence play a decisive role in the subsequent organisation of space. It is through this multi-layered system of nodalities and linkages that a loosely knit and weakly connected system of settlements gets transformed into a highly differentiated as well as integrated field of a unified home market in national space.

If these interactions are symbiotic and not exploitative, the rural areas would specialise in products which would be shipped to the urban in the form of food products and raw materials in exchange for wage goods and technological inputs into agriculture, which are the specialities of the urban manufacturing sector. Viewed thus, the exchange of commodities is intended to provide intermediate inputs and final demand requirements to both the rural and urban segments in terms of their respective economic bases.

Such a model of the spatial economic system gets operationalised through the processes of upward, downward as well as lateral movement of different commodities between the various hierarchical fields of nodes in the following manner;

The downward movement: It would consist of commodity flows from the higher orde field to the lower order and a sizeable par of such flows would consist of manufacture and semi-manufactured goods;

ii The upward movement: It would be from the lower order to the higher order fields and would mainly consist of food products for the consumption of the population and raw materials and fuels for the productive units located in the higher order urban agglomeration; and

iii The lateral movement: It would represent the exchange of intermediate and final demand goods between different nodes at each level of the hierarchical system.

It may, however, be noted that the nature and magnitude of the different kinds of flows are seriously modified by locational decisions and freight rates, on the one hand, and by social or urban bias/in the national policies, on the other. In this context, it is also interesting to observe that in the absence of a balancing mechanism in the inter-regional exchange, it is possible for a region to draw on the resources of another without a corresponding inflow into the latter from the former. Such a situation would reflect and would invariably lead to disparate rates of development in different regions. Inter-regional disparities in the national economy under such circumstances would tend to be high and the economy of the relatively backward regions would continue to remain depressed.

These features of concentration of flows from and to some specific regions, however, do suggest that in a large country like India, there will exist economic subsystems a group of regions having strong intra-group links than with regions outside the group. The identification of such groups of regions, which are functionally bound together would provide a useful framework for regional planning.

It is generally agreed that the intensity of movement and interaction tends to fall with distance. In other words, the volume of goods transported between any pair of locations is some inverse function of the distance that separates them. Weber (1929) while examining the factors associated with the location of industries assumed that the transport costs are directly proportional to distance. However, the subsequent analysts found this assumption untenable as the freight rate structure can be manipulated in such a way that the transport costs no longer remain proportional to intervening distance. The direction and the magnitude of commodity flows, thus, becomes quite sensitive to changes in the freight rate policy. a given transport rate structure can influence the spatial distribution of production activities in two ways: firstly, by changing the degree of taper through telescopic rate structure; and secondly, by discriminating between different commodities through cross-subsidisation of different classes of freight traffic. Such a policy makes it possible for a low rated commodity to move over longer distances as compared to a high rated commodity. A subsidisation in freight rates of a particular commodity may result in offsetting the friction of distance and may consequently affect the choice of its location. For example, high rail tariff for finished products as compared to raw materials would tend to move the industry away from the source of raw material towards demand centres, thus putting the resource rich regions at a comparative disadvantage. Once a resource poor region gets the advantage of initial start, it may continue to develop as an industrial centre and move up in the settlement hierarchy.

With such a model of the space economy in view, it should be possible to use commodity flows as an analytical tool for the study of the strength and weakness of the regional structure of a national economy. Looking at the Indian scene from this point of view, it is noted that the country inherited a distorted and dys-functional transport system, which had been established to meet the requirements of the imperialist suction mechanism during the colonial period. The railway network, that was established in India during the period of the growth of industrial capitalism in Great Britain was intended to facilitate, on the one hand the suction of raw-materials to the port towns from their hinterlands for onward transmission to the metropolitan country; and on the other, the diffusion of manufactured goods from the port towns to the depths of the vast interiors. This requirement led to the emergence of an essentially centrifugal system oriented towards the ports. This was operationalised through the node connecting sequence, the directional focus of the network, the multiplicity of gauges and distorted freight policies.

During the process of economic development in free India, the contradiction between the inherited railway network and the new economic tasks became apparent. The network which had been established with a view to fulfil the requirements of an imperialist suction mechanism could not become the instrumentality of consolidating the national home market. It was, therefore, considered necessary in independent India to seriously modify freight policies and the character of the network in order to make them effective instruments of national economic integration.

It would be interesting to find out whether the distortions of the transport network continue to constrain economic development even in the new phase since 1947. Such a study would be particularly useful because Berry (1966) in his pioneering work on the analysis of commodity flows in India for the early sixties had shown that the port oriented system of commodity flows continued to be the main feature of the regional structure of the national space economy.

NATURE OF RESEARCH IN TRANSPORT

A survey of research in transportation studies reveals a growing body of literature dealing with a variety of themes. A search therein for better cohesive theoretical constructs or methodological consistencies would, however, not be very rewarding. The body of literature is highly fragmented and unifying and synthesising conceptualisations are weakly developed. It is necessary therefore, to identify well-defined themes of research in the subject within the basic theoretical framework.

Transportation has been studied traditionally as a structural feature in regional studies and as a topical field in engineering, economics, geography, and planning. While in the fields of engineering and technology, the study of transport has long played a major role, its advent into the social sciences is more recent. While a mass of literature on traffic engineering, mass transit, rapid transit, hydraulic engineering and designing of bridges, choice of construction materials or pavement engineering is available in the former field, studies on systems analysis, gometric design, locational analysis and models of production—allocation dominate the latter. Within the social sciences also, the interest in trasport was primarily stirred in the discipline of economics. Broadly speaking, transportation has been conceived as an area of research and study where analysis and quantitative techniques have an edge over descriptive or qualitative approach. Economics, with its early start in quantification, provided a suitable nurturing ground within the social sciences for its germination and early growth. In Economics, major emphasis has been to develop models to determine the location of economic activity so as to minimize the transport costs. Another important area of investigation has been the determination of threshold values for different modes of transport. With the advent of the quantitative revolution in Geography, however, a new opening for transportation was created with several exciting possibilities. For example, the analysis of interaction matrices, linear programming models for the movement of commodities or gravity and entropy models fall in this category.

A systematic approach to the study of transportation in the context of spatial interaction was ushered in by the following fundamental concepts developed by Ullman (1957):

i complimentarity;
ii intervening opportunity; and
iii transferability

It was postulated by Ullman that flows in economic space occur not only because of areal differences, but also if the above conditions are satisfied. In other words, the flows of goods, people and ideas stem from the socio-economic structure of the generators and absorbers of these flows, on the one hand, and from the network efficiency, on the other. These flows take place along defined channels; and their spatial arragements provide the basis for more complex system of interactions which integrate the space economy. It is important to make a clear distinction between the existence of a channel system (routes, networks) and its intensity as well as the nature of its use. In other words, routes and networks should be distinguished from the nature and the magnitude of flows. We may, therefore, categorise transportation studies under three general heads:

i the study of transport networks;
ii the study of flows on the networks; and
iii the study of networks and flows in relation to each other and to the spatial organisation of the economy.

In the more restricted context of this survey, studies specific to the space economy in relation to transportation may be grouped as follows:

i structure and space—the study of transport networks in the space economy;
ii interactions and space—the study of flows in the space economy.

Structure and space: the study of transport networks

The study of transport networks relates to the evaluation of its structure and efficiency. Some of the questions which have been posed by regional planners relate to the level of network development in a region, the relationship between the networks of different modes of transport and their role in the intra, inter-regional and metropolitan contexts. In a large number of studies conducted around the world, these questions have been answered traditionally through the use of cartographic techniques, with the help of accessibility maps, isopleths, and route density maps.

The application of topological concepts and graph theoretical techniques to the analysis of transportation networks has also been attempted in many recent studies. With advances in such studies, several methods have been evolved to measure the efficiency of networks in their entirety or of any of its component. The indices thus developed attempt to measure different facets of network structure and have been applied both for cross-sectional as well as time series analysis.

Kansky (1963) argues that the structure of the transportation network of any area cannot be studied in isolation from the geographic chara-ctresitics of that areas. His study uses abstract graph theory concepts to analyse hypothetical relationships between the structure of transportation networks and the level of economic development. Other studies of a similar nature include works by Garrison, (1960a, 1962), Ramachandran (1973), Ibrahim (1975) and others.

Some places are more accessible as compared to others. How are these more and less accessible places distributed in a region. Is there any regularity in the pattern of their distribution. Transportation linkages serve human habitals which are either rural or urban settlements of varying sizes. An important aspect, therefore, is the analysis of the structure of the transport network in relation to the spatial organization of particular type of nodes. Studies of this type include those by Mayer (1954), Johnson (1966),

Ramachandran (1973), and Kumar (1977) Reed (1970) has worked out the levels of connectivity of Indian cities based on domestic air links. Hagget (1965) has identified various levels of nodes and a structural hierarchy on the basis of interaction attributes. Taaffe (1960) and others have examined the spatial diffusion and socio-economic growth accompanying the expansion of a transportation network.

Studies on the impact of highway development on the economy of the neighbouring regions constitute an important area of investigation in transport studies. Khan (1973) discusses the impact of improved transportation facilities for metropolitan areas from economic, social and environmental points of view. Campbell (1972) assesses the results of transportation programmes in developing countries. A study analysing the relationship between changes in accessibility to the highway network and the growth of urban centres in Sao Paulo has been conducted by Gauthier (1966, 1973). Changing nodal accessibility and its impact on urban attributes has been studied by Ramachandran (1977).

Interaction and space: the study of flows

The movement of goods and people over transport networks involves origin (generators/shippers), destination (receivers/absorbers) and routes. Each of these three elements may be studied with reference to a number of aspects. While analysing flows, researchers essentially have posed the diagnostic questions. For example, how to identify the underlying factors that generate a particular pattern of flows? Are there any similarities in the flows of different types of commodities and if so, why? Can we predict the nature and magnitude of flows? Is it possible to fit the nature and magnitude of commodity flows in a general theory of development? Answers to many of these questions may be sought by looking into the three elements involved in the movement; that is goods, people and capital.

A second set of questions is essentially prescriptive in character and deals with optimization of movement patterns. Allocation models are used to work out least cost flow patterns both in their simpler forms represented by transport models and complex forms of capacitated networks.

Other than structural analysis of flows, a group of predictive models of flow patterns, for example, the family of gravity models have been developed. These models are very useful in predicting the flow of commodities between a set of given nodes. Further the estimated flows may be distributed over different modes of transport for which a number of modal split algorithms have been developed.

Although it is recongised that the characteristics of spatial exchange of commodities in an economy reflect as well as indicate the characteristics of that economy, this important bi—directional relationship has received only scant attention from scholars. However, a small number of significant studies are now available.

The study by Ullman (1954, 1957) of U.S. commodity flows may be considered to be a significant and pioneering work. The study was conducted with the help of data relating to commodity traffic by rail and water for the year 1948. He has brought out the dominant role of the industrial belt of the North-West in the flow pattern of various manufactured commodities in the United States, and has identified the gross features of these linkages that hold the economy together in terms of a series of inter-state commodity flow maps.

Duncan and his associates (1960) describe the economy of the United States as comprising a set of metropolitan regions within which the exchange of commodities is dominated by flows to and from the metropolitan centres. They also bring out the fact that exclusive regional specialities in production results in the integration of the national market, although a prepondent share of the flows is routed between the metropolitan centres.

Theoretical as well as empirical contributions by Probst (1962), Alampiev (1959), Bedenkova (1964) and Kistanov (1965) relate to the flow of commodities and the formation of economic regions in Soviet Russia. In Germany, significant studies regarding transportation are available in the Raum and Verkher Series (1959). In the first volume prepared by W. Linden, the role of railroads in the economic development of Germany has been examined. The second volume is concerned with the movement of commodities, while the third volume of the series contains a description of the relationships between economy, circulation and transnortation.

Mitsuhashi (1970) has identified the broad patterns of spatial interconnections within the Japanese economy through application of factor analytical techniques to the movement of thirty-two commodities originating from forty-six prefectures. He concludes that the magnitude of traffic is a function of demands and supplies, on the one hand, and of the capacity of the existing transport network, on the other.

Britton (1977) has used origin-destination data on road freight flows at the city and regional level for England and Wales as a means of identifying regions linked in dominant chains and in hierarchical patterns. Wallace (1974) provides a brief survey of the nature and relative importance of the characteristics of the transport industry as they bear on the spatial behaviour of industrial products. Factors influencing the density of freight traffic are discussed at length by Wallace (1958, 1963) and Mayer (1945, 1970) stresses the role of transportation in the location and subsequent growth of cities. The study also throws light on the merits and demerits of different modes of freight and passenger transport and emphasizes the close relationship between functions of towns and commodity flows.

The structural changes of economic regions in Poland have been investigated by Chojnicki and Czyz (1973) through a factor analytic study of railway commodity flow data for the period 1958-66.

Currie (1959) presents a detailed economic survey with specific reference to the role of transportation in the Canadian economy, and highway freight transport. An analytical study of intra and inter-provincial commodity flows and their effect on the domestic demand for transportation in the Philippines has been carried out by Easton (1957). Taaffe (1960) describes rail transport in Central Asia with reference to the regional and historical setting, the development of the rail pattern during the Soviet era and the inter-regional trade of certain commodities. Williams (1962) presents a comparative study of transportation on the U.S.S.R. and U.S.A. with special reference to the composition and growth of freight transport.

Several studies on urban goods movement are available. The structure and patterns of freight movement have been analysed by Chapman (1954), Eisen (1934) and Patton (1956) An analysis of goods movement by railway has been carried out by Golledge (1963), Hare (1954), Smith (1963) and Wallace (1958).

With reference to the Indian situation, studies on commodity movements and the structure of the spatial economy are unfortunately rather rare. The classic work is that of Berry (1966) an attempt to test the veracity of Ullman's principles derived from American commodity flows in an entirely different socio-economic setting and to isolate the underlying principles determining the interaction pattern within the Indian economy. The study brings out the persistence of a set of economic regions organised around the colonial primates that are simultaneously the principal manufacturing areas of the country and the emergence of a limited number of regions with specialised production based either on ecolological differences or on the exploitation of substantial quantities of mineral resources. The book is divided into 3 sections—an atlas of Indian commodity flows for the movement of sixty-three commodities, an analysis of the relationship between commodity flows and regional economic structure and a study of regional sectoral demand and supply functions through a three region-eighteen sector model with predictive abilities.

It may, however, be mentioned that the usefulness of Berry's work was restricted on four counts, namely:

- i commodity flows were analysed in an aggregated form;
- ii the intra-regional flows were completely ignored;
- iii strength of spatial links as expressed in the number of interactions were not examined; and
- iv the pattern of spatial dispersion, as expressed in distance of flows was not taken into account.

Reed (1967) has provided a detailed picture of commodity flows in the Bengal-Bihar industrial belt. Using originating data for twentry-three stations for three months of the year 1962, he used the potential model and showed that supply/demand

and distance variables account for 33 to 66 per cent of the variations and therefore, includes the effect of intervening opportunity and competition.

Bhatt and Gidhadhubli (1971) have used rail and waterway flow data to work out a scheme of economic regions. A study of market towns and spatial development concludes that the development of an economy involves a high degree of specialisation giving rise to complex set of inter-industry flows which in turn require a widespread and in several ways hierarchical network of towns and cities. Sdasyuk (1968) emphasises the role of transport in the formation of economic regions in India. The relationship between the movement of goods and market centres in the Hadoti Plateau region has been brought out by Saxena (1975).

Johnson (1963) presents an economic survey of the Indian railways in the historical context. The sections on goods traffic as well as the contribution of the railways to agriculture, industry and commerce provide some interesting findings. Chakraborty (1978) has studied the Indian urban economic base in terms of the movement of commodities through the railways from and to the metropolitan centres.

The major limitation of the studies undertaken in the Indian context relates to their data base. These studies have mainly used data from Inland Trade Accounts. The detailed description and inadequacies of the Inland Trade Accounts. would be examined subsequently. These limitations not only affect the overall results, but also do not permit a proper analysis of intra-regional flows and to find out the spatial elasticities of demand or to test the validity of the distance decay principle.

Different aspects of commodity flows in relation to the various characteristics of the Indian economic system have been examined by a team of scholars. The investigations are based on the railway freight flow data for the year 1973-74 and significant contributions have been reported in the following areas:—

i The patterns of aggregate commodity flows in relation to the development, characteristics have been examined by Aggarwal (1979). The study also examines the impact of distance on the flow patterns of different commodities. The commodity flow data on intra as well as inter-district movement has been used in the study.

ii Ramachandran (1979) has examined the spatial organization of the Indian economy as a system where a set of nodes of different hierarchic orders are inter-linked through commodity flows. A hierarchical system of national, regional and local nodes has also been developed on the basis of commodity flow attributes.

iii The spatial organisation of the Indian economy, as reflected in the pattern of rural-urban commodity exchanges, has been examined by Kumar (1979). The study has developed a model of rural-urban commodity flows for some selected commodities.

iv Relationships between economic base and commodity flow characteristics of the Indian urban system have been examined by Khurana (1979). A functional classification of Indian urban centres has been developed by using Nelson's method. The freight characteristics of each type of functional group have been studied in detail.

v The inadequacies of the metropolitan hinterland exchange have been examined by Dutta (1979). A study by Raza, Aggarwal and Khurana (1980), examines the relationships between economic base and commodity flow characteristics. It has been shown that the essential inadequancy of the Indian metropolitan system lies in its weak economic base and a bloated tertiary sector.

The Inter-zonal movement of commodities for the financial year 1974-75 has been examined by Seetharam and Chakraborty (1979). The analysis is based on the point to point flow data but only those locations have been considered between which the total flow of a particular commodity is 100 tonnes or more. The analysis has shown that the regional inter-dependence is restricted to adjacent zones only. The inadequacy of the study lies in the fact that a very large spatial unit of observation has been selected— that is, the railway zone.

Interaction and space—the study of freight policy

The development of railway rates and governmental regulations over them also needs careful examination. The first and the most important work on railway rates was done by Ghose (1918) during the first quarter of this century. The development of railway rates and government regulations over them have been examined in the light of their impact on the economic developments of India and its industries. It may be emphasised that most of the investigations on Indian freight rate structure undertaken by different scholars in the subsequent period were essentially based on the work of Ghose (1918) The inadequacies of the railway freight rates were later examined by Mehta (1927) in his pioneering study with special reference to the Indian railways. The major focus of the study was to examine the structure of railway freight rates and the power of the government to control it. A just railway policy has been the focus of enquiry by Antia (1932). Tiwari (1937) in his study on railway rates in India came to the conclusion that the rates policy as followed by Indian railways was injurious to the development of indigenous industries. The railway rates were framed in such a way, that it favoured the export of raw material and import of finished goods. A similar study by Lefeber and Chaudhary (1971) concludes that the Indian railway rates policy was highly discriminatory. In a latest study, a critical analysis of freight rate structure of the Indian Railways has been undertaken by Aggarwal (1982).

The revision of the freight rates structure in 1948 is an important landmark in the history of Indian railways. With a view to simplify and rationalise the freight rates, a standard 15 class telescopic class rates were introduced. In view of the criticism of the 1948 freight policy, another Railway Freight Structure Enquiry Committee recommended the revision of scale of rates and the corresponding tapering of the freight rates. The committee on Transport Policy and Coordination appointed by the Govt. of India has examined the perspectives of a long term transport policy. The impact of railway freight rates on the economy has also been examined.

In the subsequent years, the Govt. of India appointed a number of enquiry committees to examine the issues related to the railway rates policy. For this purpose a reference to the proceedings and reports of differnt Convention Committees may be made. The domain of these enquiries was either to make general recommendaions about the overall structure of the railway rates, or to examine the impact of freight equalisation for some specific commodities or to report on the social burden of Indian railways. It is unfortunate to observe that inspite of its crucial importance, the railways have not undertaken any empirical study to evaluate the impact of the freight structure on the location of industries.

THE PRESENT STUDY

The present study is an outcome of a large scale research project on commodity flows. One of the salient features of the study was its wide data base as point to point commodity flow matrices were generated and analysed for the first time in India. The study was designed to remove some of the limitations of the earlier studies and to analyse the Indian commodity flows in relation to its regional structure for later period—on the basis of the data for the 70's. The major objectives of the present study were as under:

- i to develop a comprehensive methodology of commodity flows analysis; and
- ii to undertake an indepth analysis of commodity flows in relation to the regional structure of the Indian economy.

This has done by:

- i analysing the spatial organisation of the developing economies;
- ii examining the structure of transport network in India;
- iii assessing the relationship between commodity flows and economic base/other development indicators at national, regional and subregional levels;
- iv identifying the pattrns of regional specialisation as reflected through the commodity flows
- v developing a hierarchy of national, regional and local nodes in the spatial system;
- vi evaluating the nature of urban-rural exchange of commodities;
- vii enquiring into the nature and pattern of metropolitan and urban commodity flows;
- viii analysing the impact of distance on the patterns of commodity flows;
- ix bringing out the nature and patterns of interregional inter-dependencies; and
- x critically examining the freight rate structure.

With a view to help other researchers in the field, a select bibliography on commodity flows has also been presented.

2

SOURCES OF COMMODITY FLOW DATA IN INDIA

NATURE OF COMMODITY FLOW DATA

SINCE flows have, by definition, directions, the basic configuration of commodity flows take the form of a flow matrix. The use of matrix to represent flows was pioneered by economists who were interested in the study of interactions not as much between places as between the sectors of specialised functions of an economic system. It may, however, be noted that the matrix representation of inter-sectoral and inter-regional flows are essentially differentiated by the labelling of rows and columns. The rows and columns in the inter-regional commodity flow table refer to spatial units and not to production sectors of the economy as is the case with the table of inter-industry flows. The commodity flow matrix like inter-sectoral flow matrix also takes the form of a square table in which the rows indicate the various origins of a particular commodity or a set of commodities and the columns show the respective destinations. Looked at in this frame of reference, the cells of a flow matrix represent the volume of movement between a particular origin and a specific destination.

It is evident from the above, that the magnitude of data involved in any commodity flow analysis increases in geometric progression with the increase in the size of the matrix. Looking at it in the spatial context wherein a large number of origins and destinations are involved, the problems of data collection and collating become formidable indeed. A highly sophisticated system of data collection and processing is required to handle a situation wherein a large number of origins and destinations have to be dealt with. It is in view of this constraint that a comprehensive and reliable commodity flow data are not available even in most of the advanced countries of the world. In order to get the idea about the magnitude of the data base, let us take the example of India with its 10,000 location codes comprising railway stations, booking agencies, sidings and out-agencies. Any analysis based on transaction matrix for one type of flow for these locations will involve 10^8 bits of information (10,000 × 10,000). If the number of variables involved are more than one, then the information required gets multipleid by the number of variables. For example, if there are 300 commodities and for each commodity we have three types of information namely weight, freight and distance, the complete data base will consist of $300 \times 3 \times 10^8$ bits of information. Many of the cells in such a huge matrix, no doubt, would be empty, but still the amount of information involved in handling such matrices would be enormous.

The development of electronic data storage and processing systems have made it possible to store huge volumes of information on magnetic tapes and disks with the help of modern high speed data recording and processing units. It may be interesting to note that even after excluding the zero cells, the data involved in the present study consists of more than 3 million bits of information. The mere print out of this data will run into thousands of pages of computer output and it will be impossible to do any type of manual analysis on such an enormous amount of data. Thus, any type of manual processing for analysis of large commodity flow matrices is an extremely difficult task. For any meaningful analysis of such data, one has to rely heavily on computerised data processing techniques. It is in this context that the coding design and the efficient use of the existing Data Base Management Techniques becomes one of the crucial factors in developing a sound methodology for undertaking reseach in this area. The methodology involved in coding, preserving and analysis of the data relating to the present study would be discussed in greater detail while describing the data base and methodological aspects of the study.

In the following section, the sources and coverage of commodity flow data that are available in different forms in India would be discussed in detail. A brief review of the nature and type of commodity flow data available for some other countries is given in the Appendix I. While making use of the information, it should be kept in mind that it is largely based on the review of literature for the studies related to the analysis of commodity flows and it is quite possible, that some of the data bases that have not been used for any empirical analysis might have been left out of the review presented in the Appendix I.

NATURE AND TYPES OF COMMODITY FLOW DATA IN INDIA

Railways are the major instrument of long distance movement. It may be observed that while a large proportion of the industrial raw materials are moved by railways, high rated freight is usually carried through roadways. Since the inception of development planning in India, great reliance is being placed on the role of railways in carrying goods that are most needed for the economic development of the country. The growth of railway freight traffic during the last 25 years is a testimony of the leading role that the railways are playing in the development of various strategic sectors of the economy. The trade between different states or regions of India may be classified under the following heads:–

- i Rail borne trade;
- ii Road borne trade;
- iii Coastal trade; and
- iv Air borne trade

During the last decade, the share of railways in the total national freight varied from 65-75% and the remaining freight was mainly accounted for by road transport. The share of coastal shipping and air freight in the total originating freight is rather marginal. However, nowadays efforts are being made to make use of the pipelines for the movement of mineral products.

Commodity flows through Indian railways

Two different sets of data are available for the commodity flows through Indian Railways. These are available in terms of the following units:

Trade block; and
Point to point

The inland trade accounts are published annually and contain aggregated information on the quantity of trade in different commodities moving by rail and inland steamer between Trade Blocks of India. The number of trade blocks have increased over the years. For example, it increased from 20 in 1955 to 29 in 1961. The traded items are classified into 30 main groups divided into 67 major items. The trade block data on commodity flows, though very handy for statistical manipulation is constrained by the large size of some of the trade blocks and the non-availability of data pertaining to the intra-trade block flows.

The second set of commodity flows data corresponds to the information available with zonal railways headquarters. Each zone of the Indian Railways prepares a 'Goods Summary Data' on the basis of invoices issued by different railway stations falling under its jurisdiction. This information, recorded on computer magnetic tapes is available in terms of nearly 550 different commodity codes classified according to its revenue earning character– origin and final use in the economic system. The railways do not use this data for any economic analysis except for accounting purposes.

The 'Goods Summary Data' can be pooled together for all the nine railway zones to arrive at the national commodity flow matrices for each of the coded commodity. Such a process of generating the national commodity flow data is not only complete in its coverage, but also takes care of the fact that it is the most disaggregated set of data on commodity flows that can be obtained at the national level. Since the process of commodity flows through the Indian railways may originate from any of the nearly 10,000 railway stations, which include booking offices, sidings and out-agencies as well. The process of pooling the zonal data would result in a basic matrix with a dimension of nearly (10,000 × 10,000) for each commodity.

COMMODITY FLOWS THROUGH ROAD TRANSPORT

Next to railways, the road transport plays an important role in carrying commodities in India. Road traffic has acquired great significance in view of its reliability, efficiency and economies for short distance movement. This is evident from the fact that there has been a steady growth in the number of commercial vehicles which have increased from 3.06 lakhs in 1950-51 to 32.36 lakhs in 1977-78.

Precise data on the nature and volume of freight traffic covered by road transport, particularly by trucks is not available on a national scale. All the estimates of road freight are based on interpolations, by taking into account the number of trucks, their capacity and utilisation indices etc. or are based on small sample studies. It is only very recently that the Planning Commission entrusted to Rail India Technical and Economic Services Ltd. (1980), a study on comparative modal costs and traffic flows as a part of a UNDP Transport Policy Planning Project. Information collected for this study has given valuable insight into the pattern of commodity flows by three major modes of transport, namely, rail, road and coastal shipping. For estimating the nature, direction and the volume of commodity flows taking place through roadways, a special origin-destination survey was conducted by Rail India Technical and Economic Services Ltd. The data pertains to the year 1978-79 and the survey was designed to cover all the districts of the country. However, since some districts have extremely low potential for commodity flows on account of low economic activity, a number of districts were clubbed together and finally 298 nodal districts were elected. To collect information on freight traffic by roads from these nodal points, a network of 216 check posts was selected covering all the routes on national and state highways. In view of the seasonal variations, the survey has been conducted in two rounds. The idea about the scale of operation may be had from the fact that 3.7 lakh trips performed by 1.53 lakh individual goods vehicles were intercepted during the first round of the survey.

For the purpose of data collection, all commodities transported were clubbed into 37 groups. Each group comprised a commodity or a group of commodities having homogeneous transport characteristics.

COMMODITY FLOWS THROUGH COASTAL SHIPPING

The total coastal shipping tonnage increased from 2.17 lakh GRT in 1951 to 4.42 lakh GRT in 1976. Nearly two third of the traffic in coastal shipping relates to dry cargo, while the remaining one third is wet cargo. The main items of dry cargo handled by coastal shipping are coal and salt. These two commodities in 1977 accounted for over 85 per cent of the originating tonnage and 85 per cent of tonne kms.

Statistics of coastal trade are available in *Statistics of Coasting Trade of India*, published by Director General of Commercial Intelligence and Statistics (DGCIS). These statistics are based on documents that pass through customs house. The statistics contain details of movements of merchandise and treasure by coast. Indian coast has been divided into 12 blocks since 1963. The statistics are separately available for trade amongst ports between the same maritime block (called internal trade) and between two martime blocks (called external trade). Separate data is also available for Indian and foreign merchandise.

SOURCES OF DATA FOR THE PRESENT STUDY

The present study makes use of the point to point commodity flow data collected from different zonal headquarters of the Indian Railways. The originating ends of this computerised data are the various railway stations, booking offices out-agencies and sidings. Data for the reference year ending on March 31, 1974 has been utilised for our analysis. The data was duplicated on magnetic tapes from the following zonal offices of the Indian Railways.

1. Central Railway	Bombay
2. Eastern Railway	Calcutta
3. Northern Railway	New Delhi
4. North Eastern Railway	Gorakhpur
5. North East Frontier Railway	Pandu (Gauhati)
6. Southern Railway	Madras
7. South Eastern Railway	Calcutta
8. Western Railway	Bombay
9. South Central Railway	Secunderabad

The fact that the data is available in computerised form may create the erroneous impression that problems associated with data collection and processing would be rather marginal. Such an impression, however, gets corrected in the process of utilising the data for research in social sciences. It is necessary, therefore, to outline the major stages in data processing.

System of coding and technical details

The basic information on commodity flows was available on magnetic tapes in a coded form. Each railway station, out-agency, booking office or siding, from where freight is loaded or unloaded is identified with the help of a five digit code. Of the five digits the first refers to the zonal railway under whose administration the particular station falls. This code varies from 1 to 9 corresponding to the different zonal railways. The second digit refers to the code of the administrative division of the respective zonal railway which has already been identified by the first digit of the station code. The third digit corresponds to trade block. The fourth and the fifth digits of the code refer to the serial number of the stations. The stations have been coded sequentially along the railway track. Thus, the station codes are not necessarily continuous series of the numbers. Following such a method of coding for the stations, two adjacent stations lying on different tracks may have quite different codes.

The five digit code is supplemented by another one digit code that is the sixth digit for gauge of the railway track on which the station is located. However, this information was not usually available for all the zonal railways. It varies from 1 to 3 as follows:

1 Broad guage
2 Metre gauge
3 Others

The numerically arranged decoding lists are available with the respective zonal railways, whereas coding is possible with an alphabetically arranged list of all stations with their numerical code number. Such lists are periodically published and updated by the Indian Railways. Similarly commodities are also coded with three digit codes. A complete range of commodities alongwith their codes is given in Appendix II. The Indian Railways, for the accounting purposes, have classified the commodities into two broad categories namely revenue earning and non-revenue earning commodities. Non-revenue traffic includes all the commodities carried by the railways for their own use. It may be pointd out that a particular commodity could be classified into both the groups depending upon its use. For example, coal for thermal power houses has been classified as a revenue earning commodity while the coal for the use of railways has been classified as non-revenue earning commodity with different commodity code. Thus, the same commodity that is coal has two or more different commodity codes.

The data on originating freight was duplicated from the computer centres of various zonal offices. The mode of duplicating the data was magnetic tapes with 7 tracks and recording density of 556 b.p.i. in EBCDIC codes. In view of the fact that the tape density of 556 b.p.i. is usually available on IBM 1401 computer, the data tapes could not be used on other computers like IBM 360, EC 1020 and so on, where the data was analysed for this study. The tapes were, therefore, converted to 9 tracks of 800/1600 b.p.i. Tapes with these specifications are acceptable in a number of later generation of computers.

The data, as obtained from the railways, was recorded in 'blocked form' on the magnetic tapes. The blocking factor was, however, different for different zones. It may be noted that a number of records are considered as one block for the purposes of recording the information on the tape. The blocking of data records considerably reduces the length of the tape required to store data and hence also data processing time. Information about each cell of a commodity flow matrix was contained in one record. For the work of this study it was considered necessary to retrieve the following from the record:

i code of the commodity;
ii the station code from which it is shipped,
iii the station code at which it is received;
iv the weight of the transaction; and
v the freight charged for the movement.

The format of the data records varied with different zonal railways. The record length ranged from the smallest record of a transaction of 55 columns in the case of Central Railway to 120 columns of the Northern Railway. Not only did the blocking factor vary from zone to zone, but even in the same zone, the number of records varied from block to block. The description of the format followed by different zonal railways for the purposes of recording of commodity flow data is given the in Appendix III.

In the light of the differences in the formats, the details given therein also varied from one zone to another. For example, the recording format of the Central Railway does not give data on distance involved in a transaction but provides information on tonne kilometres. It was quite surprising to note that even in the case of weight, two units of measurements were adopted. While some railways record freight in quintals, the others used tonnes as the unit of recording. In terms of periodicity of recording the data, it was observed that while for some zones monthly aggregates were available, the data for other zones was recorded only in terms of annual or quarterly aggregates.

SCRUTINY OF THE DATA

An enormous data base necessarily involves a variety of coding, recording and punching errors. Owing to punching errors, for example, several alpha characters would appear instead of numerical values. While some of these errors are detectable, none of these are rectifiable, since 'correct records' are not available against which such records could be verified. However, at zonal railway level, data relating to gauge-wise originating tonnage for 7 major commodities are available. It was, therefore, considered necessary to aggregate the data in a format so that cross checking could be done with the originating freight data available with each zonal railway. As a result of the exercise, it was noticed that in practically all the zones, the originating freight showed a significant positive difference from published data. Such large values for differences may have been possible due to punching errors, particularly in the quantity of freight since even a slight displacement of a figure in a 10 digit field may have led to a difference of millions of tonnes. With a view to taking care of such errors, all those cases where a particular transaction exceeded more than 100,000 and 50,000 tonnes were printed and consistency checks were made for its validity. It was found that for a very large number of transactions both originating and terminating stations as identified from the tapes did not exist. In many such cases the commodity code was also non-existent in the master data tape. It was neither necessary nor fruitful to go into the origin of such errors. In the few remaining cases, the physical possibility of such movements was probed and a decision taken to drop the record or to include it. After making these corrections, similar scrutiny was undertaken again, which showed about 1 per cent error at the aggregate level and the recorded data nearly matched the published data not only at the national level but also for different zones and for major commodities.

RAILWAY STATIONS AND SETTLEMENTS

Since the data collected by the railways are recorded for accounting purposes, it could not be directly used in the form in which they were available for the present study. The station in terms of which data are provided, are not in themselves nodes in the space economy. A number of sidings and booking offices, for example, have different codes due to differences in gauges and zonal administration but are really a part of the settlement. Since one of the major areas of investigation in the present study relates to the examination of commodity flow characteristics and the economic base indicators of different types of settlements, it was, therefore, considered advisable that each observation be a node identifiable with a human settlement. For this purpose, the settlements as defined in the Census of India were found suitable and the same have been used in the present analysis. Thus, in many cases a number of stations were aggregated into only one or a fewer number of nodes corresponding to each Census settlement. For example, large urban agglomerations like Delhi, Bombay, Calcutta, Madras, Kanpur or even smallar industrial centres which were served by a number of sidings were each considered as one node and the data for other railway stations falling in the agglomeration were clubbed together with that of the major node. For example, 113 stations (like Lodhi Road or), Paharganj and Subzi Mandi) were identified as a part of single node, that is, Delhi. In this process, the initial 10,000 and odd stations were aggregated into 6,775 nodes each of which is a village or an urban centre identifiable with a Census settlement. In some cases, stations belonging to several zonal railways also had to be aggregated into one node and one of the zornal codes was selected to designate such cluster of stations. A base map locating all the 6,775 nodes was also prepared. Following this classificatory system of railway stations, booking agencies and out-agencies into different settlements, originating-destination commodity flow data were also aggregated in terms of these 6,775 nodes. In the analaysis that follows the words node and stations have been inter-changeably used. The station would thus correspond to each Census agglomera-ion or settlement.

ADDITIONAL IDENTIFICATORY CODES

After having generated the commodity flow matrix representing inter-nodal interactions the additional information necessary to probe into the various aspects of the problems posed in the earlier chapter was also added. The following additional information was coded for every station:

i each station was classified into rural or urban category. Since the aggregated modified stations had been equated to settlements as defined by the Census of India (1971), it was possible to classify them into various categories according their population size. Whereas urban centres were coded from U1 to U6 according to the class of towns, all the rural places were considered as one category.

ii the administrative district in which each station is located was indicated by an additional code. This procedure made it possible to aggregate data of all stations in a district to create smallar data matrices and relate it to other facets of the space economy for which districtwise data was available from other sources.

iii the levels of development of a district, in various sectors, of the country based on 1961 Census data have been worked out by Pal (1975) and the same were also included in the districtwise aggregate data so that cross-tabulation could be made to seek the flow characteristics of the districts with varying levels of development in different sectors of the economy. Although the data on which the computations are based pertain to 1961, it is assumed that major changes in the ranking of districts have not taken place in the last decade. Thus, information on the following levels of development of the districts were included in the flow matrices:

a composite level of development;
b level of agricultural development;
c level of non-agricultural development;
d level of industrial development;
e level of tertiary development; and
f level of urbanisation.

iv the structure of the work-force in terms of nine industrial categories of the Census and some other important demographic characteristics for urban areas were also coded separately. The data on distribution of workers in 9 industrial categories was taken from the Census of India publications. This has been done with a view to examine the relationship between the economic base of the Indian urban system and their freight characteristics.

During the process of study, additional information/references have also been made to a number of other sources such as Railway Board and Census of India publications.

AGGREGATION OF COMMODITY FLOW MATRICES

Even with their reduced dimension, it would have been counter productive to analyse over five hundred matrices pertaining to individual commoities for which the data is available—the wood may have been lost in the trees. Within the scope of the problem posed and to suit the theoretical framework of analysis outlined earlier it was considered necessary to aggregate the commodities in to a number of internally homogeneous groups. The purpose of grouping of commodities was not merely to reduce the number of matrices involved but to articulate the theoretical framework discussed earlier.

The urban and rural settlements that constitute the space economy interact with each other through the exchange of their produce among other media of interaction. At national and regional level, it is through the urban centres that the space economy is organised. The system of nodes and associated system of hinterlands tend to represent different types of commodities that are exchanged between them. With this in view, the following nine groups were identified:

Commodity/ Group Code	*Description*
1	Food products
2	Raw materials from primary sources
3	Inputs into agriculture
4	Fuels
5	Construction materials
6	Industrial products
7	Defence goods
8	Livestock
9	Miscellaneous

Thus, food products (except for a small proportion of processed food which is shipped from urban centres), raw materials from primary sources (including cash crops like sugarcane, cotton, jute, plantation and mineral products) and fuel (except imported crude) are essentially those commodities that should be generated from the hinterland, while inputs into agriculture, industrial products and construction materials (largely accounted for by cement) would be generated from the metropolitan and other urban centres. The undefined items are grouped into miscellanous commodities. In view of the non-availability of information about the nature of commodities moved for defence purposes, these have been treated in a separate group—defence. Similarly, livestock, which is recorded by head counts, is treated as a separate group.

The above nine categories are broad groups of commodities with single digit code. Each of these has been further classified into subgroups for detailed analysis. A two-digit code was evolved for this purpose. Depending on the nature of the product, the two digit classification provided for a larger degree of intra-group homogeneity and thus allowing for a substantial reduction in the size of commodity flow matrices. Following this method, 45 groups of commodities were identified and their description and the corresponding originating freight is given in Table 2.1. The detailed break up in terms of three digit commodities and their corresponding two digit code has been given in Appendex II.

It is evident from the two digit classification of the commodities that food products are further classified into foodgrains and non-foodgrains. Rice and wheat, being the major food grains have been considered separately while all other foodgrains have been grouped under a third category of other foodgrains. Gram and pulses have been considered as a separate group. It may be noted that these commodities are generally collected in the mandis and then stored in godowns and are shipped to different deficit parts of the country. However, it might involve some rudimentary processing as is the case with flours. Sugarcane has been considered as a separate commodity in view of its specific nature. The other group is composed of fresh vegetables and fruits which are shipped from nearest railway stations from the producing areas to a large number of destinations in different parts of the country. Fish, poultry and dairy products constitute a separate group. Plantation products are divided into two parts—one with some amount of processing and localised places of production like beverages (coffee and tea) and the others included with general provision like spices,

TABLE 2.1 : **Distribution of commodity flows 1973-74**

Sl. No.	*Description*	*Flow in (000 Tonnes)*	*Percentage share to total freight*
1.	Rice	3,577	1.94
2.	Wheat	6,241	3.39
3.	Gram and pulses	2,351	1.28
4.	Other foodgrains	2,369	1.29
5.	Sugarcane	1,692	0.92
6.	Fruits	450	0.24
7.	Fish	14	0.01
8.	Tea	216	0.12
9.	Oilseeds	1,069	0.58
10.	Cotton	678	0.37
11.	Jute	2,341	1.27
12.	Sugar	87	0.05
13.	Tobaccoo	2,960	1.61
14.	Salt/spices	260	0.14
15.	Hides/skin	232	0.13
16.	Plantations	3,110	1.69
17.	Forestry	417	0.23
18.	Edible oils	539	0.29
19.	Limestone	11,838	6.43
20.	Iron ore	20,112	10,93
21.	Manganese ore	2,102	1.14
22.	Non-ferrous metals	135	0.07
23.	Iron and steel	9,176	4.99
24.	Metal scrap	348	0.19
25.	Coal and coke	62,659	34.06
26.	Mineral oils	10,248	5,57
27.	Firewood	7,833	4,26
28.	Fodder	2,542	1.38
29.	Manure	335	0.18
30.	Fertilizers	5,300	2,88
31.	Primary building material	1,320	0.72
32.	Coal tar	1,063	0.58
33.	Cement	10,257	5,57
34.	Bricks	561	0.30
35.	Textiles	624	0.34
36.	Electrical goods	322	0.18
37.	Glassware	234	0.13
38.	Paper	879	0.48
39.	Rubber	195	0.11
40.	Chemicals	708	0.38
41.	Agricultural implements	34	0.02
42.	Transport equipment	28	0.02
43.	Miscellaneous	5,135	2.79
44.	Livestock*	183*	—
45.	Defence goods	1.395	0.76

*Value is in numbers (thousands)

cardamom and pepper. In view of their commercial nature oilseeds, cotton and jute have also been considered as separate group.

Sugar is treated separately alongwith other itmes of common use (sugarcane) like khandsari, molasses, gur etc., all involving various degree of processing. Tobacco and its manufactured products have been considered separately. Similarly, edible oils form another group and salt in various forms are considered as one group. Plantattion products, hides and skins and products originating from the forestry sector have been organised into one group. Products of the mining sector have been classified into three separate groups. These are limestone, iron ore and manganese ore. The processed output of the mining sector has been divided into three groups; namely non-ferrous metals, iron and steel and metal scrap.

Fuel is grouped into three major categories—coal, and coke, mineral oils and firewood from the forest sector. Coal and mineral products have been kept separate in view of their complimentary nature and relative importance in the economy.

Inputs into agriculture again are classified into three groups. Two of these commodities come from the agricultural sector itself. These are fodder and manure. The third commodity group that is chemical fertilizer represents the inputs into agriculture which originate from the industrial sector. Such a classification would also be very useful in understanding the rural-urban interdependencies generated through the process of rural and urban inputs into the agricultural sector.

Construction materials are classified into four categories. Unprocessed materials like tiles, lime, marble, wood and sand have been considered as a separate group. The other three groups relate to the processed materials like coal tar, cement and bricks.

Industrial products are, however, classified into eight sub categories based on the nature of raw material used, the nature of the products and their final use. Thus, we have textiles, electrical goods, glassware, paper, rubber, chemicals, electrical goods, transport equipment and other miscellaneous consumer goods. The classificatory scheme is primarily based on the differing nature of use of these products in the inter-industrial and final demand sectors of the economy.

The other three groups of commodities, viz. , defence, livestock and miscellaneous are not further classified since they remain unspecified in the original data matrix.

CREATED DATA FILES

It is evident from the preceding discussion that the basic data on commodity flows have been aggregated at different levels. Efforts were also made to supplement the commodity flow informaion with other socio-economic data. This was made possible by maintaining separate files of different types of data for various levels of spatial aggregation. A brief description of some of the important data files is as under:

Master files of basic data (point to point)

The fourteen original tapes that were duplicated from the various zonal railways were then reduced to 9 tapes by increasing the blocking factor and also by maintaining the data separately for each zone. Thus these nine tape files, each referring to different zone, are now available in a common data format with additional codes of stations with reference to their rural/urban character, districts in which they are located, and commodity code (3 digits). It may be noted that a considerable amount of time and energy was spent to bring the data to a common format. These master files have been preserved for use by interested researchers and the details fr using these tapes for data analysis are given in Appendix IV. In terms of its coverage, the point to pont data are available for 6,775 originating and terminating stations which has been further classified in the form of 534 commodities. In view of the enormity of the data, getting a complete print-out from the computer was not possible.

Master file of basic data (district to district)

The first level of aggregation in terms of the spatial unit was undertaken at the level of a district. The point to point flows were aggregated to district to district flows and at this stage no attempt was made to aggregate the data in terms of the commodities. Therefore, these data files contain data in a format which is essentially similar to point to point flow data. It may be noted that

the usefulness of this data file lies in the fact that in addition to commodity flow data, the information about the economic development indices for all the districts has also been incorporated.

Master file of basic data (region to region)

The second level of aggregation in terms of the spatial unit was undertaken at the level of a region. The National Sample Survey Regions were selected for the purpose of regional analysis. The detailed description of the NSS regions is given in Appendix V. The usefulness of National Sample Survey regions lies in the fact that a wide variety of socio-economic data is available which can be meaningfully used for examining the inter-relationships between economic base and freight characteristics of a region.

Aggregated basic data file (station to station)

A second set of data file pertains to the station to station flow data which were aggregated for two digit and single digit commodity group. The data have been recorded in terms of format given in Appendix VI and the data pertaining to single digit commodity group have been extensively used to examine different aspects of the areas under investigation in the present study.

The data files were first sorted on the originating end and then for the terminating end. This was down with a view to getting a print—out of the commodity-wise originating freight for each railway station arranged according to ascending order of the codes of the receiving railway stations. This type of output was also considered necessary for manual manipulation of the data. The data were thus got printed both for the originating stations and for the receiving stations as the sort key.

Aggregated basic data files (district to district)

The nature of the data in this file is the same as in the point to point flow matrix. However, the aggregation of data into nine commodity groups has considerably reduced its size. The size of the flow matrix was thus reduced to 335 × 335 for each commodity—335 being the number of districts having either originating or terminating flows.

Distance matrix

The information available from the basic data relates to only weight and interaction of the commodity moved. In the light of the objectives of the study, it was considered advisable to incorporate the distance variable as well, so that average lead for each station and for individual commodities could be calculated. For this purpose it was decided to take into account the linear distance from each district to all other districts. And hence a distance matrix of 335×335 was prepared showing for each district the linear distance from its centre to the centre of all the remaining 334 districts of India. This table has also been preserved on computer magnetic tapes.

DATA PROCESSING

Depending upon the availability of computer time and facilities, a number of computer systems were used for various stages of processing. The configuration of the systems used for data processing work is as under:

- i Computers located at headquarters of all the nine railway zones. These are IBM 1401 models with 7 track, 556 b.p.i. tape drives. These computers were used for duplicating the zonal data.
- ii Delhi Univesity Computer Centre (IBM 360) for conversion of 7 track tapes (556 bpi) to 9 track (800 bpi and 1600 bpi) and for updating the tapes and for tabulation purposes;
- iii Jawaharlal Nehru University Computer Centre (EC 1020) for analysis and getting basic data tables printed;
- iv Computronics India Ltd. (EC 1030) for sorting and updating the tapes; and
- v Planning Commission (Inter-data 8/32) for some intermediate processing.

Since the software support and the data handling capacities of configurations differed from one another, the necessary programming languages used covered a wide spectrum—Fortran VI, Fortran IV, Fortran II, PL/I, COBOL and Assembler. A number of consistency programmes were developed to check the acquired data and to identify non-numeric characters. Some programmes were developed to add information to the existing data. The information to be added were earlier punched, verified and loaded on tapes. Since the additional information pertained to stations as well as commodities, the data were sorted on various fields with the help of SORT and MERGE programmes.

At the time of tabulation and analysis, a number of programmes were developed for tabulation to generate summary inter-action regarding total freight handled at each station, their commodity group break up, number of inter-actions or to tabulate the matrix of commodity flow terminating at stations, or to summarise the table of inter and intra—district exchanges of freight between rural and urban sectors of the economy. Standard packages were utilised for multiple regression, stepwise regression and factor analysis at various stages of data analysis. Some packages were also modified according to the requirements of our own analysis.

SCHEME OF DATA TABULATION

Basic tabulations (station to station flows)

Necessary computer programmes were developed for tabulating and printing the station to station flows both for originating and terminating freight in terms of nine commodity groups. The tables were obtained both for originating and terminating low separately. The originating flow tables contain information on the rural/urban classification code for each originating station along with district identification code and the corresponding levels of development of the district. All the stations to which it sends goods are then listed with station identification and flows for 9 commodity groups and the total for all commodities. This table also summarises the total freight originating from a station and the number of stations it interacts with. Similar information is also available for receiving freight at each station. The format of the output is shown in Appendix VII & Appendix VIII.

The preparation of these tables took considerable energy and time. The output of these tables runs into about 30,000 pages of computer printout. These tables have thus brought out a complete flow matrix of dimension 6,775×6,775 for each commodity group, along with information about interactions in a summary form.

Summary tables

The format of the table has been shown in Appendix IX. This table contains information about each of the 6775 interacting stations, on the rural/urban nature of the station, total originating tonnage, total terminating tonnage, percentage distribution of each commodity originating in total originating freight, percentage distribution of each commodity in total terminating freight, number of interactions for originating freight, number of interactions for receiving freight, average lead (average distance) separately for originating and terminating freights.

Rural-urban interaction tables

In order to study the pattern and nature of commodity flows between rural and urban centres, data was aggregated at the district/regional level and a detailed table in the form shown in Appendix X, was got printed from the computer. We got nearly 2,000 such tables in the form referred to above. Each table is a (5×5) matrix containing information on rural-rural, rural-urban, urban-rural, urban-urban exchange of commodities, interactions and average distance. Intra-district or intra-regional flows are also shown separately in each table.

Wherever possible, all the above mentioned tables have been aggregated at the district and regional level (regions based on National Sample Survey). Besides this a number of other valuable tables have been generated, the reference to which would appear during our discussions in the subsequent chapters.

LIMITATIONS OF DATA

While interpreting the results, the following limitations of the data may be kept in view. Firstly, the whole analysis is based on only one mode of transportation, that is the railways. It may be pointd out here that the study did not take into account all the modes of transportation and hence the picture may be only a partial one. One may, however, recall that the railways accounted for about 65-70 per cent of the total flow for the period under study and it is hoped that an analysis of the commodity flows by railways would throw adequate light on the nature of inter-regional relationships inspite of this limitation. Secondly, the analysis in this study has been done in terms of weights and not in terms of their monetary value. It may be noted that there were almost unsurmountable difficulties in computing values. It would have involved a huge amount of expenditure and computer time, which was beyond the available resources. Even if resources were available, the range of prices for each commodity is so large that it would have been an enormous task to work out an average price. Even if it was possible to work out such a price its explanatory power would have been extremely limited in a study like this, wherein inter-regional differences are of the essence.

3

STRUCTURAL ANALYSIS OF TRANSPORT NETWORKS

REPRESENTATION OF TRANSPORT NETWORKS

WITH a view to facilitate the movement of men and material from one discrete node to another across space some definite channels of transport are required. These channels consist of nodes and routes connecting these nodes. Thus, the structure of transport network to a large extent, besides other things, would depend upon the settlement pattern itself. The term network may, thus, be considered as referring to spatial pattern of transportation facilities in a given region. No matter what type of system is under examination, some common geometric properties like the origin, the destination and the route joining the origin and destination may be identified. In order to describe, analyse and compare the network systems, we need to formulate methods, which are accurate as well as consistent. By using quantitative methods to measure such relations, the concept of structure can be quantified, that is, the structure of a transportation network can be defined rigorously in mathematical terms. Many recent contributions relating to the study of transportation systems are based upon definitions and descriptions expressed in mathematical form. In a simplified manner, some of the measures of transport network may be stated as under:

- i total road mileage and its derivatives such as road mileage per lakh of population or road mileage per thousand sq. km. of land area;
- ii total railway mileage and its derivates;
- iii net tonne kilometres of freight carried and its derivates:
- iv accessibility to railway network; and
- v developing least cost networks.

The measurement and analysis of the properties of a network is a very complex task. It is only by making certain assumptions that some of the characteristics can be unravelled. Some crude measures of the properties of the transport network may be based upon definitions without measurement, but the analytically efficient one require exact measurements, for example, a study of the structure of a transport network or of the relationship between the structure of a transport network and regional characteristics demand exact measurement.

A number of techniques have been developed for the analysis of transport networks. The more elementary measures like the existence or non-existence of terminals and the existence and non-existence of routes seems somewhat easier to interpret than the preparation of maps and tables listing distances, capacities, flows and such indices as network densities and isochrones. Some indices of structural aspects of the network can be developed subsequently. With a view to provide a better basis for comparison and evaluation of different networks, a number of consistent measures describing the network characteristics have been developed during the past several years. Most of these measures are based on the graph theory and the abstract concept of mathematics. Graphs are defined as sets of systematically organised points and lines.

Graphy theory, as a branch of combinatorial topology provides us with appropriate tools suitable for measurement and analysis of structural aspects of transportation network. However, the underlying assumption is that any given network can be reduced to a structure consisting of points which can be connected by a set of lines or segments. Such graphs enable us to look at the entire transport network, as well as its parts in terms of the whole.

Many social scientists have studied the structure of transport networks using graph theoretical techniques. For example, Lalanne (1963) analysed the density and pattern of the railroad network of the continental France. He observed regular tessellations of the railroad network and suggested a hierarchical relationship between the network and political divisions in France. Hexagons have held a fascination for natural scientist and mathematicians since the Greeks. Therefore, Christaller's (1933) central place theory has used hexagon as the modular unit to bring out the associations between transportation patterns and urban locations. Similar evidence is also available in the works of Losch (1940). Attention may be particularly drawn to some recent studies, which have considered the spatial pattern of transportation systems from the graph theoretical point of view. Garrison (1960) has applied some of the techniques of graph theory to analyse the connectivity of the inter-state highway system of United States for the year 1957. He has underlined the usefulness as well as some of the limitations when the methodologies of graph theory are applied to the analysis of transport network. Garrison and Marble (1961) have designed a set of measures based on concepts of the graph theory. These measures deal with theoretical and empirical investigations of what has been termed as structure of transport network. Nysteun and Dacey (1961) analysed functional connections between central place based upon communication flows in a network with the help of graph-theoretic measures to regional highway networks. Kansky (1963) has undertaken an extensive empirical analysis of transport network structures and has suggested a number of measures for analysing complex transport network structures. Kissling (1969) has examined the regional highway network for the province of Nova Scotia and has used it to identify the probable growth points in the system and more particularly to pinpoint the existing bottlenecks where improvements would yield greater benefits to the region. These studies affirm the applicability of the analytical approach, and of graph theoretic techniques to the analysis of transportation networks.

However, before dealing with different measures of network structure, a brief introduction to the following basic graph theoretical concepts, which translate the observed relationships of networks into numerical and symbolic form, may be advisable:

i *Vertices* (v): The points which form the basic elements of a graph are commonly known as vertices and are sometimes designated as nodes.
ii *Edges (e):* The lines connecting the vertices are called edges.
iii *Oriented and non-oriented graphs:* The oriented graphs recognise the direction of the link whereas in the case of non-oriented graphs no consideration is paid to the direction of the link. The existence of the link in this case is a sufficient condition and the interaction is assumed to be bi-directional.
iv *Connected and unconnected networks:* A network is said to be connected when it is possible to reach a vertex from any other vertex by following the lines or the edges connecting the different vertices. Otherwise the graph is considered to be unconnected.
v *Planer and non-planer graph:* A graph which can be mapped on a plane such that no two edges have a point in common that is not a vertex is known as a planer graph. Graphs which cannot be mapped in the manner stated above are called non-planer graphs.
vi *Circuits:* A circuit is defined as a finite, closed path in which the initial node of linkage sequence coincides with the terminal node.

Measures of network structure are measures of relative quantity. All measures dicussed below are either directly derived from graph-theory or are inferred from these concepts. Two general classes of measures will be dealt in the present study:

i measures of the transportation network in their entirety; and
ii measures of individual elements of the transportation network.

The measures of network structure derived from graph theoretical concepts may be broadly classified into two groups:

i non-ratio measures; and
ii ratio measures

NON-RATIO MEASURES

The measures describing transportation network their entirety are constructed predominantly as ratios between the whole system and its individual elements. Only two measures, abstracted directly from graph theory (the cyclomatic number (μ) and diameter (δ) of the network) are non-ratio measures. The cyclomatic number (μ) is an arithmetic comparison between individual elements of the system, and the diameter (δ) is a special form of the 'associated number'.

Cyclomatic number (μ)

The cyclomatic number is one of fundamental indices of graph theory and is defined as the count of the number of basic circuits existing in the graph. it may be written as:

$$\mu = e - v + p$$

where,

e = number of edges or routes
v = number of vertices or nodes
p = number of non-connected sub-graphs

The index has two properties important for transportation studies:

i the cyclomatic number (μ) of a linear graph G is equal to the maximum number of independent circuits of the graph G; and

ii in a connected graph G, the cyclomatic number is equal to the maximum number of fundamental circuits.

FIG. 3.1 CYCLOMATIC NUMBER

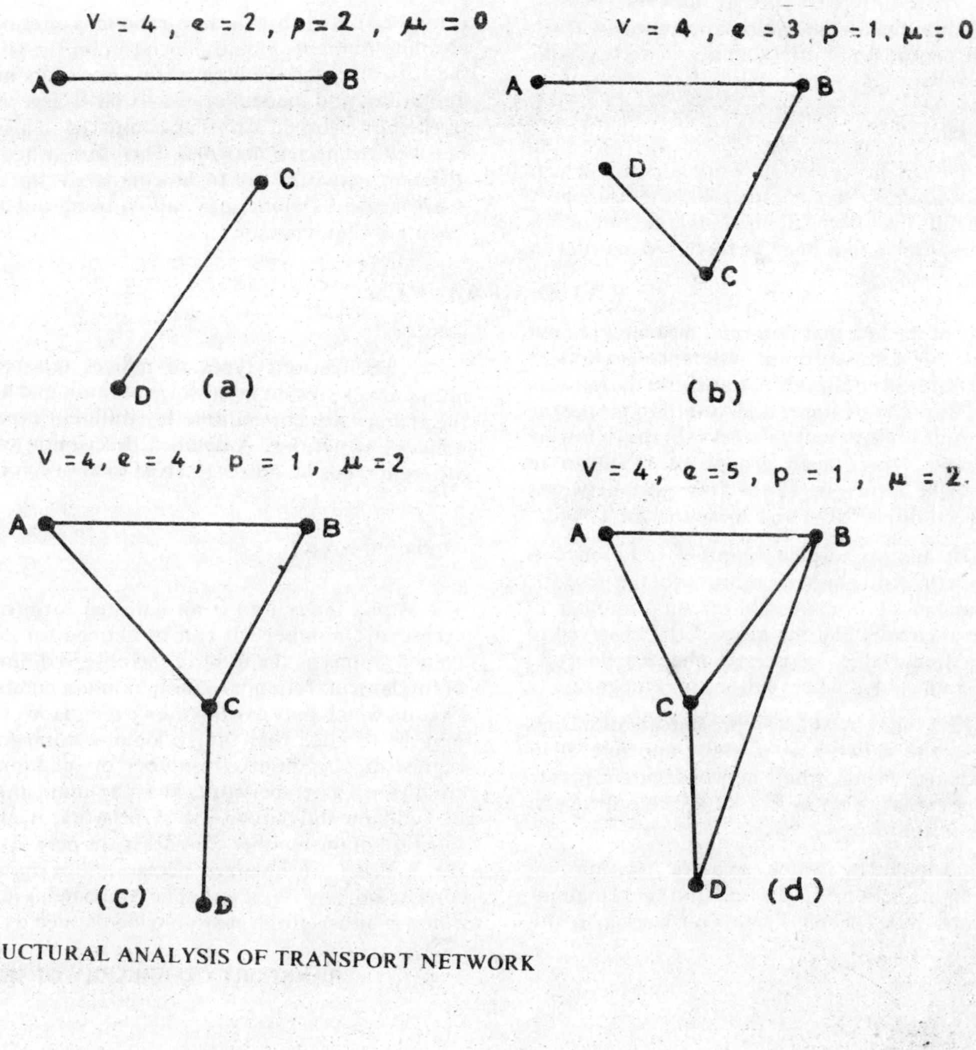

The relationship of the cyclomatic number with the network structure has been examined through Fig. 3.1. Let us consider a network consisting of 4 nodes *A, B, C* and *D*. As can be seen from Fig. 3.1, the disconnected or a tree type of graph has a cyclomatic number of *O*, whereas the graph moves closer and closer to a completely connected state, the cyclo-metric number increases.

These properties do suggest that the magnitude of the cyclomatic number which characterises the development of the transportation system of the country, would have strong association with the level of its social and economic development.

In spite of the fact that the cyclomatic number is an index of network structure which is invariant under isomorphic transformations, it suffers from some major limitations. The cyclomatic number is not an intelligible measure especially when one is concerned with the comparison of two or more different types of network systems. This limitation of the cyclomatic number arises since it depends upon the number of vertices and edges only.

Diameter

Diameter is a measure of network structure which is associated with the span of the transport system. It has been defined as the minimum number of links that must be traversed in order to move between the two points that are farthest apart. The following example illustrates the significance of this measure. Consider the network with farthest apart points being *A* & *D*. Following the above definition, the diameter of the network is 2.

FIG. 3.2 DIAMETER OF THE NETWORK

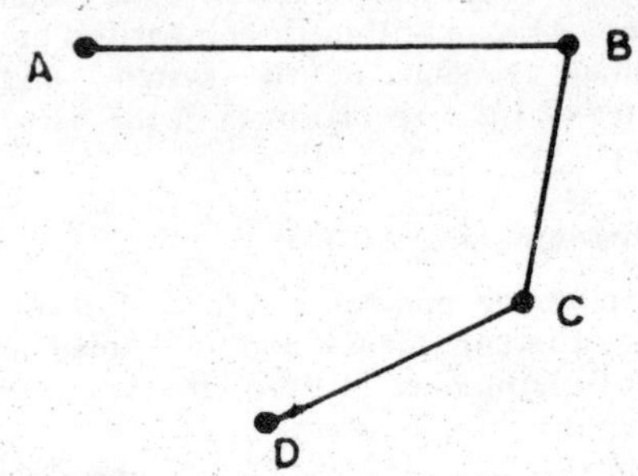

It may be noted that the non-ratio measures being absolute numbers would depend upon the size of the network. A large network in spite of its many limitations and inadequacies may have large value of the non-ratio measures as compared to a small but well connected network. Therefore, whenever different networks are to be compared, the non-ratio measures alone may fail to bring out their essential characteristics.

RATIO MEASURES

In view of the fact that non-ratio measures are not suitable for comparison of different networks, it would be ideally desirable to transform the index in such a way that its upper and lower limits take the same value for different networks. In the following paragraphs, three such groups of measures to analyse the structure of the transport networks have been discussed. These measures are :

1 Indices which express relationships between the distinguishable elements of the network, the number of fundamental circuits, number of maximal circuits and the ratio of the observed to the maximum edges/vertices. Alpha (α), Beta (β) and Gamma (γ) indices fall in this category.

2 Indices which represent relationships between the network as a whole and one of its individual elements, whole network with respect to its edges. Eta (η) and Pi (π) are two measures falling in this group.

3 Indices which express relationships between the network as a whole and the remaining elements. Iota (*i*) and Theta (θ) belong to this category.

The various types of indices referred to above are expressed in the form of ratios and hence the indices are comparable for different types of network structures. A detailed description of the different types of indices referred to above, follows:

Alpha index (α)

The Alpha index (α) is an adjusted form of the cyclomatic number . It can be defined for non—planer graphs as the ratio of the observed number of fundamental circuits to the maximum number of circuits which may exist in the system. However, it may be recalled that the cyclomatic number (μ) represents the observed number of fundamental circuits in a given network. The maximum number of fundamental circuits in a network is also a function of the number of nodes in the network and the number of linkages necessary for minimal connection between nodes. The Alpha index (α) for a non-planner graph may thus be defined as

$$\alpha = \frac{\text{actual circuits}}{\text{maximum circuits}}$$

or

$$\alpha = \frac{e - v + 1}{2v - 5}$$

The value of the Alpha index would thus vary from *O* to *1*. The value *O* would mean a minimal connected network, whereas a value of 1 would refer to a maximally connected network. For convenience, the index may be expressed in a percentage form and may be interpreted as an index representing percentage of connectivity—the maximum connectivity being 100 per cent.

Fig. 3.3 shows two networks having the same number of vertices but different structures. It may be observed from Fig. 3.3 that the maximum number of possible circuits in the two networks is only 5 that is (2v—5). In the case of the first network the number of actual circuits is zero and hence it takes the minimum value that is =*O*. In the second network only two circuits have been formed and hence 2/5 = 0.40

FIG. 3.3 α INDEX

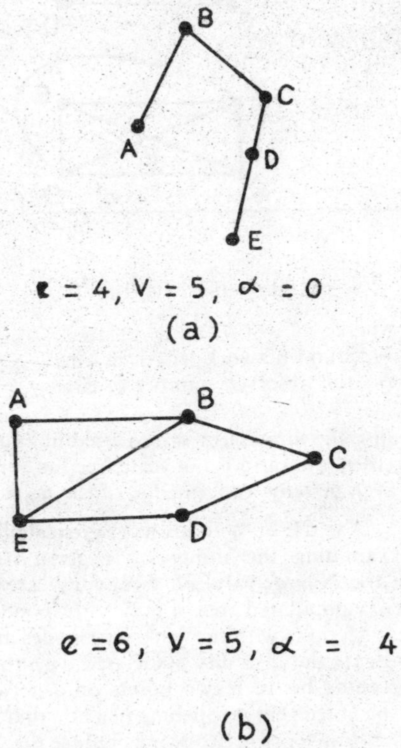

Beta index (β)

The beta index is the simplest form of the three measures which record the relation between two individual elements of a network and has been defined as :

$$\beta = \frac{e}{v}$$

The logical basis of β index is similar to that of the u and α measures. While a transport network. which is highly connected will have a high value of β a network. with a simple structure. will have a low value. Some important properties of β index are:

i β value for three types of structures and disconnected networks would always be less than 1. It would take zero value when there are no edges in the network.

ii β value for any network structure with one circuit would always be equal to 1.

iii β value exceeds 1 for a complicated network structure having more than 1 circuits.

The beta index (β) takes a value between *O* and 1 depending upon the nature of the disconnected graph. The value of β index for non-planer graphs would vary from *O* to γ; whereas for non-planer graphs, the range of β index is from *O* to 3

Gamma index (γ)

The Gamma Index (γ) is a ratio between the observed number of edges and vertices of a given transportation network. For a network, considered as a non-planer graph. The gamma index has been defined as :

$$\gamma = \frac{e}{3\,(v-2)}$$

Stated in other words, γ is a ratio of the observed number of edges (e) to the maximum number of edges in a planer graph. The index, thus, measures the connectivity in terms of the degree to which a given network deviates from an unconnected graph The connectivity as measured by *Y* index varies from a set of nodes having no interconnection to the one in which every node has an edge connected to every other node in the graph. The index gives a numerical value bounded by *O* on the lower side and *1* on the upper side. As in the case of α index, this measure may be written in the form of a percentage and would thus range from *O* to 100 A given value of γ index can, therefore, be considered as percentage connectivity. The value of 100 per cent will be ascribed to a completely connected network.

It is interesting to observe that γ index is independent of the number of vertices of a transport network; that is the value of 1 (or 100 per cent) will be assigned to all completely connected networks whatever be the number of vertices. The following figure shows the maximal connectivity

FIG. 3.4 INDEX

Vertices	*Maximum No. of edges*	*Geometric presentation*
2	1	
3	3	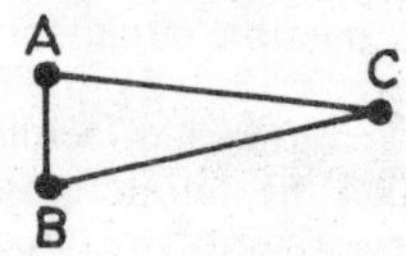
4	6	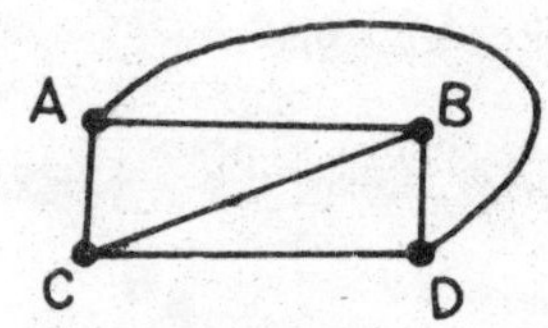
5	9	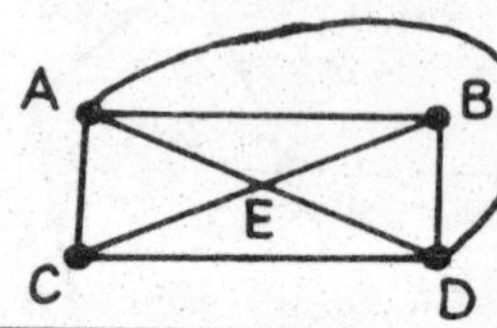

It is evident from the above Figure that for a planer graph, the addition of each vortex to the system increases the maximum number of edges by three. This proposition is true for any planer network with more than two vertices.

Eta index (η) :

The Eta index is one of two measures (η & θ) which have been designed to capture the structural relationship between the transport network as a whole and its routes as individual elements of that network. The η index has been found to be quite useful when some spatial characteristics of the network are under examination. For example, the average edge length is an indicator which depends upon the location of specific nodes in space. If the nodes are located close to each other, then η index would have low value as compared to a network having nodes located distant apart. The index is thus measured on a ratio scale and is based on the principle that network having the same ratio between the whole network and its routes should have the same value of the index. Broadly speaking, the generalised form of the Eta index for any measurable characteristic may be defined as the ratio between the total *kms* of the network and the observed number of edges or

$$\eta = \text{average edge length} = M/E$$

where
M = total network length in kms
E = the observed number of edges

Because the numerator is measured in kilometres, therefore, the ratio is not scale free but represents the average length of an edge of the network.

The use of η index has a great significance in examining the utility of a given transport network. A large value of η may indicate either a sparsely populated area or may correspond to lack of connections with the en-route nodes and thus represents the disutility associated with the space intervening between two points on a network. It may be noted that an opening of a new node within a given transport network may reduce the value of η index, thus representing, the better utility of the

FIG. 3.5 INDEX

$$\eta = \frac{180}{2} = 90 \text{ kms.}$$

$$\eta = \frac{180}{3} = 60 \text{ kms.}$$

network. The following diagram illustrates this point :

It is possible to further divide the network circuits and the η index may be compared for different circuits. Kansky (1963) has used this index in analysing the transport network data for a number of countries.

Pi index (π)

The pi (π) index has been developed to examine the relationship between a transport network as a whole and specific edges of the network. It is called π index for its logical similarity to the irrational number π . which finds extensive use in trignometery ($\pi = 3.1415$). It expresses the relationship between the diameter and its circumference *($C=\pi d$)* or area *($A = \pi r^2$ where $r = d/2$).*

A similar index has been developed for the analysis of transport networks when the focus of enquiry is to investigate the relationship between the transportation network as a whole and its diameter (Kansky, 1963). Let us assume that the total route length of a transportation system is analogous to the circumference of a circle and the total mileage of all edges of the diameter of the network is analogous to the diameter of a circle. The ratio between the length of the network and the length of the network's diameter would always be a real number, analogcus to π . Therefore, the π index may be written as :

$$\pi = \frac{C}{d}$$

where C is the total mileage of a given transportation network and d is its diameter. It may be noted that the ratio $\frac{C}{d}$ will not be constant for all transportation systems. On the contrary it would vary with variations in the level of economic development of a given area.

The application of π index to transportation network would give a numerical value which would be greater than or equal to one. Higher numerical values will be ascribed to more complicated transportation networks; therefore, higher numerical values of the π index would reflect higher degree of development of the network.

Theta index (θ)

The theta index (θ) is a modified form of η index and may be represented as follows :

$$\theta = \frac{T}{V}$$

Like other measures, it is also a ratio where, T is the total traffic flow, or the total volume of freight carried, and V is the observed number of vertices. In this case, the scale of measurement of the numerator would be either metric tonnes or quintals and the denominator is a number. Therefore, the ratio of the two would denote the volume of freight per vertex. It may be, therefore, considered as an average representing the number of tonnes of freight carried through an intersection.

One may also express the totality of transportation networks in terms of the total route length as before. The θ index written as

$$\theta = \frac{M}{V}$$

is then a measure of length per vortex. In this form it may be used as a proxy to the η index. The θ index has one important property—it offers information on the length, structure and also on the degree of connectivity of the network simultaneously. Theoretically speaking, θ seems to be a more powerful measure than η. However, application of η index to the empirical evidence revealed that long average length of an edge is a simple function of the network's structure. η is a sufficiently accurate measure if applied to large basic units of research; θ many be used as a complimentary measure, especially for smaller basic units of research.

Iota index (i)

The iota index is quite useful for the analysis of transport networks as it has been developed on the basis of the following three aspects of transportation networks :

- i structure,
- ii length, and
- iii functions

The index may be written in the following form

$$i = \frac{M}{T}$$

where, M is the total route length and T is the number expressing the total traffic flow. It is widely used in tranportation studies under the name — "Average distance per tonne", or if written in the reciprocal form (T/M) under the name "Average freight carried per km"

Another variation of the above measure corresponds to the situation when the total traffic flows are not available and may take the following form :

$$i = \frac{M}{W}$$

Where, M is the total mileage of the network and W is the observed number of vertices weighted by their function.

The index $\frac{M}{W}$ is very useful for the analysis of transport network for which no traffic flow data are available. It is based on the intuitive assumption that the structure of a transport network is a reflection of the network's traffic flow pattern. Kansky (1963) has used the index as follows. The numerator corresponds to the total number of miles of a given network, the denominator represents the sum of the networks vertices, weighted in such a way that a vertox gets a weight of two when it is the third and higher order intersection. By weighting the third and higher order intersections twice that of vertices with one or two intersections, Kansky (1963) emphasized the role of higher order vertices in the spatial setting of the given network. It was also assumed that transportation networks with a large number of high order vertices were capable of handling larger amounts of traffic flow than networks with a small number of high order vertices, because the high order intersections perform a relatively large number of functions than the low order intersections.

MEASURES OF INDIVIDUAL ELEMENTS OF TRANSPORTATION NETWORKS

A number of measures are available which are capable of assessing the relative cohesiveness of a network or the relative position of individual elements in a given transport system. By averaging the measured scores of all network elements we may also calculate scores as the representative numerical value of the whole network.

Associated number

The first measure, called the associated number of a vortex, was suggested by Konig (1936). The associated number may be defined as the maximum distance from this place to all other places.

One can consider the number of edges as an indication of topological distance. Therefore, the associated number, expressing the maximum distance between network vertices, may be interpreted as a measure of the network's topological extent.

Diameter

This concept is similar to that of network diameter discussed earlier.

Degree of connectivity

The second measure is called degree of connectivity. This measure compares the relative position of an observed network's connectivity on a scale limited by maximum connectivity ratios. If v=number of vertices and e=number of edges, then a network's maximum possible number of routes will be for non-planer graphs :

$$e = \frac{v(v-1)}{2}$$

It has been suggested that the degree of connectivity of a network for which the number of places is known may be expressed as :

$$\text{Maximum connectivity} = \frac{\frac{v(v-1)}{2}}{\frac{v(v-1)}{2}} = 1$$

Thus the maximum connectivity is always equal to 1

The minimum connectivity ratio is the other

limit which oscillates according to the number of vertices :

$$\text{Minimum connectivity} = \frac{\frac{v(v-1)}{2}}{v-1}$$

The degree of connetivity *(d. c.)* may then be written as :

$$d.c. = \frac{\frac{v(v-1)}{2}}{e}$$

Where e is the observed number of edges. Because the minimum connectivity ratio increases with the higher number of vertices, the range of this measure varies greatly (it can be proved that the range is bounded by one at the lower limit and V/2 at the upper limit). Therefore, each network, having a different number of vertices, is measured on a different scale. We can compare degree of connectivity of different networks only if we transform the degree of connectivity values into percentages.

Dispersion

Two other measure have been suggested by Shimbel (1953). The index of transport network structure called the dispersion of a network *(N)* is by difinition :

$$D(N) = \sum_{i=1}^{n} \sum_{j=1}^{n} d(i, j)$$

where d is the distance (in kilometres or in any other metric unit) from a vertex i to a vertex j. It is evident from the formula that this measure is a double sum.

Accessibility

The second measure is called the "accessibility" of a vortex i in the network N and it is by definition :

$$A(i, A) = \sum_{i=1}^{n} d(i, j)$$

It is evident that the "accessibility" measure is equivalent to the measure of "dispersion". Thus, we can characterize, the measure of dispersion as an index expressing an overall property of the network whereas the index of accessibility is a measure indicating the spatial relation between a given element of the structure and the remainder of the network.

Circuity

The last measure of this set is called the degree of circuity. Its purpose is to measure the relative location of a network's individual elements and to measure a network's over-all property. It can be visualised from the formula :

$$\text{Degree of Circuity} = \frac{\sum_{i=1}^{n} (E-D)^2}{v}$$

where E is the existing route in kms., D is the length of a desire line in kms., and v is number of vertices.

By applying this formula we may compare the difference between the existing transportation system and an imaginary transportation system which contains routes connecting all vertices by shortest possible path. The shortest imaginary line between the two given vertices (air distance) is called a "desire line". The difference between a desire line and the existing route, expressed in kms. is squared. By adding up all squared values and by dividing the total by the number of vertices we get a number indicating the degree of circuity of the transportation network relative to the given vortex. An over-all value of the network can also be calculated as an average degree of circuity of all vertices; that is, total number of all squared deviations for all vertices divided by the number of vertices.

The degree of circuity seems to be a meaningful measure. By applying it to transportation network we obtain a metric order among individual networks. The practical applicability of this index depends upon an operational definition of a vortex. Numerical values of the degree of circuity are functions of the number of vertices in the network. Thus, for the same transportation network we may derive different value of the index according to the defined number of vertices. With increase in the number of vertices the calculation of this index becomes time consuming and expensive.

MEASURES OF NODAL ACCESSIBILITY

The emphasis in the identification of spatial structure of transport network may be placed on the changes in response to the new linkage on the position of the individual nodes in the network. These changes are reflected in changes in the nodal accessibility.

The network as a matrix

Any network may be represented as a matrix with its rows as set of origins and the columns as the set of destinations. The number of rows and columns would correspond to the number of nodes in the network. Such an abstract matrix would necessarily be a square non-zero matrix. At the simplest level the cell entries may merely record the presence or the absence of a link between a pair of nodes in the network. At a more complex level of analysis, inter-regional commodity shipments may be represented by a commodity flow matrix, in which each cell would record the volume of each commodity being shipped from one node to the other.

Nodal accessibility

Summation of individual rows or columns of a matrix produces a vector wherein each value represents the total number of direct links from a given centre to all other centres and may be defined as a degree of a node. The higher the value an individual nods gets, the greater is its accessibility to all other centres. For example, in the Indian context the linkage matrix has shown that New Delhi happens to have the highest accessibility through direct train connections with other state capitals. Whereas the least accessible state capital is that of Assam and Pondicherry

The degree of a node as measured by the number of direct links has serious limitations. We may be frequently interested in knowing the accessibility of a node by taking indirect connections into account. What is needed, therefore, is a measure that takes account of both direct and indirect connections. The number of indirect connections between nodal points can be determined by matrix multiplication. Each individual cell of C^2 would be.

$$C_{ij}^2 = \sum_{k=1}^{n} C_{ik} \cdot C_{kj}$$

The procedure that has been employed to determine paths with links of two linkages can be generalised to determine paths of any length in the network. Thus, for a connectivity matrix C, C_{ij} is a path of length n between i & j nodes. When the value of n equals the value of diameter of the network, all the nodes will have path connection to all other nodes.

In determining nodal accessibility we have only considered the number of linkages and have altogether ignored the impact of other variables such as the distance between two nodes, the time of journey or the capacity of the inter-nodal connections. By suitable manipulation of the connectivity matrix, it is possible to study the impact of the above referred variables. Shortest path matrix is one such method in which accessibility is computed in terms of the distance between the nodes. Similarly, the internodal distance can be subsitituted by the journey time or the cost of movement between different nodes.

It is clear from the above discussion that from the matrix representation of a network, it is possible to derive several measures of centrality or accessibility which can be usefully employed to provide information on the structural aspects of a network.

It follows from the above discussion that the techniques of graph theory for analysis of transport network structure have played a very crucial role in broadening our understanding and have provided the basis for undertaking empirical investigation relating to the internal structure of a given network.

4

TECHNIQUES OF COMMODITY FLOW ANALYSIS

THE literature survey presented in Chapter 2 has clearly brought out that the empirical research on commodity flows has emerged on the academic scene only recently and methodologically significant contributions are particularly rare. The reasons for this lag in empirical research are at least partly connected with the complexity of the phenomenon and partly with the dearth of adequate statistical measures with which to examine its behaviour. However, with the advent of high speed data processing machines certain statistical tools have been developed recently which may be profitably used in the identification, description and analysis of interdependencies in commodity flows. Some of the statistical tools may be used even for the objective treatment of a complex set of data so as to reduce the possibility of bias in subjective judgement. The statistical techniques necessary for such an analysis have been adopted quite recently by social scientists in general and by economists and geographers in particular and have found profitable use in many areas of regional analysis. The development of large capacity digital computers have also greatly facilitated the application of a wide range of descriptive indices and sttistics, simple and multivariate inferencial techniques to large sets of data matrices ususally encountered in research in social sciences. The study also makes use of a number of statistical tools for the structural analysis of large commodity flow matrices. This chapter, therefore, presents within the conceptual framework outlined earlier, the techniques and the tools of analysis that have been used in the structural analysis of inter-regional flow matrices and the pattern of their spatial linkages.

THE CONCEPTS DEFINED

Commodity flows

The basic configuration of commodity flows takes the form of a transaction matrix in which the rows indicate the origin of movement and the columns represent their destination. As is evident from the following matrix, (i, j) cell of the matrix represents the volume of movements between i^{th} origin and j^{th} destination.

FIG. 4.1 INTER REGIONAL COMMODITY FLOW MATRIX

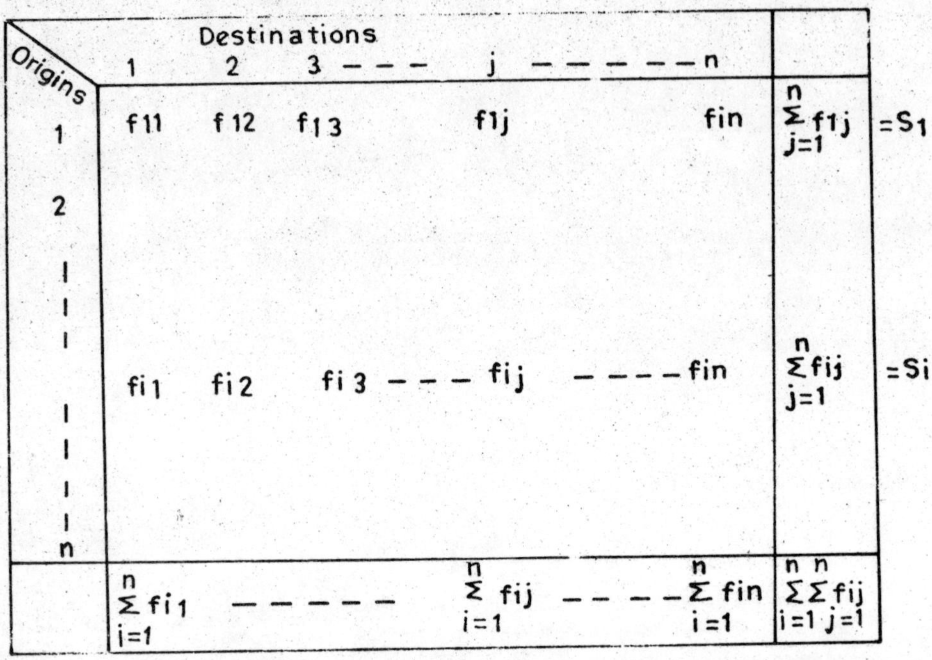

INTER-REGIONAL COMMODITY FLOW MATRIX

The following indicators may be considered for each spatial unit in the economic space :

i Volume of originating flows—commodity-wise and total
ii Volume of terminating flows—commodity-wise and total

Shipments from a district or a region have been defined as the total volume of originating freight for all the nodes falling within the district or the region. Similarly, receipts into a particular district or a regions have been defined as the total volume of freight terminating at all the nodes falling within the boundaries of the district or the region. It may be noted that at the district level both intra-district flows have been included in the total originating terminating volume of the freight. These concepts of shipments from and receipts at a particular district or a region are more meaningful as compared to the one in which intra-district or intra-regional *(Ii)* flows are usually assumed to be zero. In the analysis that follows the concepts of shipments and receipts as defined above that is, including intra-regional flows have been used. In the following notations, we shall use the district as a spatial unit of measurement. Similarly, the aggregation can be done at any other level of spatial aggregaiton.

Let S_i = Total shipments from district $i = 1, \ldots n$

T_i = Total receipts into district i

S_{ij} = Shipments from i^{th} district to j^{th} district

T_{ij} = Receipts into i^{th} district from j^{th} district

When $i = j$

$$S_{ii} = T_{ii} = I_i$$

Where I_i is intra-regional flow of the ith district.

$$\left.\begin{aligned} S_i &= I_i + \sum_{j=1}^{n} S_{ij} \; i \neq j \\ T_i &= I_i + \sum_{j-1=}^{n} T_{ij} \; i \neq j \end{aligned}\right] i, j = 1, 2, \ldots \ldots i-1, i+1 \ldots n$$

Spatial linkages

i number of interactions—originating freight
ii number of interactions—terminating freight

The number of interactions have been defined as the number of spatial links, irrespective of the volume of freights that each node establishes with other nodes during the process of freight exchange. In the case of a district such linkages would be added for all the nodes falling within its boundaries.

Spatial dispersion of flows

i Average distance—originating freight
ii Average distance—terminating freight

The average distance of shipments originating from the *i* node has been defined as under :

$$AD_i = \frac{\sum_{j=1}^{n} D_{ij} W_{ij}}{\sum_{j=1}^{n} W_{ij}} \qquad j = 1, 2 \ldots\ldots n.$$

Similarly, the average distance of receipts at j node can be defined as under :

$$ADj = \frac{\sum_{i=1}^{n} D_{ij} W_{ij}}{\sum_{i=1}^{n} W_{ij}} \qquad j = 1, 2, \ldots\ldots n.$$

Where

D_{ij}=Distance from i^{th} node to j^{th} node
W_{ij}=Volume of flow i^{th} node to j^{th} node
n=number of interactions

SPATIAL INTERDEPENDENCE OF COMMODITY FLOWS

Our earlier discussion of the commodity flow phenomenon is based on the principle of mutual interdependence of flow of various commodities. With a view of validate our hypothesis ragarding the spatial interdependence of commodity flows, the association between the aggregate levels of shipments and receipts may be examined through a correlation matrix. For example, if there are *k* commodities for which the spatial association between shipments and receipts need to be examined, then the correlation matrix would be of *(2k, 2k)* dimension and would take the form as represented below :

Since our interest primarily lies in examining the association between shipments and receipts in each region, the matrix shown in thick border would only be considered. It may by noted that the matrix under consideration would be non-systematic and *rij* would not necessarily equal *rji*. In the case of perfect spatial interdependence of all the commodity flows, the correlation in all the cells of the correlation matrix would be statistically significant, whereas in the case of perfect spatial independence, no correlation would be statistically significant. Let be the value in *(i, j)* cell of the correlation table. *rij* woul indicate the degree of spatial

FIG. 4.2 INTER CORRELATION MATRIX

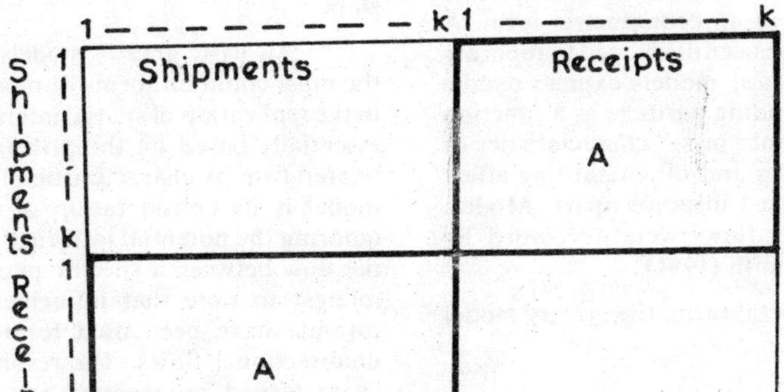

association between the shipments of i commodity and the receipts of **j** commodity.

It may be noted that within such a framework r_{ij} would indicate the strength of intra-regional flows for i^{th} commodity, whereas $(1-r^2)$ would indicate the strength of inter-regional flows.

MODELS OF COMMODITY FLOW INTERACTION

Broadly speaking, the analysis of commodity flow matrices may be undertaken at any or all of the following three levels :

i unilateral
ii bi-lateral
iii multi-lateral

Corresponding to each of these categories, we have a variety of statistical tools which may be used for understanding the nature of inter-regional commodity flows. shall briefly discuss some of the important tools of analysis for
in the following paragraph us.

Unilateral models

The type of models that have been developed to replicate the flows in relation to other variable, e.g., economic base and the development attributes of the region, can be classified as unilateral models. Despite its shortcomings, many such models have been quite useful in developing a proper understanding of the factors generating the commodity flows. The techniques of simple and multiple regression analysis are used to estimate the unknown parameters. In dealing with such models one has to be cautious since they are simplistic versions of a highly complex phenomenon and ignore the potential influence of dyadic or multi-lateral interactions. This type of models are quite useful for the analysis of aggregate commodity flow patterns.

Bi-directional models

A promising alternative line of development to the unilateral models has been the construction of spatial trade models in an econometric form. A number of models have been developed to replicate the bilateral flows. These models express dyadic interactions among trading partners as a function of theoretically relevant "mass" characteristics of the partners themselves and of a retarding effect related to their physical distance apart. Models related to commodlty flows were developed by Gould, Robert and Smith (1961).

In its most general form, the gravity model is usually written as :

$$X_{ij} = \frac{k\ P_i\ (W_i)\ P_i\ (W_j)}{w_d\ d_{ij}{}^n}$$

where

Pi, Pj are mass factors
dij is distance between points i, j
w is weighing factor
x is a scaler constant

The Poyhonen-Pulliainen model is expressed by :

$$X_{ij} = K \frac{C_i\ C_j\ P^a{}_i\ P^b{}_j}{d^n{}_{ij}}$$

Whereas the Tinbergen formula is :

$$X_{ij} = K \frac{P^a{}_i\ P^b{}_i}{d^n{}_{ij}}$$

Pi, Pi are Gross National Product of origin and destination countries, dij the distance between their main economic centres, exponents a, b and d are elasticities of trade with respect to Gross National Product and distance. K is a proportionality constant while Ci and Ci in the Finish model are indices expressing "openness to trade," such as resource endowment, tariff levels, etc. In a review of these models the Belgian economist Waelbroek has suggested that the factor of prices in origin and destination countries, and the elasticity of substitution attendant upon relative price differences be added to the gravity model.

However, these models do not allow the type of modifications which would permit their application to multi-lateral effects. The bi-lateral models can be further classified into the symmetrical and asymmetrical models. While the symmetrical models consider two way flows, the asymmetrical models express one way relationship.

All basic gravity models, which are among the most common forms of model to be employed in the replication of spatial interaction patterns, are essentially based on the principle of symmetrical bilateralism. A characteristic of the gravity type of model is its consideration of dyadic interaction ignoring the potential influence of other factors on the flow between a specific pair of points. It is of interest to note that refinements of the gravity formula have been used for the explanation of unidirectional flows. The resulting model is thus characterised by asymmetrical bilateralism. One such refinement is the making of a formal distinction between 'push' and 'pull' effect so that appropriate magnitude can be attached to origin and destination of a particular unidirec-tional flow.

Models with multivariate components

In view of the multi-lateral character of many economic interactions, is might be argued that this condition should be reflected in any model which attempts to replicate inter-regional flows. The need for the consideration of the many sided and complex nature of interactions has, in fact, been recognised and put into effect in a number of more recent empirical models. The concepts which permit the incorporation of outside influences on dyadic flows are those, which are based on the idea of intervening opportunity or interaction potential. However, models using the concept of potential for the measurement of interactions have not been an unqualified success in practical terms. The drawbacks of potential models in the explanatory framework are noted by Reed (1967), who employed the concept of potential in examining the flow of goods in a regional context in India. Reed draws attention, for instance, to an aspect of Stouffers concept of intervening opportunity, which envisages the level of interaction between points *'d'* miles apart as being proportional to total probability of interaction between each point in question and all outside points within a radius 'd'. Logically, this probability (if points are uniformly distributed) should also be closely proportional to distance *d*. Thus, the distance variable itself may be used as a surrogate for intervening opportunity measure with a fair degree of analytical efficiency.

The preceding discussion has important implications for the present study. The explict recognition of multi-lateral influences on volume of flows, whether aggregate or dyadic, has been highlighted as theoretically desirable. It has also been made evident that there are serious practical problems in the use of potential measure in models based on the explanatory power of independent vairables.

ALTERNATE FRAMEWORK FOR ANALYSIS OF FLOWS

Berry's study of Indian commodity flows is significant for more than its introduction of potential measures in a linear flow model. It is perhaps of greater interest for its pursuance of a more satisfactory way of displaying empirical relationships between dyadic flows on the one hand and economic stimuli on the other—avoiding the limitations of the essentially bi-lateral gravity based formulations. It is possible to envision the set of inter-regional economic relationships as an example of a 'field' of interaction possibilities, where the concept of a field involves the abstract notion of potential interaction among a set of regions as well as direct dyadic or bi-lateral inter-connections.

The usefulness of the field concept lies in its amenability to expression in the form of a multivariate model in which aggregate or multilateral as well as dyadic interactions, and corresponding disparities in relevant characteristics, are seen as two sets of variates between which particular relationships may be identified. The usefulness of this procedure in the present instance should now be quite clear. We can define the national economy as a field, in which the various regions are the objects, and their commodity flows are the interactions of prominent interest. Our objective being to establish the nature, significance and the direction of the mutually reinforcing relationships among the different nodes in these fields which are operationalised through commodity flows. The formal statement of concepts underlying this approach has been designated as the Field Theory, and the method by which these relationships can be unravelled is a linear algebric procedure involving the multivariate techniques of principal axis factor analysis and of canonical correlation.

The technique of factor analysis, based on the principle of mutual interdependence, seems to provide a simpler, though relatively crude alternative. The basic structural features of the situation under examination are reflected by a set of indices, often referred in literature as factors, aspects, components or dimensions. These indices, hereafter referred to as factors, are formed from the observations using the following mathematical principles:

- i those variables that are most closely inter-correlated are combined within a single factor;
- ii the variables allocated to a given factor are those that are most nearly independent of the variables allocated to the other factors;
- iii the factors are derived in a manner that maximises the percentage of the total variance attributed to each successive factor (given the inclusion of the preceding factors); and
- iv the factors are independent of each other.

Let us assume that we have n (i=1, ...n) variables to represent the m (j=1,2....m)

underlying structural features of the solution in each of the N (K=1, N) spatial units, say of a district. The factor analysis model may then be written in matrix notation form as under:

$$Z\ (n,\ N) = A\ (n,\ m)\ E\ (m,\ N)$$

where,

Z = The matrix of variables (of order $n \times N$).

However, the observations of variables are normalised.

Z_{ik} =(i=1, 2............... n. k=1..................N) with respect to their arithmetic mean and standard deviation

$$\frac{Z_{ik} - X_{ij}}{X_i}$$

A =the aspect matrix of (order $n \times m$) or the matrix of factor loading a_{ij} (i=1............n, j=1.........m)
F =the matrix of factors (of order $m \times N$) with elements f_{jk} (i=1...............m; k=1, 2...............N).

Each eigen value (λ_i) sets the contribution of its factor to the variance of all the variables (or columns) as explained by the common factors, or

$$\lambda j = \Sigma a_{ij}^2$$

where $\Sigma\lambda j = {}_m - dj^2$

and dj^2 = variance unexplained by the common factors.

The cumulative percentage is the relative contribution of each factor compared to the total contribution of all the common factors, or

$$\Sigma[(\lambda j/\Sigma\lambda j) + (\lambda j - 1/\Sigma\lambda j)]$$

The communalities (h^2) indicate the degree to which the linkages within the sample are explained by the common factor, or

$$h_j^2 = 1 - dj^2$$

The most common method of identifying the nature of the resultant factor is to examine the factor loadings matrix. The rotated factor loadings describe the relative strength of each variable in the factor. The higher the weights attached to a particular variable, the greater would be the importance of that variable in the component. The factor loadings or weights as derived are multiplied by the standardised matrix to give factor scores. These scores can be further used in identifying the functional regions which would be based on commodity flow characteristics.

Factor analytical tools in the flow analysis can be used from two view points: first, those which use factored flow data as input for further analysis, and second, those where factor analysis results constitute the foci of the study. In the first instance, the technique is used primarily to reduce the bulk of the flow data while preserving much of the statistical information. The second type uses factor analysis to regionalise a flow system, that is, to reduce a complex flow system to its components. Several studies exemplify this use. Britton (1971) in a discussion of the role of the factor analysis in a general methodology of flow analysis, describes patterns of inter-regional goods movement at a national scale for England and Wales. Aggarwal (1979) in an analysis of district-wise aggregate commodity flows in India has used factor analytical tools to demonstrate the patterns of regional specialisation. Khurana (1979) has used similar techniques to study the pattern of urban commodity flows. These studies have undoubtedly demonstrated that the factoring techniques can be effectively utilised to identify the basic factor or salient flow patterns even within a complex multi-lateral commodity flow system.

The structural analysis of flow matrices to produce the underlying structure of freight flows distinguishing groups of origin or destination regions may proceed in the following two ways:

R—mode factor analysis of commodity flow matrix

Each column of the flow matrix is correlated with every other column, and the resulting matrix of correlations showing similarities in the way destinations assemble their needs is factored. Rotated factor loadings yield groups of column (receivers) or consuming regions and the ranking of the corresponding factor scores for the originating regions indicate the most prominent sources of shipment to each group comprising a number of consuming regions which are indicated by respective factors.

Q—mode factor analysis of commodity flow matrix

Each row of the commodity flow matrix is correlated with every other, yielding a correlation matrix showing the similarities in the way origins ship their products to destinations. Factoring yields groups of origins or producing regions and the ranking of factor scores indicates the most prominent destinations of shipments from each group.

The type of analysis indicated above would enable the identification of the cluster of regions, having common origin or destination for each commodity separately.

ANALYSIS OF DYADIC FLOWS

It is evident from the above discussion, that the R and Q modes of factor analysis are useful to identify the resultant factors only if there is one interaction matrix. However, these are not amenable to the type of situation wherein the relationship under examination is essentially bilateral and the number of interaction variables are more than one. Such a situation arises when the focus of the study shifts from the analysis of flows of regions to that of specific pairwise interactions. The purpose of the present section is to develop the conceptual framework which permits the replication of commodity flow complexities in a framework of inter-connected dyads.

The above discussion relating to the theoretical underpinnings of commodity flow analysis provides the following set of concepts which should prove useful in the present context:

i the volume of exchange is regulated by the nature and relative severity of friction applying to each kind of movement.

ii since multi-lateral influences, which shape the mixes of flows, operate at the disaggregated as well as at the aggregated level; thus implying that the flows are mutually interdependent.

The basic principles of interaction as outlined above may be considered to be applicable to the more specific case of dyadic interactions. Under such a situation, dyadic factor analysis may be applied to unravel the nature of the bilateral type of spatial linkages for all the possible sets of connections and for all the variables (matrices in their case) taken together.

The analysis of dyadic interactions becomes all the more important if it is postulated that close neighbours will tend to have greater volume of interactions than pairs occupying distant locations in space. The dyadic analysis of commodity flows proceeds in the following stages.

First, the original flow matrices are converted into a second interaction matrix in such a way that the rows represent all the possible dyadic flows and the columns represent different commodities or types of flows. For example, if we have k (number of commodities) inter-regional flow matrices, each of the dimension $n \times n$ (where n represents the number of regions) there will be n^2 or $(n^2—n)$ rows in a dyadic flow matrix depending upon whether intra-regional flows are being considered or not, and k types of commodities or types of interactions would occupy the columns. Second, the new matrix of dimension $(n^2 \times k)$ or $(n^2—n) \times k$ may be treated for structural analysis like any other data matrix. The columns of such a matrix may be inter-related and, therefore, it is possible to collapse them into f dimensions using a factor analysis model $(f \leqslant k)$.

Several problems arise in using the above procedures for the structural analysis of flows. First, there is a considerable loss of information as the actual flows among the regions are not presented and the directional aspect of the individual flows is not fully ascertained. Second, the flow pattern of some regions might not be well represented by a single factor, yet such a region will be shown as belonging to a particular factor by virtue of its being forced into a particular group or category. Third, the original correlations are based on extremely skewed distributions, thus violating some of the initial assumptions of correlation coefficients. The obvious solution to this problem is to transform the original data in such a way that the skewness is eliminated. Inspite of the possibility of such transformations, sometimes it becomes difficult to offer explanation in support of such transformations, especially in the case of commodity flows. However, as compared to the usefulness of the applications of these models in flow analysis, these appear to be minor limitations. In the present study we shall extensively use these techniques of commodity flow analysis.

GROUPING OF REGIONS

The objective of grouping of regions is to place in one group those areas which are near together (homogeneous) in N dimensional space and to separate groups which are far apart (hetrogeneous) in a similar space field. The detailed review of all the methods is beyond the purview of this study.

The input for such groupings is usually the factor scores of the orthogonal factors. While grouping the spatial units, we are mainly interested in clustering or forming groups of regions on the basis of their spatial contiguity. However, in the preesent exercise, the contiguity constraint was not considered.

The present study makes use of the method developed by Ward (1963). It aims at each step to combine the two units which give the least increase to the pooled within-group sum of squares. The starting point considers the points in a 'p' dimensional space (*p* is the number of orthogonal variables) in which the sum of squared distance from each region's centroid to its component basic units can be calculated. With p orthogonal variables, *Zij* for a region with a units, we have:

$$ESS = \sum_{j=1}^{p} \sum_{i=1}^{n} \left[Z_{ij} - \frac{1}{n} \sum_{i=1}^{n} Z_{ij} \right]^2$$

$$= \sum_{j=1}^{p} \left[\sum_{i=1}^{n} Z_{ij}^2 - \frac{1}{n} \left(\sum_{i=1}^{n} Z_{ij} \right)^2 \right]$$

In the first instance, the *ESS* for all possible combinations are calculated and the combination which gives the minimum *ESS* is calculated again for each of the remaining possible pair-wise groupings. This process can continue until all units are combined into a single region.

EFFECT OF DISTANCE ON COMMODITY FLOWS

It has generally been agreed that the volume as well as the intensity of movement falls as the distance increases. While examining the role of distance in commodity flows, Raza and Aggarwal (1980) have reviewed the ways in which the pervasive and attenuating impact of distance can be measured. Distance-weight relationships for the railway freight can be studied in the context of:

- i either, the actual point to point flow matrices; or
- ii the volume of terminating freight in various distance classes.

Keeping the objectives of the present study in view, the former appears to be less appropriate as a large number of cells would be empty in the actual point to point flow matrix. The latter method has, therefore, been used; and the regression estimates of distance decay for various commodity groups have been obtained from the volume of terminating freight in diferent distance classes.

The degree of correspondence between distance category and terminating freight can be measured mathematically by the correlation coefficient and the coefficient of determination. A negative and statistically significant correlation would show the existence of distance decay effect, whereas the value of R^2 will indicate the proportion of explained variance. Techniques of multivariate regression analysis have been found to be quite useful in the study of the nature of relationship between distance and terminating weight. By using these tools, it is possible to estimate spatial elasticity of demand for different commodities.

Similarly, the spatial elasticity of interactions can be calculated by using the interaction/spatial linkage matrix instead of the flow matrix. A comparison of elasticities of demand and interactions would bring out some of the essential characteristics of the commodity flow phenomenon.

Some other techniques of analysing commodity flow matrices include the use of mathematical programming models. The most powerful analytical tool of analysis is linear programming and its variations in the form of integer programming techniques. The latest departure from the linear programming approach is the use of simulation techniques to predict the economic consequences of various policies and investment decisions. However, the data requirements for developing such models are staggering. The economic model requires a set of historical data for a number of years including input-output matrices. The corresponding transport model would require the physical characteristics of the links in the transport system. Detailed information would also be required on the volume and characteristics of vehicles and rolling stock. The existence of origin, destination and commodity flows is of crucial significance. In view of the difficulty in getting all the required information/data, the immediate application and usefulness of the mathematical programming models to many of the developing countries is limited.

It may, thus, be noted that the foregoing discussion on methodological aspects of commodity flow analysis is only explanatory in nature and efforts were made to discuss in detail only those methodological techniques which were considered to be more appropriate from the view point of our study.

5

COLONIAL UNDER-DEVELOPMENT AND THE DEVELOPMENT OF RAILWAYS IN INDIA

MODEL OF COLONIAL UNDER DEVELOPMENT

MANY of the developing nations have had a colonial history stretching till the recent years. A study of the spatial organisation of such countries which ignores the role of their colonial heritage and particularly of its strong surviving vestiges would be superficial and incapable of analysing contemporary reality. It is with this end in view that an attempt has been made to develop a model of the spatial organisation of colonial underdevelopment.

The Latin American school may be rightly considered to provide significant impetus to a scientific analysis of the spatial structure of colonial/dependent economies. There is an analogous body of literature which sets up a neatly dualistic analytical framework mutually antithetical constructs such as 'modern' sector and the 'traditional' sector; the 'urban' sector and the 'rural' sector; the 'industrial' sector and the 'agricultural' sector; the 'subsistence' sector and the 'monetised sector' etc.

The Latin American school and the Dualist School both succeeded in comprehending larger slices of reality of the colonial/dependent economies than the conventional Anglo-Saxon theories. In important respects, the Latin American School represents a breakthrough in theoretical analysis of the colonial/dependent economies. But, the Dualist School is altogether wide off the mark because of the very neatness of their antithetical constructs. In fact, the specific features of the colonial/dependent setting follow from the very fact that the 'modern' sector is really not so 'modern', nor is the 'traditional' sector entirely 'traditional', the 'subsistence' sector entirely 'non-monetised', or the 'urban' sector entirely 'urban'. The constructs are not valid even in the sense of analytical ideal types.

On the other hand, the Latin American School—often known for their 'Structuralist' approach—fail to articulate their 'structural' model of the economy in terms of the capital accumulation process operating through the interaction of different modes of generation, appropriation and utilisation of the economic surplus in its vertical as well as horizontal dimension.

The point of departure for the colonial dependent setting consists in acknowledging the following features.

i non-economic compulsions characterise the accumulation process subsisting between the metropolitan economy and the colonial/dependent economy, which serves as the overriding condition governing the nature of the economic reproduction process.

ii multiple modes of generatidn, appropriation and utilisation of surplus operate simultaneously, not necessarily in conflict with each other, and tend to precipitate a hiatus between the system of property and earning power and production responsibility, or commitment to the 'production principle' as Antonic Gramsci would put it.

iii under conditions (i) and (ii), the process of monetisation and commercialisation of the economy unleashed through the forcible penetration of the exigencies of metropolitan accumulation of claims to wealth and income with various-liquidity-ratings unrelated to their respecting real productivity-ratings.

iv as a result of (i), (ii) and (iii), the learning process does not necessarily incorporate a technical progress function, thereby disconnecting the socio-economic infrastructure from the self-regenerative growth process.

The spatial dimension of such a pattern of accumulation essentially consists in impounding even the very limited growth impulses within the socio-economic enclaves. The national market, which is the offspring of the forced intrusion of the metropolitan capital accumulation process, is not the symbiotic result of interlacing local, regional and sub-regional markets from the base upwards. The system of exchange between the metropolitan economy and the colonial/ dependent economy acts more like a cantilever bridge from whose various arms the enclaves hang down creating vortexes of exchange in the colonial-dependent economy, inter-connected by a tenuous currency and transport network. Through these vortexes the surplus is siphoned off partly to the metropolitan economy, the rest getting impounded in the enclave itself.

A simplified skeletal model of the consequent spatial structure has been shown in Fig. 5.1 and may be conceived as follows:

i the dependent enclaves are urban agglomerations acting as outposts of the metropolitan economy in the dependent/ colonial economy.

ii the Satellite centres usually constitute a cluster subserving the main enclave agglomeration as subsidiary assembly points of primary produce and labour force at a lower level of infrastructural facilities which connect them to the hinterland of primary produce

iii plantation and mining areas necessarily develop in clusters at a very low level of urbanisation so far social infrastructural facilities are concerned.

iv the hinterland of primary produce, other than plantation crops, is comprised of rural areas producing food and cash crops.

The above model of spatial organisation gets tied up with the help of the infrastructural network.

However, after attaining independence, efforts have been made to alter this structure by influencing the location of production activities in space. This is usually achieved by a considerable public investment and state sponsored economic activity in the resource rich regions. Consequently, certain modifications of the colonial economy take place and these are envisaged in Fig. 5.2. The basic categories remain the same except for the following changes.

The enclave-agglomeration is no longer a mere outpost of the metropolitan economy. It is, however, still a major trade-outlet and becomes the centre of conglomerate big business, metropolitan collaboration, capital, and major state-institutions Its basic functional character, however, remains unchanged as the focal point of commodity, income, capital and labour force flows remain as described earlier. The specific features of its pattern of urbanisation remain basically intact.

Apart from the old Satellite centres of tertiary activity and the mining and plantation areas, a new set of satellite centres of public-investment now subserve the main agglomeration. These public sector townships are different from the old Satellite centres in that they are usually location sites of heavy industry and are not centres of tertiary activity. However, in course of time, they may develop into subsidiary agglomerations with increasing weightage of tertiary activities. The growth impulses of public investment in these new centres, continue to be impounded, and fail to affect the neighbourhood substantially.

Because of the massive public investments in agriculture, focused on the water supply variable, a sharp gradation of the hinterland of primary produce takes shape. Areas of sub-marginal subsistence are mostly concentrated in the dry areas. The circumstances of sub-marginal subsistence continue to be reproduced in pockets of squalor, as before, all along the urban spectrum. In some cases, these pockets may be eliminated from the heartland of urban areas to their peripheries, because of sky-rocketing urban land values-thanks to massive public investments.

In this model, as before, the infrastructural network ties up, so to speak, the various components of the space economy involving all

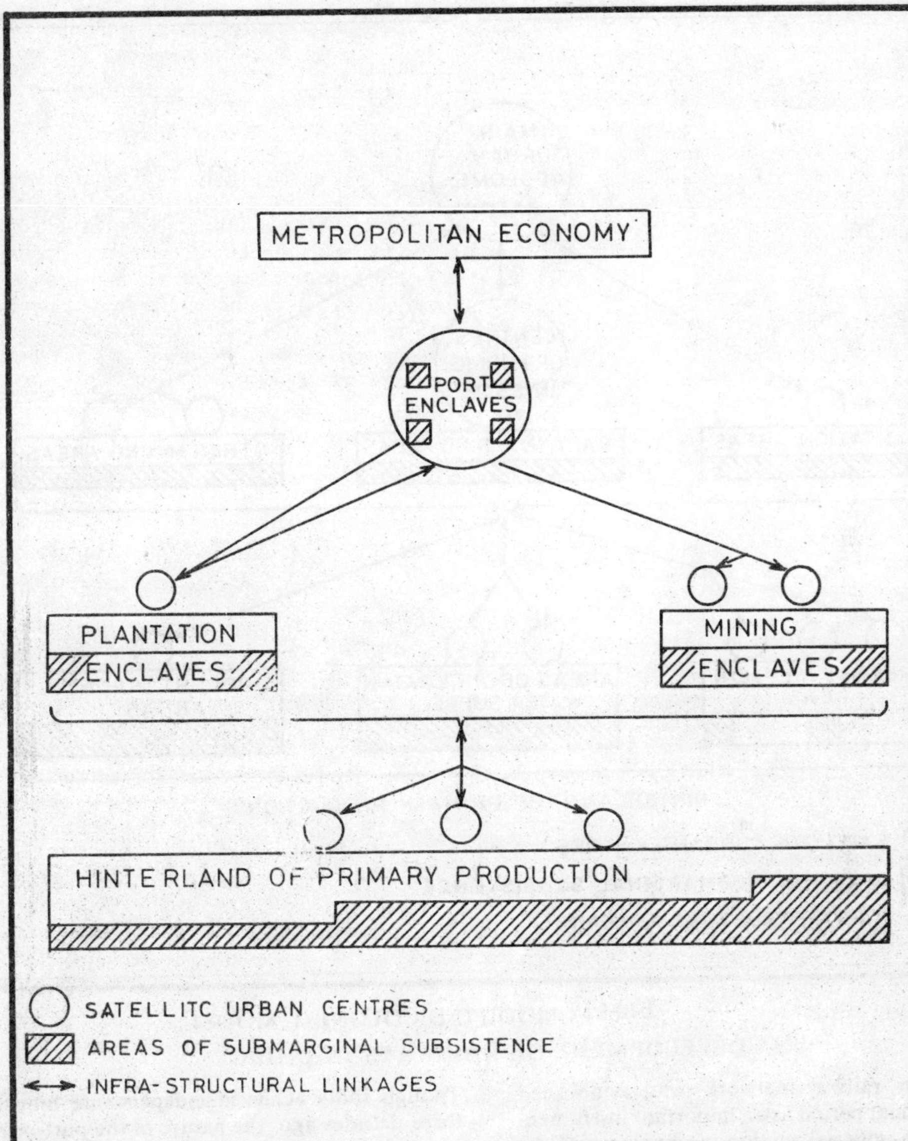

round accentuation of vertical ana horizontal disparities and associated social tensions.

One may notice in this model an implicit hierarchic arrangement where a hinterland is broken into parts of varying characteristics at the lower levels, a set of second order satellite centres again of varying characterisıtics and the metropolitan centres at the apex. Here again the possibilities of links within the hierarchic level is underplayed. With such a model of the spatial organisation of under development, let us now examine the role which the railways played in the spatial organisation of the space economy during the colonial period.

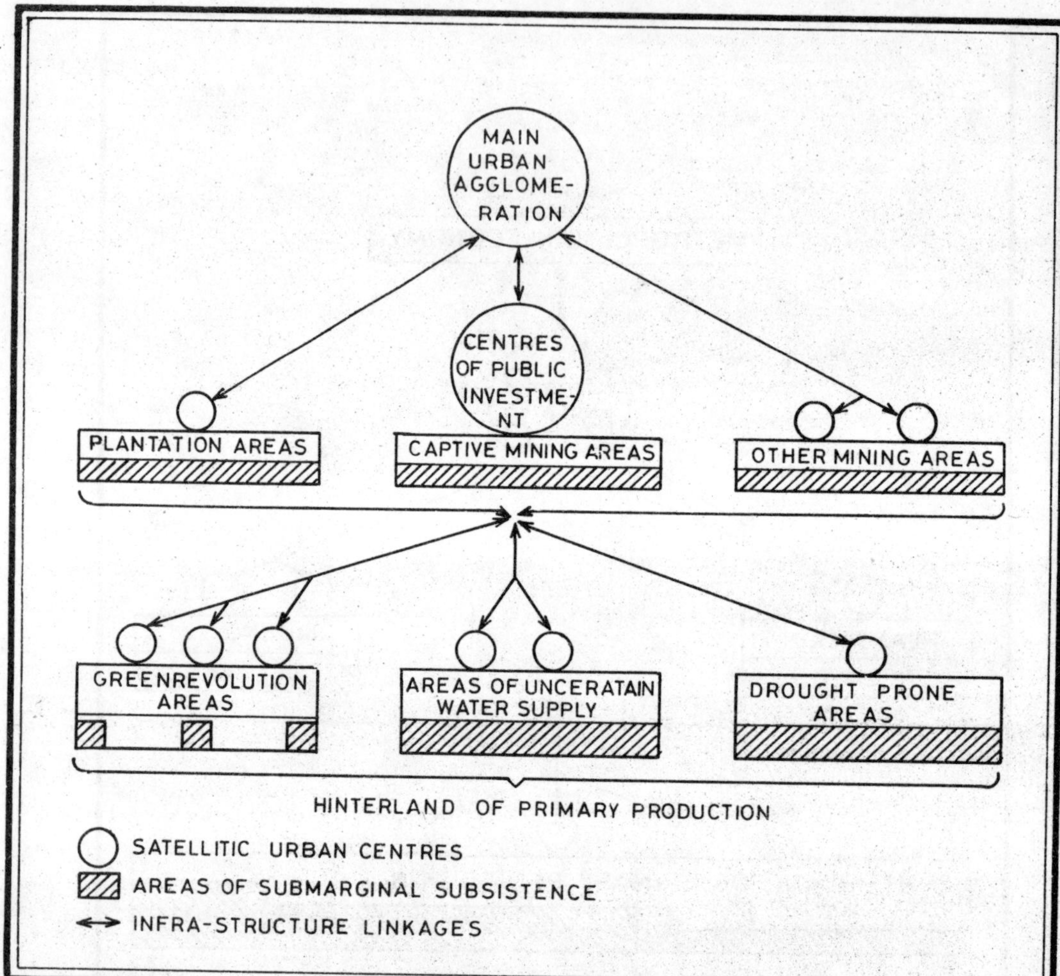

FIG 52 : MODIFIED COLONIAL MODEL

DEVELOPMENT OF RAILWAYS IN INDIA

The Indian railway network was established during colonial period as an important instrumentality of the imperial suction mechanism and the associated freight policies were evolved to operationalise the centrifugality of commodity flows over the vast tracts of the colony. The rapid expansion of the railway network in India was neither proceeded by nor inter-twined with the unfolding of an industrial revolution. The freight policies were evolved to facilitate the export of raw materials and the import of industrial goods.

Though India achieved independence more than three decades ago, the nature of the port-oriented network has only been marginally modified and some of the inequities of the traditional freight policies still persist. It is, therefore, desirable that a contemporary study of railway commodity flows and the regional structure of the Indian economy should begin with a retrospective look at the attributes of railway development in India in the context of and in response to colonial underdevelopment.

OBJECTIVES OF RAILWAY DEVELOPMENT IN COLONIAL INDIA

The economic and political objectives of the state basically determine the geographical alignment of railway network within a country. Given the economic targets, the railway alignment would connect locations with a view to counteract resource isolation to achieve the former. If trade with foreign countries has a high priority, the network tends to become port-oriented. Railway alignment is developed within the national framework, to link the surplus with the deficit regions. In the case of non-economic objective—like external threat or internal disorder, the network would connect the areas which are vulnerable to former or sensitive from the point of view of the latter.

In order to analyse the nature and patterns of the spatial interactions within the colonial economy, one must proceed by clearly identifying the major objectives, which the promoters of Indian railways wanted to achieve through the instrumentality of network alignment and with freight rates policy. These may be classified as under:

- i to provide adequate logistic support to the imperial army in meeting the challenge challenge of external threats and internal dis-satisfaction;
- ii o create avenues for private British capital investment in the Indian economy;
- iii to facilitate the export of raw materials and food from the colony to the metropole and of industrial goods from the metropole to the colony; and
- iv to contribute to famine prevention and famine relief—with a view to enable the goose that lays the golden eggs to survive.

MILITARY OBJECTIVES

Faced with the task of ruling over an unwilling people and defending the long land frontiers of their empire from rival imperialist powers, the British Government devoted considerable attention to the military, political and strategic objectives of developing the railway network in India. By the middle of the last century the situation along the land frontiers of the Indian empire was becoming fairly explosive. The military threat in the North-West from Russia and the fluid situation along the India-China borders were posing serious problems for British imperialism in India. The Russian threat, in particular, was causing great anxiety to the colonial rulers, and continued to do so up to 1907 when the inter-imperialist relations were stabilised by a convention and it appeared as if the Russian menace had been contained.

As has been correctly noted by Tiwari (1921), "strategic railways were a first charge on the total capital expenditure." From the operational point of view, the railway network was intended to enable the government to bring the main bulk of its military strength to bear upon any given point in the shortest possible time. Before the introduction of railways, the time taken to move the military from one region to the other was very large. For example, it often took a period of six months for a regiment to move from Calcutta to Peshawar. With the increasing complexities of the warfare, the colonial rulers could ill afford it anymore. The need for fast movement of military from one place to other was also necessitated in view of the increasing dis-satisfaction among the Indian rulers. They knew well that the railways, providing the most advanced transport technology as bulk carriers, would not only revolutionise military logistics but would also help them in dealing effectively with the law and order problems arising from within the country. It is, therefore, not surprising that as early as in 1846, Lord Harding had recommended that the construction of a few selected railway lines in India would lead to a saving of Rs 5 lakhs on army transport alone.

The internal problems of maintaining law and order were no less serious. Lord Dalhousie, one of the major architects of the policy of territorial expansion by conquest and annexation, had visualised the development of a transport network, which would connect strategic positions in the sub-continent with each other, so as to enable the swift despatch of troops for maintaining the territorial integrity of the empire. Being a far-sighted statesman, he was convinced that consolidation of the conquered territory was a necessary condition towards the process of empire building by conquest. He, therefore, encouraged the task of railway building and attempted to integrate scattered private schemes of railway construction into a comprehensive all India programme. He wrote:

> It can not be necessary for me to insist upon the importance of a speedy and wide introduction of railway communication, through length and breadth of India. A single glance cast upon the map recalling to mind the vast extent of the empire we hold; the various classes and interests it includes; the wide distances which separate the several points at which hostile attacks may at any time be expected; the perpetual risk of such hostility

appearing in quarters where it is least expected; the expenditure of time, of money and of life that are involved in even the ordinary routine of military movements would convince the urgency of speedy comunication.

It is of interest to note that no steps were taken in the direction of opening up of lines for purely strategic purpose before the outbreak of the Afghan War in 1878. Under its impact, however, the Government of Lord Rippon gave serious consideration to the development of the railway network from two points of view; that is of opening up of strategic lines, on the one hand, and of improving the carrying capacity of existing railway lines leading from the chief cantonments to and along the frontiers, on the other. It was only during the Viceroyalty of Lord Rippon that a definite programme for the construction of strategic railway lines was formulated with an estimated cost of over five million sterling pounds. Since the government was neither interested in nor was in a position to invest such huge sums for railway construction, it was, therefore, decided that this outlay should be derived from borrowed funds. The conversion of some railway lines from one gauge to the other was also necessitated due to strategic reasons, though it involved huge expenditure. Technical improvement in existing lines, brought about by substantial expenditure were also, by and large, defence oriented. There were, for example, some of the narrow gauge railway lines in the Indus Valley and Punjab which were converted to broad gauge.

It is clear from the above that the Britisn fully realised the significance of modern transport technology in bridging the space gap and inter-linking the far flung areas into an integrated political and administrative unit. 'Railways', wrote Sir Edwin Arnold in 1865, "may do for India what dynasties have never done—what the genius of Akbar The Magnificant could not effect by government nor by cruelty".

The mutiny of 1857, which brought into open the essential weakness of the colonial power tended to further underline the above approach of the British government towards transport development and led to the expansion of railways on a more extensive scale.

Sir John Strachey pointed out that the Indian railways "stimulated the vitality of every branch of the Administration, they brought the Empire closer together and England closer to India..." (Hunter, 1908). In order to bring "England closer to India," the railway network acquired a highly centrifugal and fragmented character, with the sea ports as its multiple foci. The task of bringing the various provinces of the empire closer together, was handled not with a view to strengthen centripetal forces and to further the politico-administrative integration of the country but with the object of interlinking the inland positions of strategic significance with each other and with the ports so as to keep an unwilling people under subjugation and to defend the frontiers from intrusions by imperialist rivals.

ECONOMIC OBJECTIVES

The programme of railway development in India during the second half of the nineteenth century was integrally linked with the rapid advance of private British capital investment in the empire. It is sometimes argued that since Indian capital was shy, British capital came on the scene only to rescue the Indian economy. The fallacy of this position is not difficult to establish; for the real aims of the British can be easily discerned in the background of the prevailing conditions of the capital market in England which were reflected in the character and composition of British investment in India as well.

Let us have a look at the British capital market during the period when railway promoters were lobbying for railway construction in India. There was a considerable surplus of investable capital in Britain. In Stracheys' words, this surplus had even in the 1830s started "burning holes in their owner's pockets", and that the investors were seeking any investment opportunity likely to yield a return of more than 3.4 per cent which corresponded to the investment in public stocks. The investment opportunities in Great Britain itself became considerably limited by the 1840s, thus creating a widening gap between the increasing availability of investable capital, on the one hand, and of the shrinking possibilities of reinvestment in the local industries, on the other

The most obvious outlet for such surplus capital that was available was investment abroad. India provided one of the safe outlet for investing this surplus capital A number of important considerations had, however, to be taken into account while seeking opportunities for capital investment outside the home market. First, the British capital export to Europe and America around 1850 accounted for more than half of its investment; but with the shift in the economic climate of the Western world, the opportunities for further investment in these countries were fast dwindling. Second, during the second phase of industrialisation in England there was a remarkable increase in the capacity of blast furnaces, which provided abundant supplies of iron and steel. The industrial revolution had reversed the economic relationship of Great Britain with India and required the opening of India as a market of the manufactured goods and primary producer of raw materials for British industry. This is clearly evident from the pattern of British investment in India. The sectorwise composition of the British capital investment in India has shown that most of it was either in the primary or in the tertiary sector of the economy. No efforts were made to invest for the development of such productive industries which would have competed with those of the mother country.

It is difficult to assess the exact quantum of capital invested in India in different branches of industry, commerce and plantations during the period under study. However, several estimates are available; but all of them lack adequate level of reliability and generally tend to be conservative. In spite of these limitations, these estimates do provide an approximate picture about the relative position of investment in the Indian railways within the framework of overall British capital investment in India. According to the estimate of Sirras presented in his evidence before the Industrial Commission-1916, the total British investment in India was of the tune of about Rs. 800 crores in 1914-15. Out of this the share of railways alone comes to about two third. Sir George Paisk in a paper, presented before the Royal Statistical Society in 1911, estimated the total British capital investment in India and Ceylon for the year 1909-10, at 365 million Sterling Pounds. Both the estimates agree on the predominant position of the railway sector in the British investments within India. This amount, according to Sir George Paisk's estimates, was broken up in Table 5.1.

In fact, a part of the investment of 182.5 million sterling pounds under 'Government and Municipal' sector should be considered as the amount invested in the railways sector. It can, therefore, be safely deduced that the export of capital from the metropolitan country to its colony was primarily intended to facilitate commercial penetration into the vast territories of the latter rather than for its economic development.

It may be argued that railway construction provided the most profitable avenue for investment — the high rates of return acting as a strong pull factor. But such was not the case. Indian railways continuously suffered deficits till the beginning of the present Century. It could not, therefore, have been the higher marginal efficiency of capital investment in India or the higher rates of profit in the railway sector which could have prompted British financiers to choose railway construction for their investment.

It is, therefore, not surprising that the father of Indian railways—Dalhousie—who was anxious to attract British capital, enterprise and initiative to India, initiated a deliberate policy of encouraging British private capital by offering to it the most favourable climate for investment. This was achieved through free grants of land and a guarantee of 5 per cent return over total capital invested. The government justified such extraordi-

TABLE 5.1 : **British investment in India 1909-1910**

S. No.	*Sectors*	*Amount in million sterling*	*%*
1.	Government and Municipal	182.5	50.0
2.	Railways	136.5	37.4
3.	Plantations (Tea, Coffee, Rubber)	24.2	6.6
4.	Tramways	4.1	1.1
5.	Mines	3.5	.9
6.	Banks	3.4	.9
7.	Oil	3.2	.9
8.	Commercial and Industrial	2.5	.7
9.	Finance, Land and Investment	1.8	.5
10.	Miscellaneous	3.3	.3
	Total	365.0	100.0

nary concessions on the ground that private capital would not otherwise take risks by investing huge sums in those enterprises which require high levels of engineering skills as would be involved in crossing central India or surmounting the Ghats.

Another important aspect of railway development in India was that the mode of investment was not uniform throughout the period under study. Several methods were tried; but each was so intricately inter-linked with British private capital that its operation can be properly understood only within the general framework of the investment goals of British capital. In the early period, that is, in the 'Dalhousie Decade' up to 1869, private companies were given free land and a 5 per cent interest on capital invested on railways was also ensured. Encouraged by this initial guarantee system, six great lines—viz., E.I.R., G.I.P.R., B.B.C.I.R., S.P.D.R., East Bengal and Madras—were started with a guage of 5'.6". After 1869, however, a new shift occurred in the policy of the government towards railway construction in India and it embarked upon the construction of railways itself side by side with the companies already engaged in similar pursuits under the guarantee schemes. In order to enable it to do so, a provision was made to the effect that the Secretary of State might raise loans on behalf of the Indian Government in London, with the Indian revenues serving as security. A number of factors prompted the colonial government to undertake the construction of railways on its own. First, the extravagance of private companies made it imperative to abandon the 'Guarantee system' Second, in the light of the strategic importance of the railways, their construction could not be left entirely in private hands. Third, the confused and unstable political conditions prevailing at that time discouraged the private investors. Fourth, railway construction, as a part of the famine programmes, did not interest the private investor and had to be initiated under the aegis of the government itself.

It may, however, be noted that in 1879 the private companies were again entrusted with the construction of new railway lines. What the government actually did was to let the companies borrow money (it was restricted to 2 million sterling pounds per annum) for the government. The Government policy during this period was directed towards the construction of branch lines by separate companies under the guarantee of a minimum return or a rebate on the invested capital.

It is clear from the above that many typical methods were adopted by the British rulers to develop the railway network in India. It is interesting to observe that not withstanding, the mode of railway construction, the basic objective of the government policy remained the same that is, to strengthen British private investment in India under the aegis of the colonial state.

The history of independent economies indicates that investments in the modern transport infrastructure is invariably intertwined with investments in industrial development; in fact, the connotation of infrastructure has relevance in such economies precisely in terms of the structure and the spatial patters of industrialisation. It is only in dependent economies that investments in railways are not accompanied or followed by industrial development. India provides the classic example of this type. While the British made considerable capital investments to develop a vast system of railway network in India, they did not encourage the development of the industrial activities. The evidence clearly shows that they invested in the infrastructure but certainly not in cotton mills, though it happened to be one of the leading industry in which the British had acquired expertise and India was also suited for the growth of this industry.

The conclusion is, therefore, inescapable that this was done to ensure that the Indian textile industry, with its absolute and relative advantages, does not emerge on the economic scene to compete with its British counterpart. What is still more surprising is that iron and steel industry, which could meet indigenously the requirement of the major input in the railway construction, was not allowed to come up even though India has one of the most favourable mix of natural resources in the world—iron ore, coal and manganese—all available in the same region. It is ironical, indeed, that the iron import bill of colonial India went on swelling and had risen by 1913-14 to Rs. 25 crores, an amount more than the total revenue earned by the railways in that year.

The foregoing discussion, thus, clearly points to the fact that the British capital investment in India was not intended to lay down the foundation of its economic prosperity by providing the transport infrastructure but to strengthen the ties of subservience and to ensure a division of labour between the metropolitan country and its colony to the advantage of the former.

What were the compelling economic factors which prompted the British investors to go in for investment in an extensive railway network in India. The answer lies in the proper assessment of the requirements of the imperialist exploitation of colonial resources during the new phase in which industrial capital had emerged on the British scene as the dominant economic force and had either liquidated or subsumed within itself the mercantile interests of the earlier period. During the nineteenth and early twentieth century, the British mercantile and political community believed that India was a jewel in the Imperial Kingdom. It was endowed with valuable products of nature but was deprived of a profitable market for want of a cheap and expeditious means of transport. Easy means of communication were required whereby the resource rich regions could be connected to other trade centres or profitable markets. The traditional land and river transport network was not only unsuitable to carry bulk commodities but was also time consuming, costly and risky.

Textile was the first export oriented industry to come up in British during the first phase of its industrial revolution. Great Britain required an alternative source to supply cotton to Lanchashire manufacturers. To facilitate the movement of cotton from the cotton producing areas to the ports for export to Britain, it was proposed that cotton growing areas should be brought on the railway map of India. Thus, search for raw materials was one of the major consideration for the extensive development of railways in many parts of India.

It should be recalled that the first few railway lines were constructed under the influence of those who were interested in the cotton trade from India to England. The demand for Indian cotton in the English market picked up during the American Civil War, which had almost completely dislocated the supply of American cotton to Great Britain and was thus threatening to paralyse its growing textile industry. Under the impact of this catastrophe, the necessity to acquire an assured supply of raw cotton became the prime necessity to sustain the industrial development in Britain. The choice for the uninterrupted supply of cotton thus naturally fell on the colonial countries as these were under the direct control of the British. India was one such country. However, the difficuity was that the cotton producing areas in India were very far off from the major ports. For a smooth and uninterrupted flow of raw cotton to England, a fast and reliable mode of inland transport became a necessity. For this purpose, a two pronged strategy was devised. Firstly, to link the major cotton producing areas with the ports and secondly, with a view to increase the total production, a network of canals was planned so as to ensure irrigation in these areas. Consequently, considerable patronage was given by the British rulers to the cause of railway development in India. With the advent of the railwys and the availability of assured irrigation facilities, Berar, Khandesh, Gujarat and Sind became more productive and India entered the markets of Europe, which was hitherto dominated by America, as a competitor for the supply of cotton.

The opening of the railway lines in the food producing areas of India, also ensured adequate and cheap supplies of foodgrains to the metropolitann economy. Such an arrangement was considered necessary as Britain was a food deficit country and consequently, they needed transport linkages with the cereal producing areas of their colonies. Britain was able to buy cereals from India at a rate cheaper than the prevailing international price and hence could maintain the standards of living of its own working class at lower costs and consequently the wages were kept low in the British market especially during the early phases of Industrial Revolution. This had invariably resulted in lowering the per unit production cost and was in turn instrumental in fetching higher profits for their products in a highly competitive world market.

The inadequate rate of expnsion of their market during the early nineteenth century was also causing considerahble worry to business interests in Great Britain. The construction of the system of modern transport network based on railways was intended to bring raw materials producing areas which were also densely populated within the reach of metropolitan capital so that two birds could be killed with one stone.

The network structure prevented each region from taking advantage of the available regional resources for enlarging their production frontiers. For instance, the mineral reesoures being in abundant in Chhota Nagpur could not make much impact on the economy of North Bihar because both were independently linked with Calcutta withoiut having mutual links.

The freight rate structure was also developed in such a way that it facilitated the exchange of commodities between the metropolitan economy and the colonial economy rather than the intra-country trade. There is ample evidence to show that the Indian Railways were indifferent to the development of local industry and to take measurees aimed at protecting it against the goods manufactured in Britain. The case of match making industry provides an interesting insight. The freight policy was formulated in such a way that special low rates were quoted for the matches originating from Calcutta, Karachi, Bombay and Madras, while no such concessional rates were applicable to matches originating from other places. Thus the indigenous match industry was put to a relative disadvantage. The position with reespect to other manufacturing industries was not much different. The commercialisation of agriculture further created a situation in which getting raw materials for local industries became much more difficult. It was easier to get goods manufactured in Britain. Consequently, Great Britain concentrated on the manufacturing activities, where the scope of the economies of production was tremendous, while the colonial economy of India was pushed to the activities where the scale economies did not exist. The effect was that by linking the two regions, the mother economy and colonial economy, as an organic part, India was compelled to become an agricultural region producing primary products for exports.

It is thus evident from the foregoing analysis that one of the aims of the railway development in India was to ensure the suply of raw materials and at the same time to find access of a potential market for the manufactured goods.

FAMINE PREVENTION

As early as in 1874, Lord Salisbury, the Secretary of State for India, had laid down three important principles of the guidance of railway construction-famine prevention being one of these. The last quarter of the 19th century witnessed a significant increase in the number and intensity of famines in the country. There were 18 famines during this period witn an estimated loss of 18 million lives. The country witnessed a number of serious widespread famines between 1874 and 1879 in the territories of Madras, Bombay and Mysore. Lack of adequate transport facilities posed a major impediment in the organisation of any type of relief work. The Famine Commission of 1880 emphasised the vital role of railways in famine prevention and considered that 5,000 miles of new railway lines were urgently needed to meet any contingency arising out of famines. The Commission underlined the fact that the country could not be considered to be safe from such calamities in the future until the Indian railway system could show an aggregate of 20,000 miles. There was, thus, an urgent need for the speedy construction of railways and revision of the hitherto policy of railway construction was called for to achieve this goal. A Select Committee was appointed to enquire and suggest ways and means for the rapid extension of railway network in India. The terms of the Committee were:

> to enquire into and report upon the necessity for a more rapid extension of railway communication in India and the means by which different objectives may be best accomplished, with special reference to the report of the Famine Commissioners, and with due regard to the financial conditions in India.

The Committee recommended a more rapid expansion of railways, primarily to protect the various regions against famine. It also recommended that the state should invite private agencies to work side by side with the government for the development of railways in India. It was, however, made clear that the Government should only undertake the construction of those railway lines which, by way of their unprofitable character in a commercial sense, or for other reasons, can not be taken up by private agencies. This led to the establishment of a very important set of famine protective railways the South Indian Railway being one of these. The period 1881-87 witnessed the construction of a far larger annual average of railway miles than any previous period.

The goal to combat famine through the provision of an inexpensive system of transport had significant impact on rapid expansion or railways. One of the salient features of such railway lines was that these were largely constructed on metre gauge. For example, a metre gauge branch line of 24 miles connecting Mathura and the Rajputana railways and a similar line connecting the Cawnpore-Farrukhabad was commenced in 1878. The construction of Bellary-Hubli and Hubli-Gadpak railway line was also recommended by the Famine Commission.

The foregoing discussion clearly brings out the fact that the development of the Indian Railways was not necessitated by the requirements of the internal development processes but was primarily governed by the requirements of the internal development processes but was primarily governed by the requirements of the colonial suction mechanism. The achievement of the above objectives was operationalised through a complex strategy of network development and freight policies which exterted a profound impact on economic space in India. The node connecting sequence and the directional focus of the network were determined with a view to strengthen the bias in favour of the ports. The adherence to the principle of inter-nodal competition rather than of complimentarity and of the multiplicy of the gauges rather than of uniformity led to the distortion of the port-hinterland relationship and the fragmentation of the home market. The railway lines of the Indian network acted like cantilever bridges between the interior nodes and the ports and strengthened the centrifugal elements of the system of spatial interactions.

The port oriented nature of the freight policy accentuated the distortions generated by the network on the economic map of India. The special port rates created the pattern of traffic characteristics of colonial economics, wherein it flows almost exclusively in two streams: raw materials moving towards the ports for export and imported manufactured articles moving up country from the ports. As a consequence, the region forming processes of intra and inter-regional flows were seriously constrained by the heavy weight of port oriented flows. Sure Canel has described a similar sitution for West Africa in the following words:

> Each economic region corresponds of a 'one line economy' an axis based externally, on a port where import and export were conducted and comprising a series of adjacent branches which subdivided in turn until they peter out in the bush. The axis and branches were followed by an ascending current, that of exportable. products. Each region resembled a kind of lung with its system of veins and arteries running parallel, receiving its oxygen at the level of agricultural production. But the heart was placed outside, far beyond the seas, the impulses that regulated the nature and the intensity of the flow were external ones.

In the case of colonial India as well, the heart was, indeed, placed outside, far beyond the seas. It is thus, clear that independent India inherited a railway system which had emerged on the economic map to operationalise the internal fragmentation and external integration of the colonial economy. The essential centrifugality of the system was a serious constraint on the consolidation of the national home market. The requirements of an independent and self reliant economic development demanded a basic change in the railway system to bring it in line with the new tasks of the new phase. It is our endeavour in this study to assess the successes and failures of the national effort in this direction.

PART TWO

COMMODITY FLOWS AND ECONOMIC DEVELOPMENT

6

DISTRIBUTION OF TRANSPORT NETWORK FACILITIES IN INDIA

A transport network is established with a view to facilitate economic and social interaction in space—both at the intra and inter-regional levels. But once it is established, it plays an important role in shaping the space economy itself. The potential of interaction among the various nodes in the space economy that stems from the nature and magnitude of spatial complementarities and intervening opportunities takes the form of flows through transferability. While complimentarity and intervening opportunities are determined essentially by the location of economic activities, the magnitude of transferability is governed by the nature of the transport network. The flows take place from one descrete node to another and not along a spatial continum as is the case with surface flow in a stream. The national transport network, thus, responds to the processes of regional specialisation and reflects the consolidation of the national home maket articulated through the complex and hierarchical system of sub-regional and regional networks. However, if the impulses of development processes are weak, distorted and ill-balanced, inter-regional disparities in the availability and utilisation of network facilities emerge on the scene and may continue to persist over time. This negative attribute is further accentuated by the governmental policies of socio-economic development which may be biased towards the urban areas. Consequently, the urban-rural differentials tend to become more and more sharp.

We have already examined the basic structural aspects of the transport network. It has already been noted therein that the intra and inter-regional interactions between different nodes are operationalised through the routes. Thus, transport networks represent the functional association between the dominant and the subordinate centres. The maximum possible limits to the amount of interaction between the node and the hinterland is determined by the availability of network facilities. However, once a transport network comes to be established in an area, it is considered as a neutral agency providing equal accessibility to all the nodes connected by it. The differentials in accessibility are brought out by the relative location of the nodes with reference; firstly, to each other in terms of geometrical centrality and aggregate travel distances; and secondly, to the network as a junction—an intermediary point or a terminal. A location may, thus, appear to be well connected just by virtue of its nearness to a higher order node. The neutrality of the network, notwithstanding, it has been the governmental practice to alter the inter-nodal accessibility differentials through policies relating to transport licensing, freight rates and location of economic activities. A critical examination of the structure of the railway freight policy also becomes crucial in this context. However, in the present chapter we shall restrict ourselves to the analysis of network structure only.

Since the present study is concerned with the analysis of flows and interactions, it may be advisable to have a close look at the accessibility differentials in the space economy, which provide the base for the movement of goods. Although the present study is concerned with freight movement by railways, the other modes are also utilised in the process of spatial interaction. These are roads, inland waterways, airways and pipelines. These modes in many cases act as feeders to the railway service. Each of these modes plays a specific role in the transportation of commodities from one node to the other. It would, therefore, not be advisable to rank them in order of their importance or merits. Rail transport requires greater initial investment per unit of track and greater maintenance cost as compared to other modes; it can, however, move much larger load over large distances. Inland water transport requires minimum energy to move a tonne-kilometre. Road transport has greater flexibility. Air transport though most expensive has the relative advantage of minimising travel time. The pipelines have been found to be ideal for moving petroleum products. Keeping in view these features of spatial organisation of transport network, it may be useful to analyse its accessibility and connectivity characteristics as a whole covering all the modes through which commodity flows take place. In the present study we have considered railways, roadways, waterways—both coastal and inland and airways for detailed investigations.

In order to nave a comparative assessment of transportation facilities available in various territorial units of the country, a multi-modal network has to be reduced to a uni-modal network where the various modes are weighted according to their importance in terms of some common criteria.

The simplest method of measuring the connections of a node is to compute some measure of the routes converging on it. In view of the fact that each mode of transportation has its own route and a number of different types of routes may be converging on the same node, the problem of determining suitable weights for each type of mode becomes important. The weights may be derived on the basis of capital cost, capacity, travel time or freight rate or all of them taken together. In the present study, we have used the capacities of different modes, the time taken per unit distance. the freight charges per unit weight and energy required to move a tonne-kilometre to determine the weight for various modes and have used it as a multiplier for the corresponding number of connections at each node. Once a system of weightages is worked out on the basis of some common criteria, the composite score of the weighted values may, then, be taken as an indicator of the accessibility connectivity attribute of a particular node.

It may be assumed that the space economy is organised at the meso and macro levels through

TABLE 6.1 : **Weightage allocated to different transport modes**

Indices	*Railways*			*Roads*		*Coastal*		*Air*	*Inland water Transport*	
	Broad gauge	*Metre guage*	*Narrow gauge*	*National highways*	*Other roads*	*Major ports*	*Other ports*		*Perennial*	*Seasonal*
Capacity (tons/day)	24,508	16,755	7,292	15,000	6,000	5,167	1,000	—	—	—
Time per Km. (minutes)	2.0	2.0	2.0	1.5	1.5	6.7	6.7	0.7	10.0	—
Charge (paise/Km.)	4.6	6.0	19.5	16.8	16.8	17.0	17.0	122.0	8.5	—
Energy (tonne Km)	750	750	750	2,400	2,400	500	500	6,300	500	—
Composite Index	6.0	5.9	5.2	5.7	5.6	1.9	1.8	2.3	1.0	0.5

*The weights for the seasonal waterways have been taken just half of the perennial waterways.

the system ot urban centres. A matrix of the number of routes converging on each of the urban centre was constructed for the various modes of transportation. Following this procedure, the connectivity matrix specifying the linkages between all the centres for five different modes of transport was obtained. Based on the four features as noted above, Table 6.1 gives the weights allocated to different modes. It may be noted from Table 6.1 that the composite weighted index varies directly with the efficiency of the mode of transport that is, higher the weightage, the better the efficiency of that particular transportation system would be. In the context of the present analysis, the railways have emerged as the most efficient mode of transport followed by roadways, air-ways, coastal and inland waterways. The number of routes of various modes converging at each of the urban centres in the coutry is multiplied by its corresponding weight. The summation of the

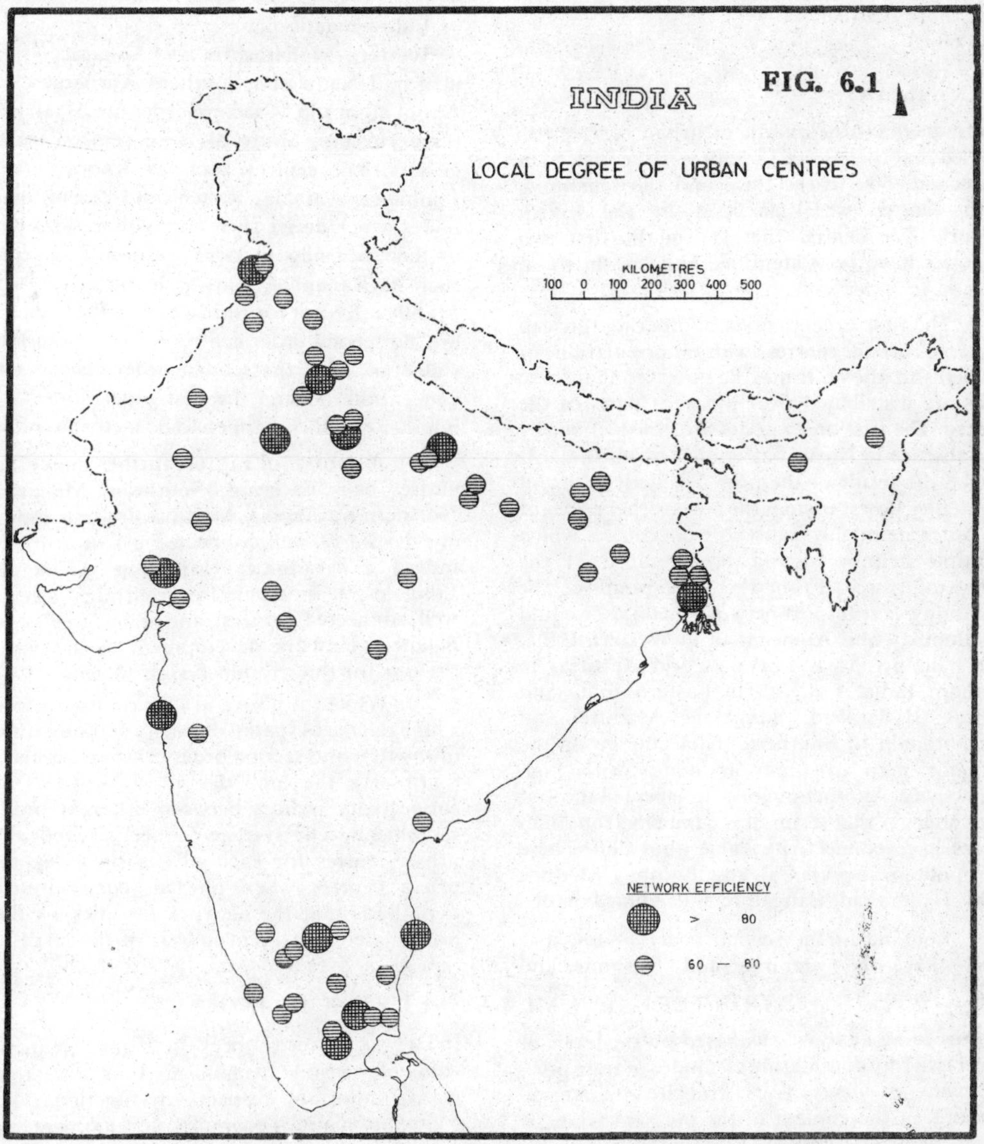

FIG. 6.1

individual row of the weighted matrix has been taken as the composite connectivity level of the relevant node which is based on the multi-modal facilities available therein.

The composite values were then arranged in a descending order and the corresponding frequency distribution curve was obtained. The following three thresh-hold points and consequently four categories were identified on the basis of the values of the composite index:

i more than 80
ii 60-80
iii 45-60
iv less than 45

The frequency distribution of urban centres has revealed that there were 13 centres in the first, 54 in the second, 300 in the third and the remaining urban centres were classified in the fourth category. The centres that fall in the first two categories have been identified and are shown in Fig. 6.1.

The first order centres numbering thirteen are large urban centres with a population of 1,00,000 and above. It may be observed that these nodes are distributed over different parts of the country. The first order nodes are conspicuous by their absence in North Eastern & central India. It may be the result of the port oriented nature of commodity flows. Besides the ports, other nodes of first order are mainly transshipment centres which sometime acquire significance because of the change of gauge. From the view point of the availability of transport network facilities, we find that Bombay and Ahmedabad in Western India, Delhi, Jaipur, Agra, Lucknow and Amritsar in Northern India, Calcutta in Eastern India and Madras, Hyderabad, Bangalore, Madurai and Tirucharapalli in Southern India emerge on the economic map of India as nodes with high connectivity. Another interesting aspect of the first order nodes is that seven of the nine metropolitan centres have connectivity value above 80. These metropolitan cities are Calcutta, Bombay, Madras, Delhi, Hyderabad, Bangalore and Ahmedabad.

Looking at the second order nodes, it is noted that while Jammu and Kashmir and Himachal Pradesh have none of the second order nodes, Gauhati and Jorhat are the only two centres in North-Eastern India with the composite score of connectivity between 60 and 80. Madhya Pradesh and Rajasthan have also a few centres of the second order—the former having Jabalpur, Gwalior, Indore and Udaipur, Jodhpur and Bikaner fall in the latter state. The map shows some well formed clusters of the second order nodes which may be grouped into the following regions:

i Indo-gangetic plain
ii Western Maharashtra and Gujarat
iii Tamil Nadu and Southern Karnataka

About 40 of the 54 second order nodes fall in these three clusters. Many of these centres are either large urban centres such as Kanpur, Meerut. Ludhiana, Ambala, Ranchi and Salem. or those nodes which derive their large connections because of their nearness to large metropolitan centres—such as Ranaghat, Katwa, Panipat. Rewari and Mandya. Except for Burdwan and Ranaghat. there are no second order centres in the hinterland of Calcutta. Thus the second order centres tend to concentrate around the first order nodes, a large number of which happen to be metropolitan cities.

A perusal of Fig. 6.1 further shows that the entire belt covering Southern Maharashtra, Northern Karnataka, Madhya Pradesh and Orissa are devoid of well connected urban centres. It is indeed a paradoxical situation, where central India despite its geometrical centrality is devoid of well connected centres, and it testifies to the ill balanced network development of the past. The reasons for this are not far off to seek.

While the above discussion points towards a high degree of spatial disparity in the distribution of the first and second order centres, it is alarming to observe the high degree of skewness in the connectivity indices between different orders of settlements. The average connectivity index of the urban centres for each of the six categories of urban centres when plotted, corroborates the hypothesis that the network facilities are disproprotionately biased in favour of the large urban centres.

STRUCTURE OF RAILWAY NETWORK IN INDIA

The foregoing analysis was based on the levels of connectivity by considering all modes of transport. However, in view of its crucial importance, especially in the context of the preesent study, it was considered desirable to examine the structural aspects of the railway network separately. The development and expansion of railway network in India was meant to meet the requirements of the colonial suction mechanism. It is, therefore, in many important respects dysfunctional in the context of planned economic development and the consolidation of the home market in independent India. It would be useful to look back into the colonial period and identify the genesis of these dysfunctional attributes of the network.

Independent India inherited an extensive railway network of about 59,000 kms— the fourth largest railway system in the world with capital-at-charge of Rs. 3,890 crores. Though quantitatively the system was impressive indeed, and was capable of being utilised for economic development in independent India, it had serious distortions and limitations from the qualitative point of view. In the light of the specificities of the Indian situation which it shares, in its essential features, with the entire under-developed world, it is worthwhile to study in some depth the exogenous as well as endogenous forces which moulded the pattern of railway network in colonial India.

Since India was a colony of an island power situated across the seas, the transport network projected to the interior from the sea ports. The main railway lines were laid from the newly established major ports to the interior parts of the country. But little effort was directed towards tying up the four port-oriented systems into a national network, capable of consolidating the home market. Relatively little attention was paid to the construction of branch lines from the main lines. Use of different gauges also hampered the free development of communication within the vast hinterland. While the major ports were interconnected by broad gauge lines, vast areas in the interior and a majority of the princely states were served by metre and narrow gauge lines.

The main objective of the establish ment of a railway network in India was to connect ports with the tracts producing raw materials for British mills as well as food for its people and with tracts of high population density which could absorb large quantities of British manufctured goods. The first railway line was constructed at the instnce of powers interested in the cotton trade from India to England. As we have noted earlier, Indian cotton received a tremendous demand in the English market during the American Civil War, which almost cut off the supply of Amnerican cotton to Great Britain paralysing her textile industry

The railway network spread like the branches of a tree from the major sea ports of Bombay, Calcutta, Madras and Karachi. The main feature of the network expansion during the period 1853 to 1880 was that the railway lines started from the port towns and penetrated into the interior like the white explorers unravelling the mysteries of the dark continent moving from the outlet to the source of a Nile, a Congo or a Niger. The pattern of railway network acquired a distinctly dendrite character. Although all the port towns became apex points of railway network, each railway system had, so to say, its one semi-closed hinterland to operate in without any competition.

The Indian railway network had already acquired its essentially colonial pattern by the end of the First World War. There emerged on the econmic man of India a system of alignments which was incapable of establishing healthy linkages between different regions of the country. Each railway network had its own territory with a port as its 'core node'.

RAILWAY NETWORK DEVELOPMENT SINCE INDEPENDENCE

Three decades appears to be too short a time for correcting the cumulative distortions of a century of railway construction with a colonial objective. Understandably, the addition of about 7,000 kms to the inherited network after independence just about makes a dent in the railway network system.

The nation has a length of 60,666 kms (1976-77) of railway routes of which about 35,000 kms is of broad guage and the rest of metre ad narrow gauge lines. Side by side with enlarging the route length of 7,000 kms an additional 8,000 and odd kilometres have been doubled. With a view to meet the social, administrative and economic needs of a developing economy, a number of new lines have been constructed. Broadly speaking, there are three major considerations for opening new railwy lines. These may be stated as:

a railway lines for opening up backward areas;

b railway lines for utilisation of mineral resources through large industrial enterprises and exports; and

c strategic lines for defence purposes.

It may be noted that some of the new railway lines have been opened in backward and underdeveloped aereas and were thus not economical from the view point of returns. The changed political situation and the resultant demands of the economy warranted gross changes in the pattern of investment in new lines. The earlier conventional methods[1] of project appraisal which involved only an assessment of financial return on investment was replaced by the discounted cash flow method[2] of project evaluation not only on the basis of economic but also of social cost benefit analysis.

Since independence nearly 50 new railway

lines have been opened. Some of these lines have been opened with a view to link some of the backward areas with the trunk routes. It was considered that such infrastructural investments are necessary for initiating development in backward regions. The list of railway lines opened since 1950 has been given in Table 6.2. The detailed analysis, of the achievement of objectives for construction of new railway lines has shown that a large number of these lines are grossly under utilised-the level of utilisation being less than 50 per cent. Some of the lines are considered as of national importance despite the likelihood of their being uneconomical for quite some time. For example, Pokran-Jaisalmer or Rangapara North-Lakhimpur are some of the lines which have been constructed for specific reasons or with a long term objective of their use.

TABLE 6.2 : **Railway lines longer than 20 kms. constructed since 1950**

Sl. No.	*Particulars of new lines*	*Gauge*	*Length in Kms.*	*Cost in Rs. crores*	*Year of commencement*	*Year of completion*	*Percentage utilisation*
1	2	3	4	5	6	7	8
1.	Chunar-Robertsganj-Churk	B.G.	79.07	2.02	1951	1954	40.6
2.	Mukerian-Pathankot	B.G.	42.98	3.77	1950	1952	81.5
3.	Arantagni-Karaikudi	M.G.	27.31	0.41	1950	1952	33.0
4.	Gandhidham-Deesa	M.G.	272.06	5.74	1950	1952	63.3
5.	Gop-Karaikudi	M.G.	32.37	0.41	1954	1955	58.8
6.	Barham-Etah	B.G.	61.80	1.34	1955	1959	48.0
7.	Khandwa-Hingoli	M.G.	302.48	12.49	1954	1961	82.5
8.	Quilon-Eranakulam	M.G.	154.48	5.56	1953	1956	85.0
9.	Champa-Korba (including Extension)	B.G.	50.70	2.47	1953	1956	55.6
10.	Indore-ujjain	B.G.	70.77	3.22	1955	1958	80.0
11.	Fatehpur-Churu	M.G.	32.88	0.65	1955	1957	37.5
12.	Raniwara-Bhilai	M.G.	69.79	1.50	1955	1958	45.2
13.	Barasat-Hasnabad	B.G.	33.06	2.56	1957	1962	43.8
14.	Bukhtiarpur-Rajgir	B.G.	53.84	2.56	1959	1962	41.8
15.	Chandrapura-Muri-Ranchi-Hatia	B.G.	143.30	13.37	1957	1961	63.6
16.	Khejuriaghat-Malda	B.G.	37.00	3.91	1959	1961	115.8
17.	Robertsganj-Garhwa Road	B.G.	163.27	21.34	1958	1963	124.6
18.	Kumedpur-Barsoi	B.G.	25.00	1.00	1958	1959	37.1
19.	Bondamunda (Rourkela)-Dumard	B.G.	67.00	7.38	1956	1960	91.0
20.	Bhilai-Dhallirajhara	B.G.	85.00	4.30	1956	1958	65.4
21.	Noamundi-Banspani	B.G.	28.05	2.89	1955	1958	37.1
22.	Bauridand-Karonji	B.G.	85.10	6.91	1958	1962	65.7
23.	Sambalpur-Titlagarh	B.G.	182.00	15.59	1959	1963	61.5
24.	Bimlagarh-Kiriburu	B.G.	41.23	5.94	1960	1963	78.6
25.	Rangapara North-North Lakhimpur-Morkongselek	M.G.	327.93	30.38	1960	1965	40.0
*26.	Bondamunda-Nowagaonpura Pani	B.G.	27.71	2.65	1958	1964	63.6
27.	Diva-Panvel-Uran	B.G.	54.22	2.16	1961	1966	48.0
28.	Butibori-Umrer	B.G.	34.00	2.35	1963	1965	42.0
*29.	Hatia-Nowagaon	B.G.	137.45	13.95	1960	1964	63.6
30.	Hindumalkot-Sriganganagar	B.G.	27.26	1.17	1961	1970	54.5
31.	Singrauli-Obra	B.G.	56.57	11.41	1961	1970	60.8
32.	Singrauli-Katni	B.G.	246.26	24.37	1962	1975	44.3

1	2	3	4	5	6	7	8
33.	Ghaziabad-Tuglakabad including second Yamuna Bridge	B.G.	54.30	5.99	1958	1966	61.3
34.	Kalkalighat-Dharmanagar	M.G.	31.36	2.30	1961	1964	45.0
35.	Siliguri-Jogighopa	B.G.	265.00	32.50	1963	1965	69.1
36.	Manmadurai-Virudhunagar	M.G.	66.10	2.53	1962	1964	30.0
37.	Sangalore-Salem	M.G.	299.33	8.50	1962	1968	72.9
38.	Hassan-Mangalore	M.G.	189.21	42.00	1964		N.A.
39.	Panskura-Haldia Port	B.G.	69.61	8.25	1963	1976	52.3
40.	Guna-Maksi	B.G.	193.21	10.00	1964	1976	38.9
41.	Udaipur-Himmatnagar	M.G.	215.00	11.41	1960	1965	24.1
42.	Jhund-Kandla	B.G.	230.84	16.53	1964	1969	71.8
43.	Kottavalasa-Bailadilla	B.G.	447.00	56.68	1961	1968	70.0
44.	Kathua-Jammu	B.G.	77.00	13.82	1968	1972	100.0
45.	Cuttack-Paradeep	B.G.	84.31	10.00	1967	1973	65.0
46.	Pokaran-Jaisalmer	M.G.	105.00	2.50	1966	1968	21.0
47.	Tornagullu-Mudukulapenta	B.G.	24.00	3.30	1971	1976	N.A.
48.	Dasla-Singhana	M.G.	32.90	2.80	N.A.	1974	10.0
49.	Sabarmati-Gandhinagar	B.G.	27.85	2.85	1973	1976	16.5

*These are part of Ranchi-Bondamunda Section.

Since the railway network in India is composed of varying gauges, the broad gauge, metre gauge and narrow guage systems have been mapped separately in figure 6.2. The connections between areeas served by metre and broad gauges are possible only through change of gauge necessitated along the following major lines:

a Madras-Trivandrum
b Delhi-Bombay
c Delhi-Calcutta

An examination of Fig. 6.2 reveals that the main concentration of broad guage lines continues to be over the food and agricultural raw materials producing areas of the Gangetic Plain. One of the denesest networks of broad gauge lines is to be noticed in the Gangetic Plains connecting the areas of Punjab through Uttar Pradesh and Bihar to Calcutta port

The rest of the country is served by a skeletal network of broad gauge lines wherein few lines probe into the interior from Bombay including the one reaching the Punjab. Inter-metropolitan connections between Calcutta-Delhi, Delhi-Bombay, Calcutta-Bombay Bombay-Madras, Calcutta-Madras and Madras-Delhi provide the basic structure for the broad gauge system.

Tenatcles of branch lines lead into the interior from this skeletal frame. Even the inter-metropolitan connectins were later additions to the network. In contrast the hinterland of each metropolitan centre was very well connected with it. The inter-metropolitan connections through broad gauge double lines were further strengthened in independent India by laying down of the alternative routes. Many of the important industrial centres like Tatanagar and Asansol and recently established ones like Durg-Bhilai and Rourkela, fall on these trunk lines. The importance of these lines may be realised from the fact that while these lines comprised only 25 per cent of the total route kilometre, they carried 74 per cent of the total freight traffic in India during 1973-74.

A quick glance at the broad gauge network of Indian railways reveals that Rajasthan, Gujarat, Gangetic Plans, north of the Ganges, part of Southern India and North-Eastern India are completely devoid of broad guage. Parts of these regions, however, are covered by metre guage single lines. These routes are generally disjointed and many of these routes either join the major broad gauge line with the interior or peter out without forming well connected circuits.

Three sub-systems of metre guage are identifiable:

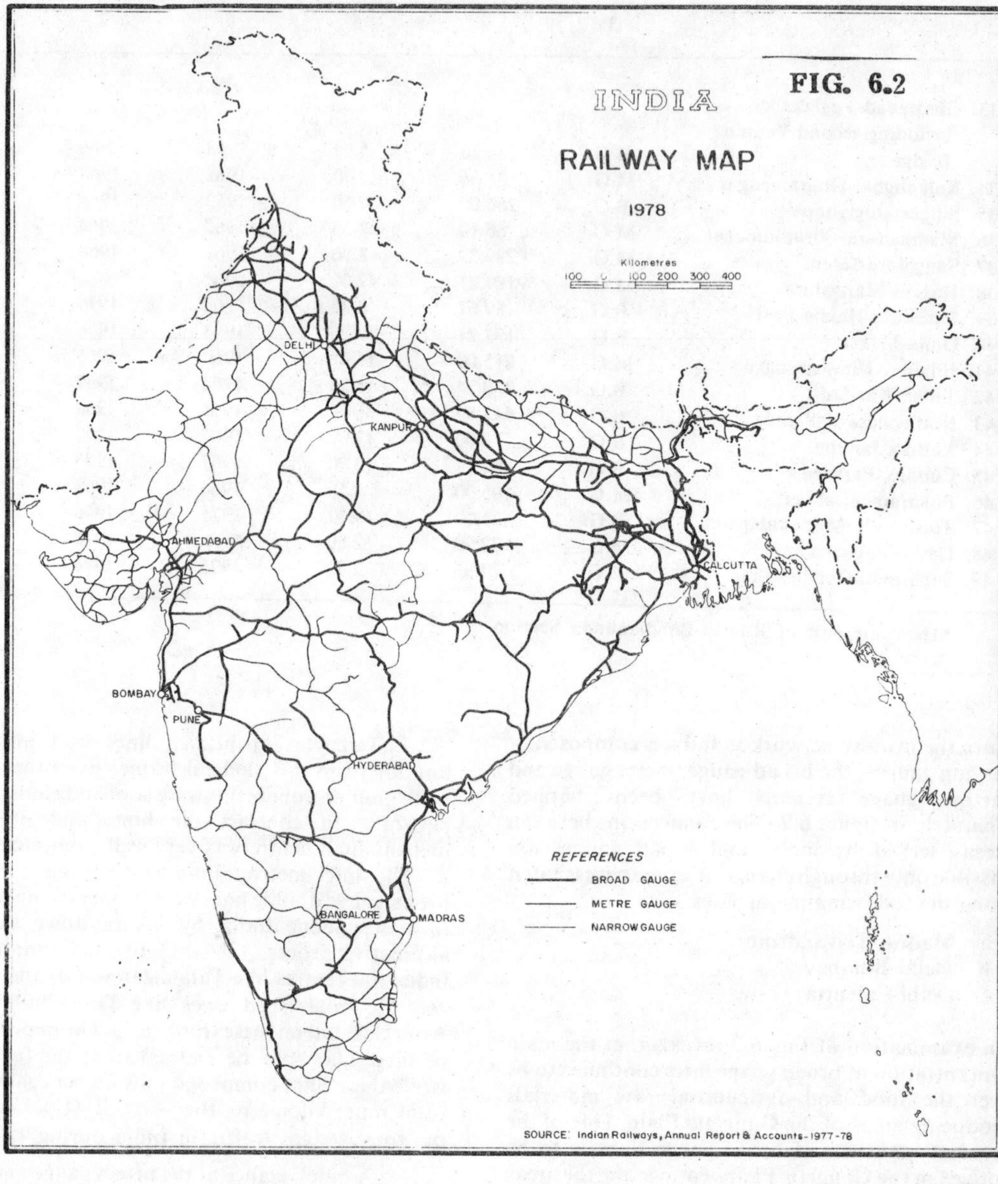

i Western Rajasthan and Gujarat;
ii Himalayan foot-hills and Gangetic plain north of Ganga running into Brahmaputra valley; and
iii Southern India.

The structure of the network, such as it is, helps in understanding the patterns of interactions as would be seen in later sections. With such a pattern of network, weak inter-connections of places in Rajasthan with other parts of the country may be expected. Similarly, the areas served by metre gauge network in southern India would find it difficult to interact with other parts of the country but convenient to interact with Madras, the metropolis of the south.

Railway facilities unlike those of the roadways are not available at all points along the line but become accessible to the human settlements at railheads represented by railway stations. The regional variations in the distribution of railway stations, therefore, bring out another

TABLE 6.3 : **Inter-zonal variations in the availability of railway facilities**

Zone No.	*Railway zone*	*No. of Railway station in*			*Density of stations per 100 sq. km.*			*No. of stations per*		
		Villages	*Towns*	*Cities*	*Village*	*Town*	*City*	*Village*	*Town*	*City*
1.	Central Railway	532	168	264	0.05	3.14	9.11	.018	0.66	3.44
2.	Eastern Railway	517	128	235	0.57	8.26	14.29	.011	0.70	4.04
3.	Northern Railway	1,121	281	387	0.42	1.00	16.67	.032	1.12	4.42
4.	Rorth Eastern Railway	566	83	79	0.45	1.00	16.67	.008	0.93	3.32
5.	North East Frontier Railway	735	51	23	0.11	3.33	8.09	.020	0.72	2.72
6.	Southern Railway	735	195	288	0.30	4.17	9.69	.027	0.53	3.56
7.	South Eastern Railway	296	81	60	0.12	4.56	8.09	.008	0.55	4.03
8.	Western Railway	1,000	254	183	0.19	4.17	7.69	.023	0.72	3.01
9.	South Central Railway	469	157	170	0,12	3.70	9.09	.030	0.48	3.13
	All India	5,611	1,398	1,689	0.36	5.26	11.11	.026	0.91	4.23

facet of the railway network facilities in the country. Three indices ie.e, density of stations per 100 sq.km. of village, town and city area were obtained by dividing the total number of stations serving each of the three settlement levels by the total area under these settlements.

Table 6.3 gives variations in the availability of railway facilities for the nine railway zones Highest density of stations for all the three types of settlements is observed for Eastern, Northern and North Eastern Railways comprising the states of Punjab, Haryana, Uttar Pradesh, Bihar, West Bengal and western part of Rajasthan. Low density is observed in Central and South-Central Railway comprising parts of Madhya Pradesh and parts of Karnataka and Andhra Pradesh respectively. The reasons for these variations at the zonal level of aggregation appear to be the same as noted at the district level: that is, the density is a function of the number and magnitude of higher order urban centres and the kilometrage passing through the zone. It may, however, be noted that the relationship does not indicate the direction of causation, which calls for a closer examination. With a view to probe further, the values for three indices were calculated for each district. Spatial variations in the density for three types of settlements have been illustrated in Fig. 6.3, Fig. 6.4 and Fig. 6.5.

The corresponding data in the tabular form is given in Appendix XI. The district-wise density of roads is also shown in Fig. 6.6. These maps bring out the following significant features of railway development in India.

The pockets which show high value of these indices normally correspond to the districts with large urban centres in general and with the location of metropolitan cnetres in particular.

Medium type of accessibility in terms of the indicators defined above are to be noticed in those districts which either surround the pockets of high accessibility or lie along the trunk routes. Thus, the districts along the east coast line connecting Madras to Calcutta and the districts on Poona-Bombay-Ahmedabad trunk route have higher densities. Similar clusters are noticeable along Bombay-Ahmedabad-Delhi, Bombay-Gwalior-Delhi, Calcutta-Delhi-Amritsar and Calcutta-Bombay route. This phenomenon gives some support to the hypothesis of development corridors formulated by some regional planners.

Since the railway network serves the settlements in the space economy and since the spatial distribution of the settlements is not uniform, it is desirable to assess the efficiency of the railway network with reference to the distribution of settlements. This is made possible by calculating the number of stations connecting each of the three types of settlements. Appendix XI gives the value of these indices for each district. The four largest metroplitan centres score high in this respect since these four centres are served by a number of stations and booking offices through which freight can be loaded or unloaded. On the other hand, the dense network of Gangetic plain records low to medium degree of connection for the three types of settlements because of dense

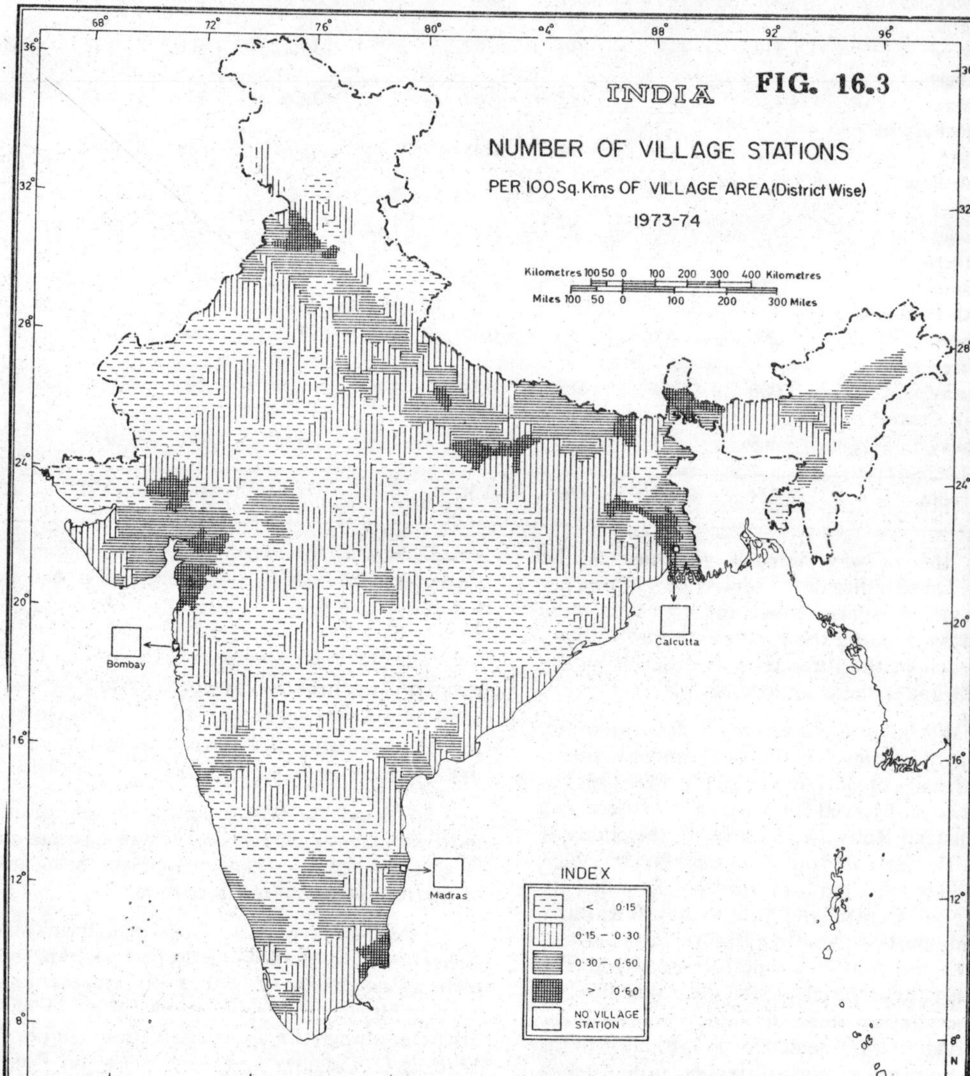

The territorial waters of India extend into the sea to a distance of twelve nautical miles measured from appropriate base line.

FIG. 6 3

population and large number of settlements. This is reflected in the low number of stations per village, town and city in the case of Eastern, Northern and North-Eastern Railways. In contrast the Central Railway zone presents a much better poicture for the three types of settlements with respect to these indicators, because of the fewer number of settlements in this zone. Similarly, in the North-East Frontier zone, the poor connectivity gets reduced ;in dimension in respect of these indicators.

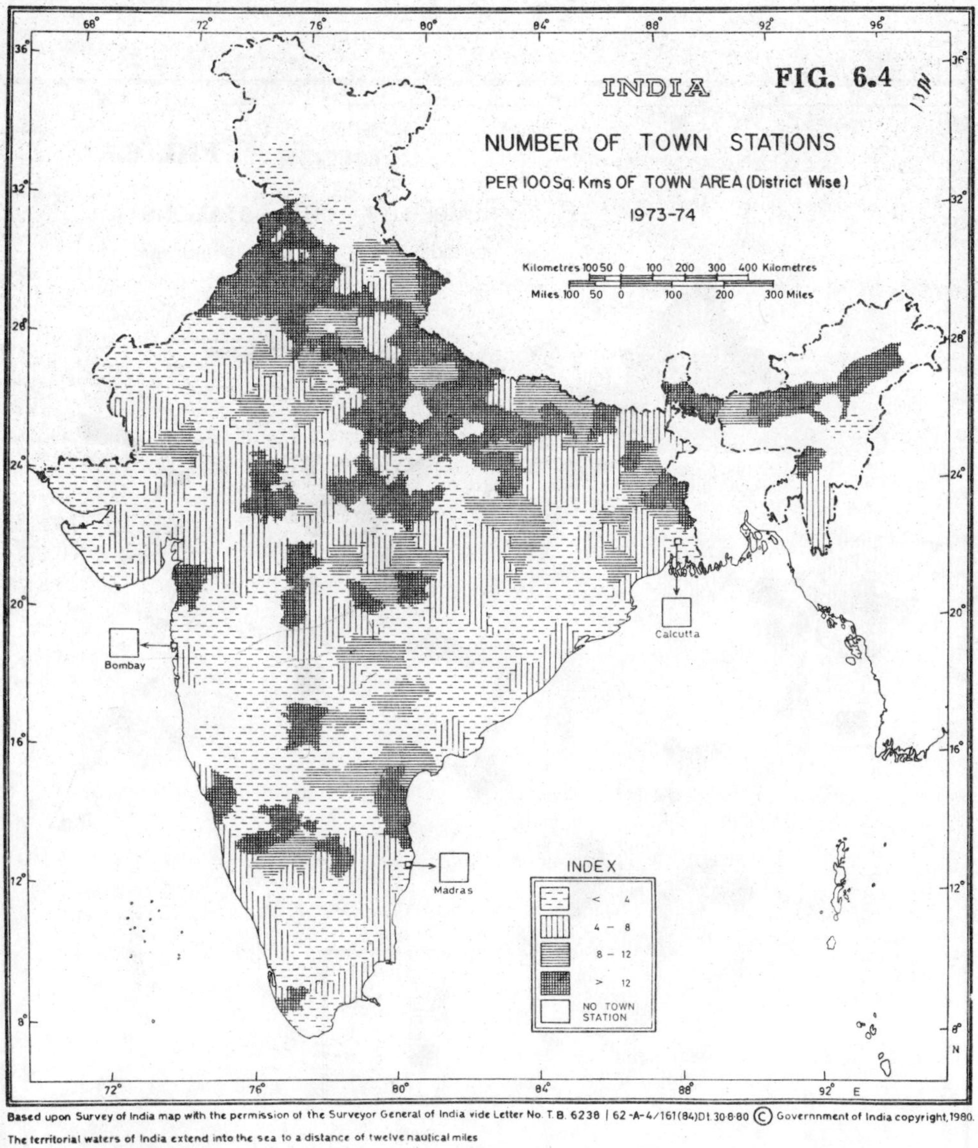

FIG. 6.4

SUMMARY

The analysis ,of transport network structure indicates the concentration of well connected centres in a few pockets of the Indian space economy and are usually associated with large metroplitan centres and cites, wherein the pivotal role of the metropolitan centres in shaping the regional pattern of network efficiency becomes apparent.

The growht of new industrial centres, which have been established since independence, happen to be on the major trunk lines. Therefore, only the

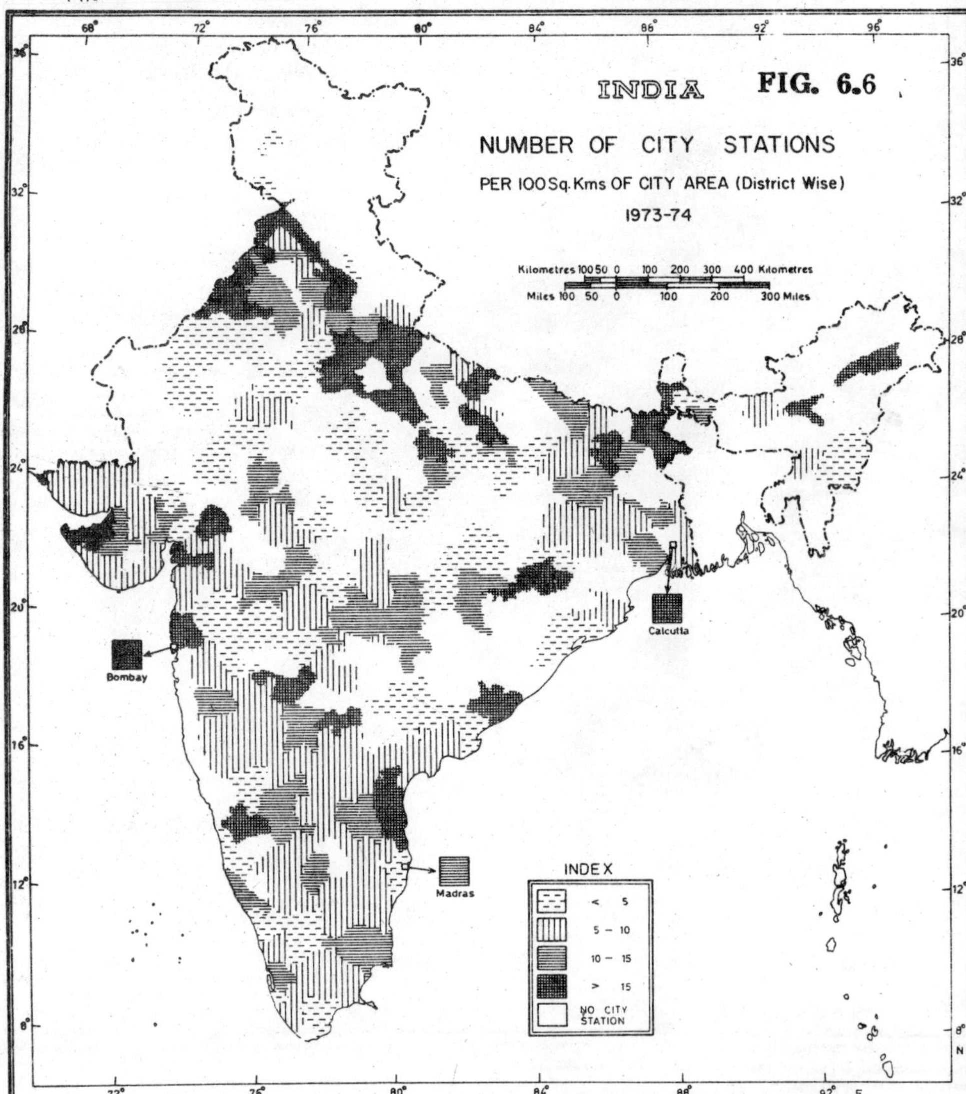

The territorial waters of India extend into the sea to a distance of twelve nautical miles measured from appropriate base line.

FIG. 6.5 ; NUMBER OF CITY/STATIONS

orientation of commodity flows was changed without bringing a structural change in the railway network. Consequently areas rich in minerals and forest resources seem to be poorly connected with differentt parts of the country but such areas continue to be served by routes connecting them to the metropolitan centres directly or through the large industrial centrees on the trunk lines.

The spatial variations in the network density of different order of settlements is a function of their relative location with respect to the higher order centres and the alignment of major trunk routes. Thus, the settlements of the three types (villages towns and cities) have a high density along the Gangetic plains and around the metropolitan and large urban centres.

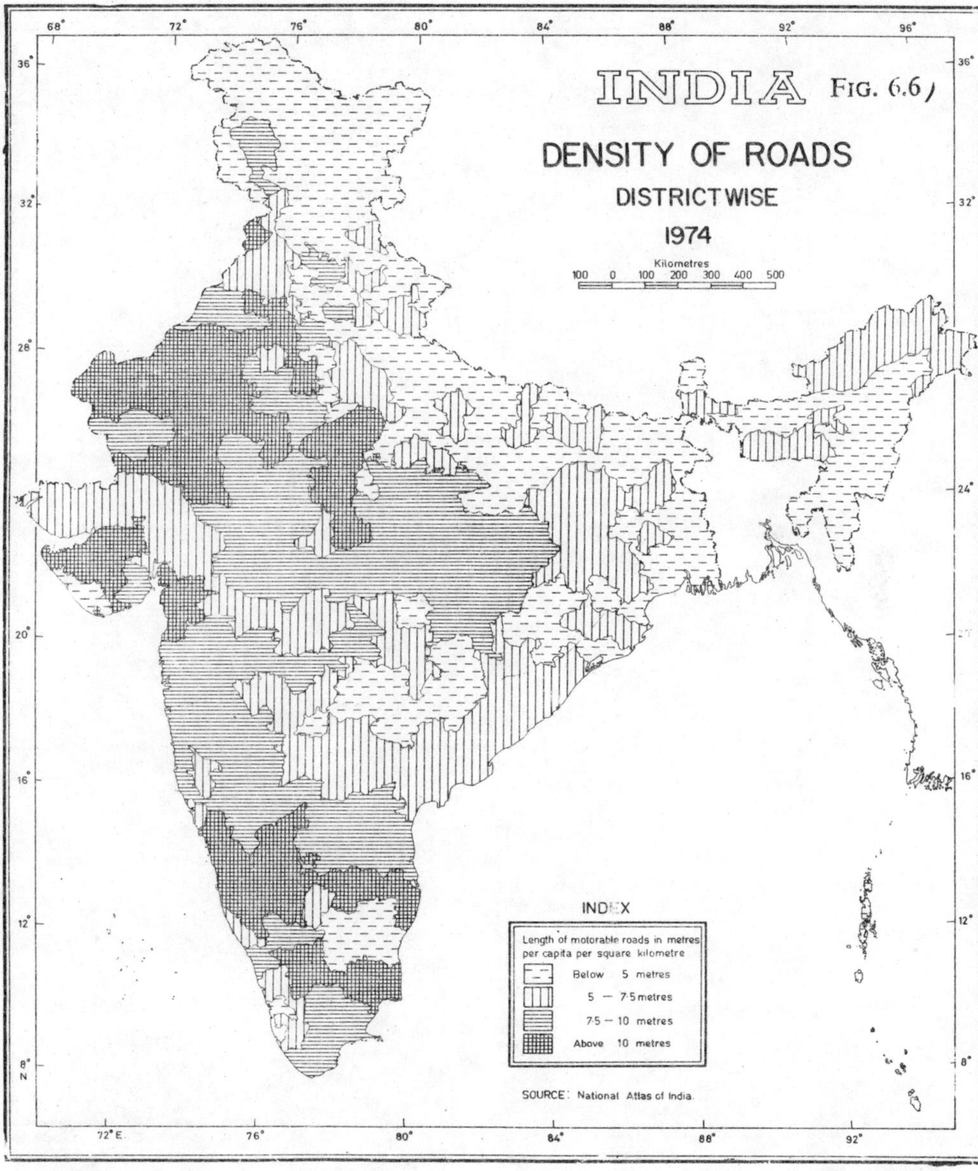

References

1. The method of appraisal involved computation of financial returns on the investment in the 6th, 11th and 16th year after commissioning of the lines. A project was considered to remunerative, if it was able to yield a return of 6.75 per cent per annum on the capital investment ;in the 6th year after commissioning.

2. For a life of 30 years a project is considered remunerative, if the returns are 10 per cent or more. Social needs are kept in view but have not been included at the time of appraisal.

7

ECONOMIC DEVELOPMENT AND FREIGHT CHARACTERISTICS

RAILWAY FREIGHT FLOWS AND INTEGRATION OF THE SPACE ECONOMY

THE analysis of inter-regional commodity flows within a country should begin with an examination of the relationship between freight characteristics and the overall economic development of the country. This is particularly so because railways are most suitable to carry bulky and heavy goods across the vast territories of countries like India, China, USSR or Canada. Railways with their high speed and large carrying capacity can meet the formidable challenge posed by the rapidly growing traffic in the process of economic development of a vast country like India.

As an essential part of the strategy for planned development launched since independence, the Indian Railways were entrusted with the task of carrying goods which were important inputs in the development process. The draft Five Year Plan (1978-83) stated that "Indian Railway system has been and will continue to occupy a key position in the strategy of building up the basic infrastructure required for a growing and diversified economy" With a view to establish the fact that the Indian Railways are playing a significant role in national development, the following propositions need to be examined:

- i **intensification of economic activity leads to the strengthening of the inter-dependence among regions and hence to increase in railway freight;**
- ii the composition of the traffic reflects the nature of the growing regional interdependence
- iii the average lead of total traffic would tend to fall as a consequence of the emergence of largely self-sufficient geographically compact production complexes in the national economic space which would imply a rise of short distance haulage; and
- iv the average lead of total traffic would tend to rise due to either increase in the movement of goods among metropoles which are situated at the extremities of the country; or to the pulling in of more remote sources of raw materials to the metropoles to sustain their increased economic acitivity.

As has been noted earlier, quite detailed information on indicators relating to the movement of goods traffic are compiled by the Indian Railways. The indicators appropriate to the phenomenon under investigation are as follows:

- i statistics relating to the total volume of originating goods traffic both for revenue and non-revenue earning groups;
- ii statistics relating to the net tonne kms. both for revenue and non-revenue earning traffic; and
- iii statistics relating to average lead, which are derived from (i) and (ii) above.

While indices of industrial production, mining, agricultural production and national income are indicative of the level and nature of economic acitivity in a country, the volume and the average lead of the rail freight reflects the level of activity of the railways. A correspondence or otherwise between the indicators of economic acitivity and of railway freight would indicate the nature and magnitude of inter-relationships between the two. If increase in economic activity leads to a corresponding increase in the volume of the originating freight then a high correspondence between the indicatiors of economic activity and of railway freight is expected. This has been established by the following analysis.

Time series data on the indices of rail freight, industrial production, mining output, agricultural production and national income has been presented in Fig. 7.1 and Table 7.1. All the indices relate to the base year 1950-51 and have been taken as 100. An examination of Table 7.1 and Fig. 7.1 reveals that all the four indices of economic development are positively related to the index of railway freight and hence move in the same direction. The correlation coefficient of the index of railway freight was calculated separately with each of the indices of industrial production, mining production, agricultural production and national income. It was observed that the correlation coefficient between the index of railway freight and the indices of industrial production, mining production, agricultural production and national income were all very high and statistically significant. It varied between 0.90 and 0.98.

The foregoing analysis has thus shown that with the intensification of economic activity ;in different parts of the country, the inter-dependence between different regions has increased. The examination of the total volume of originating freight shows that the volume of traffic handled by the Indian Railways has been showing considerable increase during the last 25 years. It has increased from 93 million tonnes in 1950-51 to 239 million tonnes in 1976-77.

It is expected that with the change in the structure of the economy, the commodity composition of the total freight would also undergo changes thus reflecting the trends of economic development in the country. Information on total freight, net tonne kms. and average lead for the originating freight in India is presented in Table 7.2. It is possible to infer the following from the table:

i Incresed scale of operations has led to high efficiency in the utilisation of railway assets since revenue earning traffic. The share of revenue earning traffic in the total has increased from 78 per cent in 1950-51 to 89 per cent in 1976-77.

ii The increased use of railways for long hauls is suggested by the increase in the average lead over the years. This also perhaps suggests that instead of the emergence of technologically integrated industrial complexes, we are witnessing the development of a few isolated nodes or enclaves. The average lead has, however, started falling after 1974-75. This may be partly explained by the large share of commodities like ores and fuels in the total freight. Bulk of these commodities move over shorter distances.

Growth rates of total freight and net tonne kms. have been worked out separately for different sets of base and terminal years. Table 7.3 shows the growth patterns of freight for various years. The following points emerge from Table 7.3.

i There are wide variations in the growth of goods traffic during the three decades of planned development. An overall growth rate of 3.7 per cent per annum has been achieved for 1950-51 to 1976-77. The positive sign of the growth rates for different periods shows that the use of railways as freight carrier has been increasing over time.

ii The maximum growth rate, both for revenue earning and total volume of traffic, has been achieved during the fifties and there has been a steep fall in the growth rate of freight during the sixties

New industries such as iron and steel, machinery, petroleum and chemicals were set up during fifties as a part of the programme of industrialisation in India. Consequently, the originating freight grew at a very fast rate during the fifties. Large public investments in these industries were made to build the industrial base of the country. The tempo of economic growth could not, however, be sustained during the sixties, and there were serious shortcomings in industrial production after 1965. Some other important events such as the devaluation of the Indian rupee, the Indo-Pak war and the severe drought during

RAIL FREIGHT AND ECONOMIC INDICATORS

(BASE 1950-51 = 100)

FIG. 7.1

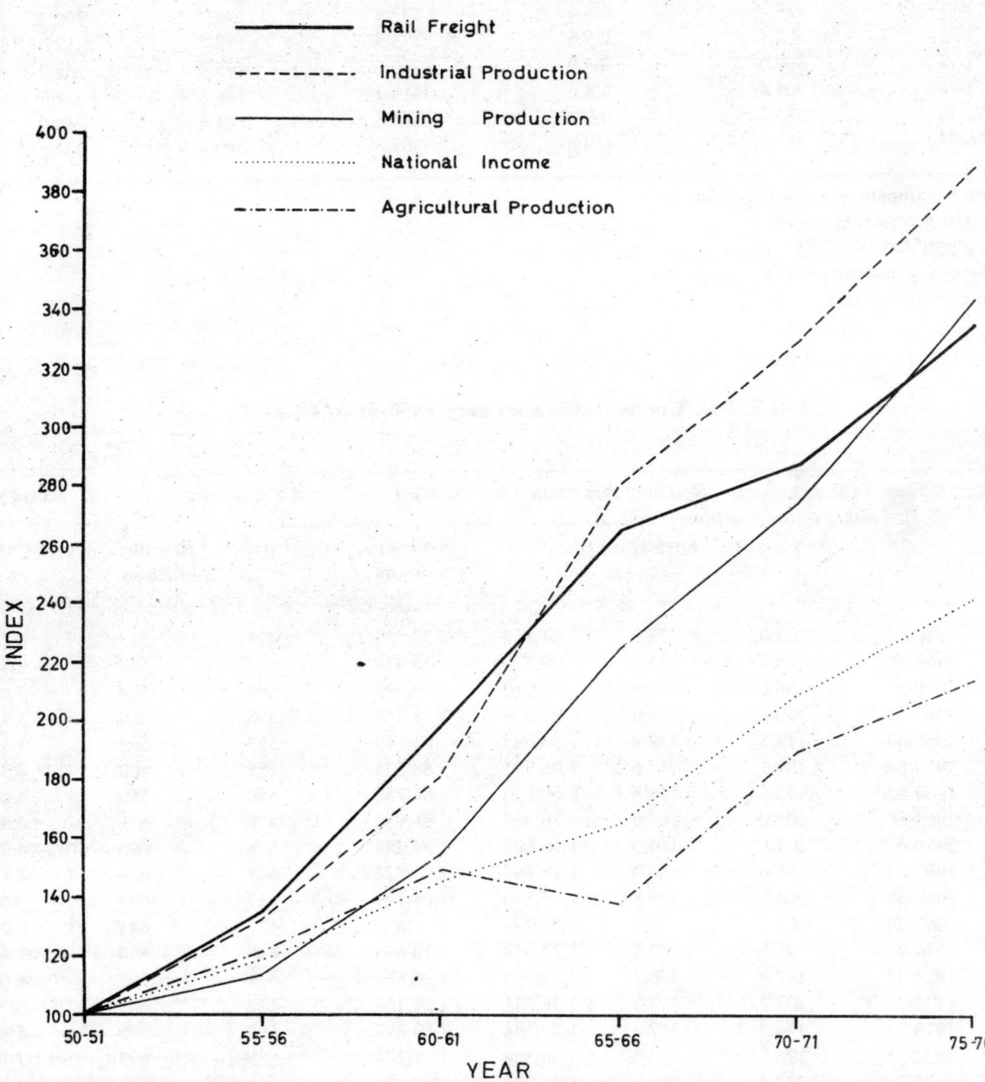

TABLE 7.1 : **Rail freight and economic indicators**

(Base 1950-51 = 100)

Year	*Index of rail freight*	*Index of ind. prod.*	*Index of mining output*	*Index of agri. production*	*Index of national income*
1	*2*	*3*	*4*	*5*	*6*
1950-51	100.0	100.0	100.0	100.0	100.0
1955-56	135.0	132.7	113.8	122.5	119.4
1960-61	198.7	182.5	153.8	149.1	145.8
1965-66	265.1	280.7	233.8	139.0	165.8
1970-71	288.7	329.6	273.8	190.7	209.2
1971-72	302.1	339.6	273.8	190.2	212.0
1972-73	309.5	363.9	280.0	175.0	208.7
1974-75	304.4	374.6	314.4	186.1	221.6
1975-76	336.0	389.4	345.5	214.6	240.9
1976-77	355.3	430.7	369.8	200.3	244.2

Correlation Coefficient of railway freight with
(i) industrial production = 0.98
(ii) mining production = 0.98
(iii) agricultural production = 0.92
(iv) national income = 0.90

TABLE 7.2 : **Goods traffic summary 1950-51 to 1976-77**

Year	*Total originating tonnes (mn.)*	*Revenue earning (mn. tonnes)*	*Net tonne kms (millions)*		*Average lead*		*Average rate per tonne km*
			Total	*Revenue earning*	*Total*	*Revenue earning*	
1950-51	93.0	73.2	44,117	37,565	474	513	3.71
1955-56	115.9	92.2	59,576	50,435	574	547	3.52
1960-61	156.2	119.8	87,680	72,333	561	604	3.88
1961-62	160.5	125.6	91,218	75,353	568	600	3.98
1962-63	178.8	139.4	1,00,693	83,140	563	596	4.12
1963-64	191.1	147.6	1,06,841	88,624	559	600	4.36
1964-65	193.8	148.8	1,06,570	88,752	550	596	4.49
1965-66	203.0	162.0	1,16,936	98,978	576	611	4.57
1966-67	201.6	164.0	1,16,607	99,284	578	605	4.71
1967-68	196.6	162.4	1,18,860	1,01,122	605	623	4.84
1968-69	204.0	170.8	1,25,140	1,08,129	613	633	5.08
1969-70	207.9	173.8	1,28,248	1,11,826	617	643	5.17
1970-71	196.5	167.9	1,27,358	1,10,696	648	659	5.43
1971-72	197.8	170.1	1,33,265	1,16,894	674	687	5.61
1972-73	201.3	175.3	1,36,531	1,21,164	678	691	5.74
1973-74	184.9	162.1	1,22,534	1,09,391	662	675	5.89
1974-75	196.7	173.6	1,34,304	1,21,374	683	699	7.16
1975-76	223.3	196.8	1,48,219	1,34,874	664	685	8.12
1976-77	239.1	212.6	1,59,756	1,44,030	656	677	8.86

TABLE 7.3 : **Growth of goods traffic 1950-51 to 1976-77**

(Compound annual growth rates)

Period	*Total freight*	*Revenue earning freight*	*Net tonne kms*	
			Total	*Revenue earning*
1950-51 to 1960-61	5.3	5.0	6.8	6.8
1960-61 to 1970-71	2.3	3.4	3.8	4.4
1970-71 to 1976-77	3.3	4.0	3.6	2.7
1950-51 to 1976-77	3.7	4.2	5.0	5.5

1965-67 also contributed to the sluggish growth of the economy. The final end product was a sharp decline in the growth of originating traffic during the sixties. With the overall improvement in the economic situation in the beginning of seventies, the freight picked up again.

The foregoing analysis has thus shown that with a given network structure, the level of originating freight has been consistently increasing since independence. However, the increease in the magnitude of freight has been greatly effected by the economic situation in the country.

Commodity composition of freight flows

In order to have a better understanding of the role of railways in the national economic development process, it is necessary to investigate the nature of commodities carried by the railways. Indian railways classify the commodities into two major groups:

i bulk commodities, which include coal, ores, foodgrains, cement, mineral oils, iron and steel, fertilizers and lime stone.

ii other than bulk commodities, which include salt, sugar, tea, jute, oilseeds, sugarcane and textiles.

An important feature of the railway freight flows is that the composition of total freight has also changed considerably during the period under review. The details of traffic composition and average lead for bulk and other than bulk commodities for various years are presented in Table 7.4.

Bulk commodities alone are accounting for most of the increase in the volume of freight since the total volume of other than bulk freight has not increased significantly. The share of bulk commodities in the total traffic has moved up from 58.2 per cent in 1950-51 to 83.6 per cent in 1976-77. The 1977-78

TABLE 7.4 : **Bulk and non-bulk composition of the railway freight**

Year	*Volume of traffic*		*% Share of*	*Net tonne kms.*		*Average lead*	
	Bull commodities	*Other than bulk commodities*	*Bull commodities*	*Bull commodities*	*Other than bulk commodities*	*Bull commodities*	*Other than bulk commodities*
1950-51	54.1	38.9	58.20	NA	NA	NA	NA
1960-61	113.7	42.5	72.79	47790	39890	420	938
1965-66	156.3	46.7	77.00	66167	40769	423	885
1970-71	156.8	39.7	79.80	81627	45731	550	1152
1975-76	184.9	38.6	82.80	101021	47198	546	1222
1976-77	199.9	39.2	83.61	109290	47466	547	1211

NA = Not available

Annual Report and Accounts of the Indian Railways show that the share of bulk commodities in the total originating tonnage has further gone upto 84.5 per cent.

The average lead for bulk commodities is much less than the average lead for other than bulk commodities. This shows that the commodities constituting other than bulk commodities move over longer distances than the bulk commodities. Bulk commodities mainly constitute raw materials, industrial inputs and fuels and are transported over shorter distances as compared to other than bulk commodities, which are mainly manufactured product like textiles, tea, sugar, chemicals, clothes and paper.

The foregoing analysis thus shows that there is a relative concentration of basic manufacturing activities near the source of raw materials. The fini hed products move over longer distances to meet the final demand in the economy.

Since the bulk commodities continue to influence the overall pattern of railway freight, an analysis of the patterns of commodity wise distribution of the freight may be quite revealing. With this end in view, Table 7.5 was constructed, showing the relative share of principal commodities carried by the Indian Railways from 1950-51 to 1975-76. An examination of the distribution pattern of total freight reveals the predominance of coal therein. Its share in the total originating freight has remained at the one third level during the period 1950-51 to 1975-76 though there has been substantial increase in the volume of its traffic.

There has been a slight fall in the share of foodgrains, raw jute, oil seeds and sugarcane in the total volume of freight. With the bringing in of more areas under cultivation and improved practices of farming, the regional imbalances in the production of foodgrains seem to have been reduced. In quantitative terms, the growth rate of agricultural production between 1961 and 1976 was 2.10 per cent per annum as compared to 4.30 per cent per annum for the output of the secondary sector.

The share of some commodities like cement, iron and steel, metallic ores, mineral oils and chemical fertilizers in the total freight has been increasing at a rate higher than that of the averages increase in freight. The share of these commodities in the total freight increased from 12.4 per cent in 1950-51 to 30.5 per cent in 1975-76 The total volume of these commodities during this period has grown at the compound rate of about 7 per cent per annum as compared to 3.7 per cent for the total freight.

It is interesting to note that while the highest growth rate of 12.8% in the originating freight was recorded by the metallic ores during the early phase, that is, in 1950-65, chemical fertilisers and mineral oils relegated metallic ores to the third position during the later phase, that is, 1965-75. This shift may be seen in the context of the fact that the development of heavy and basic metal industries occupied an important position in the economic sphere during the fifties and the early sixties; but the focus shifted to the green revolution during the later half of the sixties, necessitating large scale movement of chemical fertilizers. The average lead for fertilizers has also increased considerably during this period, from 752 kms. in 1965-66 to 988 kms. in 1977-78. This indicates that while there was spatial diffusion in the use of fertilizers on a considerable scale, the spatial spread of production centres did not keep pace with this process.

Commodities like iron and steel, cement, chemical fertilizers, metallic ores and mineral oils are used as intermediate inputs in various productive sectors of the economy. This fact is clearly brought out by an examination of the inter-industry transaction matrix or input-output table. The input-output matrix for India pertaining to the year 1968-69, has been used here to analyse the sectoral output disposal pattern of some of the important commodities.

It is only with the help of an input-output table that the share of the output of each sector that is being used for intermediate consumption in other sectors of economy can be worked out. The ratio of total intermediate consumption to its gross output is a measure of the forward linkage of any productive sector in the inter-sectoral transaction matrix of the input-output table.

Mathematically,

$$U_i = D_i / X_i$$

where

U_i is a measure of forward linkage of ith sector

D_i is the total intermediate demand for the output of ith sector, and

X_i is the gross vaule of output of the ith sector.

The value of forward linkage of some important sectors of the input-output table is presented in Table 7.6

Two groups of commodities can be identified from the above table; those with high value and those

TABLE 7.5 : **Principal commodities carried by railways : 1950-51 to 1975-76**

(000 Tonnes)

Commodity	*1950-51*		*1960-61*		*1965-66*		*1973-74*		*1974-75*		*1975-76*	
	Vol.	*% Distr.*	*Vol.*	*% Distr.*	*Vol.*	*% Distr.*	*Vol*	*% Distr.*	*Vol.*	*% Distr.*	*Vol.*	*% Distr.*
(1)	*(2)*	*(3)*	*(4)*	*(5)*	*(6)*	*(7)*	*(8)*	*(9)*	*(10)*	*(11)*	*(12)*	*(13)*
Coal	30,911	33.26	50,396	32.26	66,741	32.88	62,062	33.56	70979	36,08	80,518	36.06
Cement	2,471	2.66	6,348	4.19	8,649	4.26	10,021	5.42	9,187	4.67	11,597	5.19
Iron and steel	2,750	2.96	7,588	4.86	10,077	4.96	9,282	5.05	9,819	4.99	10,758	4.82
Metallic ores	3.055	3.78	11,140	7.13	18,623	9.17	21,107	11.42	22,627	11.50	26,933	12.06
Manganese ore	881	0.95	1.230	0.79	1,497	0.74	1,080	0.58	1,355	0.69	1,331	0.60
Foodgrains	7,805	8.39	12,629	8.10	14,514	7.15	14,648	7.92	13,666	6.95	16,184	7.25
Raw jute	470	0.91	644	0.41	763	0.38	591	0.32	485	0.25	632	0.28
Tea	265	0.28	250	0.16	203	0.10	199	0.11	198	0.10	116	0.05
Paper & paper products	193	0.21	442	0.28	670	0.33	199	0.11	875	0.44	899	0.04
Jute manf.	271	0.29	263	0.17	275	0.14	842	0.46	346	0.18	548	0.25
Raw cotton	525	0.56	536	0.34	485	0.24	447	0.24	340	0.17	382	0.17
Cotton textiles	477	0.51	380	0.24	308	0.15	148	0.08	141	0.07	123	0.06
Oilseeds	1,595	1.72	1,517	0.97	1,470	0.72	1,021	0.55	1,055	0.55	1,168	0.52
Sugarcane	2,819	3.03	3,237	2.07	2,717	1.34	1,818	0.99	1,688	0.86	1,491	0.62
Sugar	933	1.00	1,488	0.95	1,543	0.76	1,382	0.75	1,566	0.80	2,038	0.91
Salt	1,576	1.69	1,981	1.27	2,569	1.27	1,339	1.27	2,694	1.51	2,904	1.30
Chemical manure	589	0.63	1,393	0.89	2,452	2.21	5,315	2.87	5,976	3.04	7,169	3.21
Mineral oils	2,692	2.89	4,700	3.08	7,495	3.69	2,994	5.41	10,751	5.47	11,663	5.22
Others	32,722	35.18	49,807	31.89	61,949	30.52	42,422	22.94	42,682	21.70	47,115	21.10
Total	93,000	130.00	1,56,200	100.00	2,03,000	100.00	1,96,900	100.00	1,96,700	100.00	2,23,300	100.00

TABLE 7.6 : **Forward linkages for some selected commodities**

S.No.	*Sector Description*	*Ui*
1.	Coal and lignite	.94
2.	Iron ore	.52
3.	Petroleum products	.84
4.	Cement	.94
5.	Iron and steel	.86
6.	Fertilizers	2.34*
7.	Food crops	.16
8.	Sugar	.18
9.	Cotton textiles	.30
10.	Machinery except electrical	.27
11.	Woolen textiles	.17
12.	Leather and leather products	.15

*Because of high imports of fertilizers, intermediate consumption of fertilizers is much more than the production within the country.

with low value of forward linkage. Commodities with high forward linkage (greater than. 0.50), are mainly used as intermediate inputs in other sectors of the economic system and their use in final demand is small These sectors also have low value added per unit of output. While the value of forward linkages for the other set of commodities is low (less than .50), it has high value added per unit of output.

It is interesting to note that 40 out of a total of 60 sectors in the inter-industry transactions matrix use coal as one of the basic inputs (fuels) is their production process. Thus, whatever be the nature of location of these industries, coal has to be provided to them depending upon the nature and size of the plant. Similarly, iron ore is a basic input for iron and steel producing industry. Petroleum products are also used in almost all the sectors of the economy in one way or the other. Iron and steel is mainly used for construction, metal production and machinery manufacturing sectors. Fertilizers are now one of the basic inputs in agriculture, the activity which is also spatially diversified.

Thus, the level of conomic activity is determined by the freight of commodities like iron and steel, cement, chemical fertilizers, metallic ores and mineral oils. Consumption of cement alongwith commodities like iron and steel show the extent of construction activity which is an element of the capital formation in the economy.

The growth of the Indian economy during 1950-51 to 1976-77 is thus clearly reflected in the increase in the total volume of traffic; and the sectoral growth of the economy over the period is reflected in the growth of traffic in commodities like cement, iron and steel, metallic ores, mineral oils and chemical fertilizers.

Average lead statistics for some important commodities are presented in Table 7.7 The average lead for commodities like coal, foodgrains, iron and steel, cement, fertilizers and mineral oils has shown different behaviour over time. It has increased over the period suggesting a more wide use of these commodities.

Cement has recorded very high increase in the average lead—an increase of 48.25 per cent during 1965-66 to 1977-78. This shows that while manufacturing of cement may have remained concentrated, the market has expanded in space. Other commodities for which average lead had increased at a high rate are fertilizers (31.38%), foodgrains (46.78%) and iron and steel (23.59%).

In the case of coal, the increase in average lead has been marginal (2.63%) for two reasons. Firstly, the movement of coal for washeries, which are located very near to the extraction point, do not result in any substantial change in average lead. Secondly, only marginal locational chanages have taken place in the case of the major users of coal like steel plants, fertilizers plants and thermal power houses.

The average lead for raw materials from primary sources has also increased by more than 20 per cent. This is because more remote areas are being exploited to get raw materials for higher levels of production and partly due to the location of industries away from the sources of raw materials.

TABLE 7.7 : Growth of commodity-wise average lead for revenue earning traffic during 1965-66 to 1977-78

(In Kms.)

Commodity	*1965-66*	*66-67*	*67-68*	*68-69*	*69-70*	*71-72*	*72-73*	*73-74*	*74-75*	*75-76*	*76-77*	*77-78*
Coal	571	540	589	575	585	605	537	562	595	586	576	586
Foodgrains	808	792	853	859	887	1059	1181	1114	1110	957	940	1186
Iron and steel	852	913	968	935	967	1028	992	1016	1069	1009	1000	1053
Cement	456	462	484	527	583	617	614	635	663	741	672	676
Mineral oils	598	576	515	576	564	595	614	638	642	607	604	626
Fertilizers	752	675	775	828	809	332	809	753	801	861	923	988
Lime stone dolomite	218	215	204	213	232	217	237	241	287	277	274	272
Other stones	336	328	317	326	312	351	355	327	338	326	319	333
Total freight	611	605	623	633	643	687	691	675	699	685	679	714

The above analysis has thus shown that increased economic activity leads to increase in railway freight and the freight composition reflects the nature of inter-dependence of various regions. Increase in average lead of different commodities do suggest that the formation of large and self-sufficient geographical industrial complexes has not taken place so far in the Indian space economy.

8

COMMODITY FLOWS AND THE CONCENTRATION OF ECONOMIC ACTIVITIES IN SPACE

NATURE OF REGIONAL IMBALANCES IN THE SPACE ECONOMY

THE similarities and dis-similarities between the developed and the developing countries with reference to their spatial patterns of inter-regional trade would depend upon the organisation of the space economy of the two, on the one hand, and upon the nature of the commodity under examination, on the other. Since production activities in both the types of economies are more concentrated in space than consumption activities, the relative concentration of originating freight is expected to be more than that of the terminating freight. There would, however, be exceptions to this general rule as in the case of commodities like metallic ores, which are collected from a larger hinterland and are processed at one point; and, consequently, receipts tend to be more concentrated as compared to shipments. Taking the total freight movement into consideration, it is expected that the degree of concentration would ordinarily be higher in underdeveloped countries because of the high concentration of economic activities at only a few locations or because of dependence on imports. This chapter is devoted to the analysis of spatial patterns of freight distribution and to measure the extent of spatial imbalances in shipments and receipts of various commodities.

Constrained by the resource endowments and the relationship between exchange, cost and distance, various areas of the economic system specialise in different activities and exchange their specialities with each other depending upon the demand for the specialised commodities of the others. Commodities would, therefore, originate from the areas of production and terminate in the areas which are either points of intermediate consumption, final demand or are the points of transhipment. Viewed thus, it is not necessary that all the regions of a system participate in the exchange procees to the same extent or in the same manner. While there are areas with rich mineral resources wherein almost all the requirements of minerals are met locally, there are other areas in the economic system which are either only at the receiving end as far as these commodities are concerned or do not participate in their exchange at all. Thus different areas, depending upon their economic base, tend to have different participation rates in the flows of different commodities. The extent of participation can be measured by the share of a particular area in the total originating/terminating freight.

There will be wide regional variations in originating and terminating freight depending upon the ecological and the socio-economic conditions of each region and upon the political economy of inter-regional relationships. The differential impact of these combined forces leads to a situation wherein some areas play an active role with high participation rates while others remain passive.

An examination of inter-district flow matrix reveals that 317 of the 355 districts in India participate in the rail freight exchange process. The remaining districts do not take part in it because they are either outside the railway network or are not directly linked through a railway station. Most of these districts have a hilly and mountaineous terrain and low levels of economic development. It has further been observed that even those districts which participate in the process of exchange of commodities do not do so for all commodities. While, some districts send/receive goods of one group only, others like Bombay, Calcutta and Delhi send/receive many types of commodities and thus may be considered to have a diversified freight pattern.

Regional variations in the originating freight will also differ from one commodity to another. It is expected that while there would be concentration of originating and terminating freight in the case of some commodities, the movement pattern of others would show a diversified pattern. Since balanced regional development has been one of the national objective in India, it would be interesting to analyse the reasons behind the large concentration in the receipt pattern, which is indicative of relative concentration of economic activities at a few nodes in space.

In the context of the nature of economic development in India, it may be expected that the following attributes may characterise commodity flows in the country :

i First order processing of bulk commodities like raw materials will show high concentration ratio both for originating and terminating freight.

ii Since the manufacturing points are more concentrated in space than the consumption points, commodities like fuels, industrial products, construction material and inputs into agriculture will have high concentration ratio for originating freight as compared to the terminating freight. The difference in the concentration ratio of originating and terminating freight of such commodities are expected to be very large in a diversified market economy.

iii The movement of food products depends upon the agricultural situation during a particular year. As agricultural development proceeds, different areas tend to specialise in the production of various crops. The relative concentration of originating and terminating freight in the case of foodgrains will be high because of the differential impact of drought on different regions in different years or the extent of population concentration as well as due to the regional specialisation as a result of the green revolution.

COMMODITY COMPOSITION OF ORIGINATING FREIGHT

The distribution of the total originating freight in terms of commodity groups in India during 1973-74 has been shown in Table 8.1. The following conclusions may be drawn from the study of this table :

Fuels account for 41.17 per cent of total originating freight. This is followed by raw materials from primary sources, with a share of 23.05 per cent. These two groups dominate the scene of commodity flows—their combined share accounting for as high as 64.22 per cent of the total originating freight. The commodities falling in these two groups are either fuels or basic inputs into various manufacturing processes and only a very small proportion of these commodities goes into the final demand sector of the economy. The

TABLE 8.1 : **Distribution of originating freight for 1973-74**

Sr. No.	*Commodity*	*% freight*
1.	Food products	11.17
2.	Raw materials from primary sources	23.05
3.	Coal & fuel	41.17
4.	Inputs into agriculture	7.07
5.	Construction material	7.41
6.	Industrial products	6.68
7.	Miscellaneous	3.45

Indian Railways are thus playing a key role in providing basic raw materials to different manufacturing units.

The share of food products in the total originating freight is only 11.17 per cent. Food products generally move from surplus areas to deficit areas; and there are wide annual fluctuations depending upon the agricultural situation in the country.

Fertilizers and manures, which constitute the main component in the agricultural inputs are again meant for consumption in different regions.

Construction materials account for 7.41 per cent of the total originating freight and include cement, bricks and tiles, which go in for creating capital stock.

Industrial products including metals, machinery (both electrical and mechanical) account for 6.68 per cent. Most of these commodities are either intermediate demand goods or investment goods for capital formation.

Miscellaneous commodities account for only 3.45 per cent. This also includes the movement of goods for defence purposes whose share being 0.74 per cent.

A study of the commodity composition of the originating freight has thus clearly brought out that a major part of exchange relates to the movement of fuels and raw materials which go as intermediate inputs in other productive sectors of the economy.

SPATIAL DISTRIBUTION OF ORIGINATING FREIGHT

Figure 8.1 shows the district-wise spatial distribution of total originating freight in India during 1973-74. Thirty-seven districts have been identified wherein shipments exceeds 10 lakh tonnes each. The dominance of mining and industrially advanced areas is clearly reflected in the originating freight.

Three type of areas can be identified within this group and these are :

i areas like Dhanbad, Burdwan, Hazaribagh and Bhilai specialising in mineral and basic heavy industries;

ii important ports like Calcutta, Bombay, Madras, Kandla and Vishakhapatnam;

iii industrially advanced nodes like Kanpur Baroda, Ahmedabad, Pune and Jamnagar,

These 37 districts with very high shipments taken together account for 74.89 per cent of the total originating freight. Nearly 30 per cent freight originates from Dhanbad, Burdwan, Hazaribagh, Durg (Bhilai), and Singhbhum. These districts constitute areas with high mining potential and form a contiguous belt of basic and heavy industrial activity along the common borders of West Bengal, Bihar, Orissa and Madhya Pradesh. Thus the dominance of mining and industrial manufacturing belt is clearly reflected in the total originating freight.

There are 145 districts wherein the total shipments range from one lakh tonnes to ten lakh tonnes per year. They are located in the coastal districts of South India, Western Rajasthan, Punjab, Haryana and some areas of Western Uttar Pradesh. The share of shipments from these districts to the total originating freight is only 22.47 per cent.

Most of the areas with high shipments either specialise in the production of agricultural commodities or in large and medium scale industrial activity. While the major agricultural commodities which originate from the former category are wheat, rice cotton and oilseeds, the major industrial products which originate from the latter category are cement, fertilizers, sugar, cloth, petroleum and petroleum products.

It may be noted from the map that the relatively underdeveloped areas of Jammu & Kashmir, Himachal Pradesh, parts of Madhya Pradesh, Gujarat, North-Eastern region and Uttar Pradesh have shipments varying from low to very low levels. Areas with shipments lying below one lakh tonnes constitute the lowest two categories. The aggregate shipments from these areas account for only 2.64 per cent of the total originating freight.

The foregoing analysis thus clearly shows that the 37 districts with very high levels of originating freight are really the nerve centres of all types of economic activity in India. Their locations vary from highly backward but rich in mineral resources to highly advanced districts of the country.

SPATIAL DISTRIBUTION OF TERMINATING FREIGHT

Figure 8.2 depicting the distribution of terminating freight presents an entirely different picture as compared to Figure 8.1. The comparison of two maps shows that the commodities get more evenly

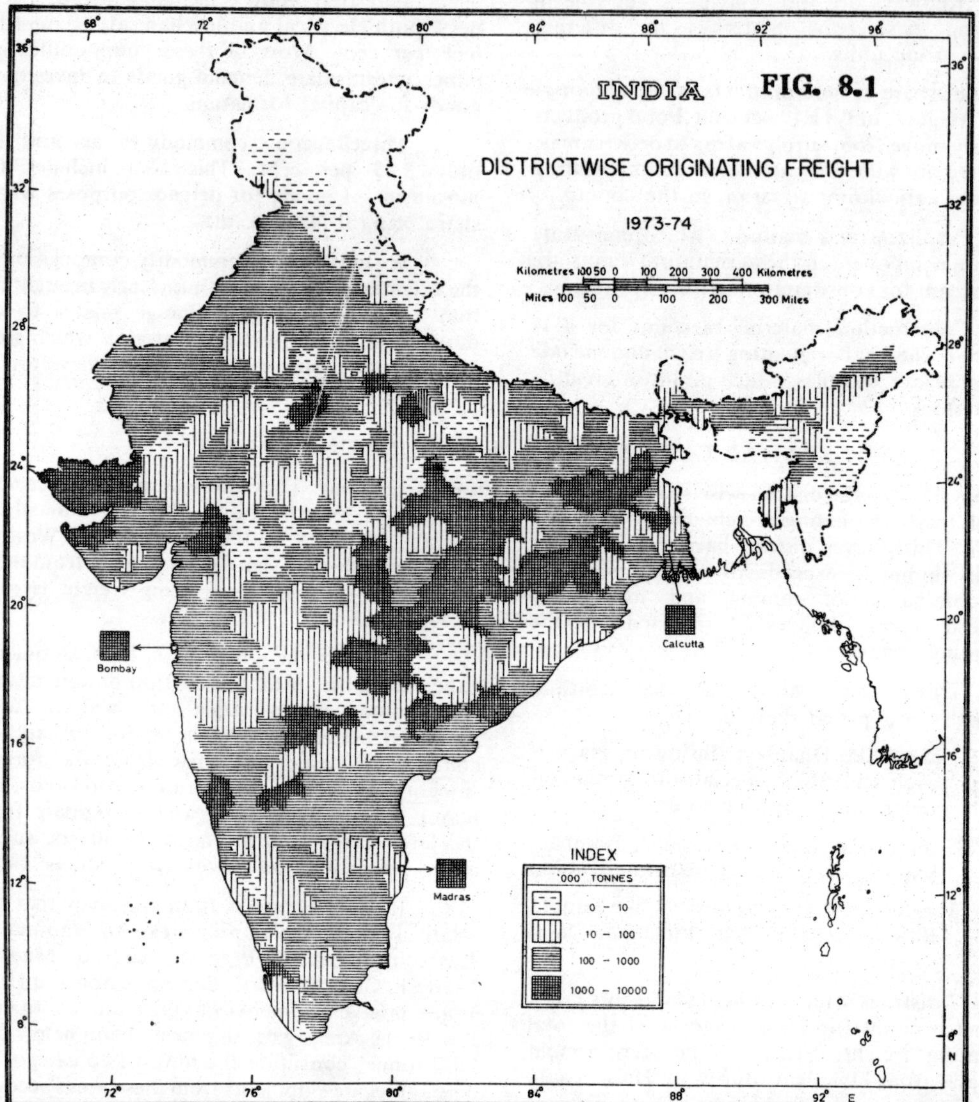

The territorial waters of India extend into the sea to a distance of twelve nautical miles measured from appropriate base line.

distributed as compared to the originating freight. It may be noted that the areas with large receipts of freight are more evenly distributed over the country and, therefore, the patterns of receipts may be said to be more diversified over the country and, therefore, the patterns of receipts may be said to be more diversified than those of shipments.

Examination of the regions falling in the high receipt areas bring out that at least two major industrial belts around the principal port towns of Bombay and Calcutta are clearly disernible; the first comprising the districts of Bombay, Thana, Nasik, Jalgaon and Pune; and the other is spread over Calcutta, Hoogly, 24 Pargana, Burdwan, Dhanbad and Hazaribagh. In addition to these major industrial belts, geographically compact industrial complexes around Delhi, Madras,

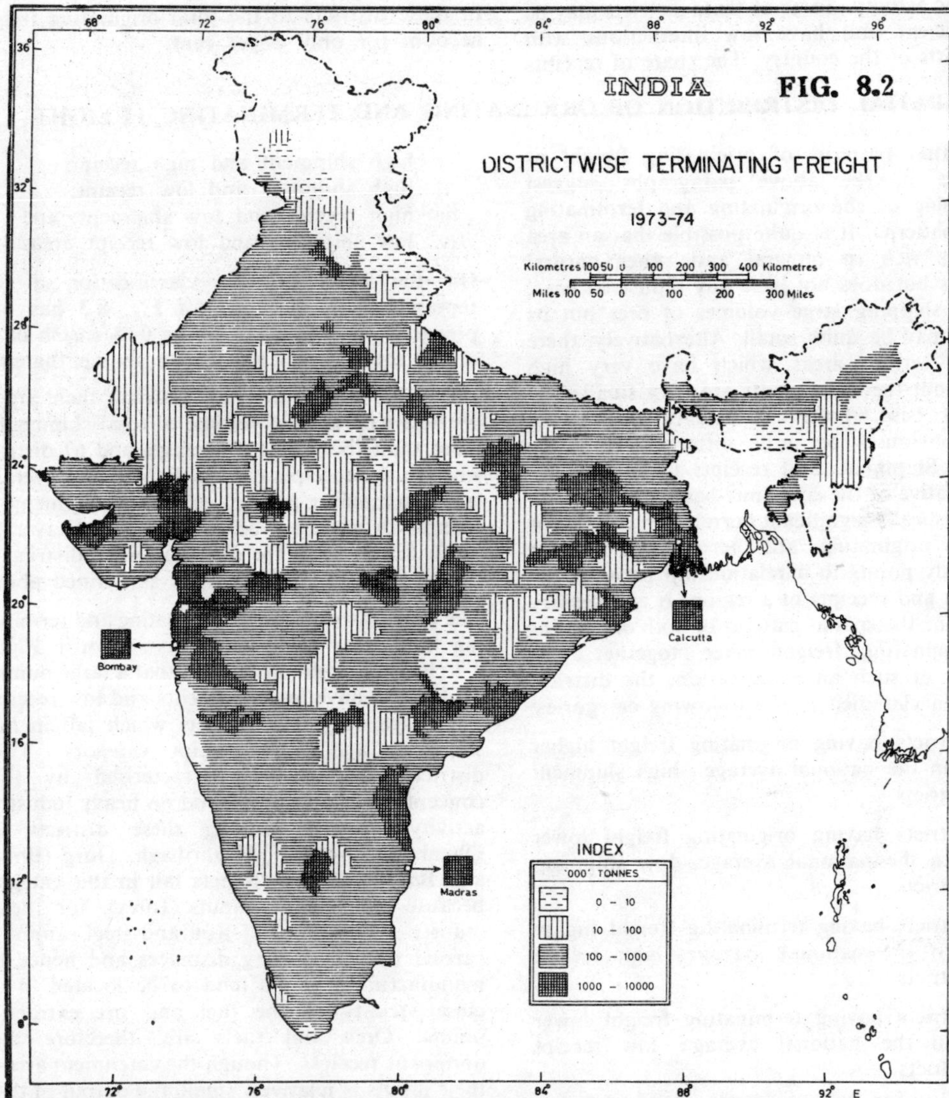

Vishakhapatnam, Ahmedabad, Khera, Bangalore, Ambala and Durg form small clusters of high receipt areas. Since these connurbations concentrate on industrial manufacture of either the specialised or the diversified type, they receive large quantities of basic inputs for their production requirements.

The districts falling in the second category have their receipts ranging from one lakh tonnes to ten lakh tonnes and account for only 30 per cent of the total receipts. The number of such districts being 181. Agriculturally advanced regions of Punjab, Haryana, Andhra Pradesh, Kerala, Tamil Nadu and coastal Maharashtra fall in this category.

The districts falling in the third and fourth category are essentially those with low level of economic activity. Some of these districts may be self-sufficient and have low interactions with other parts of the country. The share of receipts in these districts to the total originating freight account for only 2 per cent.

SPATIAL DISTRIBUTION OF ORIGINATING AND TERMINATING FREIGHT

The spatial patterns of originating freight as discussed in the above paragraphs suggest overlapping of the originating and terminating freight patterns. It is quite possible that an area which is rich in mineral and other natural resources but does not have any industrial base, may be shipping large volumes of ores but its receipts may be quite small. Alternatively, there may be certain areas which have very high receipts but their shipments are very small. The economic base of the two category of regions would obviously be quite different from one another. Shipments and receipts taken together are indicative of the economic base of the region. The statistically significant correlation coefficient between originating and terminating freight definitively points to a relationship between the shipment and receipts of a region. It is necessary to examine the spatial patterns of both originating and terminating freight taken together. For purposes of such an examination, the districts have been classified in the following categories:

- i districts having originating freight higher than the national average—high shipment districts
- ii districts having originating freight lower than the national average—low shipment districts
- iii districts having terminating freight higher than the national average—high receipt districts
- iv districts having terminating freight lower than the national average—low receipt districts

It may be mentioned here that the national average of originating and terminating freight will be the same. When originating and terminating freight categories are cross tabulated, we get a (2x2) table, with their respective cells as:

- i high shipment and high receipt;
- ii high shipment and low receipt;
- iii high receipt and low shipment; and
- iv low shipment and low receipt areas.

On the basis of this classification a map represented in the form of Fig. 8.3 has been prepared and the areas falling under each of the above four classes have been shown therein.

Out of a total of 317 districts, there are 57 districts wherein the volume of total shipment is more than the national average, and 67 districts wherein the receipts exceed the national average. In the remaining districts either the shipments or receipts or both are below the national average. Table 8.2 presents the distribution of districts in the various freight categories as defined above.

The areal distribution of originating and terminating freight for each district as shown in Figure 8.3 clearly brings out the fact that a large number of districts have low shipments and low receipts. There are very few districts which fall in high shipment and high receipt category. These districts are usually characterised by their concentration on mining and on heavy industrial activity. Notable among these districts are Dhanbad, Burdwan, Hazaribagh, Durg (Bhilai) and Baroda. These districts fall in this category because the basic inputs (ores) for heavy industries like those of iron and steel cannot be carried over very long distances and hence the manufacturing plants tend to be located in the close vicinity of the fuel and ore extraction points. Ores and fuels are, therefore their dominant receipts. Though the catchment area of their inputs is relatively small, the output of these industries serve the national market. The fact that average lead for inputs is much less than that for their output indicates that the industries which get located in these areas are essentially resource based. Whereas the average lead for

TABLE 8.2 : **Distribution of districts according to freight characteristics**

Originating	*Terminating* *High*	*Low*	*Total*
High	32	25	57
Low	35	225	260
Total	67	250	317

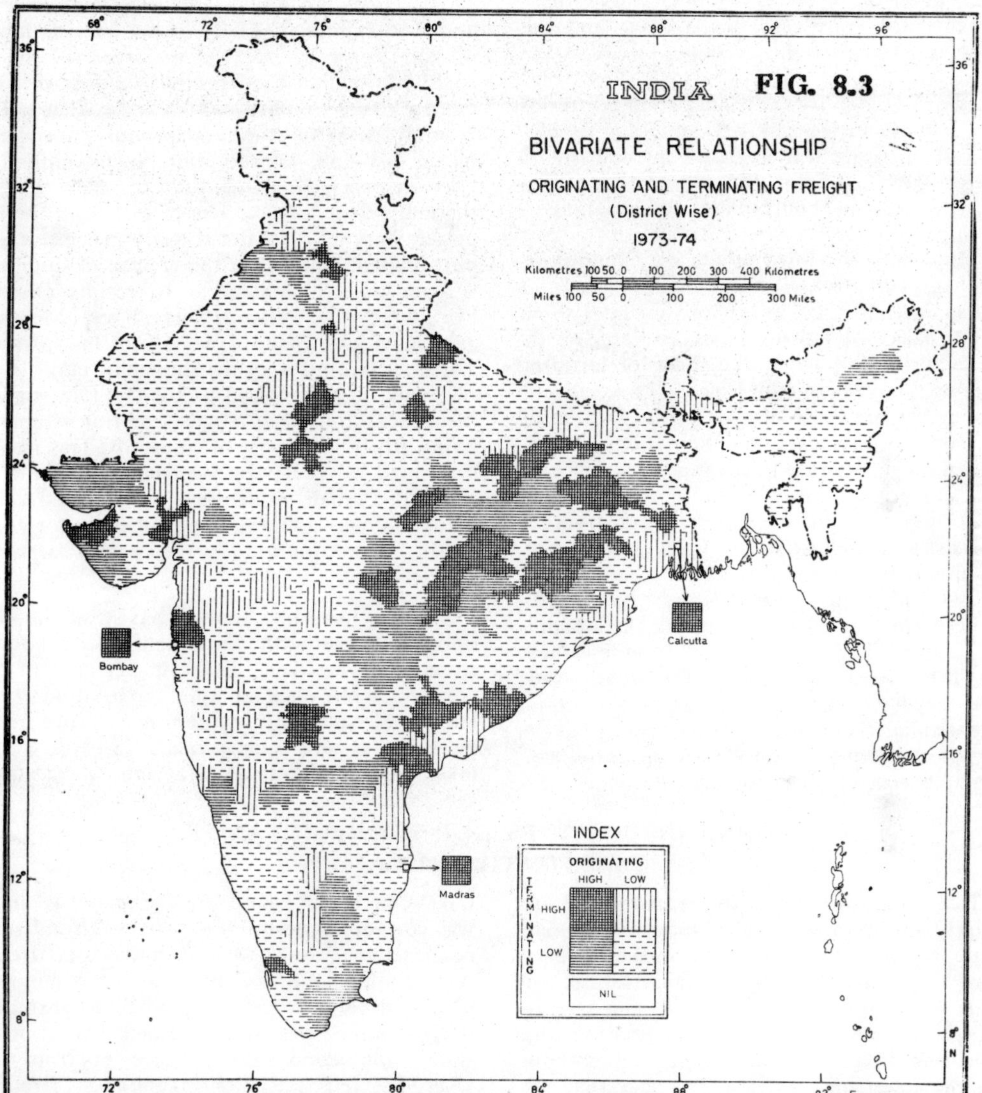

Based upon Survey of India map with the permission of the Surveyor General of India vide Letter No. T.B. 6238 | 62-A-4/161(84)Dt.30-8-80 © Government of India copyright, 1980.

The territorial waters of India extend into the sea to a distance of twelve nautical miles measured from appropriate base line.

receipts of iron ore and coal for steel plants was 329 kms and 357 kms respectively, the average lead for the shipment of iron and steel was 1016 kms.

Other areas, which fall in the high shipment and high receipt category, have a developed commercial and manufacturing sector, are generally engaged in the manufacture of machinery and durable goods including those for household consumption. This sub-set includes some of the large urban settlements of the country like Madras, Calcutta, Bombay, Delhi, Kanpur, Patna and Nagpur. Quite a few of these districts happen to be the locations of important ports which perform trans-shipment functions on a considerably high scale.

Out of a total of 57 districts with high shipments, 25 have low receipts. Thus, this group of 25 districts represents those areas where shipments are more than the average and the receipts are less than the average. A look at the location of these districts on a map shows that these are located at some distance from centres of heavy manufacturing industry and thus usually supply them either raw materials in the form of ores or fuels. Raipur and Sarguja are two districts in the neighbourhood of Bhilai falling in this category. Some other districts which have high shipments and low receipts are Chindwara, Keonjhar, Adillabad, Shahdol, Karimnagar and Santhal Pargana. This group also includes some of the backward districts where large scale manufacturing industries like those of fertilizer and cement have been established. The receipts in these regions are those of food products to meet the food requirements of their popoulation. Some of the agriculturally advanced districts also have similar attributes because those areas import inputs into agriculture, construction materials and industrial products and export food products to deficit areas on a substantial scale. This phenomenon is illustrated by districts like Ferozepur, Ludhiana, Sangrur, Dhenukanal and Tirunelveli. The exports of food products from these areas are quite substantial; and, hence, they have high shipments and low receipts. For example, the analysis of originating freight has shown that more than 95% of rice produced in Punjab was exported outside the state.

There are 35 districts with high receipts and low shipments. Many of the districts falling in this category receive a large volume of commodities like food products along with raw matrials from primary sources and coal as well as other fuels. While the food products are mainly meant for final consumption, high volumes of coal are received in many of these districts for thermal power houses. The output from thermal power stations does not directly generate transport demand and hence the volume of shipments is quite low as compared to its receipts. Districts like Darbhanga, Saharsa, Surat, Khera, Mehsana, Jalpaiguri and 24 Pargana fall in this category. The high receipts and low shipments may also be explained in some cased by the fact that some of these areas are rail terminals, and trans-shipment points for other modes of transport. This may be illustrated by the case of Gurdaspur district in the state of Punjab, which has very high receipts because it acts as trans-shipment point for goods meant for consumption in the state of Jammu & Kashmir.

The foregoing analysis has strong implications for planning the movement of commodities from and between different regions of the country. While deciding upon the location of new industries, such information may prove to be quite useful and appropriate measueres can be taken to avoid bottlenecks at subsequent stages.

MEASURING INEQUALITIES IN INTER-REGIONAL TRADE: A QUANTITATIVE APPROACH

The foregoing analysis has shown that there are relatively few areas with high shipments and high receipts, while many districts fall in the category of low shipments and low receipts. The relative dominance of mining, manufacturing and agriculturally advanced areas in the originating and terminating freight has also been brought out from the foregoing analysis. The fact that the spatial pattern of inter-regional trade is dominated by relatively few areas suggests that the distribution of commodities are skewed in favour of a few regions of the economic system. Areas of high shipment and high receipt account for 53.46 per cent of the shipments and 52.50 per cent of the total receipts. The dominance of commodities with high weight and low value is also clear from the fact that all the areas in the category of high shipment and high receipt are generally specialising in mining or heavy industrial activity. Raw materials and fuels dominate the flow pattern in such areas.

In order to have a clearer picture about inter-regional imbalances in the freight receipt, it was considered desirable to work with individual commodities rather than with the total freight. An additional reason in favour of commodity-wise analysis was that it might help to distinguish those commodities which, by their nature, would show a high concentration of receipts from those where the relatively high magnitudes of receipts may be the result of inter-regional disparities. The following two techniques have been applied to measure the inequalities in the spatial distributon of originating and terminating freight:

i coefficient of variation
ii Lorenz curve and Gini coefficient

Though both the measures essentially serve the same purpose of measuring relative variation, coefficient of variation is less sensitive to extreme values than the corresponding Lorenz curve.

Table 8.3 gives the average weight, standard deviation and coefficient of variation for originating as well as terminating freight, there will be wide variations in the standard deviation and the coefficient of variation depending upon the spatial links formed by the originating and terminating freight in economic space. While the distribution of average weight per district will follow a pattern similar to that of the share of each commodity in the total freight, the values for standard deviation and coefficient of variation of different commodities would give some indication about the spatial concentration or dispersion of various economic activites associated with each commodity.

An analysis of the coefficient of variation of shipments and receipts will indicate the extent of forward spatial links generated by each commodity. Index of Forward Spatial Distribution (SD) has been worked out by using the coefficient of variation for shipments and receipts for each commodity. Table 8.3 presents the index of spatial distribution for all the commodity groups under consideration. A commodity with high value of the index will show a more dispersed pattern of spatial dispersion as compared with that of a commodity having a low value of the index. This is illustrated by the high value of the indices of spatial distribution corresponding to inputs into agriculture as well as for coal and fuels. This is so in view of the fact that these commodities originate from a relatively small number of nodes but are usually received at a very large number of spatially dispersed nodes.

It has been observed from Table 8.3 that though food products and raw materials from primary sources originate from a large number of nodes especially in surplus areas they are received usually in bulk at a smaller number of locations. It may sometime happen that the same node may be getting its supplies from more than one region. In such circumstances, the pattern of shipments would tend to be more dispersed than the receipts. There may be many reasons for this. Concentration in receipt may be either due to the consumption oriented nature of the commodity or the node may itself be acting as a transshipment point for different modes of transport.

The low value of the *index of spatial dispersion* for raw materials can be attributed to the fact that they are usually received at a single point (manufacturing plant) although they orginate from a variety of nodes. For example, iron ore would be despatched from a large number of nodes in the mining areas and would be received only at the plant location.

High values of coefficient of variation (C.V.) suggest that there are marked inter regional differences between shipments and receipts of various commodities. Since C.V. does not give any idea about the shape of the distribution curve, it was decided to draw Lorenz curve for individual commodities, so that the relative dominance of some specific districts could be brought out. Gini coefficient for different commodities has also been computed separately for shipments as well as for receipts. A comparison of Gini coefficient for originating and terminating freight gives an idea about the extent of the spatial concentration or diversification of one in relation to the other.

In order to draw the Lorenz curves, the district-wise commodity-wise data was arranged in descending order and the relative share of each district in the total freight was calculated. Lorenz curve was drawn by taking percentage freight (cumulative) on X axis and the corresponding value of percentage districts (cumulative) on Y axis. Lorenz curves for both shipments and receipts for each commodity have been drawn on the same graph so that their relative position may be compared.

TABLE 8.3 : **Commodity-wise average weights, standard deviation and coefficient of variation**

S. No.	*Commodity group*	*Average wt. (000 Qts.) Orig./Term.*	*Standard deviation*		*Coefficient of variation*		*Index of spatial distribution*
			Orig	*Term.*	*Orig.*	*Term*	
1.	Food products	647	1047	687	1.62	1.66	0.976
2.	Raw materials	1335	5185	5199	3.88	3.89	0.997
3.	Fuels	2384	14427	6937	6.05	2.90	2.086
4.	Inputs into agriculture	410	3006	2945	4.33	2.18	1.986
5.	Construction material	429	1269	743	2.96	1.73	1.711
6.	Industrial products	387	1879	1173	4.86	3.03	1.604
7.	Misc	200	598	502	2.99	2.51	1.191

TABLE 8.4 : **Commodity-wise distribution of originating freight**

Cumulative per cent of districts	*Cumulative per cent of freight*							
	FP	*RM*	*Coal*	*IA*	*CM*	*IP*	*Misc*	*Total Freight*
1	*2*	*3*	*4*	*5*	*6*	*7*	*8*	*9*
2	22.05	55.01	70.74	61.74	36.42	67.66	35.30	33.86
5	40.29	71.09	88.48	75.79	62.00	79.98	49.09	53.50
10	57.23	80.81	98.41	85.33	85.44	87.65	63.96	71.41
15	67.43	86.13	99.25	89.33	93.47	92.06	73.18	78.98
20	75.17	89.62	99.58	92.22	96.84	94.96	79.96	85.13
25	80.84	92.41	99.75	94.27	98.23	96.71	85.07	88.19
30	85.14	94.25	99.85	95.58	98.93	97.64	89.00	90.99
35	88.52	95.59	99.91	96.58	99.32	98.23	91.99	92.96
40	91.40	96.73	99.95	96.67	99.53	98.74	94.39	93.68
45	93.76	97.60	99.97	98.25	99.74	99.10	96.08	95.22
50	95.86	98.42	99.98	98.87	99.86	99.41	97.42	96.71
60	98.06	99.27	99.99	99.45	99.95	99.72	98.69	98.24
70	99.41	99.78	100.00	99.82	99.99	99.90	99.51	99.31
75	99.73	99.89	100.00	99.92	100.00	99.95	99.73	99.62
80	99.92	99.97	100.00	99.97	100.00	99.98	99.88	99.85
90	100.00	100.00	100.00	100.00	100.00	100.00	99.99	99.99
100	100.00	100.00	100.00	100.00	100.00	100.00	100.00	100.00

FP = Food production
Coal = Coal and other fuels
CM = Construction material
Misc = Miscellaneous

RM = Raw materials from primary sources
IA = Inputs into agriculture
IP = Industrial products

TABLE 8.5 : **Commodity-wise distribution of terminating freight**

Cumulative per cent of districts	*Cumulative per cent of freight*							
	FP	*RM*	*Coal*	*IA*	*CM*	*IP*	*Misc*	*Total Freight*
1	*2*	*3*	*4*	*5*	*6*	*7*	*8*	*9*
2	25.91	54.52	34.75	50.19	21.17	36.48	31.63	28.49
5	38.84	74.93	57.59	58.31	34.56	54.70	47.87	50.88
10	51.82	83.17	73.21	67.00	48.34	69.76	64.70	64.60
15	61.17	87.80	80.39	73.11	57.03	78.46	73.24	73.82
20	69.12	91.02	85.35	78.48	64.67	83.97	80.12	78.11
25	75.42	93.12	89.47	82.90	70.89	87.58	85.16	82.58
30	80.38	94.69	92.52	86.55	76.24	90.30	88.72	85.94
35	84.22	95.88	94.47	89.36	80.62	92.37	91.32	88.62
40	87.62	96.91	96.07	91.83	84.55	94.17	93.53	91.06
45	90.47	97.75	97.26	93.81	87.86	95.66	95.26	93.07
50	93.11	98.53	98.35	95.66	91.16	96.96	96.73	95.03
60	96.04	99.30	99.35	97.68	94.95	98.29	98.23	97.24
70	98.26	99.77	99.85	99.14	97.83	99.28	99.30	98.93
75	99.05	99.89	99.93	99.56	98.77	99.60	99.60	99.43
80	99.66	99.96	99.98	99.82	99.47	99.84	99.84	99.75
90	100.00	100.00	100.00	100.00	99.99	99.99	99.99	99.91
100	100.00	100.00	100.00	100.00	100.30	100.00	100.00	100.00

FP = Food products
Coal = Coal and other fuels
CM = Construction materials
Misc = Miscellaneous

RM =Raw materials from primary source
IA = Inputs into agriculture
IP = Industrial products

Table 8.4 and Table 8.5 show the commodity-wise distribution of per cent freight (cumulative) and the corresponding share of districts (cumulative) both for shipment and receipts respectively. Lorenz curves for shipments and receipts of each commodity and for the total freight are show in Figure 8.4 and Figure 8.5.

The nature of Lorenz curve for each commodity group is quite distinctive from each other. Even within the same commodity group, there are wide variations in the distribution of shipments and receipts. The value of Gini coefficient for each commodity group both for shipments and receipts has been presented in Table 8.6.

A reference to Figure 8.4 reveals that the distribution pattern of total freight is highly skewed. It may be noted that very high value of Gini coefficient for different commodities as well as for total freight point to the dominance of relatively small number of districts in shipments as well as in receipts. The extent of this dominance may be gauged from the fact that eight districts account for 35 per cent of shipments and 31 per cent of receipts of the total

LORENZ CURVE DISTRIBUTION

ORIGINATING & TERMINATING FREIGHT (1973–74)

FIG. 8.4

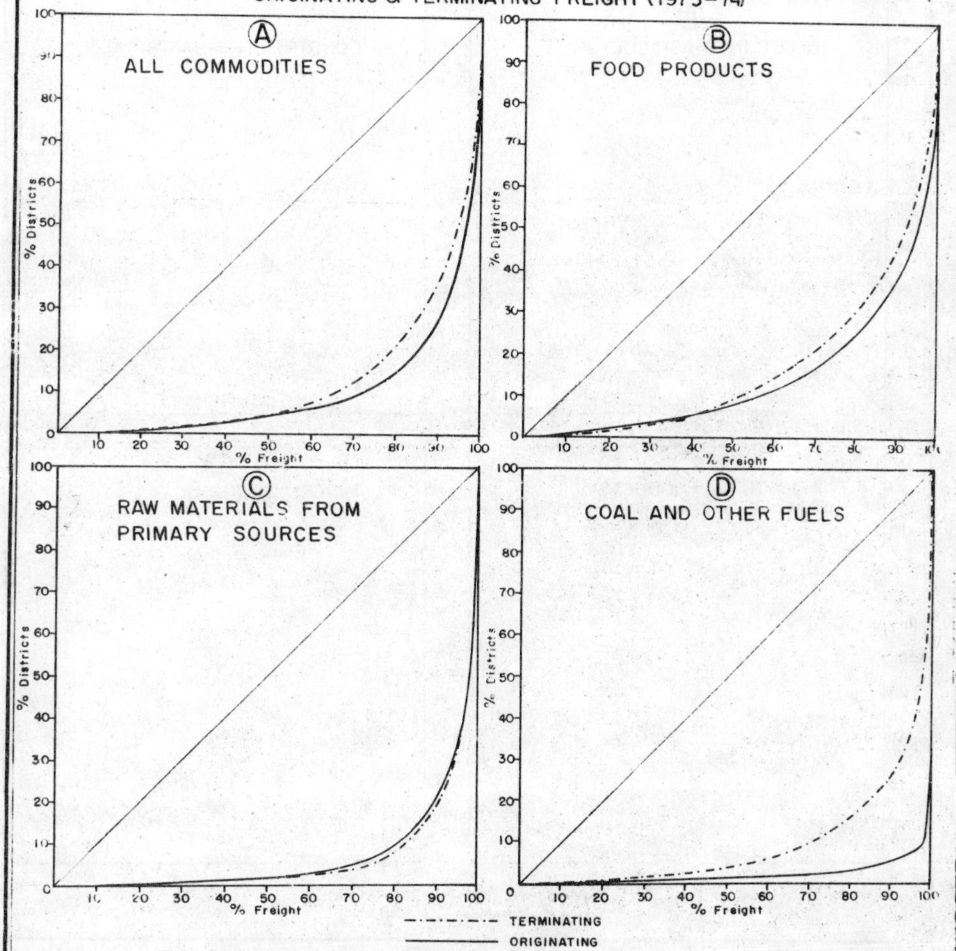

freight. At the lower end of the ladder are the 100 districts, wherein only 0.50 per cent of the total freight originates and only 0.70 per cent of the total freight is received.

In order to advance our analysis at a more disaggregated level, it was decided to shift the focus of attention to individual commodity groups. It is noted that the distribution of shipments is more skewed than the distribution of receipts. This is true in the case of all commodities except raw materials from primary sources. It is the other way round in the case of raw matrials from primary sources, that is the concentration is high in terminating freight because the distribution of receipts is more skewed than that of shipments. This is due to the fact that there are only a few centres where metallurgical plants are located and their basic inputs like ores, which fall in the category of raw materials from primary sources, come from their neighbourhood. This leads to slightly higher concentration in the case of receipts as compared to originating freight for raw materials from primary sources. The Gini coefficient for the

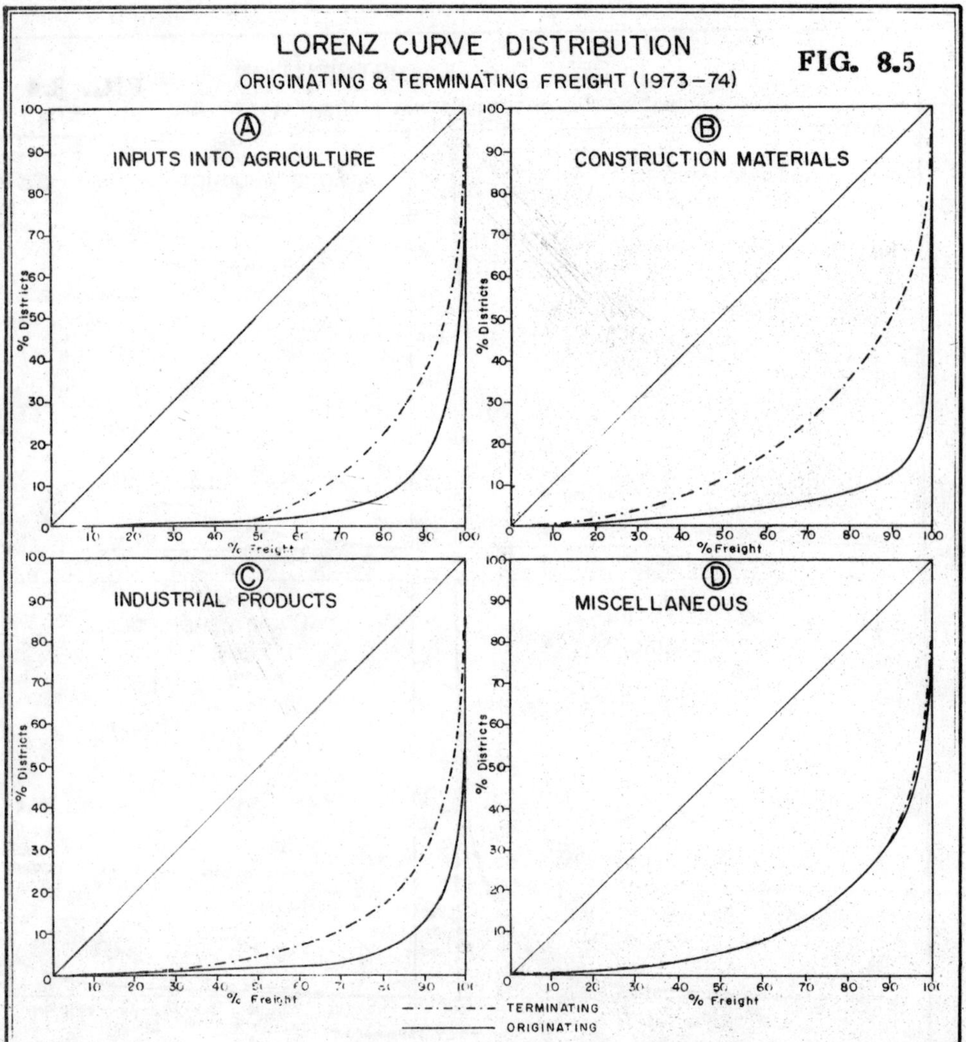

TABLE 8.6 : **Gini coefficient for originating and terminating freight**

S. No.	Commodity Group	Gini Coefficient	
		Originating	Terminating
1.	Food Products	.72	.68
2.	Raw Materials from Primary Sources	.86	.87
3.	Coal and Fuels	.95	.82
4.	Inputs into Agriculture	.89	.82
5.	Constrution Material	.90	.63
6.	Industrial Products	.91	.81
7.	Miscellaneous	.82	.81
8.	All Commodities (Total Freight)	.80	.76

originating freight is 0.86 as compared to 0.87 for terminating freight. This is indicative of the fact that the processing of bulky raw materials can be done efficiently near their extraction points. This type of skewness is an indicator of the emergence of territorial production complexes based on the regional resource base and is a welcome phenomenon for economic development.

The Lorenz curve distribution for food products is shown in Fig. 8.4. It shows that the distribution of receipts, which is immediately (bottom left corner) more skewed than that of shipments gets transformed into its opposite later. The six districts with large metropoles and large urban population namely Calcutta, Bombay, Delhi, Madras, Bangalore and Hyderabad are obviously deficit in food and receive more than 25 per cent of total originating food products. In view of their large population, their food requirements have to be met from the surplus of far more than seven districts. This is well illustrated by intersection of originating and terminating freight curves. Looking at the lower end of Table. 8.4 & 8.5, it has been observed that the 135 districts with lowest values are shipping only 2 per cent and receiving only 4 per cent of the total freight in food products. The values of the Gini coefficient are 0.72 and 0.68 for shipments and receipts respectively. We should be cautious in deriving generalisations by comparing these Gini coefficients, since the two Lorenz curves cut each other, thus rendering these coefficients of not much use for any type of generalisations.

In the case of coal and fuel, the spatial concentration of shipments is of extremely high order. There are four districts namely Dhanbad, Burdwan, Hazaribagh and Surguja, which taken together account for nearly 60 per cent of the total originating freight in coal and other fuels. This is indicative of the dependence of the remaining regions on these four districts not only for ores but also for their fuel requirements. In the case of receipts of these items, however, one would expect a relatively even distribution since almost every region requires coal and diesel. It is, therefore, surprising to note that the demand for coal and other fuels is also highly skewed. The major users of coal and other fuels are steel plants, thermal power houses and Indian Railways. These taken together account for nearly 60 per cent of the total demand for coal. The value of Gini coefficient for orginating freight is 0.95 and for terminating freight, it is 0.82. The 135 districts at the lowe end of the distribution receive only 0.65 per cent of the total originating freight.

In the case of inputs into agriculture, the value of Gini coefficient for originating freight is 0.89, which shows a very high level of unevenness in its distribution. The high level of imports as well as of the transshipment activities at the port towns has also led to a high concentration of originating freight. It may be noted, for example, that nearly 46 per cent of total fertilizer requirement was met by imports in 1973-74. The distribution of terminating freight for inputs into agriculture is less skewed as compared to the originating freight. But still the lowest 135 districts are accounting for only 2.5 per cent of the total freight receipts. This clearly shows that the use of fertilizers is restricted to only a few regions. These lie mainly in the belt of Punjab and Haryana and in Andhra Pradesh. It is hoped that with the spatial diffusion of agricultural development based on adoption of modern farming practices, the concentration ratio of the receipts of inputs into agriculture may get reduced.

The Gini coefficient for terminating traffic is lowest in the case of construction materials, which mainly comprise the movement of cement. This shows that the consumption of cement is more equitably distributed as compared to that of any other commodity. However, as far as originating freight is concerned, the value of Gini coefficient is as high as 0.90, which shows that the location of cement manufacturing plants is spatially concentrated.

Industrial products also show a high degree of inequality in the distribution of both originating and terminating freight—the corresponding values of Gini coefficient being 0.91 and 0.81 respectively. The concentration of both shipments and receipts appears to be of high magnitude. The examination of commodity-wise origin-destination data has shown that high shipment areas are also the high receipt areas. This shows that the activities related to the industrial sector are concentrated only at a few centres. Some of these districts are not only producers of industrial products, but also exchange it among themselves without allowing for downward flows in the settlement hierarchy. We shall examine these features in detail during the subsequent analsis. The six top ranking districts account for 34 per cent of the total terminating freight in industrial products; and these, as expected, are Calcutta, Bombay, Delhi, Madras, Ahmedabad and Burdwan.

There is practically no difference in the distribution pattern of originating and terminating freight for miscellaneous commodities. It is, however, interesting to note that the top ranking districts in terms of originating as well as terminating freight are invariably industrially advanced. This suggests that the behaviour of the miscellaneous commodities is quite similar to that of industrial products as it is comprised of all those commodities especially manufactured products which cannot be classified anywhere else.

SUMMARY

The above analysis has thus shown that the pattern of inter-regional trade is highly skewed in the case of all major commodity groups. Production centres are relatively more concentrated in space as compared to consumption centres. This is evident from the fact that the distribution of the originating freight is more skewed than that of terminating freight. The skewed nature of the spatial spread of the production as well as distribution of certain commodities may be indicative of the healthy process of industrial developmet especially in the case of such processes wherein the location of natural resources, economies of scale and technological constraints of the production process warrant the location of industries at few specific points in space. Ores, mineral oils, and other basic metal industries are expected to have highly skewed distribution both in originating and terminating freight in view of locational considerations. The highly skewed distribution, of commodities like iron and steel, cement, fertilizers and other industrial products cannot, however, be interpreted in this manner. They show the degree of disparity between the few top consumers and the remaining areas in the economic bsystem. High value of Gini coefficient for shipments and receipts of these products are an indication of the imbalances in regional development. The high values for such disparities in the sphere of production as well as consumption are danger signals and call for effective intervention in the light of the national objective of balanced regional development.

9

COMMODITY FLOW INTER-RELATIONSHIPS AND THE REGIONAL STRUCTURE OF THE INDIAN ECONOMY

AN analysis of the patterns of commodity flows in an economy is of considerable significance in assessing the levels of regional development. This follows from the role played by commodity flows in changing the geographical position of goods in two ways; firstly, by moving the intermediate inputs to locations where these can be processed more economically; and secondly, by distributing the goods to various demand centres for final consumption. Inter-regional trade in a number of commodities like food products, raw materials and manufactured goods gets stimulated within the national economy due to the existence of a common currency and transport network, on the hand, and the absence of tarrif barriers, on the other. The direction and magnitude of inter-regional trade, however, depends upon the requirements of the development processes and the system of national priorities related to them.

It is evident from the discussion in the earlier chapters that the inter-regional movement of commodities reflects the linkages among the sectoral as well as territorial components of the national economy, which assume the form of direct input-output type of relationships between the production system of a given region and the final demand sector located within other. The production of goods and services involves the bringing together of various intermediate inputs to territorial production system from different sectors and from a range of distances. Within the limits imposed by transportation costs and political or cultural barriers these intermediate inputs are then transformed into products, in demand in the same or other regions of the economy. The exchange of goods between the producing and consuming centres results in a regular pattern wherein the commodity flows get linked with one another. One would, for example, expect a high correspondence between the receipts of sugarcane and shipments of sugar as also between receipts of iron ore as well as of lime-stone and shipments of iron and steel. The identification and analysis of these patterns of inter-linked commodity flows may thus throw light on the nature of regional economies and their strong and weak points. It is not our intention here to lay stress on the factors influencing locational decisions, but to examine the inter-relationships in the commodity movements based on the territorial organisation of the productive forces and to identify the patterns of regional specialisation within the economic system.

A review of literature reveals that most of the commodity flow studies are primarily based on railway freight flows. We have already noted the contributions made by Berry (1966) and Hashim (1966). Both Berry and Hashim have used the trade block data. Due to the aggregative nature of the data and the non-availability of the data on inter-regional flows, these studies were neither able to catch the diversities of and the disparities in the production processes as well as in consumption levels nor were they able to properly bring out the elements of the regional structure. With the availability of point to point commodity flows data, it is now possible to undertake an indepth analysis of commodity flows at the national, regional and sub-regional levels. The present study is a step in this direction. An attempt has been made in this chapter to identify the spatial patterns and areas of regional specialisation based on shimpents and receipts of different types of commodities.

Commodity flow inter-relationships may be examined with the help of a correlation matrix. Seven variables each for originating and terminating freight, with district as the unit of observation, were derived for this purpose.

Yet another meaningful dimension of the commodity flow analysis pertains to the use of quantitative techniques for identification of spatial clusters with similar freight characteristics. One of these—the technique of factor analysis—has been profitably used in many areas of regional science. This has been done in our study as well with a view to identify spatial clusters with identical behaviour in terms of originating freight.

COMMODITY FLOW INTER-RELATIONSHIPS

Commodity flow inter-relationships have been examined with the help of a correlation matrix. As noted earlier, 14 flow variables were considered—7 corresponding to originating freight and another 7 corresponding to terminating freight. The inter-correlation matrix is presented in Table 9.1 The table shows the follwing :—

- i originating freight of raw materials from primary sources has significantly high correlation with the originating freight of industrial produets. Thus, industrial products and construction materials mainly originate from the areas which are resource rich in terms of ores and limestone. It is also evident that because of high transport cost of movement of raw materials, the industries for the first round processing of ores and other primary materials are located near the sources of raw materials;
- ii originating freight of industrial products, in addition to shipments of raw materials, is also significantly related with the shipments of coal and other fuels. This shows that the industrial products, the major component of which is iron and steel, are being manufactured mainly in the areas which are rich both in raw materials (ores) as well as in coal and other fuels;
- iii the correspondence between the shipment of fuels and that of construction material is weak as compared with the correspondence between the shipments of raw materials and that of construction materials. This clearly indicates that nearness to the sources of raw materials is relatively more important in the locational decisions pertaining to the manufacture of construction material (mainly cement) as compared to proximity to coal and fuel;
- iv the flow patterns of miscellaneous commodities are quite similar to those of industrial products. The originating and terminating freight of miscellaneous commodities has a significantly high correlation with the shipments and receipts of industrial products and construction material. This clearly shows that miscellaneous commodities, industrial products and construction materials have common origin. This is partly explained by the fact that all the commodities meant for defence use have been classified under the miscellaneous category and commodities like cement, iron and steel, machinery and industrial products dominate the defence movement;
- v the location of major steel plants near the sources of raw materials and coal, leads to large volume of intra-district flows of these commodities. This has been reflected in a significantly high correlation between the originating freight of the raw materials from primary sources and that of fuels;
- vi the dominance of a few regions in intra-district trade of industrial products is clearly brough out by a significantly high correation between the originating and terminating freight of industrial products.

vii input-output type of relationships between raw materials and fuels as inputs and industrial products as output have also been established by the high correlation between the receipts of raw materials and fuels, on the one hand, and of the shipments of industrial products, on the other. It has also been noted that areas which receive industrial products also receive construction material, fuels and raw materials, as is evident from the inter-correlations between the movement of these commodities.

The above analysis has clearly brought out the freight characteristics of various commodities and the nature of inter-relationships in their flow patterns. However, this type of analysis fails to identify the regions with similarities in their freight characteristics. The identification of such regions and their spatial distribution would definitely add a new dimension to our understanding of the regional structure of the Indian economic space.

COMMODITY FLOW CHARACTERISTICS AND AREAL SPECIALISATION (SHIPMENTS)

We have already examined the inter-relationships in commodity flows in the previous section . We, therefore, now turn to develop the classificatory scheme for various districts based on the commodity flow inter-relationships.

Following the procedure mentioned earlier, the relationships between various combinations of shipments of seven commodity groups have been examined with the help of factor analysis. Three eigen values were obtained, which taken together were able to explain 60 per cent of the total variation. Three factor loadings were obtained corresponding to three eigen values. The eigen values, and the corresponding factor loadings are presented in Table 9.2.

As is clear from Table 9.2 that 29 per cent of the variation is being explained by the first factor singly. The examination of the corresponding value of factor loading for each variable shows that the commodity groups related with industrial activity (e.g., industrial products) have high factor loadings. The first factor may, therefore, be considered to represent industrial activity. Thus all the high factor scores corresponding to the first factor may be taken to represent the dominance of shipments of industrial freight. The second factor, which is able to explain about 16 per cent of the total variation, has high positive loadings for food products and inputs into agriculture. Thus the second factor may be taken to represent the dominance of agricultural activity. The third factor which explains about 15 per cent of the total variation corresponds to the shipments of coal and other fuels. Thus the third factor shows the dominance of fuel producing areas in the originating freight. In view of the above findings three significant groups of shippers can be identified on the basis of originating freight. These are:

i areas specialising in the shipment of industrial products (Ist Factor);

ii areas specialising in the shipment of agricultural products (2nd Factor); and

iii areas specialising in the shipment of coal and other fuels (3rd Factor).

Factor scores were obtained for all the three groups by using the factors loadings following the method described above. The district-wise values of factor scores are given in Appendix XII. The ranking of factor scores for a particular factor loading matrix shows the relative position of each district in terms of activity represented by the particular factor. Factor scores for all the three factors have been ranked and a frequency distribution curve was obtained to identify the cut-off points. For each factor, the relevant scores have been plotted on a map. The results are discussed below:

Areal specialisation of industrial activities: Factor I

The pattern of spatial distribution of factor scorers of the first factor has been shown in Fig. 9.1. The districts have been classified into 5 mutually exclusive categories. The first group of very high level of industrial activity picks up the metropolitan districts of Bombay and the locations of basic processing industries. The districts of Burdwan, Durg, Singhbhum and Dhanbad, which specialise in the first round processing of bulk commodities, like coal and ores, fall in this group.

Group 2, comprises the districts in the neighbourhood of the districts falling in the first group. These districts have high scores in view of their resource base. These districts normally ship large quantities of ores and other bulky inputs for the basic processing industries located in the districts

TABLE 9.1 : **Correlation matrix of originating and terminating freight for each commodity group**

		Originating							*Terminating*						
		FP	*RM*	*COAL*	*IA*	*CM*	*IP*	*MISC*	*FP*	*RM*	*COAL*	*IA*	*CM*	*IP*	*MISC*
OR	FP	1.000													
IG	RM	—.005	1.000												
IN	COAL	—.023	.018	1.000											
AT	IA	.043	.006	.038	1.000										
IN	CM	—.013	.205	.087	.046	1.000									
G	IP	—.038	.575	.421	.076	.188	1.000								
	MISC	.074	.074	.217	.167	.335	.372	1.000							
TE	FP	.111	.061	.169	.002	.045	.117	.237	1.000						
RM	RM	.060	.465	.354	.093	.198	.817	.296	.145	1.000					
IN	COAL	.007	.295	.469	.041	.152	.623	.266	.262	.540	1.000				
AT	IA	.057	.057	.006	.022	.024	.037	.108	—.001	.060	—.007	1.000			
IN	CM	.137	.081	.230	.160	.165	.469	.656	.284	.459	.465	.081	1.000		
G	IP	.065	.097	.218	.160	.205	.541	.705	.193	.484	.445	.089	.919	1.000	
	MISC	.080	.207	.193	.167	.311	.611	.765	.210	.564	.458	.098	.859	.875	1.000

FP = Food products
COAL = Coal and other fuels
CM = Construction materials
MISC = Miscellaneous
RM = Raw material from primary sources
IA = Inputs into agriculture
IP = Industrial products

TABLE 9.2 : **Factor loadings—shipments**

(All Commodities)

S. No.	*Variable*	*Factor-I*	*Factor-II*	*Factor-III*
1.	Food products	.00296	.50507	—.42360
2.	Raw materials from primary sources	.57044	—.50069	—.48403
3.	Coal and fuels	.53151	.02343	.68788
4.	Inputs into agriculture	.20951	.59612	.02662
5.	Construction materials	.52336	.14109	—.35312
6.	Industrial products	.83534	—.25124	.08819
7.	Miscellaneous commodities	.64973	.43526	.02664
	Eigen values	2.04566	1.13417	1.02079
	Cummulative percentage ot eigen values	29.2	45.4	60.0

belonging to first group.

Prominent among the districts in the third group are Calcutta, Madras, Hyderabad, Shahabad, Jamnagar, Bilaspur, Hazaribagh and Sambalpur. It may be noted that these areeas specialise in the manufature of a variety of industrial products. Districts with low or very low levels of manufacturing industries are fairly scattered all over India.

The role of the metropolitan system in production base of the Indian economy as reflected through commodity flows, is essentially weak in character. It is evident from figure 9.1, that the productive base of the Indian metropoles varies from low to very high level of industrial activity. While, Bombay has very high level of industrial activity, Calcutta, Madras and Delhi show the declining trend. The essential weakness of the Indian metropoles which substantially contributes to the distorting role played by them in the organisation of economic space, lies in their economic base, with a weak secondary and a bloated tertiary sector.

An examination of the pattern of spatial distribution of factor scores for industrial activities (refer Fig. 9.1) also reveals that it is possible to demarcate a number of well defined production complexes, in the Indian economic space, with varying degree of industrial activity. These production complexes have been classified into three categories depending upon their specialisation and location characteristics. These are:

i spatial clusters of industrial activity in and around mining areas;

ii spatial clusters of industrial activity in and around principal ports; and

iii other scattered nodes of the industrial activity

The following clusters of industrial activity are easily discernible from Fig. 9.1:

i the most dominant spatial cluster comprises the areas of West Bengal Orissa, Madhya Pradesh and Bihar. These ares specialise in mining, heavy and basic industries;

ii Bombay, Pune, Thana and Nasik industrial belt is also well marked and is clustered around the port town of Bombay;

iii Ahmedabad, Baroda and Bhavnagar constitute another spatial cluster specialising in cotton textiles, industrial products and petro chemicals;

iv Bangalore, Tumkur, Salem, Coimbatore, Tiruchirappalli and Ramanathpuram constitute another industrial belt specialising in the manufacture of construction material and industrial products; and

v in addition to well marked clusters, some nodes like Delhi, Agra and Kanpur also emerge as important centres of industrial activity.

The above analysis has clearly brought out the dominance of Orissa, Bengal and Bihar in commodity flows through Indian Railways. It is interesting to note that most of the spatial clusters of industrial activity have emerged in and around the major port towns. A number of other spatial clusters and scattered nodes with varying level of industrial activity have also been

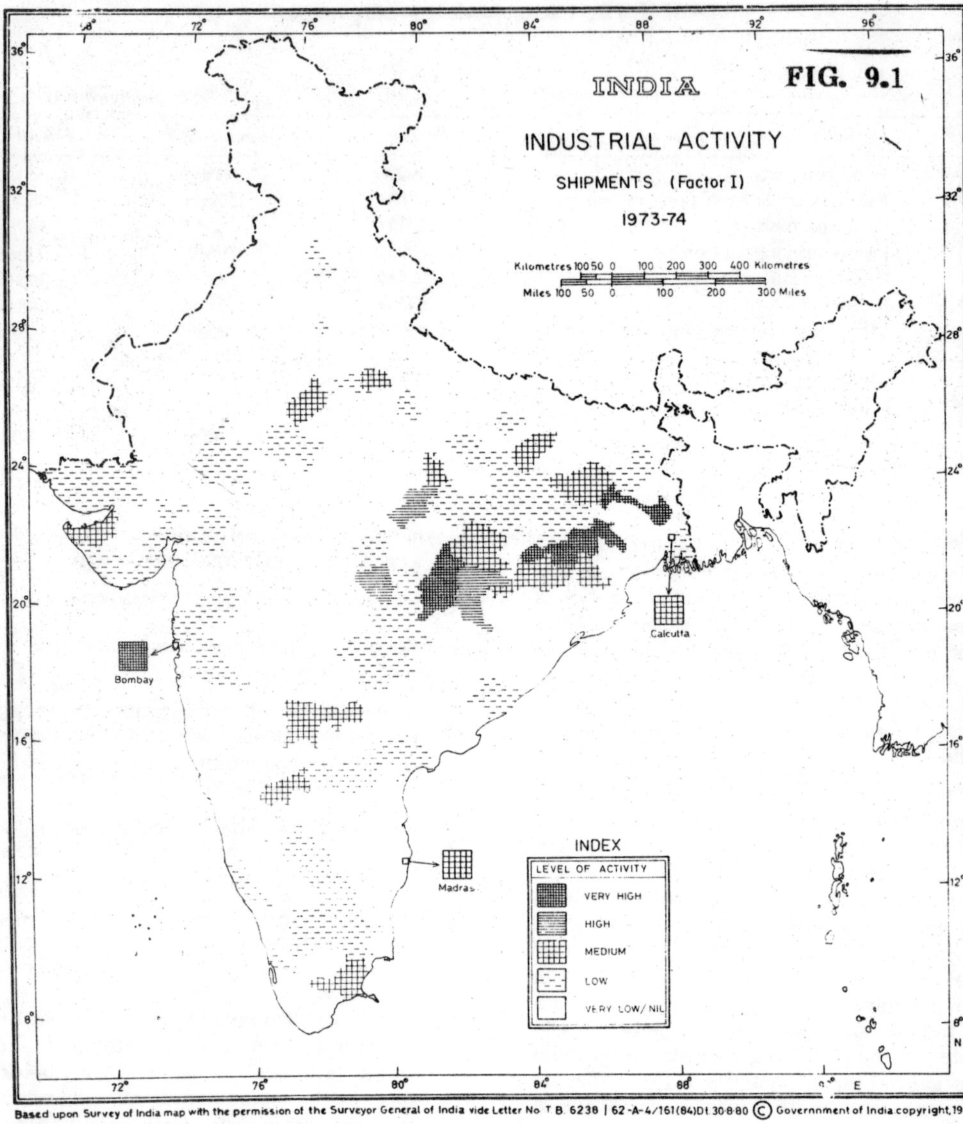

identified on basis of shipments.

Areal specialisation of agriculture oriented activity: Factor II

From the view point of the second factor, the agricultural and associated activities include the shipments of food products and inputs into agriculture like fertilizers, fodder and manure. The factor loadings corresponding to the second factor have clearly brought out the dominance of these activities in the originating freight (refer Table 9.2). Since the factor loadings for both food products and inputs into agriculture exceed 0.50, the dominance of various districts in these activities will be brought out by their respective factor scores. It has been observed that two types of regions dominate the originating freight of commodities associated with agricultural activities

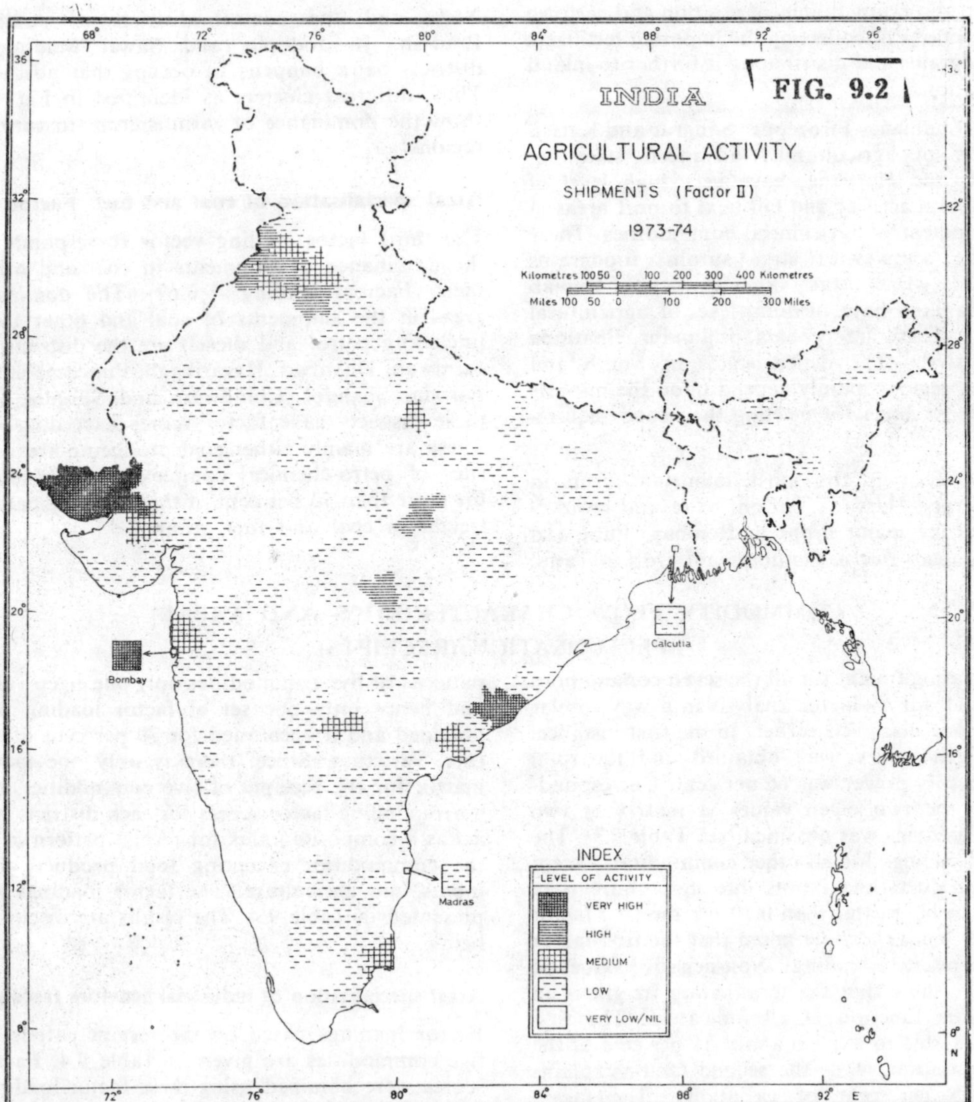

FIG. 9.2

and these are:

i port towns which are not producers of any agricultural products but happen to account for a large proportion of shipments.

ii agriculturally advanced and surplus producing areas specialising in the production of one or more crops.

Factor scores of the second factor representing agricultural activity for each district have been plotted on a map (Refer. Fig. 9.2). The port districts of Bombay, Vishakhapatnam and Kandla have very high positive scores and thus show their dominance in the originating freight for inputs and outputs of the agricultural sector. Though these areas are not major producers of agricultural products, yet in view of the crucial importance of international trade, these places happen to occupy dominant position and perform the functions of collecting the imported fertilizers & foodgrains and distributing it further to inland destinations.

Ludhiana, Firozepur, Sangrur and Karnal districts of agriculturally advanced states of Punjab and Haryana, have very high level of agricultural activity and fall next to port areas in the shipment of agricultural commodities. These are the areas with large surplus foodgrains especially wheat. Many other districts of Punjab and Haryana have medium level of agricultural activity. These are Ambala, Jullundur, Bhatinda and Patiala. The deficit states of South and Eastern regions mainly depend upon the imports from these areas for meeting their food requirements.

Wheat is the most important crop in Punjab and Haryana; cotton, bajra and groundnut are the major crops in Bombay, Pune and Ahmedabad; rice is the dominant crop in Tamil Nadu and the coastal districts of Andhra Pradesh. In Jodhpur and Sawai Madhopur districts bajra happens to occupy that position. Thus, different clusters as identified in Fig. 9.2 show the dominance of various crops in various regions.

Areal specialisation of coal and fuel: Factor III

The third factor loading vector corresponds to the dominance of shipments in coal and other fuels (Factors loading = 0.69). The dominant areas in the shipments of coal and other fuels (including petrol and diesel) are the districts of Burdwan, Dhanbad, Hazaribagh, Punchmahalas, Baroda, Shahdol, Chindwara and Surguja. All these districts have factor scores exceeding +1. These are mainly either coal producing areas or sites of petro-chemical complexes and account for more than 72 per cent of the total originating freight in coal and fuel group.

COMMODITY FLOW CHARACTERISTICS AND AREAL SPECIALISATION (RECEIPTS)

Terminating freight for all the seven commodities was analysed by factor analysis in a way similar to the one discussed earlier. In the first instance, two eigen values were obtained and the total explanatory power was 66 per cent. Corresponding to the two eigen values, a matrix of two factor loadings was obtained (see Table 9.3). The factor loadings for all other commodities except food products and inputs into agriculture were found to be greater than 0.50 for the first factor matrix. It may also be noted that the first factor has no negative loadings. Non-negative values of loadings show that the terminating freight is an increasing function of all indicators. The first factor is able to explain about 51 per cent of the total variation, while the second factor explains only 15 per cent of variations. The factor loadings for the second factor show that inputs into agriculture have a very high weight as compared to other commodities, while food products have negative loading or weight.

Since the areas which receive food also receive very large volume of raw materials, fuels, construction materials and industrial products, separate cluster of districts could not be identified for the receipts of food products only. In order to improve the results further, it was decided to drop the two variables, namely the receipts of food products and inputs into agriculture and the exercise was repeated with the remaining five commodities. Based on the receipt patterns of five commodities only one eigen value and hence only one set of factor loading was obtained and it accounted for 70 per cent of the total variation. Since, there is only one factor matrix for the receipts of five commodities, the corresponding factor scores for each districts will act as a composite index for receipt pattern of all the commodities excepting food products and inputs into agriculture. The factor loadings are presented in Table 9.4. The results are discussed below:

Areal specialisation of industrial activities (receipts)

Factor loadings based on the receipt pattern of five commodities are given in Table 9.4. Factor scores were obtained using these factor loadings and all the districts were arranged in descending order on the basis of their respective scores. Factor scores have been plotted on a map and is presented as Fig. 9.3. It distinctly brings out three types of spatial clusters and these are:-

i port towns which act as traditional outlet for improts and exports;

ii industrially advanced areas receiving mainly raw materials, basic inputs and fuels; and

iii areas specialising in the production of agriculture but receiving large volumes of non-agricultural products.

TABLE 9.3 : **Factor loadings—receipts**

(All Commodities)

S. No.	*Variable*	*Ist Factor*	*IInd Factor*
1.	**Food products**	.35009	—.44990
2.	**Raw materials from primary sources**	.69632	—.05709
3.	**Coal and fuels**	.66819	—.25092
4.	**Inputs into agriculture**	.11381	.85196
5.	**Construction materials**	.91616	.06490
6.	**Industrial products**	.91347	.12031
7.	**Miscellaneous commodities**	.91758	.10745
	Eigen Values	3.58259	1.02471
	Cummulative percentages of eigen values	51.2	65.8

Districts with very high level of receipt activity are mainly the port areas of Calcutta, Bombay, Madras and Vishakhapatnam. The other non-port districts having very high scores are Delhi, Burdwan and Durg. Burdwan and Durg receive large quantities of raw materials and fuels, because big iron and steel plants are located in these districts. Very high scores for the metropolitan districts of Calcutta, Bombay, Delhi and Madras indicate large demand for industrial products in these centres. Our earlier analysis of shipments has also shown that the Indian metropoles have weak production base. The available evidence on commodity flows, thus, corroborates our earlier finding that the relative weak involvement of the metropoles in the production system of the country gives them the character of the major centres of consumption rather than of production.

Industrially advanced areas in manufacturing processes (as identified on the basis of Factor I of shipments) also happen to be the areas with high receipts. The districts with high receipts are Hazaribagh, Singhbhum, Dhanbad and Burdwan. These areas specialise in the basic and heavy manufacturing industries. The major component of receipts in these areas are fuels and raw materials. It is interesting to note that these districts taken together account for about 23 per cent of the receipts of raw materials and 28 per cent of fuels.

Bombay-Thana industrial belt, specialising in medium and large scale industries, emerges as one of the dominant receipt centre. It ranks next to the areas specialising in basic metals and allied manufacturing activities.

Many districts of Punjab, Haryana and Western Uttar Pradesh also show high receipts. These districts specialise in the production of agricultural commodities (as identified in the case of originating freight), and are not highly specialised in industrial activities. Fuels, inputs into agriculture, construction materials and modern industrial products (including heavy machinery) are, therefore, imported therein. Thus, these areas emerge as big receivers of products manufactured elsewhere.

Areal specialisation and multiple activities

Since it is possible for a region to specialise in more than one type of activity, it was considered necessary to examine the extent of complimentary specialisation. In the preceding analysis, we have identified three distinct types of activities associated with shipments—industrial, agricultural and mining. It has been observed that areas specialising in more than one activity are very few and practically no area specialises in all the three types of activities. No area has been identified which specialises both in mining and agricultural activities. However, some regions with both industrial and agricultural or with both industrial and mining activities have been identified. While Bombay, Hyderabad and Jabalpur fall in the former; Burdwan, Dhanbad and Hazaribagh fall in the latter category.

Trends in industrial and agricultural activity for the districts with positive factor scores have been plotted and are shown in Fig. 9.4. It has been observed that places like Dhanbad, Burdwan, Durg, Hazaribagh have very high level of industrial activity and very low level of agricultural activity. Areas with high levels of agricultural activity are the states of Punjab and Haryana which happen to have low level of

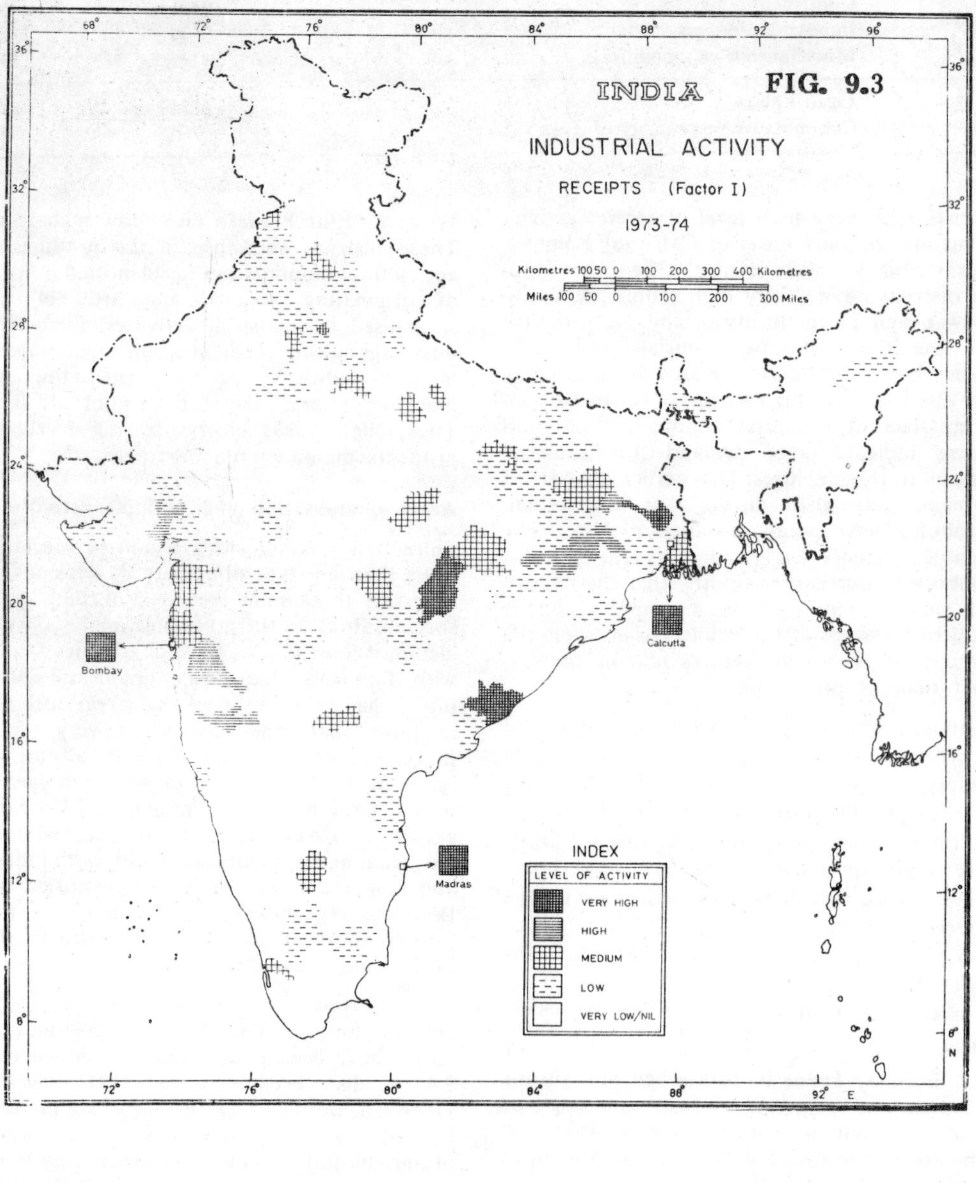

INDIA
FIG. 9.3
INDUSTRIAL ACTIVITY
RECEIPTS (Factor I)
1973-74
Kilometres 100 50 0 100 200 300 400 Kilometres
Miles 100 50 0 100 200 300 Miles
Bombay
Calcutta
Madras
INDEX
LEVEL OF ACTIVITY
VERY HIGH
HIGH
MEDIUM
LOW
VERY LOW/NIL

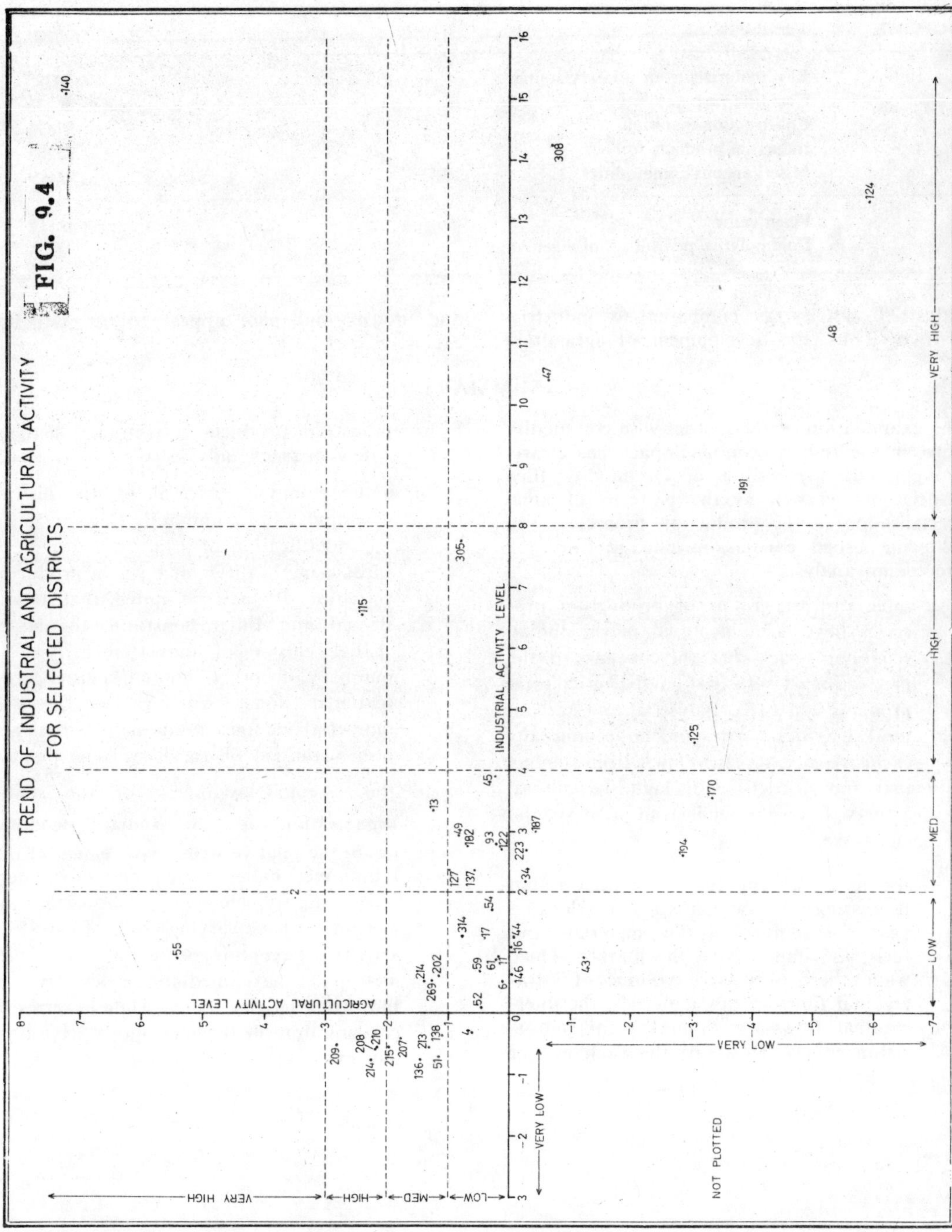

FIG. 9.4

TREND OF INDUSTRIAL AND AGRICULTURAL ACTIVITY FOR SELECTED DISTRICTS

TABLE 9.4 : **Factor loadings—receipts**

(For industrial activity only)

S. No.	*Variable*	*Factor loadings*
1.	Raw materials from primary source	.70393
2.	Coal and fuels	.66273
3.	Construction materials	.91624
4.	Industrial products	.92268
5.	Miscellaneous commodities	.92499
	Eigen value	3.48117
	Cummulative percentage of eigen values	69.6

industrial activity as compared to industrial districts. Thus, the development of agriculture and industry in space appear to be mutually exclusive.

SUMMARY

The examination of the district-wise commodity flows in the Indian economic space has clearly brought out the nature of commodity flow associations as well as the patterns of areal specialisation in the production processes. The following broad conclusions emerge from the proceeding analysis:

i three distinct groups of production processes have been identified in the Indian economic space and these relate to the production of industrial goods, agricultural products and fuels. Industrial and agricultural activities are by and large, mutually exclusive in space. It follows, from the fact that the districts with high agricultural activity have low industrial activity and vice-versa.

ii the industries engaged in the first round processing of raw materials are located near the sources of raw materials and fuels, as compared to the market. Thus, while there is a large volume of intra-regional flows of raw materials, the inter-regional flows are dominant for industrial products. However, the exchange of industrial products is restricted between a few districts only.

iii another important result of the district-wise analysis of commodity flows relates to the identification of production complexes specialising in different types of productive activities It may be noted that Orissa, Bengal and Bihar constitute the largest spatial cluster of industrial activity. A number of other spatial clusters and scattered nodes with varying level of industrial and agricultural activity have also been identified on the basis of shipments.

iv the essential weakness of the spatial organisation of the Indian economy lies in the relative weak involvement of the Indian metropoles in the production system of the country. The analysis shows that the metropoles have varying levels of industrial activity. Excepting Calcutta, the other metropoles have medium or low level of Industrial activity index, while in terms of consumption all the metropoles have high indices.

10

COMMODITY FLOWS AND LEVELS OF DEVELOPMENT IN INDIA

A Districtwise Analysis

THE process of economic development in the developing countries leads to the consolidation of the home market and consequently to increased exchange across regions and to greater inter-regional dependence. It follows from the above; first that the structure of the economy manifests itself in the level and pattern of inter-regional commodity flows; and second, that the pattern of shipments and receipts of commodities reflect the economic base of the region. In the absence of a balancing mechanism in inter-regional exchange, it is possible for a region to draw on the resources of another without a corresponding inflow into the latter from the former. Such a situation would reflect and would invariably lead to disparate rates of development in different regions. Inter-regional disparities in the national economy under such circumstanes would tend to be high and the economy of the relatively backward regions would continue to remain depressed. The analysis of inter-regional commodity flows may, therefore, be considered to be a valid and useful tool of probing into such suction mechanisms within the economy.

Both production processes and consumption levels in different regions are associated and causally linked with the development processes therein and with the nationsl economy as a whole. There is enough evidence to indicate that the production processes tend to concentrate in space due to the factors of geographical specialisation as well as of the economies of scale and agglomeration. This is, however, not true of the consumption patterns and levels which tend to be relatively ubiquitous.

In terms of commodity flows, production activities may be considered to be associated with shipments and consumption patterns with receipts. Since consumption and production reflect and affect the pattern of regional development, it would be interesting to examine the correspondence between levels of development and commodity flow indices.

The present study is an attempt to examine this relationship and test the following hypotheses :

i there exists a statistically significant positive correspondence between the total volume of shipments the receipts in a district, on the one hand, and its level of development on the other;

ii the level of regional development is more effectively reflected in patterns of receipts as compared to those of shipments; and

iii urban centres continue to dominate the Indian economic system, both in terms of commodity flows as well as levels of regional development.

The district has been indentified as the unit of investigation for purpose of this analysis on the assumption that intra-district variations in the development patterns are not significant. It may, however, be noted that a district-wise analysis presupposes the use of a huge volume of data for each district both on the volume of shipments and receipts of various commodities and of the levels of development.

For the purpose of this study, station to station commodity flow data has been aggregated at the level of district. The indices of development, by Pal (1975) have been utilised to examine the relationships between commodity flows and the development processes. While interpreting the results note should be taken of the fact that the levels of development pertain to the year 1961. It would, however, be not wrong to assume that the relative position of the districts has not changed significantly since 1961 and hence the results are not going to be substantially affected.

To determine the various levels of development of a district, the method of first principa component of a group of related variables identifying specific characteristics was used by Pal (1975) in his study. Seventeen variables were selected for the study from four specific groups-agriculture, industry, tertiary activities and urbanisation. Using these variables, fro each district, the following six composite indices of development were developed :

- i composite index of development
- ii index of agricultural development
- iii index of non-agricultural development
- iv index of development in secondary activity
- v index of development in tertiary activity
- vi index of urbanisation

The data on each of the six indices were then classified into the following six levels in order of their value. The quantitative difinitions are given in Table 10.1 and the classes were defined as :

- i extremely high
- ii very high
- iii high
- iv medium
- v low
- iv very low

The above indices and levels of development have been found to be quite useful for inter-district comparisons of the development process.

The quantitative values for each of the six composite indices alongwith the commodity-wise shipments and receipts were tabulated for all the districts. It was noted that there are wide regional variations in the total volume of the freight and also that of the commodity composition of originating and terminating freight. The variations are ususally dependent upon the natural and socio-economic conditions of each district and upon the political economy of inter-regional relationships. While some areas play an active role with high level of participation in the economic activities, others are relatively passive. It was noted that only 317 districts participated in the process of rail freight exchange and only these have been taken into consideration. The remaining 38 districts do not have a railway network in their territories.

TABLE 10.1 : **Classification of indices**

					Class Interval of indices	
Class Symbols	*Z*	*X*	*Y*	*Ys*	*Yt*	*Yu*
(1)	*(2)*	*(3)*	*(4)*	*(5)*	*(6)*	*(7)*
VL	below 0.60	below 0.85	below 0.70	below 0.63	below 0.76	below 0.66
L	0.60—0.88	0.85—0.95	0.70—0.90	0.63—0.87	0.76—0.92	0.66—0.89
M	0.88—1.16	0.95—1.05	0.90—1.10	0.87—1.10	0.92—1.07	0.89—1.12
H	1.16—1.44	1.05—1.15	1.10—1.30	1.10—1.34	1.07—1.22	1.12—1.35
VH	1.44—2.00	1.15—1.35	1.30—1.70	1.34—1.82	1.22—1.53	1.35—1.81
EH	above 2.00	—	above 1.70	above 1.82	above 1.53	above 1.81

VL=very low, L=low, M=medium, H=high, VH=very high, and EH=extremely high

Z = composite index of development — *Ys* = index of development in secondary activities

X = index of agricultural development — *Yt* = index of development in tertiary activities

Y = index of non-agricultural development — *Yu* = index of urbanisation

PATTERNS OF TOTAL SHIPMENTS/RECEIPTS AND THE LEVELS OF DEVELOPMENT

In order to determine whether the level of economic development of a district is more related to production process or consumption levels within the district, the volume of total shipments and receipts were related to the corresponding indices of development of the district. The correlation matrix is presented in Table 10.2. From Table 10.2, the following conclusions emerge :

i all indices of development are associated more significantly to the total volume of receipts rather than to the corrresponding volume of shipments. It may, therefore, be stated that, in general, it is not the production base, but the consumption pattern which reflects the levels of development of various districts in India;

ii of considerable interest is the highly significant negative correlation between the index of agricultural development and the volume of terminating freight. This clearly indicates that the terminating freight remains low in the agriculturally developed regions as compared to agriculturally less developed regions. This indicates the relative self-sufficiency of agriculturally advanced areas;

iii urban bias in the development process is quite clear from the fact that a significantly high correlation exists between urban development and terminating freight. Of all the indices of development, the highest positive value of correlation is observed between the level of urbanisation and the volume of receipts in the district. Thus the dominance of the metropoles and the large towns in the Indian economy is indicated.

TABLE 10.2 : **Correlation matrix for shipments, receipts and indices of development*****

S. No.	*Index of development*	*Correlation coefficient with the volume of**** *Shipments*	*Receipts*
1.	Composite	.150*	.339*
2.	Agricultural		—.225*
3.	Non-agricultural	.183*	.387*
4.	Industrial	.229*	.400*
5.	Tertiary	.101*	.275*
6.	Urbanisation	.191*	.427*

* Significant at 1%
** Significant 5%
***Only significant correlations are considered

PATTERNS OF COMMODITY-WISE SHIPMENTS/RECEIPTS AND LEVELS OF DEVELOPMENT

It may be argued that the nature of development of the district will be better represented by the type of commodities that it ships to and receives from other regions, rather than by the total volume of shipments and receipts. A commodity-wise analysis is also desirable because of the wide variations in the commodity composition of total shipments and receipts for various districts. In view of this, it was decided to test the validity of the above conclusions by examining the relationship between commodity-wise shipments, receipts and various indices of development.

This analytical framework resulted in a set of 20 variable for each district consisting of 7 variables for shipments (each commodity group constituting a variable), 7 variables for receipts (one for each commodity group) and 6 variables referring to the indices of development. Because of the skewed distribution of shipments and receipts, commodity flow variables were log transformed. Based on this data, a (20 x 20) correlation matrix was obtained and the correlation coefficients relevant from the point of view of this study are presented in table 10.3. The Table brings out the following :—

i the phenomenon that receipts, in

general, have a significantly higher correlation coefficient with all the indices of development as compared to shipments, which had been noticed for total freight, is also found to be true for each commodity group. It is observed that the correlation values are considerably higher for receipts for every commodity as compared to the corresponding values for shipments. This phenomenon is true for all the six indices of development. Thus, it has been established that irrespective of the nature of commodity composition, the receipts are more associated with the levels of development of a district than shipments;

ii since the receipts of various commodities is expected to influence the development pattern of districts differentially, the relationship of commodity-wise receipts with the indices of development is expected to unravel the nature of development. We find that of all the six indices, it is the index of urbanisation that has the highest positive correlation with the receipts of each of the seven commodity groups. This clearly shows that higher the level of urbanisation, the higher is the level of receipts of all the commodities irrespective of the other development patterns of the district;

iii the fact that the receipts of industrial products play a major role in the development process as compared to the receipts of other commodities is indicated by the finding that of all the commodities, it is in the case of receipts of industrial products that the highest degree of correspondence has been observed with all the indices of development. The relationship between level of urbanisation and the receipts of industrial products is shown graphically on a semi-logrithmic scale in Figure 10.1. The data for top most 65 districts in terms of commodity flows accounting for nearly 83 per cent of the total receipts of industrial products have been plotted.

iv the correspondence between levels of development and the commodity-wise shipments is quite different from that of receipts. It shows the following :

a for shipments, the index of urbanisation has the highest degree of positive correlation with the shipments of food products, raw materials, inputs into agriculture and miscellaneous commodities. This clearly shows that urbanisation is mainly associated with collection and distribution of commodities which are mainly imports into port areas or are the produce of the hinterland. During 1973-74, for example, nearly 46 per cent of the total fertilizer demand was met by imports and it was further distributed from the port towns to the inland consumption centres.

b the highest degree of correspondence of shipments of construction materials, fuels and industrial products is with the level of industrial development in the region. Thus the manufactured products mainly originate from the developing industrial centres where massive public investment has been made.

v the significantly high positive correspondence between the index of composite development and the degree of urbanisation shows the associational relationship between urban development and the overall level of development of the district. All the million population cities taken together account for 18.6 per cent of total receipts and 7.5 per cent of total shipments.

The above analysis has, therefore, clearly shown that the urban centres forming the dysfunctional enclaves within the so called developed regions are continuing to appropriate a disproportionate segment of the economic surplus. The analysis also establishes the fact that the regional structure of underdevelopment, established by the imperial power to meet the requirements of its exploitative mechanism during the colonial period, still persists in many of its essential characteristics.

RECEIPTS OF INDUSTRIAL PRODUCTS AND THE LEVELS OF DEVELOPMENT

In the foregoing analysis, we have considered only the associational type of relationships

TABLE 10.3 : **Matrix of significant correlations for commodity shipments, receipts and indices of development**

Index of Development	*Shipments*							*Receipts*						
	FP	*RM*	*FUEL*	*IA*	*CM*	*IP*	*MISC*	*FP*	*RM*	*FUEL*	*IA*	*CM*	*IP*	*MISC*
Composite	.320*	179*	.215*	.327*	.235*	.457*	.460*	.393*	.384*	.380*	.371*	.433*	.538*	.464*
Agriculture			—.118**	—.134*	—.120**	.128**	—.158*							
Non-agricul-ture	.507*	.349*	.248*	.505*	.285*	.569*	.486*	.597*	.558*	.573*	.588*	.643*	.704*	.634*
Secondary	.431*	.319*	.285*	.485*	.305*	.588*	.459*	.552*	.532*	.545*	.550*	.583*	.668*	.595*
Tertiary	.459*	.257*	.153*	.374*	.196*	.440*	.374*	.506*	.436*	.473*	.490*	.560*	.588*	.526*
Urbanisation	.546*	.397*	.241*	.558*	.281*	.572*	.530*	.621*	.600*	.605*	.627*	.672*	.722*	.661*

Note : FP = Food products
FUEL = Coal and fuel
CM = Construction materials
MISC = Miscellaneous commodities
*Significant at 1%
** Significant at 5%
RM = Raw Materials from primary sources
IA = Inputs into agriculture
IP = Industrial products

between the development process and the commodity flow indices. At this stage of analysis, it was considered necessary to examine the causal type of relation-ship between the various indices of development and the commodity-wise receipt patterns. The essential purpose of this exercise is to identify the relative strength of the various commodities in influencing the degree of development. This type of analysis has been made possible through the application of stepwise regression technique considering the commodity-wise receipts. (i.e. all seven commodity groups) as

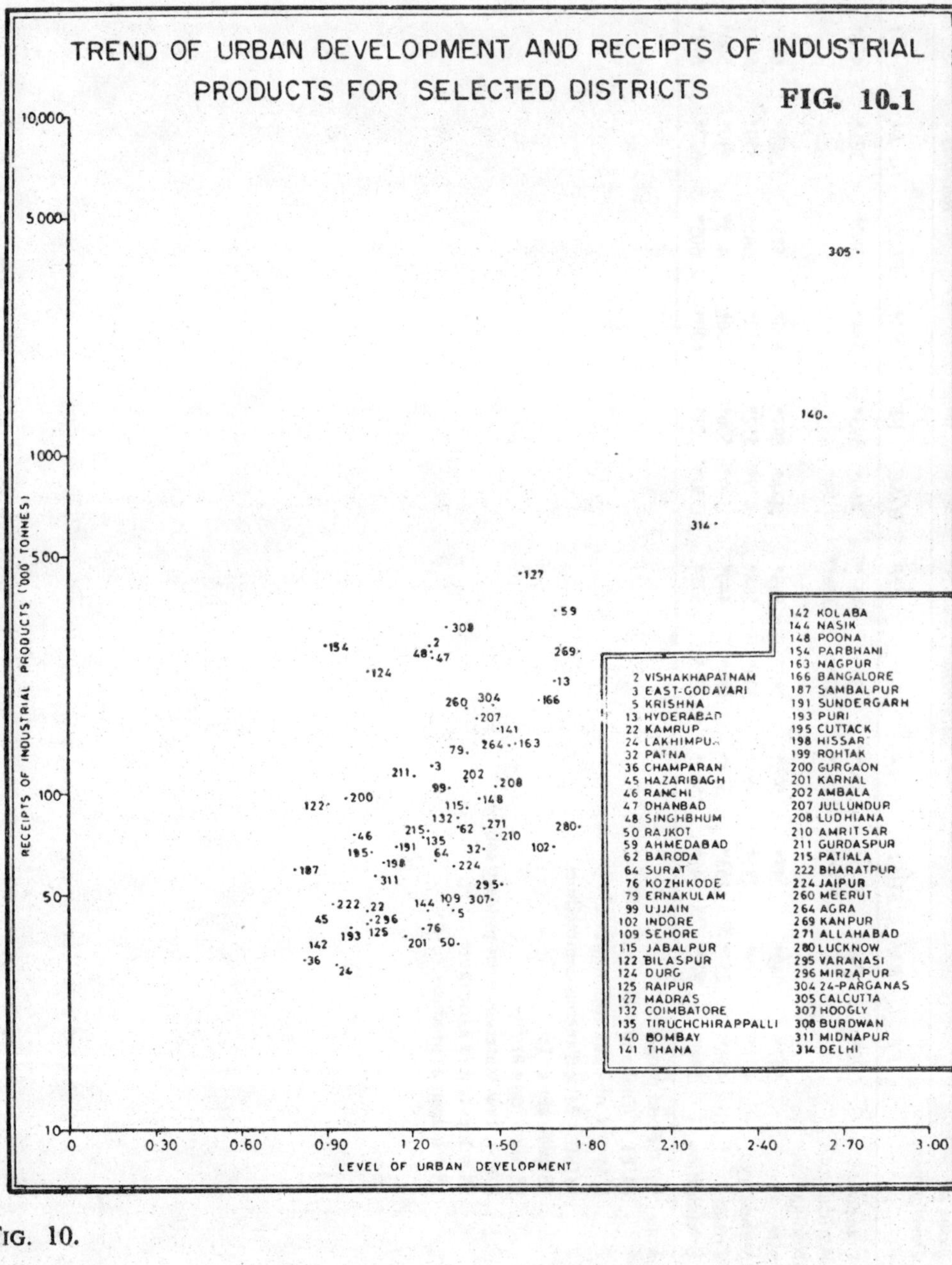

FIG. 10.

independent variables and the indices of development as dependent variable taken one at a time. The relevant results of the stepwise regression analysis are presented in Table 10.4. The examination of Table 10.4 brings out the following :

i that the receipts of industrial products constitute the major determinant of the development process. The positive sign of the regression coefficient shows that the higher the receipts of industrial products, the higher will be the level of composite, non-agricultural, industrial, tertiary and urban development in the district. The regression coefficients show the incremental impact of receipts of industrial products with the various indices of development.

ii the most significant result corresponds to the relationship between urbanisation index and receipts of industrial products, where the value of explained variance is highest (52%) and the 'beta' coefficient is relatively high as compared to non-agricultural, industrial and tertiary development levels. The relationship as shown graphically in Fig. 10.1 clearly brings out that the urban centres and their receipts of industrial products continue to play a dominant role in the development process.

TABLE 10.4 : Stepwise regression analysis results

S. No.	*Dependent variable (Index of Development*	*Step No.*	*Independent variable entered (Commodity-wise receipts)*	R^2	*Intercept (a)*	*Regression coefficient (b)*	*F Value*
1.	Composite	1	Industrial Products	.28	.503	.131	126.43*
2.	Non-agricultural	1	—do—	.51	.548	.107	313.63*
3.	Industrial	1	—do—	.45	.470	.122	257.59*
4.	Tertiary	1	—do—	.35	.667	.077	168.70*
5.	Urbanization	1	—do—	.52	.463	.128	347.31*

*Significant at 1 per cent level.

SUMMARY

The above study has indicated that the following hypotheses stand validated

i **there is a strong association between the economic base and the commodity flow patterns of a district;**

ii **the development process is more reflected in the receipt patterns as compared to shipments;**

iii urban centres continue to dominate the Indian economic system, both in terms of commodity flows as well as in levels of regional development;

iv of all the commodities the receipts of industrial products have the highest degree of association with the various indices of development.

11

RAILWAY FREIGHT FLOWS AND DISTANCE DECAY

DISTANCE DECAY IN COMMODITY FLOWS

COMMODITY flows constitute the basic instrument-ality whereby economic space of a country in the modern world is transformed into the national home market. This procees gets operationalised in two ways :

First : the flows take place from a discrete node to another in the network of an interactive system and not along a spatial continuum as is the case with surface flow in a stream. Viewed thus, the vertical dimension of the system of inter-sectoral linkages, as expressed in input-output matrices, finds its horizontal manifestation in freight exchange between different categories of settlements within economic space. The system of inter-settlement linkages provides the form of the process of integration of the national home market; the content is provided by the system of intra and inter-sectoral interactions.

Second : in view of the territorial division of labour and the consequent regional differentiation, which accompanies and is instrinsically linked with development, the national economic field emerges in space through a process of the multi-level nesting of sub-fields—from the local, through the sub-regional and regional to the national level. The model is neither of the number of fields existing at the basal level as closed systems nor of an undifferentiated monolith, but rather of a hierarchical system of fields within fields; of a system of interdependencies nesting into a larger system of interdependencies.

Such a model of the space economy is essentially operationalised through the differential range and rate of distance decay in commodity flows. While the range refers to the intervening distance upto the terminal where such interactions cease; the rate refers to the lapse in freight with distance within the range. It is no doubt true that spatial interaction is inversly related to distance. What is, however, crucially important in economic analysis of flows is not the search for the ideal curve of decay but the identification and explanation of differentials in the range and the rate of distance decay in the flows of different types of commodities and from nodes at different levels in the national fields of economic activities.

While the range of interaction would be greatly influenced by factors like agglomeration tendencies, differential accessibility and patterns of concentration; the rate would be mainly determined by the nature of vertical or inter-industry linkages. Both are inter-related to the extent that one determines the other through the patterns of spatial distribution of freight. In a normative system, for example, the weight losing raw materials or intermediate inputs would tend to have a steeper distance decay curve as compared to finished products; and the distance decay curve for a first order node would be less skewed as compared to that of the second or third order nodes. For similar reasons; high concentration of production activities and consumption processes in space may result in a curve which may reveal quite a weak impact of distance and yet the range may be large. As opposed to this, the decay rate would tend to be high and the range small when both production and consumption are ubiquitous.

The spatial elasticities of flow and interactions will also vary under the influence of the freight tariff structure. It may affect the magnitude and the nature of inter-relations and may thus offset the impact of distance. A policy of subsidisation in the freight rates of a particular commodity may, for example, neutralise the friction of distance and may consequently lead to changes in the spatial elasticities of movement and interaction.

In the light of the above, an analysis of the role of distance as well as of other related variables in the patterns of commodity flows would provide meaningful insights into the nature of regional inter-dependence through the organisation of economic activities in space.

It is unfortunate that an adequate number of empirical studies on distance decay in the context of commodity flows are not available. There are only a few indepth studies wherein variations in distance have been analysed in relation to variations in the volume of terminating freight. Smith (1962) and Gould (1960) have studied the flow of commodities by rail from the major ports of Australia and Ghana respectively. Both found that intervening distance has only marginal effect on the volume of goods shipipped from the port to towns in their hinterland. In the case of the flows from Sydney and Melbourne to towns in southern New South Wales, for example, distance (in miles) was found to be weakly correlated with receipts (in tonnes). Similarly, in the case of commodity flows to hinterland towns from the port of Takoradi in Ghana, it was noted that the range of the distances involved was too small and that it did not exert significant impact on the volume of flow. It is, however, important to note that in the case of these regions, a very high proportion of variations in the receipts from port towns could be explained in terms of the variations in the population of the receiving town.

It would not be correct to infer from these findings that there is no inverse relationship between distance and magnitude of flow. The weakness of the distance effect in some of these cases only suggests that the friction of distance may be effectively offset by a particular organisation of economic space or a particular structure of the costs of operating specific modes of transport. In other words, distance decay would not operate only if, under the impact of exogeneous factors, the share of movement costs as compared to terminal costs tends to acquire a marginal significance. Intervening distance would have little or no effect upon the volume of flows to a set of destinations if:

- i there is but one major originating source, as in the case of a port with a relatively closed hinterland;
- ii all the destinations are located relatively close to their source of supply so that operating costs are mainly terminal costs;
- iii all the destinations are at relatively equal distances from the source; and
- iv transport subsidies are available so that the friction of distance is minimised.

In situations, where the above factors do not operate—such as a set of destinations with many competing sources of supply, located at substantially varying distances from each source—one would expect that variation in distance would have considerable effect upon the volume of goods which a set of destinations will receive from any source. For example, the pervasive and attenuating influence of distance on commodity flows both at the inter-regional and inter-national level in the USA is clearly brought out by Isard and Peck (1954). Ray (1965), found that, within the large Canadian economy, 58 percent of the variation in volume of commodity flows by rail from Southern Ontario to points throughout the rest of Canada could be accounted for simply by variation in the distance to receiving points. The distance decay exponent was 1.55 when distance was measured in terms of cost per tonne and 1.45, when measured in miles. Reed (1967), in his study on commodity flows of the Bengal-Bihar industrial area in India, noted that the relationship between originating freight and intervening distance was quite weak—R^2 ranging from 4 to 7 per cent. This finding has been explained in terms of governmental control over the distribution of certain important commodities like iron and steel, on the one hand, and of the over powering pull of Calcutta metropole, on the other.

This analysis, based on commodity-wise data will not only be complete in terms of its coverage, but would also allow for the possibility of examining the differences in the distance decay patterns of various commodity groups. Commodity-wise analysis becomes much more useful since, sometimes, the composition of the total freight may be such that the distance decay does not seem to operate for total freight while for some of the commodities it may have significant decay rates as compared to others.

Distance-weight relationships for the railway freight can be studied in the context of :

i either, the actual point to point flow matrices; or,

ii the volume of terminating freight in various distance classes.

Keeping the objectives of the present study in view, the former appears to be less appropriate as a large number of cells would be empty in the actual point to point flow matrix. The latter method has, therefore, been used; and the regression estimates of distance decay for various commodity groups have been obtained from the volume of terminating freight in different distance classes.

The degree of correspondence between distance category and terminating freight can be measured mathematically by the correlation coefficient or the coefficient of determination. A negative and statistically significant correlation would show the existence of distance decay effect, whereas the value of R^2 will indicate the proportion of explained variance. The technique of multi-variate regression analysis has been applied to study the nature of relationship between distance and terminating weight. For each commodity group, two types of distance decay models have been tested and these are :

i simple linear regression model of the form;

$$Y = \alpha + \beta X$$

ii log linear or double log regression model of the form;

$$Y = \alpha \; X^{\beta} \text{ or } Log\, Y = Log\, \alpha + \beta\, Log\, X$$

Where,

Y=Volume of terminating freight in thousand tonnes;

X=Average distance in kms.

The best fit of the regression model will be determined by the spatial distribution of the forces of demand for and supply of various commodities. The spatial elasticity of demand (Sd) will be given by the exponent of the negative exponential distance decay function. The greater the distance exponent (Sd), the more local would the traffic be. The values of spatial elasticity of demand in the above analytical frame would be indicative of three mutually exclusive situations :

i $|Sd| > 1$: wherein changes in the volume of terminating freight is less than proportionate as compared to corresponding changes in distance; and, wherein intra-regional flows would tend to be low as compared to inter-regional flows;

ii $|Sd| = 1$: wherein changes in the volume of terminating freight proportionately correspond with changes in distance; and

iii $|Sd| < 1$: wherein changes in the volume of terminating freight in more than proportionate as compared to corresponding changes in distance and wherein flows would be of an intra-regional or local type.

TABLE 11.1 : **Interdependence of commodity freight and distance**

S. No.	*Commodity group*	*Correlation coefficient of freight with distance*	*Coefficient of determination (R^2)*
1.	Food products	—.857*	.74
2.	Raw materials from primary sources	—.726*	.52
3.	Coal and other fuels	—.730*	.53
4.	Inputs into agriculture	—.808*	.65
5.	Construction material	—.857*	.73
6.	Industrial products	—.645*	.41
7.	Miscellaneous commodities	—.954*	.91
8.	All Commodities (Total freight)	—.824*	.68

*Significant at 99 per cent level of confidence.

REGRESSION ESTIMATES OF DISTANCE DECAY

Using point to point data for each commodity group, a table, with the volume of terminating freight for each distance class was generated for each group and for total freight. On the basis of these tables eight graphs were plotted on a linear scale. These are shown in Fig. 11.1 and Fig. 11.2. Since the shape of the distance freight curve for different commodities invariably reveal a significant distance impact on the volume of terminating freight, it was considered desirable to probe deeper into the nature and magnitude of this relationship.

The fall in the volume of terminating freight may be attributed to change in the pattern of spatial demand and can be measured by the change in the volume of terminating freight with change in

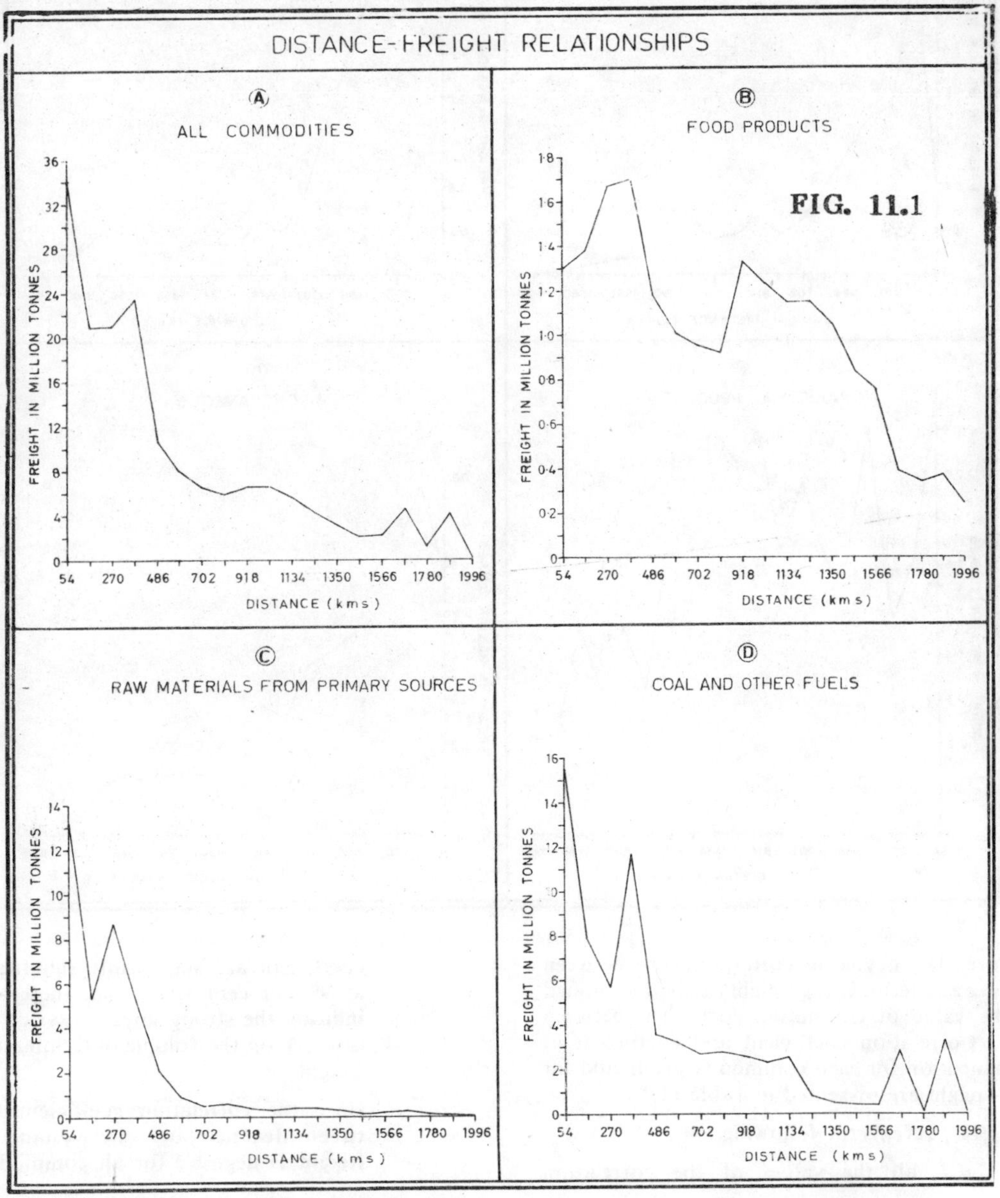

FIG. 11.1

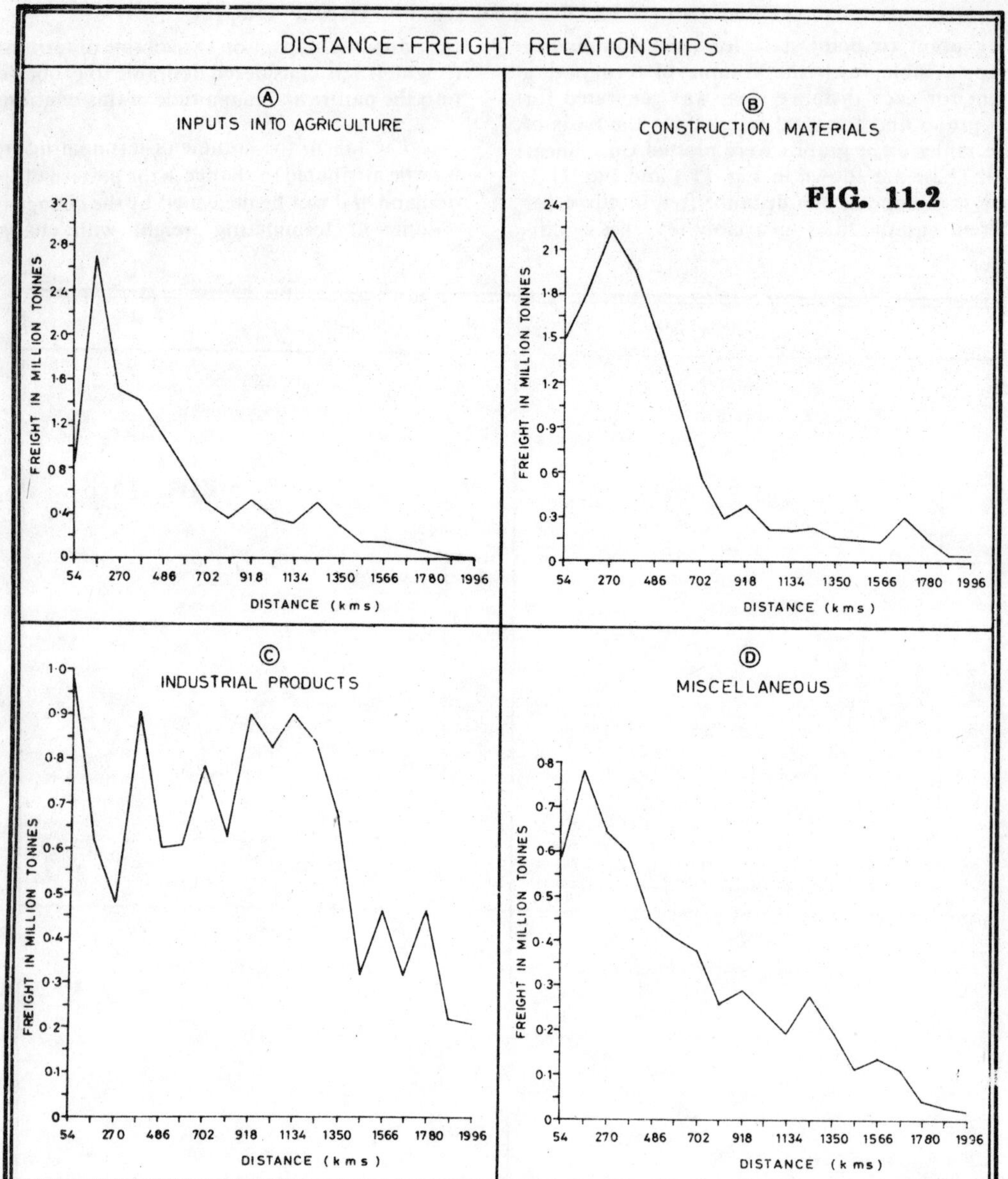

FIG. 11.2

distance. The degree of correspondence between distance and terminating freight can be determined by the value of correlation coefficient between them. Correlation coefficient and coefficient of determination for each commodity group and for total freight are presented in Table 11.1.

Table 11.1 reveals the following :

i all the values of the correlation coefficient are statistically significant at 99 per cent level, and, therefore, indicate the strong impact exerted by distance on the volume of terminating freight.

ii since the correlation coefficient between distance and the volume of freight is negative for all commodity groups as well as for total freight (ranging from —.645 to —.954), an inverse relationship between distance and terminating freight is strongly indicated.

iii it may be inferred from the high values of the coefficient of determination that the variations in the volume of terminating freight in the case of all commodity groups and of total freight may be substantially explained by variations in distance alone. The coefficient of determination is greater than 50 per cent in the case of all the commodity groups except industrial products. Its value in the case of the total freight is as high as 68 per cent. The conclusion is, therefore, inescapable that the variations in the volume of inter-regional exchange are mainly due to the friction of distance. It would, therefore, be erroneous to under play the role of distance in inter-regional trade models.

In view of the strong impact of distance observed in inter-regional commodity flows in India, the nature and type of best fit regression model was determined.

The regression results of both the linear and log linear models for each commodity are presented in Table 11.2 and 11.3. The following may be inferred

TABLE 11.2 : **Performance of simple linear regression model ($Y=\alpha+\beta X$)**

Sr. No.	*Dependent variable*	*Correlation coeff.*	R^2	*Intercept*	*Regression coefficient*	*F-Value*
1.	Food products	—0.857	.74	1613.54	—0.598	47.168**
2.	Raw materials from primary sources	—0.726	.52	6473.04	—4.263	18.970**
3.	Coal and fuels	—0.730	.53	8613.66	—4.898	19.397**
4.	Inputs into agriculture	—0.808	.65	1549.51	—0.891	32.035**
5.	Construction materials	—0.851	.73	1730.42	—1.015	44.830**
6.	Industrial products	—0.645	.41	873.73	—0.251	12.096**
7.	Miscellaneous commodities	—0.954	.91	665.34	—0.347	173.50**
8.	Total freight	—0.824	.68	21574.04	—12.262	36.059**

Note : **Significant at 99 per cent level of confidence
Y = freight in thousand tonnes
X = distance in kms.

TABLE 11.3 : **Performance of log linear regression model ($\text{Log } Y = \alpha+\beta \text{ Log } X$)**

Sr. No.	*Dependent variable*	*Correlation coeff.*	R^2	*Intercept*	*Regression coefficient*	*F—value*
1.	Food products	—0.64	.41	9.33273	—0.384	11.834**
2.	Raw materials from primary sources	—0.93	.86	17.18642	—1.632	107.841**
3.	Coal and fuels	—0.72	.52	15.47255	—1.216	18.335**
4.	Inputs into agriculture	—0.78	.60	12.90575	—1.064	26.085**
5.	Construction materials	—0.84	.70	12.79450	—1.065	40.790*
6.	Industrial products	—0.52	.27	8.02796	—0.255	6.165*
7.	Miscellaneous commodities	—0.77	.59	10.93439	—0.838	23.939**
8.	Total freight	—0.17	.75	14.922	—0.946	53.585**

Note : ** Significant at 99 per cent level of confidence
* Significant at 95 per cent level of confidence
Y = freight in thousand tonnes
X = distance in kms.

from these tables :

i the fact that the terminating freight tends to decrease for all commodity groups as the distance increases is clearly brought out by the similarities in the regression coefficients, all of which are negative.

ii these regression models have been able to explain a very high proportion of variations in data except in the case of industrial products. While lthe coefficient of determination is less than 50 per cent for industrial products, it is more than 50 per cent for all other commodities. The fit, which is not so good in the case of industrial products, may be attributed to the relatively stronger influence of some variables other than the friction of distance, for example, the industrial licensing policy of the government and or the biased freight rate structure in the case of some commodities carried by the Indian railway.

In the next stage of analysis, the performance of both the regression models was compared and the best fit model was determined for each commodity group. The results are presented in Table 11.4. The analysis of Table 11.4 shows that :

i the best fit of the model is determined by the nature of the commodity. Log linear model gives best fit for commodities which are mainly used as intermediate inputs. These are coal, fuels and raw materials from primary sources. The simple linear relationship holds good for all other commodity groups—food products, inputs into agriculture, construction materials, industrial products and miscellaneous commodities.

ii the bulk movement of raw materials and fuels takes place over relatively shorter distances since the log linear model has been found to be the best fit for these commodity groups. Most of the raw materials move over much shorter distances as compared to fuels since the values of both the intercept and regression coefficient are higher for raw materials as compared to fuels.

iii the elasticity of spatial demand is greater than unity for fuels, inputs into agriculture and construction materials, whereas it is less than unity for the food products, industrial products and miscellaneous commodities. Thus the latter group of commodities shows greater spatial dispersion as compared to the former.

iv the basic metal industries and other industries based on primary raw materials tend to concentrate near the sources of raw materials rather than the market. The distance impact is less pronounced in the case of all other groups as compared to the raw materials.

TABLE 11.4 : **Distance-weight regression model for each commodity group**

Model 1 : Simple linear regression model ($Y = \alpha + \beta X$)	
Commodity group	Regression line
Food products	Y = 1613.54—0.598X
Inputs into agriculture	Y = 1549.51—0.891X
Construction materials	Y = 1730.42—1.015X
Industrial products	Y = 873.74—0.251X
Miscellaneous commodities	Y = 665.34—0.347X
Model 2 : Log linear regression model ($\log Y = \alpha + \beta \log X$)	
Raw materials from primary sources	logY = 17.18642—1.632 logX
Coal and other fuels	logY = 15.47225—1.216 log X
Total freight	log Y = 14,922 — 0.946 logX

The marked differences in the spatial elasticity of demand of various commodity groups do suggest that there are significant variations in the spatial demand patterns for each commodity. It would be desirable, both from the theoretical and the planning perspective, to identify the value of range or critical distance beyond which the expected movement of a particular commodity becomes zero. The greater the value of such distance, the greater would be the spatial despersion of demand of that particular commodity. The reverse proposition would also hold good. The critical distance at which the expected value of movement becomes zero, may be disignated as the Critical Range of Spatial Demand (Cr). In a simple linear regression model of distance decay, the volume of terminating freight at a particular distance is determined by :

i bulk character of the commodity(α_1); and

ii the friction of distance (β_1).

The critical range of spatial demand is thus defined as;

$$Cr = \frac{\alpha_1}{\beta_1}$$

The index of spatial dispersion(Cd) for ith commodity group is defined as;

$$Cd_i = \frac{Cr \text{ of the commodity}}{Cr \text{ of the total freight}} \; 100$$

The values of Cr and Cd for each commodity group have been derived from Table 11.2 and are presented in Table 11.5.

Table 11.5 shows the follwing :

i the fact that the Cd is highest for industrial products and lowest for raw materials indicates that the basic processing industries are located near the sources of raw-material rather than the market for their output;

ii Cd for food products, industrial and miscellaneous commodities is greater than 100. It follows from this that any inter-regional relocation of these industries is likely to affect the inter-regional exchange patterns significantly.

The above analysis has clearly shown that while distance impact is quite strong in the case of inputs into agriculture and construction materials, the inter-regional flows of industrial products reflect it minimally. It follows from this that there are factors other than the friction of distance which exert relatively greater influence in the inter-regional flow of industrial products as compared to that of other commodities. An enquiry into the operation of these factors may provide useful insights into the nature and patterns of inter-regional flow of commodities.

With a view to probe further in this direction, we shall consider three important commodities namely fertilizers, cement and iron and steel. It would be appropriate to assume that the distance decay rates for these commodities would be the same as those of the commodity group to which they belong. This assumption is not only based on the relative homogeneity of the group but also on the fact that each of these commodities constitute nearly 75 per cent of the total flow of the group concerned. The production and distribution of these three commodities is substantially influenced by the industrial and

TABLE 11.5 : **Critical range and index of spatial dispersion of demand for different commodities**

Sr. No.	*Commodity group*	*Cr*	*Cd*
1.	Food products	2898	153.4
2.	Raw materials from primary sources	1518	86.3
3.	Coal and other fuels	1753	99.7
4.	Input into agriculture	1739	98.9
5.	Construction material	1704	96.8
6.	Industrial products	3341	189.9
7.	Miscellaneous commodities	1917	108.9
8.	All commodities	1759	100.0

freight policies of the government in the following ways :

i provision of cash subsidies to industries at particular locations; and

ii provision of transport subsidies in the movement of either raw materials or finished product or both.

Though it is not possible to find out the impact of cash and transport subsidies separately on the inter-regional exchange patterns with the existing data, yet the role played by these factors in the spatial organisation of the economy would become evident from distance decay rates. In the case of fertilizers and cement, for example, distance decay rates are quite strong as compared to those of iron and steel. A high distance decay rate($Sd>1$)would indicate an efficient organisation of production activities and consumption patterns in economic space, whereas, a low distance decay($Sd<1$)rate would be indicative of the concentration of the production at a few places and may consequently be a manifestation of the economic organisation of space. Looked at in this frame of reference, the available evidence suggests that the production and consumption are more efficiently organised in space in the case of cement and fertilizers as compared to those of iron and steel.

A careful study of the inter-regional exchange patterns shows that while the producing units for fertilizers and cement have come up in the neighbourhood of demand centres, this is not so in the case of iron and steel. For example, the average lead for iron and steel is 1016 kms. as compared to 644 kms. for the remaining commodities taken together. The average lead for cement and fertilizers is 635 and 753 kms. respectively. Thus bulk of steel mainly moves over longer distances. It has been observed that nearly 54 per cent of steel was carried beyond the average distance of 1016 kms. in 1973-74. The corresponding values for cement and fertilizers are only 38 and 39 per cent. A large proportion of the total receipts of iron and steel are concentrated at metropoles of Bombay, Calcutta, Delhi, Madras and Ahmedabad. All these places are at large distances from the originating points and the friction of distance is reduced because of freight equalisation. Thus the metal based industries have been located at places which are far away from the metal producing regions thus putting resource rich regions at a comparative disadvantage in the production of these commodities.

SUMMARY

The following summary emerges from the above analysis :

i the statistical evidence on flow of individual commodities clearly indicates the pervasive and attenuating impact of distance. The coefficient of determination is more than 50 per cent for all commodities except industrial products.

ii in the case of industrial products, the influence of factors other than distance seems to be greater as compared to the friction of distance. The low value of explanation ($R^2=41\%$) can partly be due to the consequence of the industrial and the freight policy of the government of India.

iii rates of distance decay vary from commodity to commodity depending upon its final use in the economy. Bulky raw materials tend to have higher distance decay rates as compared to their output. Since the decay is very fast in such commodities, the logrithmic type of regreession mode has been found suitable, whereas, for other commodities linear relationship holds good.

iv that the basic processing industries tend to locate near the sources of raw materials rather than the market centres is clearly shown by the Index of Spatial Dispersion which has the highest value for industrial products and lowest for raw materials from primary sources.

v food products, industrial products and miscellaneous commodities have greater spatial dispersion as compared to coal and fuels, raw materials, inputs into agriculture and construction material.

12

DISTANCE AND FREIGHT RATE STRUCTURE

COMMODITY FLOWS AND TRANSPORT COSTS

THUS far, our analysis has been based on the assumption that space is adequately represented by distance and its impact on the freight flows has already been examined in the preceeding chapter. Recognising the fact that human behaviour in space may be interpreted as a continuous attempt to minimize the effort involved in overcoming the friction of distance, we find that such conventional measures of distance as kilometres and miles may not necessarily be the most appropriate measure for this. In order to examine the impact of some other related vairables, it was considered necessary to relax the condition that intervening distance is a true measure of the friction of distance.

The location of industries which consequently leads to a definitive pattern of commodity flows, is itself influenced by several factors other than distance. Firstly, in view of the inter-linkages in the technological factors, it may be economical to produce some commodities at specific locations; secondly, the relatively more developed infrastructural facilities in certain regions would often result in the reduction of the cost of production and would attract new industries to its fold; and thirdly, the transportation costs as reflected through freight rate structure play a definitive role in motivating locational decisions and thus would be critical to the resulting spatial patterns of economic activities in space. Lastly, the public sector investments, the industrial licencing policies, and other fiscal policies can also be usefully employed to achieve the desired pattern of industrialisation in the country.

It may be noted that the freight rate policy is only one of those instruments that may be operated differentially to achieve the desired pattern of industrialisation. For example, a subsidisation in the freight rates of a particular commodity may result in offsetting the friction of distance and high tariff rate for the finished products as compared to the raw materials would tend to move the industry away from the sources of raw materials to the demand centres and vice-versa. The location of industries away from the resource rich regions may result in a comparative advantage to the resource poor regions as compared to the resource rich regions. As a consequence, the resource poor regions would continue to develop at the cost of resource rich regions.

An examination of the structure of the railway freight policy acquires added significance since the development and expansion of the railway network in India was not in response to the requirements of the internal economy but was primarily governed by the requirements of the colonial suction mechanism. In order to achieve these objectives, the British formulated a tariff policy which can at best be described as port oriented freight rate policy. Freight rates were manipulated in a manner so that the direction and magnitude of commodity flows could be regulated to facilitate the export of raw materials and food products from the colony to the metropole and of the industrial goods from the metropole to the cololny. Thus the freight rate policy created favourable conditions for industrial locations at zone-centroids which were ports. The port locations acquired nation wide significance bacause of being locations of several types of industries and showed the signs of industrial complexes without its characteristics. The effect of such a tariff policy on the industrial economy of India was so uneven and distorted, that the present day problems of lopsided development and irrational distribution of productive forces can be traced back to the colonial era. These developments, in their turn, have resulted in a dual character of the Indian economy.

In view of these specificities of the Indian situation, which it shares, in its essential characteristics with the entire colonial world, it is worthwhile to undertake, in the first instance, a brief survey of the development of the Indian freight rate policy and then to examine the relationship between transport costs and distance so as to explain some of the peculiarities of the railway freight rate policy as is being followed today. It may be noted that, in the present chapter, we shall consider freight rates to be the function of weight and distance and the effect of other factors between the particular destinations and origins is ignored.

At this stage of analysis, it is necessary to point out that the freight rates do not constitute the wnole cost of transport. In addition to the freight rates charged by the hauliers, there are certain other costs which the user is expected to pay. To a user, the total transport cost of movement for a commodity will not only consist of, for example, the freight rates charged by the railways but would also include the cost incurred in getting the goods from and to the railway station. This fact is simple and obvious but it acquires added importance when one compares the total transport costs for different modes of transport. However, the analysis in the present chapter is mainly restricted to transport costs that are reflected through the freight rates and no attempt has been made to examine the cost of providing the transport services from the hauliers points of view. More specifically, the present chapter aims at the following :

i to identify the instruments through which the freight rate policy may be operationalised;

ii to present major characteristics and a brief historical review of the railway rate making policy in India;

iii to examine the present structure of freight rates in India;

iv to determine the relationship between distance and freight rates; and

v to examine the impact of the present freight rates on the pattern of commodity flows in India.

DISTANCE AND TRANSPORT COSTS

The impact of any transportation system upon regional specialisation is necessarily transmitted through the structure of transportation rates; which in its turn are related to the distance. Freight rates charged by carriers, such as railways, provide a direct measure of the cost of overcoming distance and may be manipulated to the advantage or disadvantage of a given region in the following manner:

Grouping of commodities

The characteristic shape of transport rates over distance would be that of a stepped, upward convex curve. However, the level of transportation cost varies markedly according to the general characteristics of the commodity involved. Thus, there may be a considerable degree of discrimination between different commodities in the level of their freight rates. Such a discrimination can be attriuted to two basic casues; firstly, to the differences in the cost of providing a transportation service for various commodities; and secondly, due to the ability of various types of traffic to stand high transportation charges.

It is thus evident that the first departure from the distance principle is based on the need to arrive at freight rates, ususally by the grouping of commodities and sometimes by sets of origins and destinations. There is a long and complex history of the commodity grouping for the railway freight rates and some of present day problems of the lopsided development of the Indian economy can be traced to the colonial period when the principle of class rates covering large group of commodities was enforced. Special point to point rates were manipulated to suit the interests of the British monarchy.

Tapering freight costs

The second departure from the distance principle is

he tendency for tapering of the railway freight rates. Generally speaking, freight rastes are tapered so that total transport charges increase with distance, but at a declining rate. Expresed in terms of costs per unit, it is, therefore, cheaper to travel long distances than short distance.

In reality, transport costs or freight rastes are generally less than proportional to distance. The main reason for this is to be found in the fact that there are some fixed costs of transportation facilities that are incurred regardless of the length of journey. Thus, interest on capital invested, cost of maintaining plant and equipment and depriciation costs must all be covered. In addition there are handling costs which although variable between different modes of transport, are again not dependent upon the length of the haul. These basic costs can be termed collectively as "terminal costs". Variable costs include such items of expenditure as fuel and wage bills which are incurred during a particular journey. These costs do increase with distance. Although terminal costs are not dependent upon the length of the journey, they greatly influence the total transportation costs because, as the length of haul increases, terminal costs are spread to a greater extent than on a short journey. The result is that the cost of providing the transport facilities per kilometre tends to decline with increasing distance. This leads to the inescapable conclusion that any tariff rate related to costs must, therefore, be tapered.

Thus tapered railway tariff is the one in which the charges increase less than in proportion to the distance. An excessive taper can however, result in loss to the railways and or induce movement of traffic which would not otherwise be carried.

The tapered freight rates are not confined to any particular mode of transport. However, the relative importance of fixed and variable costs differ between different modes of transport. The distinction between terminal costs and haulage costs goes some way towards explaining why one mode of transport may be favoured over another for a particular journey distance. Truck transport has small terminal costs relative to rail transport and as a result truck transport will be more economical for short haults. However, truck transport has large haulage costs relative to rail transport. After a certain distance, the initial terminal cost advantage of truck transport is lost because of large haulage costs. Rail transport may then have an economic advantage over truck transport.

It is thus evident from the above discussion, that the railways' freight structure can be manipulated to the advantage or disadvantage of particular region either through grouping of commodities into different class rates and or by differential tapering of freight rates.

RAILWAY FREIGHT RATES IN INDIA : A HISTORICAL OVERVIEW

It has already been observed that the development of the Indian railways was not based on the internal requirements of the Indian economy, but was mainly governed by the requirements of the colonial suction mechanism. It was in this context that during the early phase of development, the railway freight rates were not based on any scientific considerations. As a result of the changing specificities of the suction mechanism, the railway freight rates also underwent considerable alterations. It may also be noted that alternative modes of transport, such as roadways, were kept under check through governmental regulations.

Since the political and military consideration were uppermost during the early phases of railway development and with the backing of a governmental guarantee of five per cent return on the capital outlay, the railway companies fixed their own rates. The freight rates fixed by these companies were not uniform since there was neither effective government control nor there was any competition between various railway companies operating at that time. So long as the monopoly persisted the demand on the reduction of freight rates and the maxima and the minima freight rates were introduced. During the early years of rate making, the commodities were divided into a maximum of 5 classes, the rates being lowest for Class I and highest for Class V commodities. However, there were a number of defects in this policy. For example, railway companies were free to change the classification by transferring the commodities from one class to the other. Thus, in the initial stages of its development, the rate policy remained the ultimate choice of the private companies only. It was only after 1880, that the competition among the railway companies resulted in the evolution of a new frame of freight rates.

From the view point of the railway rates, the period after 1880 acquires added significance since the opening of a number of new railway lines resulted in a competition among the different railway companies. For example, the Rajputana-

Malwa railway (1881) brought Bombay nearner to the grain producing districts of Northern India; secondly the opening of Cawnpore-Achnere railway in 1884 resulted in competition between Eastern India & O & R.R. companies for carrying important Sambhar salt; thirdly, the opening of Indian Midland Railway (IMR) in 1889 opened up an alternative route for traffic between Northern Indian and Bombay on broad gauge and brought competition among BBCI and GIPR for the Bombay traffic and between IM R & EIR for Calcutta traffic. These railway connections brought particularly the ports of Calcutta and Bombay in a sharp clash to win over the export traffic from the interior.

There were several reasons for the prevailing high rates. Firstly, the cost of operation was very high due to large costs of constructing the railway tracks; secondly, there was no competition between the railway companies and lastly, there was no governmental control over the rate making process. However, the competition between various railway companies to win over the port oriented traffic resulted in a significant development in railway rate making and it was realised that the cost of transport by rail was a figure variable with the volume of tonnage and the distance covered. The principal of 'cost of service' and 'what the traffic will bear' were accepted to determine the maximum and minimum limits of the railway freight rates. The tapering system of rates was recognised as legitimate in all cases where the particular traffic would be lost without such rates.

The immediate consequence of the competition between different railway companies and the administration's desire to rationalise the freight rate structure was that in 1887, the Government of India, divided the freight charges into mileage rates and terminal charges and maxima and minima charges were fixed for mileage rates. This resulted in the establishment of a pattern of rates which was too low to and from ports. The freight policy favoured the flow of raw materials to the main ports and the movement of imported manufactured goods to inland centres connected with their system.

The major defect of the telescopic schedule rates, which existed rarely, was that these rates were applicable only on distances within the boundary of a particular railway and thus there was a discontinuity of mileage when calculating telescopic rates on a traffic passing from one railway to another.

Whilst the pressure of war-time demands compelled the railway administration to enhance rates further within their prescribed maxima, the demand of additional finances led the Government of India in 1917, to impose surcharges tax of one pie per *maund* on coal, coke and firewood and of two pies per *maund* on all other goods carried by rail. The surchange was further enhanced in 1921 to 2½ *annas* per rupee of freight payable on all goods excluding grains and pulses, firewood and fodder but including all coaching traffic other than passangers (Indian Finance Act VI of 1921). The imposition of the surcharge was disliked by the public, on the one hand, and by the railways, on the other.

The Acworth Committee appoited in 1921 disapproved of the surcharge and recommended a substantial increase in the rates and fares charged over the Indian Railways. The matter was further persued by Indian Railway Conference Association and some of the proposals finally accepted by the Railway Board were :

i to increase the number of classes and raise and maxima rates as this would bring in an increased revenue;

ii to allow suitable alterations in the classification of goods so as to place the revised rates on an equitable basis.

It was in view of the above recommendations that the number of classes were increased to 10 with four additional classes being interpolated into the then existing classes. While the maxima rates were raised from 15 to 25 per cent, the minima rates were left unadjusted. The new classification, which was brought into force from 1st April, 1922 alongwith the previous one is given in Table 12.1

The classification of goods introduced in 1922 remained in force for fourteen years. It was pointed out that the classes were not evenly spread, and a proper relativity did not exist between the rates at railways risk and owners risk. From May 1936, revised classification with the number of classes increased from 10 to 16 was introduced. The new classification was again not free from defects. The grouping of commodities was again done arbitrarily and the increase in the number of classes was not a significant improvement. The continued existence of 'exceptional classes rates' and 'adjusted class rates' was the major instrument in the hands of the railway companies by which the rates could be manipulated.

The second world war brought considerable traffic for railways. In order to increase the railways contribution to General Revenues, an additional surcharge was levied. However, no significant changes were made in classification of goods till the new freight rate policy was introduced in 1948.

TABLE 12.1 : **Railway freight rates : A comparison of 1922 and earlier classifications**

(Rates in pies per maund per mile)

OLD CLASSIFICATION			*NEW CLASSIFICATION*				
					% Surcharge over		
Class	*Maximum rate*	*Minimum rate*	*Class*	*Maximum rate*	*Existing class*	*Previous class*	*Minimum rate*
1st ...	0.333	0.100	1st ...	0.38	14 over 1st	...	0.100
			2nd ...	0.42	26 over 1st	11	,,
			3rd ...	0.58	16 ,, 2nd	38	0.166
2nd ...	0.500	0.166	4th ...	0.62	24 ,, 3rd	7	,,
			5th ...	0.77	16 ,, 3rd	24	,,
3rd ...	0.666	,,	6th ...	0.83	23 ,, 3rd	8th	
4th ...	0.833	,,	8th ...	1.04	25 ,, 4th	8	,,
5th ...	1.000	,,	9th ...	1.25	25 ,, 5th	20	,,
X ...	1.500	,,	10th ...	1.87	25 ,, X	50	,,

Source : Railway Board

A review of the rate policy of India prior to 1947, reveals that the classification of goods was not based on scientific principles and had adversely affected the trade and industry. The rating systems were multiple-class rates, schedule rates and station to station rates. The rates were based on a flat rate system. They did not include terminal short distance and trans-shipment charges which were leviable at different scales on different railways.

The salient feature of the new freight rate policy was that alongwith the introduction of new freight rates, standard wagon load scales were also introduced in replacement of the different schedule rates quoted on different railways. A 15 class commodity classification with three legs of distances were introduced. Apart from 15 class rates, there were 13 wagon-load scales which were all lower than the first class rates. Generally, the wagon load scales were recommended for the commodities with substantial social utility and of comparatively low value. A very important feature of the wagon load scales was that they had a sharper taper than the class rates, and the rates were applicable uniformly over all railways and on a continuous mileage basis. In order to discourage the short distance traffic by railways, to the class and wagon-load rates were added separate terminal and short distance trans-shipment charges. The 1948, classification of goods and the telescopic rates are given in Table 12.2

Although the 1948 revision was a major step towards simplification and rationalisation of the rate structure, yet it was to achieve uniformity rather than absolute rationalisation. Certain shortcomings were noticed in the new freight rate policy. In view of their new role in the process of national development a complete revision of the 1948 rate policy was alo necessitated during early fifties. The railways were entrusted with the task of carrying goods associated with the development activities undertaken during the processes of planned development.

The Railway Freight Structure Enquiry Committee (1955-57) examined the whole question of freight structure in the light of the new role which the railways were expected to play and recommended a revised rate structure which was built around a percentage system with two separate basic rates known as Class 100-A and Class 100-B. All the rates are expressed as percentages of these basic rates. 100-A Class represents the freight which was previously charged at wagon-load scales, while 100-B Class represents the other freight rates. Coal in wagon-load was to be charged on a separate scale. The percentage system proposed above makes for greater simplification and flexibility and it was possible to incorporate new classes as and when necessary. The Railway Board reassessed the whole set of recommendations and proposed the freight rates, at a substantially lower figure. The salient features of the revised rate structure were as follows :

i the commodities were classified into 45

TABLE 12.2 : **Freight rates based on 1948 classification**

Class	*Basis of telescopic class rates* — *Pies per maund per mile* — *For the 1st 300 miles*	+ *for the next 300 miles*	+ *for distances beyong*	*Minimum pie per maund per mile*	*Maximum pie per maund per mile*	*Maximum rate per maund exclusive of terminal, transshipment and other extra charges* Rs.	A.	P.
1st ...	.49	.45	.40	.16	.49	3	4	0
2nd ...	.54	.49	.45		.54	3	10	0
3rd ...	.58	.54	.49		.58	4	0	0
4th ...	.63	.58	.54		.63	4	6	0
5th ...	.68	.63	.58		.68	4	12	0
6th ...	.73	.68	.63		.73	5	2	0
7th ...	.78	.73	.68		.78	5	9	0
8th ...	.84	.78	.73	.20	.84	6	0	0
9th ...	.90	.84	.78		.90	6	7	0
10th ...	.97	.90	.84		.97	6	14	0
11th ...	1.04	.97	.90		1.04	7	6	0
12th ...	1.11	1.04	.97		1.11	7	14	0
13th ...	1.18	1.11	1.04		1.18	8	8	0
14th ...	1.41	.18	1.11		1.41	9	4	0
15th ...	2.11	1.41	1.18		2.11	11	0	0

Source : Railway Board

classes as compared to 45 Class rates prevailing earlier. Out of these 14 classes were called Class-A commodities which indluded commodities of social utility, raw materials, food-grains and the rest 31 classes belonged to other commodities, and were called Class-B commodities. Besides Coal, the commodities listed under categories upto 40 per cent of scale-A of the railway tariff schedule has been treated as low rated commodities. Commodities included in categories above 40 per cent on scale-A and those in scale-B have been taken to be high rated.

ii Instead of three leg scale, the new rate structure envisaged a 8 leg distance scale. This was done in order to achieve more progression of the rates as the distance increases.

iii it was also recommended that the separate level of terminal, transshipment and short distance charges be abolished since this was taken care of while formulating the new rates.

There has been a continuous rise in the rates and fares of railways ever since the new rate structure was introduced. In August 1967, important changes were made in the classification of goods. Class A and B were reserved for wagon loads and a new Class-C having 17 class rates was then introduced for small consignments. Thus the total number of Classes became 71. This classification was again revised in April 1970 and the distinction of Class A, B and C was done away with and only two classes were constituted. The first class included 30 class rates meant for bulk consignments weighing more than 10 qts. and the second list included 17 Class rates meant for small consignments weighing less than 10 qts. In 1972-73, minimum weight condition for some commodities was again revised.

PRESENT FREIGHT RATE STRUCTURE

From the above discussion, it is very clear that the freight policy of the Indian Railways as has been evolved over a period of time is more related to the principle of 'what the traffic will bear' rather than to the 'cost of service' principle. Under such circumstances, it would be interesting to examine the extent of taper in various commodities and the degreee of cross-subsidisation due to the grouping of various commodities.

A preliminary investigation into this aspect can be made through the casual examination of the

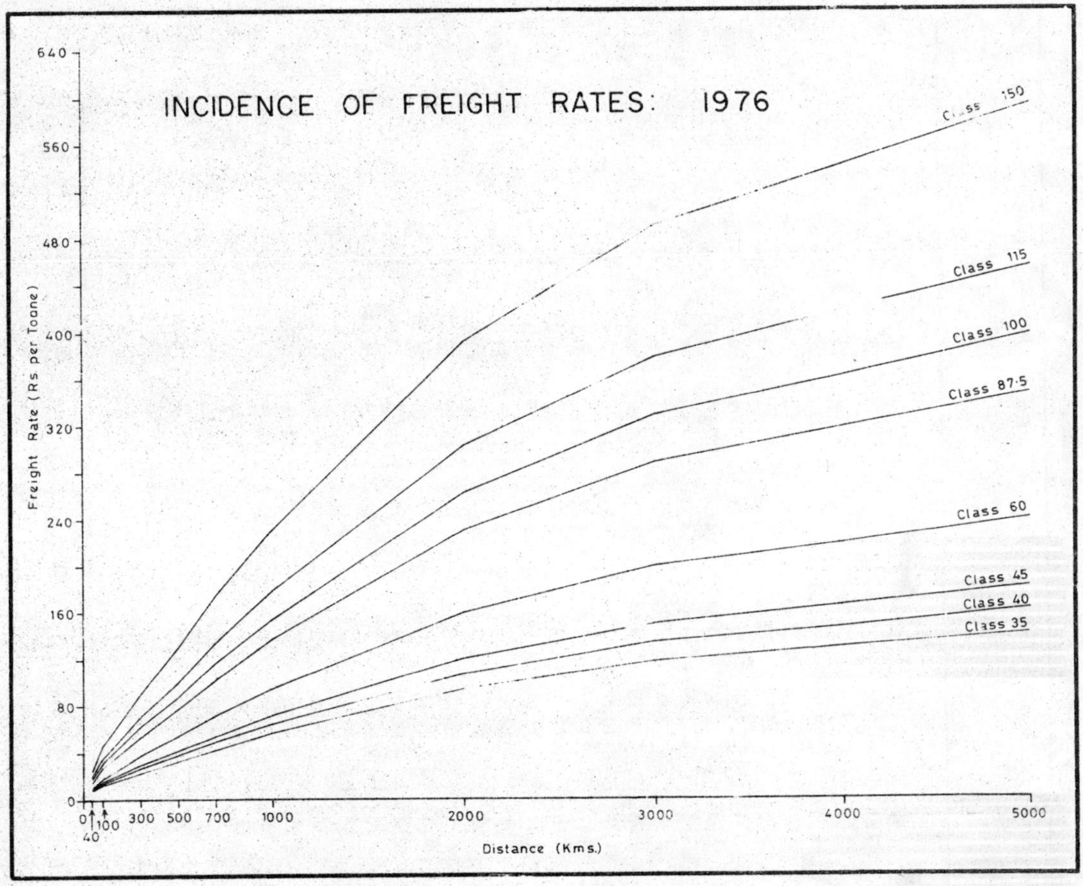

freight rates corresponding to different distance slabs. Such an analysis would clearly bring out the basic characteristics of the rate policy. The relationship between distance and cost can be further examined through suitable regression model. A further insight into the freight structure would be provided through regression estimates of cost based on distance slab statistics. Such analysis allows us to measure the long haul and commodity bulk economies. In the regression equation the smaller the exponent, the greater the economy.

Incidence of freight rates

The freight rates corresponding to different slabs as prevailing in 1976-77 have been considered for this study. Besides the basic rates, the freight was subjected to certain supplementary charges also. The distance-freight rate relationship for goods in wagon loads for certain selected classes has been presented in Fig. 12.1. Such a presentation would clearly bring out the differentials in tapering of different classes as well as the basic differences in their rates. The following points emerge from the examination of Fig. 12.1.

i there are wide differentials in basic of different classes and it goes on becoming more and more acute as the distance increases. For short distances, the rates for class 150 are 3.2 times the rates for class 35 commodities and this ratio further increases as the distance increase. At a distance range of 5000 kms. the rates for class 150 are 4.2 times that of class 35.

ii as the distance increases, the indicence of freight also increases. However, the increases in freight is not directly proportional to the increase in distance. In view of the economies of scale in the operation processes, the freight charges are less than the proportionate increase in distance. It may be observed

TABLE 12.3 : **Distance wise Freight Charges for Different Commodities**

Commodity / Distance (Km.)	Coal	Cement	Sugar	Food-grains (A)	Mineral Oil	Iron & Steel (A)	Iron Ore	Ferti-lizer (A)	Tea	Edi-ble Oil	Ce-ment Manf.	Cot-ton Raw	Oil Seeds
0.50	0.90	1.16	1.28	0.90	1.90	1.76	0.98	1.16	1.90	1.38	1.46	2.24	1.16
100	1.30	1.72	1.93	1.30	2.91	2.70	1.44	1.72	2.91	2.07	2.21	3.47	1.72
150	1.59	2.12	2.39	1.59	3.64	3.37	1.77	2.12	3.64	2.57	2.75	4.35	2.12
200	1.89	2.54	2.87	1.89	4.38	4.06	2.11	2.54	4.38	3.08	3.30	5.25	2.54
250	2.18	2.91	3.33	2.18	5.10	4.73	2.43	2.92	5.10	3.57	2.83	6.11	2.91
300	2.45	3.31	3.75	2.45	5.75	5.32	2.74	3.31	5.75	4.03	4.32	6.91	3.31
350	2.70	3.66	3.98	2.70	6.39	5.90	3.02	3.66	6.39	4.47	4.78	7.68	3.66
400	2.98	4.04	4.56	2.98	7.05	6.51	3.33	4.04	7.05	4.92	5.27	8.46	4.04
450	3.22	4.39	4.96	3.22	7.68	7.09	3.61	4.39	7.68	5.36	5.74	9.23	4.39
500	3.47	4.74	5.37	3.47	8.31	7.68	3.89	4.74	8.31	5.79	6.21	9.99	4.74
600	4.14	5.65	6.41	4.14	9.94	9.19	4.64	5.65	9.94	6.91	7.42	11.96	5.65
700	4.62	6.33	7.19	4.62	11.18	10.32	5.19	6.33	11.18	7.84	8.33	13.46	6.33
800	5.11	7.02	7.97	5.11	12.42	11.47	5.75	7.02	12.42	8.60	9.24	14.96	7.02
900	5.59	7.67	8.72	5.59	13.60	12.55	6.28	7.67	13.60	9.42	10.11	16.38	7.67
1000	6.05	8.32	9.46	5/05	14.77	13.67	6.81	8.32	14.77	10.22	10.98	17.81	8.32
1100	6.50	8.97	10.20	6.50	15.95	14.71	7.33	8.97	15.95	11.02	11.85	19.23	8.97
1200	6.97	9.61	10.94	6.97	17.12	15.79	7.86	9.61	17.12	11.82	12.70	20.64	9.61
1300	7.38	10.19	11.60	7.38	18.15	16.75	8.32	10.19	18.15	12.53	13.47	21.90	10.19
1400	7.80	10.77	12.26	7.80	19.20	17.71	8.78	10.77	19.20	13.25	14.24	23.17	10.77
1500	8.21	11.35	12.92	8.21	20.24	18.68	9.25	11.35	20.24	13.96	15.01	24.42	11.35
1600	8.61	11.52	13.58	8.61	21.29	19.63	9.72	11.92	21.29	14.68	15.77	25.69	11.92
1700	9.03	12.49	14.24	9.03	22.33	20.89	10.19	12.47	22.33	15.38	16.54	26.95	12.49
1800	9.44	13.08	14.90	9.44	23.38	21.56	10.65	13.08	23.38	16.10	17.31	28.22	13.08
1900	9.75	13.51	15.38	9.75	24.16	22.28	11.00	13.51	24.16	16.64	17.90	29.17	13.51
2000	10.07	13.94	15.88	10.07	24.95	23.01	11.36	13.94	24.95	17.18	18.47	30.12	13.94
2100	10.37	14.38	16.38	10.37	25.74	23.73	11.71	14.38	25.74	17.73	19.06	31.09	14.38
2200	10.69	14.81	16.88	10.69	26.52	24.46	12.07	14.81	26.52	18.26	19.64	32.04	14.81
2300	10.99	15.25	17.39	10.99	27.32	25.18	12.42	15.25	27.32	18.80	20.22	32.99	15.25
2400	11.31	15.69	17.87	11.13	28.10	25.91	12.76	15.69	28.10	19.34	20.80	33.94	15.69
2500	11.52	15.97	18.20	11.50	28.62	26.39	13.01	15.97	28.62	19.69	21.18	34.57	15.97

SOURCE: Goods Tariff No. 34 Part II. Goods Rate Tables (Inforce from 15th September, 1974) (Indian Railway Conference Association the goods rates herein are published with the authority of the Central Government) that for class 35, the freight increases by 16.5 times only when the corresponding distance shows an increase by 100 times. This we have already referred to as a taper in the freight rates. The examination of the figure further reveals that the degree of taper also varies from one commodity to another. Corresponding to an increase in distance by 100 times (40 kms. to 4000 kms.) the freight for class 35 increases by 16.5 times and for class 150 by 21.5 times.

iii since the essential items and most of the intermediate inputs are classified into different commodity classes and thus the extent of subsidisation of freight on such items would have limeted impact. However, it is the degree of taper or telescopic rates that really provides relief for long distance movement.

The preliminary examination of the freight rate structure thus reveals that the railway freight rates are based on the telescopic freight rate principle. In view of this, the relationship between freight rates and distance takes the form of a curvillinear relationship. The relationship between distance and freight rates has been examined through log linear regression model. The freight rates for 1974 published by Indian Railway Conference Association have been used in the present chapter. (refer Table 12.3). The postulated model is :

$$Y=\alpha X^{\beta}$$

where Y= freight rate per quintal
X= distance in kms.

The results of the regression analysis are presented in Table 12.4 which reveals the following :

i it has been observed that the coefficient of determination is very high for almost all the commodities. It can thus be stated that the log linear function is a good fit to the freight cost-distance data. Stated in other words, we can say that the tariff rates of the Indian Railways are not based on unmodified distance. The tapering of freight rates may considerably neutralise the impact of distance.

ii the regression coefficient for each commodity is significantly different from zero. Thus the fact that there is a taper in the freight rates for each commodity is confirmed.

iii the regression coefficient is different for different commodities thus showing that there are differentials in the degree of taper. For example, one may observe from the table that in the case of iron and steel, the doubling of distance increases the freight payable only by 87 per cent, while for coal, the freight cost increases by 83 per cent with a similar increase in distance.

Freight equalisation

It may be noted that in the context of industrial development, the balanced regional development has been one of the major policy objectives of the Indian planning strategy. Freight equalisation was one of the policy measures that was considered to be a useful tool to promote industrial development of the areas located further away from the major sources of raw materials and production centres. From this view point, the freight equalisation was confined to industrial commodities only. However, it may be observed that freight equalisation is not the only instrument to achieve the balanced regional development. Other policy measures such as public sector investments, industrial licencing policies and other fiscal and monetary controls can be exercised by the planners to guide both the rate as well as the pattern of regional development. Thus the freight equalisation can act as an additional instrument for fostering the industrialisation along the desired lines. In the discussion that follows, we shall try to examine the extent to which the freight equalisation schemes have fulfilled their objectives.

A careful examination of the railway freight policy shows that the freight rates as fixed by the railways have also inherent in them the characteristcs of freight equalisation, which gets operationalised, firstly, through the telescopic freight rates where the short distance traffic subsidises the long distance movement and secondly, by charging the differential freight rates for different commodities. In the preceding discussion we have already examined the basic characteristics of the freight rates as are being followed by the Indian Railways.

Freight equalisation schemes are essentially concerned with the equalisation of freight charges. In the operation of freight equalisation scheme, the freight carriers do not give any direct subsidy towards the transport charges of the commodity covered under the scheme. The carriers do charge for freight at normal rates and as such do not incur any direct operational losses on account of the operation of these schemes. The modus operandi of the freight equalisation scheme is that the short

TABLE 12.4 : **Freight and distances : the functional relationship**

Commodity	*Constant (Log α)*	*Regression Coeff. (β)*	R^2
Coal	—3.7353 (0.1995)	0.8370 (0.0270)	0.9716 (958.306)
Cement	—3.5460 (0.2237)	0.8562 (0.0267)	0.9737 (1036.820)
Sugar	—3.4747 (0.2297)	0.8648 (00268)	0.9737 (1039.425)
Foodgrains (A)	—3.7347 (0.1994)	0.8369 (0.0270)	0.9716 (958.850)
Mineral oil	—3.1308 (0.2873)	0.8801 (0.2614)	0.9759 (1133.712)
Iron & steel	—3.1998 (0.2738)	0.8785 (0.0267)	0.9757 (1126.325)
Iron ore	—3.6749 (0.2039)	0.8457 (0.0268)	0.9727 (998.784)
Fertilizer (A)	—3.5504 (0.2173)	0.8570 (0.267)	0.9436 (1031.029)
Tea	—3.1305 (0.2871)	0.8800 (0.0261)	0.9760 (1134.173)
Edible oil	—3.4061 (0.2348)	0.8662 (0.0264)	0.9746 (1075.447)
Cement manufactured	—3.4497 (0.2649)	0.8370 (0.0307)	0.9716 (826.713)
Cotton raw	—3.9823 (0.3248)	0.8858 (0.0259)	0.9766 (1168.716)
	(0.2173)	(0.0267)	1030.431

Note:

1. All the coefficients are significantly different from zero as shown by their magnitudes and standard errors.
2. Bracketed figures under regression coefficients are their standard errors and under R^2, it is F value denoting the overall significance.

distance movement pays for the long distance movement.

The freight equalisation scheme, in the Indian context, is operated by pooling the freight charges through self financing accounts, for which the excess amount paid by the long distance hauls are drawn for which credits are made available when the freight is moved over less than the average distance. The weighted average expenditure on freight based on the expected lead distances and the corresponding tariff rates are estimated in advance to be added to the ex-factory price and this also provides the basis for the operation of freight equalisation fund.

The freight equalisation scheme are usually applicable to the commodities moved through railways. In some cases, where the rail head do not exist, the road transport has also been covered. In such cases rail freight up to rail head and road transport charges upto the terminal point are adjusted and equalised.

The freight equalisation scheme is at present functioning for iron and steel, cement and petroleum products. The scheme is also operating for fertilizers for which not only freight but total production costs are also equalised by means of a subsidy resulting in a fixed pool price for sale. Similarly, foodgrains are also distributed in different areas with a built in subsidy through which the prices are equalised. The distribution of foodgrains is currently being managed by the Food Corporation of India. Under the freight equalisation scheme for petroleum products the whole country has been divided into 13 primary and secondary distribution centres and each consumer is entitled to take the delivery from the point nearest to him. The scheme for freight equalisation in petroleum products was introduced in 1969. The cost of transportation from the nearest point to the consumption point is borne by the concerned consumer.

It is also possible that sometimes various manufacturers industries, of their own, can also undertake freight equalisation by fixing the f.o.r. destination prices. Such a process may help the particular manufacture industry in capturing the national home market and to eliminate the competition. For example, some of the leading cotton textile manufacturers follow this policy. Regional differentials in the prices of such commodities, if any, are generally due to the variations in the local taxes.

Besides freight equalisation for raw materials and intermediate inputs, there has been a growing demand for extending the scheme to consumer goods also. Some of the state governments have also demanded freight equalisation for raw cotton. The demand was particularly made by the governments of West Bangal and Tamil Nadu and it was pointed out by these governments that the cotton textile industries in these states are suffering from disadvantages on account of high freight rates on cotton. Attention was also invited to the difficulties faced by small scale units scattered in other remote areas. Some state governments have also pointed out that heavy transport charges are incurred in providing essential consumer goods in inaccessible areas thus raising the price of such commodities. The question was examined in detail by the working group on freight equalisation (Govt. of India, 1977). The working group not only rejected the plea for freight equalisation on essential consumer items but also suggested that the scheme of freight equalisation should be phased out since it might lead to in-optimal location of industries.

We have already examined the nature and patterns of regional inter-dependencies for the commodities covered under freight equalisation and it was conclusively shown that the consumption of iron and steel is mainly concentrated in metropolitan centres (for detailed discussion refer Chapter 11). It has been shown that the major beneficiary of the freight equalisation are those poeple who have comparative advantage in terms of other infrastructural facilities also. It is in this context that the freight equalisation schemes appear to be marginally effective as a device for reducing the competitive disadvantage of unfavourable locations.

The evidence brought out before the Inter-Ministerial group on freight equalisation has also shown that even when the average lead of movement is more than 2,000 kms., the price advantage as a result of freight equalisation is only marginal. It has been calculated that the price advantage for movement beyond 2000 kms. is only 1 per cent for ammonium sulphate, 0.3 per cent for machine tools, and about 2.6 per cent for steel structures.

In view of the above discussion, it appears that freight equalisation by itself is not an optimal policy for achieving the objective of the balanced regional development.

SOCIAL BURDEN ON INDIAN RAILWAYS

A review of the freight rate making processes of Indian Railways and the structural analysis of its existing freight rate policy suggested that, historically, railway rates were based on the principle of 'What the traffic can bear.' Such a process of rate making has evidently resulted in a differential rate structure, which leads to subsidisation in the transport costs either due to direct subsidy operationalised through low freight rates or indirectly through the operation of freight equalisation schemes. The continued existence of a highly differentiated rate structure can not only be attributed to economic factors and is justifiable only on the consideration of public policy. Though it is not an easy task to evaluate the exact impact of such policies on the regional patterns of development, the continued existence of such a freight policy may consequently act as a catalytic agent resulting in a high degree of regional disparities by offering locational advantage to some specific regions. The subsidisation of traffic and its financial effects have been concealed during the time when no attention was given to the movement costs of particular traffic and when the absence of effective competition allowed the cross-subsidisation of un-remunerative by remunerative traffic.

The Indian railways being a public utility service connot refuse to carry any goods offered to them. The Indian Railways Act, 1890 makes it obligatory to provide reasonable facilities for receiving and forwarding traffic without any undue preference or discrimination against any person or class of goods. On the other hand, the road transporters are free to choose the type of commodities which they wish to carry. Under these circumstances the roadways would prefer the traffic which can bear high transport costs and would leave the other traffic for the railways. Such a situation would invariably result in operational losses for the railways. During 1974-75, the average freight earned by the railways was Rs. 50.35 per tonne against the average lead of movement of 699 kms. A comparison with the freight rate table shows that average freight was pain by the commodities in class 40—45, the rates for which are substantially lower as compared to class 100 commodities. The commodity-wise analysis of the losses incurred by the railways for the financial year 1977-78 shows that nearly 60 per cent of the total losses were incurred in the movement of foodgrains only. The commodity-wise breakup of the losses for the year 1977-78 are given in Table 12.5.

As noted earlier, the railways have so far found it sufficient to meet their out of pocket expenses with a greater part of overhead or joint costs falling on commodities which are high priced and can bear high transport charges and the remaining part is partly left uncovered specially in the case of long distance traffic. In view of their basic importance, low rates were generally fixed for commodities such as coal, important raw materials and foodgrains. An analysis of the patterns of the railway freight flows in India suggests that the proportion of low rated commodities is steadily increasing. Thus the railways have conventionally endeavoured to cover their operational costs through cross-subsidisation and by pricing their output on the basis of 'what the traffic can bear' principle.

Such a situation, however, presumes monopoly position in the market for the producer in question. With the recent expansion and modernisation of the road transport in India, the railways are no longer in a position to maintain their monopoly position in the matter of inter-regional freight flows. As a result of severe competition from the road hauliers, the railways are losing a considerable volume of high rated traffic in favour of roadways. Though the problem of revenue losses dur to social burden on the finances of the Indian railways has not yet acquired a serious dimension, but it has definitely led to a serious thinking on the subject of bringing railway rates closer to costs. Most railways in the world—and this applies particularly to America and Great Britain—which are faced with the problem of competition, are now placing emphasis on the cost of service basis for fixing rates. In most of the countries, the railways are compensated for losses they incur in consequence of their public service obligations.

There are only two ways by which the railways can endeavour to eliminate losses on the movement of goods traffic. These are firstly, to

TABLE 12.5 : **Revenue losses due to social burden on Indian railways 1977-78**

Sl. No.	*Commodity*	*Revenue loss (Rs. Crores)*	*Percentage*
1.	Foodgrains	40.88	58.82
2.	Fodder	3.84	5.53
3.	Salt for edible use	9.46	13.63
4.	Fruits and vegetables	2.04	2.94
5.	Oilseeds	1.16	1.67
6.	Gur, shakkar and jagree	3.78	5.45
7.	Bamboo	1.50	2.16
8.	Firewood and charcoal	2.59	3.73
9.	Livestock	1.31	1.89
10.	Ores other than iron and manganese	0.33	0.48
11.	Edible oils	1.86	2.68
12.	Molasses	0.67	0.96
	Total (1 to 12)	69.42	100.00

Source : Report of High Level Committee on Social Burdens on Indian Railways continue with the present freight rate policy based on the principle of cross-subsidisation of goods traffic and secondly, 'to suitably modify the freight rates and bring them closer to costs. We discuss below the implications of these possible alternatives.

Scope for cross-subsidisation of goods traffic

The goods traffic carried by the Indian railways can be placed in certain well defined categories as under

i Essential raw materials like coal, iron ore, limestone, lime, sand and gypsum etc., which are being carried by the railways at the rates which are very much below the corresponding costs of movement. The justification for fixing low rates for these commodities is that they cannot bear heavy freight rates since these commodities are of low value. The proportion of such commodities in the national freight comes to about 50 per cent.

ii Basic necessities like foodgrains, salt, sugar, fruits, and vegetables etc., are also carried at low rates on social and political considerations. These commodities account for nearly 15 per cent of the total railway freight.

iii Certain commodities like fertilizers, paper, cement, livestock, sugarcane and soda ash etc., are carried at low rates in view of the overall interest of national economy since most of these commodities are essential inputs in the vital sectors of the economy. These commodities also account for nearly 15 percent of the railway goods traffic.

iv The high rated traffic consists of commodities like cotton, timber, jute, electrical goods, leather, paints and varnishes and so on. However, over the years, the railways have been losing the traffic in these commodities. The loss of railway traffic in these commodities has further limited the railways capacity to meet their overhead on operational expenses through cross subsidisation.

v Iron and steel and mineral oils constitute another group of high rated commodities. The classification of these commodities is already very high and the incidence of freight on prices is substantial. For P.O.L. products, now pipelines are being laid while the competition from road hauliers is becoming very stiff for iron and steel.

In view of the above discussion, it is clear that there is a little scope for railways to eliminate their losses by following the policy of cross-subsidisation of goods traffic since the freight rates for nearly 80 per cent of traffic are fixed on public policy considerations and for the remaining there is already stiff competition from road hauliers. The introduction of Container and Quick Transit Service (QTS) for high rated commodities might help railways to attract high rated commodities to its fold. However, such measures would have only marginal impact.

Cost based railway tariff

It is evidently clear from the foregoing discussion that if the railways are to eliminate losses on goods traffic, the only alternative is to increase the freight rates on carrying of such commodities which are presently being transported at below cost.

It is unfortunate to observe that inspite of its crucial importance, the railways have made no systematic attempts to collect data on movement costs of differet commodities. However, the importance of establishing accurate data on costs is now increasingly realised even when a commodity moves only by a single mode of transport. Where the commodity moves to a destination by more than one mode of transport, accurate cost data are required to determine the choice between alternative modes or combination of modes of transport. It is only very recently that a study on inter-modal transport costs has been undertaken at the instance of the Planning Commission (RITES 1979).

In view of the lack of precise data on transport costs, it is not possible to find out the exact incidence of cost oriented freight rates on the prices. However, it has been estimated by the railways that the cost oriented freight rates would marginally increase the price of these commodities. For example, the price increase in the case of foodgrain, salt, gur and edible oils has been estimated to be 4 to 5 paisa per Kg. as against 2 or 3 paisa per Kg. for oilseeds, firewood, charcoal and other related items. Efforts are now being made to streamline the railway freight rate structure in the light of the recommendations of the Rail Tariff Enquiry Committee (1980). It is expected that the railways in their own interest would evolve suitable costing techniques for their services, which will enable them to determine accurately the losses due to social burden.

SUMMARY

The analysis in the present chapter is based on the assumption that the patterns of commodity flows are influenced by several factors other than distance and the trasportation costs as reflected through freight rate structure play a definitive role in motivating locational decisions. It has been recognised that freight rate policy is one of those instruments which may be operated differentially across the regions to achieve the desired pattern of industrialisation. The follwing points emerge from the structural analysis of the freight rates as are followed by the Indian Railways :

i The impact of any transportation system upon regional specialisation is necessarily transmitted through the freight rate policy. The cost of overcoming the friction of distance may be manipulated to the advantage or disadvantage of a given region firstly by grouping commodities in different classes and secondly by suitably tapering the freight rates.

ii Historically, the freight rates were manipulated in a manner so that the direction and magnitude of commodity flows could be regulated to facilitate the requirements of the colonial suction mechanism. The expansion of the railway network was not governed by the requirements of the internal economy but were manipulated to the advantage of the British empire.

iii The analysis of the existing freight rate structure shows that the increase in freight rates is not directly proportional to increase in distance. For example, for class 35, the freight increases by 16.5 times when the corresponding distance shows an increases by 100 times.

iv Similarly thre are wide differentials in the basic rates of different commodities It may be noted that the rates for Class 150 are 3.2 times the rates for Class 35.

v The exponential model fits well between distance and freight rates. It is interesting to note that for low rated commodities, the tapering of freight rates considerably neutralises the impact of distance.

iv The freight equalisation schemes appear to be marginally effective as a device for reducing the competitive disadvantage of unfavourable 'locations. It also appears that freight equalisation by itself is not an optimal policy for achieving the objectives of balanced industrial development.

vii Historically, the railways, in view of their monopolistic position, have been basing their charges on the principle of 'What the traffic will bear', and no consideration was given to the movement costs of different commodities. However, the development of road transport has radically changed the situation and the cross-subsidisation of the unremunerative by remunerative traffic is becoming increasingly difficult. An analysis of traffic carried by Indian railways shows that during 1974-75 the average freight was paid by commodities in Class 45—50, the rates for which are substantially lower as compared to class 100 commodities.

viii The commodity-wise break up of losses for 1977-78 shows that nearly 60 per cent of total loss was incurred in the movement of foodgrains only.

ix It has also been shown that there is very little scope for cross-subsidisation of goods traffic since the freight rates for nearly 80 per cent of traffic are fixed on public policy considerations and for the remaining there is already stiff competition from road hauliers. The only alternative is to increase the freight rates on carrying of such commodities which are presently being transported at below cost.

PART THREE

COMMODITY FLOWS AND THE REGIONAL STRUCTURE OF THE INDIAN ECONOMY

13

URBAN-RURAL COMMODITY FLOWS

URBAN-RURAL interactions constitute the basic links which unite diverse elements of the space economy into a functioning, dynamic and hierarchical system. It is an important element in the continuous process of the re-organisation of space through the kaledioscopic change in the system of settlements as a response to the changing character and level of man-nature interactions through which development proceeds. Looked at in this frame of reference, the changing spatial patterns of settlements reflect the dynamics of social transformation. Urbanisation is a specific process of the re-organisation of space and can be properly analysed only within an eco-developmental frame. It may be defined as the process of re-organisation of space through spatial redistribution of population among a hierarchical system of settlements in response to vertical shifts within the work force. The accelerated growth of modern industrialisation, unleashed since the beginning of the nineteenth century, brought about a qualitative change in the organisation of space on a global scale through the progressive concentration of population in urban settlements (Raza, Habeeb & Aggarwal, 1983).

It may, however, be noted that the process of re-organisation of space did not proceed uniformaly over the globe. The period of rapid industrialisation witnessed, on the one hand, the integration of the world market; and, on the other hand, its basic fragmentation between the ceveloped countries, with high levels of industrialisation and the countries of the third world, engaged largely in the extraction or production of primary products. This process of essentially bi-polar differentiation exerted a profound impact on the urban processes and led to high magnitude of disparities in the levels of urbanisation as between the two segments.

The specificities of the nature of urban-rural interactions in the Indian context flow out of this fragmentation of the world in two segments. They are essentially rooted in the colonial heritage of the continent. It is with this end in view that the basic features of the distorted regional structure of colonial India is presented below :

First, the centripetal pulls exerted by the inter-settlement linkages, which had evolved over time, were replaced by the centrifugal pulls generated by the metropolitan economy through the establishment of new port towns and orientation of the internal commodity flows towards them. The horizontal re-distribution of population generated by the emergence of this port-oriented suction mechanism greatly distorted the process of urbanisation in India, seriously disrupted the node-periphery relationship and strengthened the centrifugal forces in the Indian economy.

Second, the symbiotic relationship between a large number of handicrafts, service and commerce-based towns, on the one hand, and their small hinterlands of primary production on the other, which had historically evolved, was disrupted and the former were either allowed to die out like Mursnidabad or were brought within the ambit of the suction mechanism as centres of collection and or primary processing. Instead of serving as nodes from where impulses of growth were induced in the periphery, they by and large, performed a satellitic role *vis-a-vis* the ports, which were themselves satellitic to the metropolitan economy. The substitution of an essentially interactive and symbiotic by a one-sided and an exploitative relationship led to the fragmentation of the urban-rural continuum.

Third, the requirements of imperialist exploitation thwarted economic development in India, acted as an impediment in the path of technological advances in agriculture, did not permit the emergence of a self-reliant industrial sector; and, consequently acted as a serious constraint on the inter-sectoral transfer within the work-force from the primary to the secondary sector, at best permitting "the development of under-development". The horizontal movement of people from the rural to urban areas was, therefore, not in response to vertical shift within the work force, but was, to a large extent, in the nature of out-migration of "refugees" from an indigent hinterland. Multitudes of the rural poor, pushed our from a tettering agricultural sector, came to the large conurbations which did not have the capacity to assimilate them. The twin processes of denudation of the working force in the village and its forced induction into the large city gave to the process of urbanisation a highly spurious character.

Fourth, the imposition of a cultural infrastructure in the urban areas, which was not rooted in the folk ethos, led to the fragmentation of tradition along the rural-urban interface.

The multi-layered components of the system of Indian settlements are depicted in Fig. 13.1.which is based on Table 13.1. It clearly brings out the essential fragmentation of the system along the urban-rural interface. The rural pyramid meets the inverted pyramid of the urban at weak and infirm fulcrum. These are two semi-closed sub-systems connected by tenuous and, as we shall see later, essentially uni-directional links.

Urban culture did not smell of the earth and was no longer a developed, sophisticated or urbanised form of culture of the people but became something different and alien to the latter. Unranism cut off from the basic source of its strength, became anaemic, imitative and rootless. 'Ruralism', on the other hand, got bogged down in the narrow world of petty production and

URBAN–RURAL HIERARCHY OF SETTLEMENTS IN INDIA **FIG. 13.1**

1971

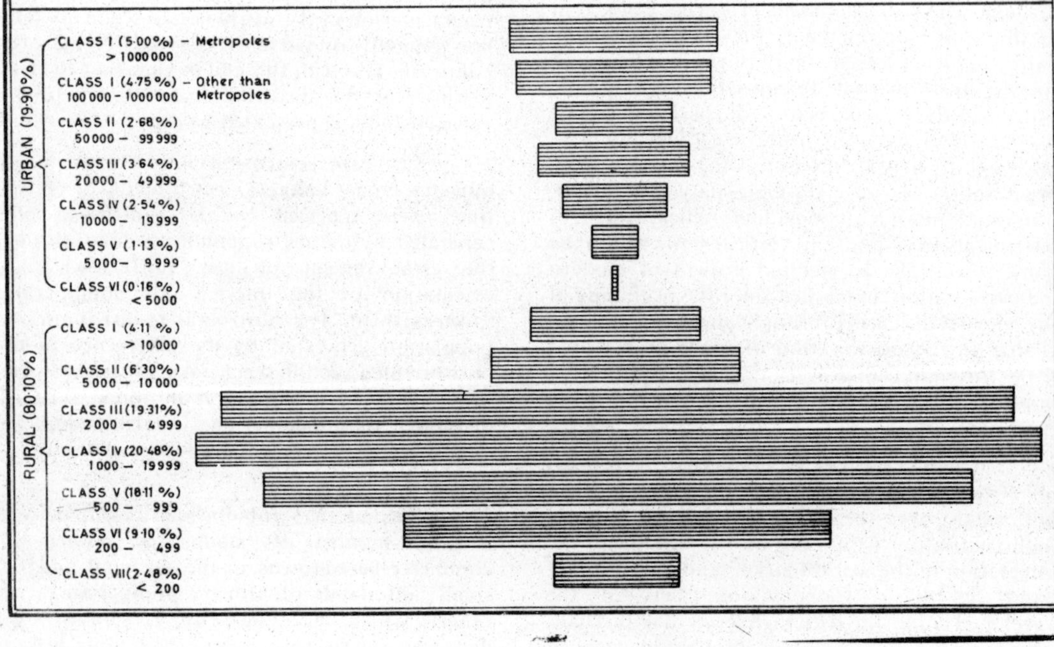

TABLE 13.1 : **Rural-urban distribution of population in India 1971**

Class of settlement	*Population size*	*% to total population*	*%to sub-group population*
URBAN		19.90	100.00
Class I	> 1,00,000	9.75	48.99
II	50,000—99,999	2.68	13.47
III	20,000—49,999	3.64	18.29
IV	10,000—19,999	2.54	12.76
V	5,000—9,999	1.13	5.68
VI	< 5000	0.16	0.80
RURAL		80.10	100.00
Class I	> 10,000	4.11	5.13
III	2,000—4,999	19.51	24.35
IV	1,000—1,999	20.48	25.56
V	500—999	18.11	22.61
VI	200—449	9.10	11.36
VII	< 200	2.48	3.10

languished under the burden of superstition, obscurantism and parochialism. Instead of sustaining each other along a continuum, both the urban and the rural segments drooped and wilted in isolation.

The current fragmentation of the urban-rural continuum in India is the direct consequence of the historical hiatus between the twin processes of industrialisation and urbanisation and between vertical shift and horizontal mobility. It is of significance of note that the impact of this hiatus on the urban and the rural segments was not uniform. While the traditional industry was liquidated or forced into a condition of decaying stagnation along the entire spectrum of settlements, the village and the small towns had to bear a heavier brunt in the process. First, they provided refuge to the unemployed astisans of the city and, as a consequence, their dependence on agriculture to a considerable degree. Second, the exogenous imposition of modern industry on the traditional enonomy was almost entirely concentrated in a few of the larger cities—generally in port conurbations, which acquired the character of islands in a vast ocean of technological backwardness in the countryside. The inherited end-product of the long drawn process of horizontal mobility unbacked by vertical shift within the colonial economy in India is characterised by serious distortions in the economic organisation of space.

The process of decolonisation (or is it neo-colonisation, at least in some cases!) spread like wildfire over the continent of Asia after the Second World War. The non-economic constraints on the development process were by and large removed. The adoption of different strategies for development has led to to a fairly large degree of international differentiation over the continent. A number of countries like China, Vietnam of North Korea have opted out of the capitalist world market and the problems of urban-rural interactions are being posed therein within the framework of a socialist economy. A number of countries like South Korea, Taiwan or Singapore have achieved a high rate of industrialisation with the help of international capital. The urban-rural relationships are being operationalised in these bridge-heads of the core and the periphery within the framework of metropolitan dominance and primacy. The rest of the Asian countries are still within the orbit of underdeveloped capitalism, with a significantly high share of the primary sector in the work force either being constant over time or decreasing at a snail's pace. Rural-urban interactions are getting articulated in these countries within the spatial structure of modified under development. In the light of the nature and magnitude of these diversities, a study of the urban-rural interactions especiallty those of commodities those of commodity flows within a comparative frame would contribute to theoretical generalisations of great value and lead to significant inputs for policy formulations.

Urban-rural interactions reflect inter-sectoral interactions and are essentially derived from the latter. It is only in this context that the urban-rural interactions acquire socio-economic meaning. While the form of the interactions is inter settlement, its content is essentially inter-sectoral. The histogenesis of urban settlements in most parts of Asia clearly indicated that the earliest towns emerged within the womb of neolithic communities in response to the emergence of inter-sectoral diversifications therein, a process accompanied in most cases by the generation of agricultural surpluses and its appropriation by the owners of land. With the growth of handicraft industries and of tertiary activities, the urban segment acquired a position of significance in the settlement hierarchy during the ancient and the medieval periods. There were, for example, 3,200 towns *(qasba)* and 120 cities *(shahar)* in the India of 1586. It has been suggested that the proportion of urban to total population in India was higher at the end of the seventeenth Century than at the end of the nineteenth. It was this historically determined process of urbanisation going hand in hand with the growth in non-primary activities, which was disrupted during the colonial period.

The vertical dimension of the system of inter-sectoral linkages, that are expressed as input-output matrices, finds its spatial manifestation as freight exchange between different category of settlements in the space economy. As we have discussed earlier, the freight exchange may be of the following three forms :

i upward flows;
ii downward flows; and
iii lateral flows.

If the rural-urban interactions are symbiotic and not exploitative, the products of the primary sector would be shipped from the rural to the urban sector in the form of food and raw materials in exchange for wage goods and technological inputs into agriculture, which would be shipped from the urban to the rural sector. The upward, downward and lateral flows thus reinforce and provide the necessary inputs for a coordinated growth of all types of settlements. In the context of such a normative model, it should be possible to assess the empirical situation of a country or a region within it. The development processes since independence were directed towards the elimination of these distortions in the structure of the economy and that of the settlements. How does one proceed in the analysis of urban-rural interactions as a response to inter-sectoral inter-relationships? This can be done in two ways—through an analysis of commodity flows and of migration streams. In the present study we shall confine ourselves to the analysis of commodity flows.

The present study is, thus, an attempt to examine the nature and pattern of urban-rural commodity flows. For this purpose, urban areas have been further divided into two groups that is cities and towns. It was considered that combining large cities with small towns in one group would hide may features of spatial interaction among different layers of the settlement hierarchy and thus the analysis would not be able to bring out the specificities of their flow patterns

The Census of India identifies six classes of urban areas in accordance with their population size. In the present study, first two urban classes are added together and referred to as cities (population> 50,000) and last four categories of urban centres have been referred as towns (population<50,000). However, this classification was found unsuitable for the analysis of districtwise data. The reason being; firstly, the districts are not large enough to have all three types of typologies within their boundaries and secondly, the encatchment area of the cities and towns or the impact of their diffusion processes is expected to extend beyond the district boundaries. Keeping in view these factors, the NSS regions were found to be quite suitable for this type of analysis. We have, therefore, in the present study, considered NSS region as the unit of analysis.

URBAN-RURAL DISTRIBUTION OF ORIGINATING/TERMINATING FREIGHT

Before undertaking an indepth analysis of urban-rural commodity flow matrices, it was considered advisable to examine the spatial patterns of originating and terminating freight for different types of settlements. Table 13.2 presents the region-wise distribution of originating and terminating freight for different types of settlements. Table. 13.2 presents the region-wise distribution of originating and terminating freight for city, town and rural settlements. The follwoing points emerge from the examination of Table 13.2 :

i It has been observed that only those regions have high magnitude of originating freight which are important raw material producing centres. The rural areas thus participate in the exchange process by sending raw materials. This is evident from the fact that the rural areas of the seven regions namely Southern Bihar, Central West Bengal, Eastern Madhya Pradesh, Western Uttar Pradesh, Northern Orissa and Inland Gujarat account for more than 70 per cent of originating freight from rural areas.

ii The major receipts in rural areas are also concentrated in a few regions only. It has been observed that the receipts in the rural areas of Inland Western Maharashtra, Central Uttar Pradesh,

Southern Bihar and Coastal West Bengal account for more than 50 per cent of the total receipts in rural areas.

iii The position with regard to small towns is not much different from those of rural areas. More than one third of total originating freight from towns is accounted for by the towns of only two regions namely Southern Bihar and Eastern Madhya Pradesh. The corresponding pattern of receipts in respect of towns located in other regions is more dispersed.

iv In the case of cities, more than 50 per cent freight originates from 4 regions only. These are Coastal Maharashtra, Inland North Andhra Pradesh, Southern Bihar and Central West Bengal. Three of these regions correspond to the port cities and the fourth represents the location of heavy industrial plants. Figure 13.2 presents the spatial distribution of originating freight for different regions. A look at Fig. 13.2 clearly reveals the important role played by the rural areas in the originating freight from a region.

TABLE 13.2 : **Region-wise distribution of rural-urban freight flows**

Region Code	*Rural*		*Urban 1*		*Urban 2*		*Total*	
	Orig.	*Term.*	*Orig.*	*Term.*	*Orig.*	*Term.*	*Orig.*	*Term.*
1	2	3	4	5	6	7	8	9
1	0.00	0.05	0.03	0.27	0.01	0.19	0.01	0.20
2	0.00	0.00	0.00	0.00	0.00	0.00	0.00	0.00
3	0.00	0.00	0.00	0.02	0.00	0.00	0.00	0.01
4	0.04	0.03	0.04	0.04	0.00	0.03	0.03	0.03
5	0.71	1.39	1.16	1.76	1.23	1.38	1.31	1.61
6	0.27	0.63	1.16	0.54	2.33	2.14	1.18	0.83
7	0.44	0.86	0.90	0.95	1.38	3.34	0.87	1.32
8	0.11	0.16	0.16	0.35	0.62	0.68	0.27	0.36
9	0.00	0.00	1.04	4.84	0.00	0.00	0.36	2.86
10	1.49	1.23	0.10	0.19	0.53	0.30	0.73	0.63
11	1.68	1.12	0.51	0.64	2.24	4.78	1.44	1.44
12	0.30	0.22	0.19	0.13	0.07	0.30	0.20	0.18
13	0.81	0.99	0.32	0.23	0.93	0.69	0.68	0.49
14	0.30	0.24	0.24	0.15	0.23	0.44	0.26	0.22
15	8.63	3.45	2.65	4.25	0.93	2.44	4.32	3.76
16	1.42	12.55	1.95	2.49	0.36	2.65	1.29	4.98
17	2.02	3.51	0.47	3.69	2.96	8.53	1.76	4.44
18	0.25	0.09	0.36	0.16	0.33	0.45	0.31	0.19
19	11.40	1.10	3.96	8.15	12.70	1.82	9.21	5.38
20	1.91	0.41	1.98	0.69	4.41	3.51	2.66	1.09
21	2.29	1.05	0.18	0.29	4.05	1.60	2.08	0.69
22	0.04	0.68	0.51	2.10	0.30	2.07	0.32	1.74
23	0.37	0.65	0.11	0.14	0.31	0.34	0.26	0.30
24	7.49	11.35	3.35	2.49	3.42	2.49	4.88	4.66
25	0.97	0.51	1.85	1.47	1.87	3.49	1.53	1.57
26	0.28	0.83	9.43	5.67	0.40	0.58	3.47	3.65
27	0.43	15.97	0.48	3.05	0.13	1.49	0.36	5.96
28	0.07	0.18	0.31	1.92	0.43	2.46	0.26	1.58

1	2	3	4	5	6	7	8	9
29	0.03	1.25	0.12	0.28	0.05	0.18	0.07	0.50
30	0.43	2.30	1.37	1.18	1.69	1.01	1.12	1.42
31	1.20	0.41	0.50	0.16	0.95	0.78	0.89	0.33
32	0.08	0.11	0.19	0.19	2.49	0.28	0.28	0.19
33	0.06	0.02	0.44	0.45	1.09	0.12	0.20	0.29
34	0.12	0.58	0.54	1.33	0.61	0.74	0.41	1.05
35	4.61	0.64	2.16	1.30	1.72	1.57	2.92	1.18
36	0.21	1.10	0.14	0.23	0.13	0.26	0.16	0.45
37	0.03	0.47	2.16	1.02	0.54	0.87	0.91	0.86
38	0.07	0.22	4.04	4.77	0.26	0.51	1.49	2.95
39	0.21	0.17	1.89	0.68	0.88	0.48	0.99	0.52
40	0.25	0.52	1.93	1.51	0.85	1.12	1.00	1.21
41	1.10	1.39	3.67	5.97	1.45	5.95	2.09	4.85
42	0.49	0.34	11.11	1.75	9.17	5.65	6.68	2.05
43	0.21	0.08	0.42	0.34	1.31	0.91	0.60	0.37
44	0.22	2.49	0.17	0.49	0.25	1.31	0.21	1.11
45	0.17	0.27	0.00	0.00	0.15	0.38	0.10	0.13
46	8.44	9.85	3.07	1.79	5.12	1.49	5.62	3.72
47	17.63	4.07	18.72	11.50	23.11	10.15	19.60	9.46
48	1.07	2.10	0.08	0.36	0.76	4.83	0.64	1.52
49	0.76	1.28	1.30	0.73	1.15	3.36	1.06	1.30
50	0.49	0.70	0.39	0.37	0.06	0.35	0.33	0.45
51	0.24	0.48	0.16	0.25	0.25	0.98	0.22	0.42
52	15.46	6.95	11.09	15.52	2.82	1.84	10.27	11.17
53	0.75	0.68	0.06	0.29	0.12	0.80	0.33	0.47
54	1.33	1.19	0.69	0.72	0.62	2.13	0.90	1.07
55	0.02	0.10	0.00	0.00	0.00	0.04	0.01	0.03
56	0.00	0.00	0.00	0.00	0.00	0.00	0.00	0.00
57	0.06	0.38	0.00	0.00	0.00	0.00	0.02	0.09
58	0.00	0.00	0.00	0.01	0.00	0.00	0.00	0.01
59	0.00	0.00	0.00	0.00	0.00	0.00	0.00	0.00
60	0.45	0.57	0.13	0.11	0.22	2.70	0.27	0.50
61	0.00	0.00	0.00	0.00	0.00	0.00	0.00	0.65
Total	100.00	100.00	100.00	100.00	100.00	100.00	100.00	100.00

The foregoing analysis has provided the essential background to our understanding of the urban-rural commodity flows. The following analysis of commodity flow matrices is expected to provide further insights in to the phenomenon.

URBAN BIAS IN COMMODITY FLOWS

After having noted the broad features of the urban-rural interaction processes, we now proceed to make a detailed analysis of the commodity flow matrices representing the aggregate patterns of exchange between different layers of the settlement hierarchy as it would provide the basis to sharpen our understanding about the role of the different types of settlement structures in the organisation of the economy. The detailed investigation along these lines would be taken up by using region-wise commodity flow matrices. With a view to highlight the imbalances and the uni-directional nature of commodity flows between the hinterland and the core regions of the Indian economic space we have

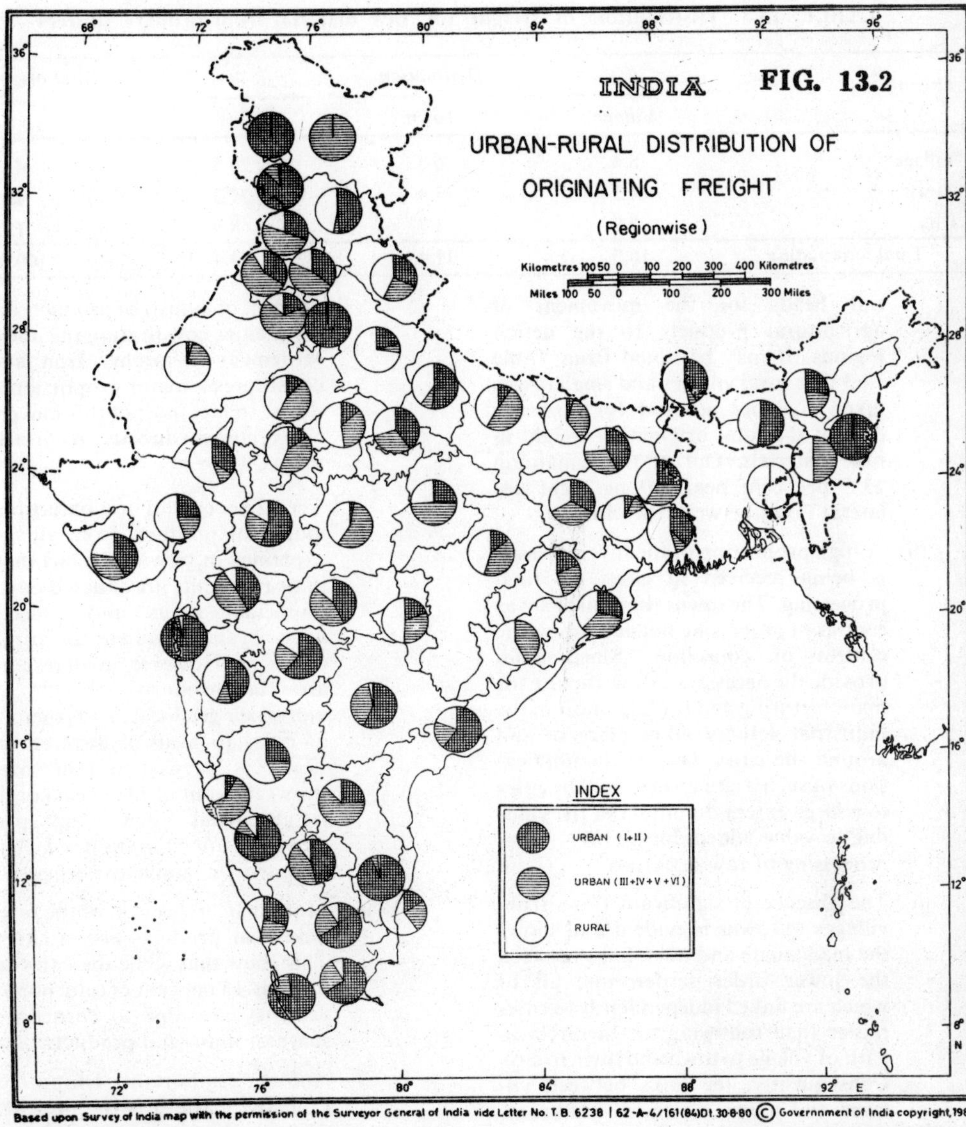

Based upon Survey of India map with the permission of the Surveyor General of India vide Letter No. T.B. 6238 | 62-A-4/161(84)D1.30-6-80 © Government of India copyright, 1980.

The territorial waters of India extend into the sea to a distance of twelve nautical miles measured from appropriate base line.

selected only two commodities that is industrial products and raw materials from primary sources. The important commodities constituting the group of raw materials are minerals like iron ore, manganese ore, limestone and dolomite and agricultural raw materials like cotton, jute, sugarcane and groundnut. The village-town-city transaction matrix for these two commodities has been presented in Table 13.3 and Table 13.4 and these flows are also represented with the help of Fig. 13.3 and Fig. 13.4.

A close examination of Table 13.3 and Fig. 13.3 indicates the following :

i. As expected, most of the raw materials originate from rural areas and small towns. The rural areas ship mining products whereas the small towns function as the centres of collection or agricultural materials and thus act as

TABLE 13.3: **Distribution of freight for raw material from primary sources**

Origin	*Destination*			*Total originating*
	Village	*Town*	*City*	
Village	8.4	6.3	26.5	41.2
Town	4.7	3.4	37.2	45.3
City	2.9	1.7	8.9	13.5
Total terminating	16.0	11.4	71.4	100.00

rail heads for the movement of agricultural products to the deficit regions. It may be noted from Table 13.3 that rural villages and small towns taken together account for 86.5 per cent of the total originating freight in raw materials. Out of the remaining 13.5 per cent nearly 9 per cent are lateral flows between the cities.

ii A high proportion of the raw materials is being received in cities for final processing. The towns thus fail to act as centres of processing but act only as the centres of collection. Since cities provide the necessary infrastructure for manufacturing and trading, most of the industrial activity takes place in and around the cities. One of the implications of such a situation is that the cities to a large extent do impound the gains due to value added during the processing of raw materials.

iii The absence of significant flows from villages to towns is evident and shows the inadequate and weak links between the lower order settlements, all of which are linked independently to cities rather than following the hierarchical path of village to town and town to city. Consequently, the links between villages and towns are much weaker as compared to those of town and city linkages.

The examination of village-town-city flow matrix for industrial products as presented in Table 13.4 and Fig. 13.4 brings out the follwing :

i in terms of originating freight nealry 80 per cent of industrial products originate from cities constituting the apex of the settlement hierarchy. Iron and steel constitutes a major proportion of such flows. In fact most of this movement to cities comes directly from the steel plants.

ii The 12 per cent of originating freight of industrial products from villages gets explained in view of the fact that many industrial units are situated outside the municipal limits and consequently have been classified as rural area locations. However, in all respects they are the products of cities. Many industries get located on the outskirts of cities to avail of dirrerent concessions. A perusal of the first row shows that out of 12 per cent orginating freight from villages 6.9 per cent terminates in cities itself, which further supports the above hypothesis.

iii More than 70 per cent of the receipts of industrial products are in cities only. This show that while the cities account for only 13 per cent of total population, yet they are able to corner a major share of industrial products.

iv Another important feature of the exchange pattern is the persistence of city-city flows in industrial products. Nearly 59 per cent of the total originating flows of industrial products are between the cities itself, thus, depriving the vast hinterland of the basic inputs for their modernisation.

SUMMARY

On the basis of the foregoing analysis, the following conclusions can be drawn :

i The villages are playing their normative role by shipping 86.5 per cent of the total originating freight of raw material, whereas 58.7 per cent of shipment of industrial products from cities take place to other cities alone and only 9

FLOW OF RAW MATERIALS FROM PRIMARY SOURCES: MACRO SPATIAL INTERACTIONS FIG. 13.3

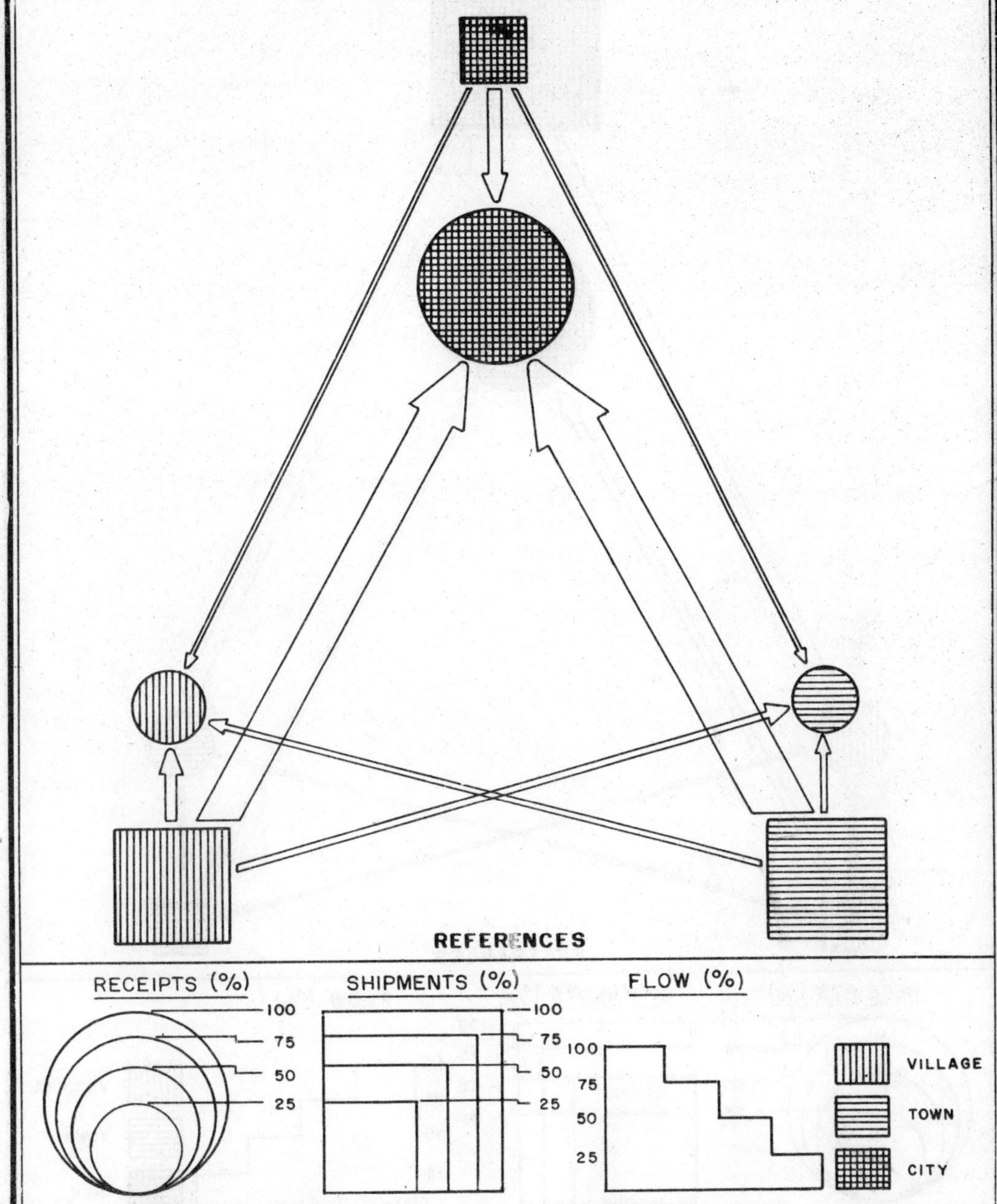

FIG. 13.4

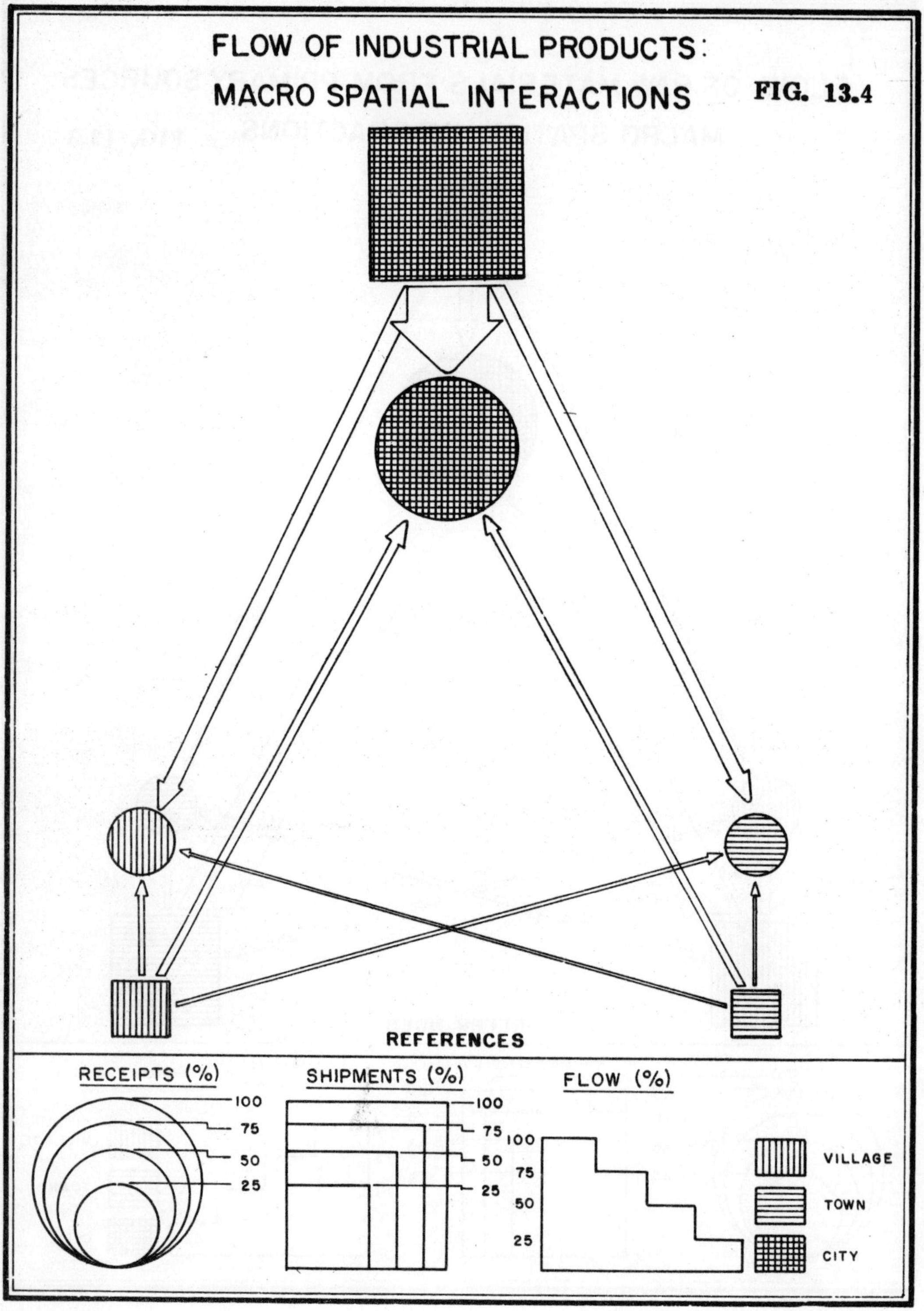
FLOW OF INDUSTRIAL PRODUCTS:
MACRO SPATIAL INTERACTIONS
REFERENCES
RECEIPTS (%)
100
75
50
25
SHIPMENTS (%)
100
75
50
25
FLOW (%)
100
75
50
25
VILLAGE
TOWN
CITY

TABLE 13.4 : **Distribution of Freight for industrial products**

Origin	*Destination*			*Total originating*
	Village	*Town*	*City*	
Village	3.6	1.6	6.9	12.1
Town	1.1	1.3	5.8	8.2
City	12.0	9.0	58.7	79.7
Total terminating	16.7	11.9	71.4	100.00

per cent trickle down to towns and 12 per cent to villages. It is thus evident that while raw materials flow from lower to higher order nodes, the flow of industrial products remains restricted to a large extent within the urban sector itself. While there is a strong upward flow, the corresponding downward flow is weak and anaemic. This has happened inspite of large distaces between the large cities in India. The freight policy of the government of India has also to some extent played a crucial role in distorting the spatial organisation of the economic space. The policy of freight equalisation for some commodities like iron and steel has effectively offset the disadvantage due to large inter-city distances. The average lead for cities is 951 kms as compared to 651 kms. for towns and 375 kms for villages.

ii Small towns instead of becoming as nodes for the diffusion of growth impulses, have become weak and anaemic. We have already noted that one of the consequence of the colonial legacy has been the decay of the historically evloved process of traditional growth. However, since independence a number of efforts have been made to change the inherited structure of production through massive investment in public sector undertakings and by providing the infrastructure in backward areas. The foregoing analysis of commodity flow matrices clearly reveals that a significant dent could not be made during the nearly thirty years of planned development. The analysis of data on the location of industrial activity would clearly reveal the immensity of the problem that we are facing. It has been observed that nearly 44 per cent of total number of factories are located in only five states— Maharashtra, West Bengal, Tamil Nadu, Punjab and Delhi. Within Maharashtra itself as much as 50 per cent of the total units are located in the two cities of Bombay and Pune.

14

ECONOMIC BASE AND COMMODITY FLOWS : A Case Study of the Indian Urban System

WE find in the corridors of time that the emergence of non-agricultural production, trade and service within the womb of undifferentiated palaeolithic communities played a crucial role in the histogenesis of early urban settlements; and it was the strengthening of these activities which sustained the urbanisation process through its various phases. What distinguishes the primitive from the modern systen of exchange is its intensity, its product range and its spatial reach rather than its essential nature. The growth of the urban centres constituting the upper levels of the settlement hierarchy is essentially a product of the reorganisation of space and the system of settlements in response to changes in the structure of the economy generated through socio-economic instrumentalities.

Thompson (1967) has recognised five stages in the process of growth; the first is characterised by self-sufficient subsistence; the second by the widening of its economic base and the consequent commencement of export; the third by economic maturity and the operation of the multiplier effect; the fourth by an increase in the range of functions and the coming up of higher order nodes which get interconnected with and bring neighbouring urban areas under their orbit of influence; and fifth by the emergence of national nodes on the basis of special functions.

It follows from the above that the reorganisation of space accompaying the urbanisation process is based, firstly, on the transformation of a uniform surface of settlements into the multi-layered surfaces comprising anticlynes and synclines, and secondly, on the strengthening of the interactive mechanisms operating both horizontally among settlements at the same level and vertically among settlements at different levels. The latter mechanisms are crucial, particularly in the developing economies, as they articulate the interactions between the large sub-stratum of the rural hinterland and the upper crust of urban settlements. In the previous chapter, we have seen that if these interactions are symbiotic and not exploitative, the products of the primary sector would be shipped from the rural to the urban sector in the form of food products and raw materials in exchange for wage goods and technological inputs into agriculture, which would be shipped from the urban to rural sector. With such a model of urban-rural interactive system of commodity flows in view, it should be possible to critically assess the role played by the urban layers of the hierarchy of settlements in the regional as well as in the national economy.

The specificities of the nature of urbanisation in the Indian context is essentially rooted in the colonial heritage of the country. The exogenous imposition of modern industry on the traditional economy was almost entirely concentrated in a few of the large cities generally in port conurbations, which acquired the character of islands in a vast ocean of technological backwardness in the countryside. It may be noted that the port oriented railway network established by the British in India was a potent instrument of implementing the policy of transforming the colonial economy into a source of raw materials and a market for the manufactured goods of metropolitan Britain. It did not emerge in response to the requirements of the indigenous development impulses but was intended to act as a suction mechanism. The inherited end product of this long drawn process is reflected in the persistence of the weak economic base of the Indian urban settlements and the consequent distortions in the organisation of space. Since the economic base of a settlement greatly influences the quantum and the type of commodity flows, patterns of spatial dispersion of demand and the nature and magnitude of their spatial linkages with both rural and urban settlements in the space economy, an exploratory analysis of the relationships between the economic base of the Indian urban settlements and their freight characteristics would provide a meaningful insight into the nature of inter-dependencies generated through the organisation of economic activities in space.

It is unfortunate that this crucial relationship has not attracted the attention of many scholars. Berry (1966) in his pioneering study of commodity flows in India, was not primarily concerned with and did not focus attention on the role of urban commodity flows in the organisation of space economy. Chakraborty (1978), though focusing attention on the relationship between urbanisation and economic processess restricted his scope to the pattern of cammodity flows of the nine metropolitian cities only. The role of the metropolitan commodity flows in the spatial organisation of the Indian economy has also been empirically examined in a study by the authors (Raza & Aggarwal, 1980b). The study has clearly brought out the fact that the essential weakness of their symbiotic interactions, which is rooted in their economic base, is characterised by a weak secondary and a bloated tertiary sector. The distorting role played by them in the organisation of the national economic space is a function of their essential infirmity. It is clear from the above that either the relationship between urban attribute and commodity flows has not been examined at all or is has been studied only within the restricted frame of the metropolitan centres. The role of the system or urban settlements as a whole has not been analysed so far. The present study is a halting first step in the direction of examining the relationships between the economic base of urban settlements and their freight characteristics. Within this framework, the following relationships are formulated :

(a) Indian urban system continues to be, by and large, stultified and dysfunctional—mainly concerned with services rather than production.

(b) While the functional attributed of urban settlements determine the nature of commodity flows and the pattern on spatial linkages, they are themselves largely determined by their economic base.

i Urban settlements specialising in primary activities other than mining ten to have small shipments and receipts, to interact with a few nodes, to send just one or two dominant commodities and to receive a wide range of commodities.

ii Urban settlements, where mining is the dominant activity, tend to have large originating but small terminating flows and to send just one or two commodities but receive a greater variety of goods. Their spatial linkages depend on the type of mineral extracted. If a town has captive mines, for example, dolomite or limestone, the number of spatial linkages would tend to be small; but if a commodity like coal, which is used ubiquitously, is the dominant produce, the sptial interactions would tend to be large.

iii Manufacturing centres tend to have large originating and terminating flows; the number of their spatial linkages tend to be large; and the commodity mix of both originating and terminating freight tend to be diversified.

iv The freight characteristics of settlements specialising in tertiary activities tend to be indefinitive and fluctuate between those of the above two categories.

ANALYTICAL FRAME

The study of commodity flow characterstics in relation to economic base and the functional attributes of the Indian urban system presupposes the availability of a huge volume of data, for each urban centre, both on commodity flows and on the occupational distribution of the work force. Indian railways provide the data on commodity flows and the data on the occupational structure of settlements has been obtained from the Census of India, 1971.

The following interaction variables were extracted for each urban centre using the point to point commodity flow matrices referred above :

Y_1 = Total shipments (Qts)
Y_2 = Number of spatial linkages—shipments
Y_3 = Total receipts (Qts)
Y_4 = Number of spatial linkages—receipts

The attribute of the urban settlements relating to their economic base have been derived from the structure of the work force as obtained from the Census of India, 1971. Two of the industrial categories, that is, cultivators and agricultural labourers have been added together to obtain the share of agricultural workers in the total work force. The proportion of labour force engaged in a particular activity is one of the few measures which is comparable from activity to activity and from one year to another, this is one of the few variables or urban activity for which fairly reliable data is available in India.

The selected variables relating to the economic base of urban settlement are as follows :

X_1 = Population of the urban settlement
X_2 = Proportion of workers employed in agricultural activity.
X_3 = Proportion of workers employed in extractive activities other than mining
X_4 = Proportion of workers employed in mining and quarrying
X_5 = Proportion of workers employed in household industry
X_6 =Proportion of workers employed in manufacturing sector (N.H.H.)
X_7 =Proportion of workers employed in construction activities
X_8 =Proportion of workers employed in trade and commerce
X_9 =Proportion of workers employed in transport and storage
X_{10}=Proportion of workers employed in other activities

It is possible on the basis of the distribution of work-force engaged in different activities to identify groups of urban settlements with similar occupational structure. Once such groups are identified, the freight characterstics of each group can be analysed in relation to their functional character. In this exercise, the method suggested by Nelson (1955) for functional classification of urban cities has been used. The choice of the method rests upon its simplicity and universal acceptance. To calculate this index, the percentage of workers in each activity in each town is calculated and the mean and standard deviation is derived. Any town exceeding mean plus one standard deviation in any activity is taken as specialising is that particular activity. Thus, using this method it is possible to classify each town as mono-functional, multi-functional or diversified.

The cut-off point for each function was identified following the Nelson's (1955) method as explained above and their values for each category are given in Table 14.1 :

The functional categories identified using the above criterion are :

i agriculture
ii extractive activities other mining
iii mining
iv household manufacturing
v other than household manufacturing

TABLE 14.1 : **Cut-off values for various functions using Nelson's method**

S. No.	*Function*	*Cut-off percentage*
1.	Agriculture	36.06
2.	Extractive	5.51
3.	Mining	8.17
4.	House-hold (HH) manufacturing	13.49
5.	Non house-hold (NHH) manufacturing	26.66
6.	Construction	7.93
7.	Trade	27.45
8.	Transport	16.59
9.	Other services	34.23

iv construction
vii trade and commerce
viii transport and communications
ix other services
x bi-functional
xi diversified

The relationships between commodity flow indicators and urban attributes have been examined by employing the techniques of stepwise regression analysis, wherein the urban attributes have been considered as a set of independent variables and the commodity flow indicators as dependent variables, being taken one at a time.

FUNCTIONAL ATTRIBUTES AND THE INDIAN URBAN ECONOMIC BASE

The urbanisation process in India has been essentially constrained by the anaemic agricultural base and the weak and the disarticulated process of industrialisation in the country. Indian urban system continues to be, by the large, stultified and dysfunctional—mainly concerned with services rather than with production. Efforts, were, no doubt, made in the period since independence to alter this structure through massive investments in public sector undertakings and through the system of controls imposed on the private sector. The end product of these efforts, spread over the last thirty years is the persistence of a weak secondary and a bloated tertiary sector. The continued existence of such a phenomenon in the urban sector is revealed by the analysis of the occupational structure and the functional characteristics of the different categories of urban settlements.

URBAN ECONOMIC BASE

The analysis of the 1971 Census data on the occupational structure of the urban centres clearly reveals that the essential weakness of the Indian urban system lies in its weak economic base. The detailed results are presented in Table 14.2. It is interesting to observe that the number of workers employed in the tertiary sector is not only greater than those in the secondary sector, but it far exceeds even combined strength of the primary and the secondary sectors also—the ratio of the former to the latter being 1.4. Within the tertiary sector also, "other services" account for nearly 25 per cent of the total work force. Trade and transport absorbs nearly 30 per cent of the workers—share much larger than the share of the manufacturing sector itself (22.8%). Such a distorted distribution of work-force for the urban settlements is a manifestation of the fact that the large non-productive superstructure of the Indian urban system rests on a weak productive base.

There are wide differentials in the sectoral distribution of workers between the various strata of urban centres as characterised by their population size. It is evident from Table 14.2 that as the size of the urban centre increases, there is a progressive shift from primary and extractive activities to secondary and tertiary activities—the share of primary and extractive sector ranging from about 30 per cent in small towns (U4 + U5 + U6) to only 4 per cent in cities (U). The reverse trend may be observed in the case of secondary and tertiary activities. While the share of the tertiary sector in the small towns is around 49 per cent, it goes up to 62 per cent in the case of cities. The share of the manufacturing sector also ranges from about 18 per cent in small towns to about 33 per cent in cities. The available evidence, thus, clearly points not only to the anaemic economic base of the Indian urban system but also to the fact that the intensity of the infirmity goes on becoming more and more acute as we go down the hierarchy in the system.

FUNCIONAL CHARACTER OF THE INDIAN URBAN SYSTEM

This assessment of the Indian urban system is also corroborated by the analysis of the functional characteristics of urban settlements. As stated earlier, the functional character of each settlement has been determined by Nelson's method. The first stage of analysis resulted in the classification of the settlements into mono-functional and multi-functional categories. Out of a total of 1464 urban settlements served by Indian railways, nearly 65 per cent were identified as mono-functional and the remaining 35 per cent were classified as multi-functional. The functional distribution of settlements and their population has been brought out in Fig. 14.1. and the distribution of settlements specialising in various functions according to their size category is given in Table 14.3.

A study of the distribution of settlements in the various functional categories reveals that the number of settlements specialising in the tertiary sector are more than double the number of settlements specialising in the manufacturing

TABLE 14.2 : Size of towns and their occupational structure 1971

Size of Urban Centres	Percentage of workers in								
	Agriculture	Extractive activities (Other than mining)	Mining	Household manu-facturing	Manufacturing (Other than household)	Construction	Trade	Transport	Other services
Class I	3.35	1.01	0.67	3.69	29.19	3.69	20.46	11.40	26.51
Class II	10.95	2.82	1.06	5.65	18.72	3.53	21.55	9.89	25.79
Class III	10.23	2.09	2.09	6.29	15.73	3.84	19.58	8.74	22.37
Class IV	29.10	2.73	0.68	7.19	11.98	3.42	18.49	6.50	19.86
Class V	29.93	2.72	1.70	7.48	11.90	3.06	16.66	5.79	20.74
Class VI	22.46	8.22	1.89	8.22	9.81	6.01	16.77	6.32	27.84
All Urban Centres	11.10	1.70	1.00	4.90	22.80	3.50	20.10	10.00	24.90

Source : Derived from General Economic Tables, Series I, India, Part II - B (i), Census of India, 1971

TABLE 14.3 : **Settlement size and functions**

Functional categories	*Proportion of settlements falling in each size category*						*Functional distribuion of total settlements*
	I	*II*	*III*	*IV*	*V*	*VI*	
Mono-functional							
Agriculture	0.00	1.73	18.69	44.34	29.99	5.21	230
Extractive	3.57	25.00	21.42	25.00	25.00	0.00	28
Mining	4.00	8.00	48.00	20.00	20.00	0.00	25
H.H. manufacturing	9.09	9.00	33.76	33.76	11.68	2.59	77
Non H.H. manf.	26.92	11.53	28.46	20.00	10.00	3.07	130
Construction	3.84	7.69	30.76	38.46	15.38	3.84	26
Trade	2.10	15.26	28.42	27.89	21.05	5.26	190
Transport	17.46	7.93	33.33	30.15	7.93	3.17	63
Others	18.18	19.88	30.68	20.45	9.66	1.14	176
Multi-functional							
Bi-functional	9.34	9.34	22.42	24.29	28.03	6.54	107
Diversified	10.19	11.89	32.76	30.33	13.34	1.45	412
Distribution of total settlements by size	144	165	420	435	254	46	1464

sector. The number of the former is roughly equal to the number of settlements specialising in primary and secondary activities taken together. This relationship in terms of the number of settlements may at the first instance appear to be a crude index of measuring the relative dominance of the tertiary sector in the Indian urban system.

It may be argued that the settlements vary in size and each functional type of settlement requires a particular mix of work-force. With a view to examine the validity of this argument, the functional character of settlements in each size category was examined through Table 14.3, which clearly reveals the existence of the weak economic base of the settlement at each level of the hierarchy.

Agricultural settlements normally tend to be small in size. Nearly 75 per cent of the agricultural settlements have population varying from 5 to 20 thousand—class IV and class V settlements having a dominant share in this category. About 50 per cent of the settlements specialising in the extractive activities are small towns falling in the category of calss IV or below. Household manufacturing activities are mainly concentrated in class III and class IV towns, their share in the total number of household manufacturing settlements being 67 per cent. It is only in the case of manufacturing settlements that the cities acquire significance—26.92 per cent of such settlements being cities.

In view of the fact that certain functions tend to coalsce with other functions and as a consequence, settlements tend to specialise in more than one function, the existence of such functional combinations in the economic system may play an important role in the organisation of the national home market. The multi-functionality of an urban settlement is the mechanism through which either the productive base of a town coalesces with the ancillary non-productive services, or one sector of the production process gets integrated with its another sector in a system of vertical, horizontal or diagonal linkages. The former leads to the coming together of the tertiary sector in combination with either the primary or the secondary sector, the latter is based on the technological links between the primary and the secondary sector.

The interactive system of multi-functional settlements can be looked upon in a multi-dimensional space, wherein a 'n' functional settlement is a point in *n* dimensional space. In the present exercise, our analysis is restricted to bi-functional settlements in 2-dimensional space. The distribution of such settlements is presented in Table 14.4. It may be observed that nearly 55 per cent of the bi-functional settlements have other

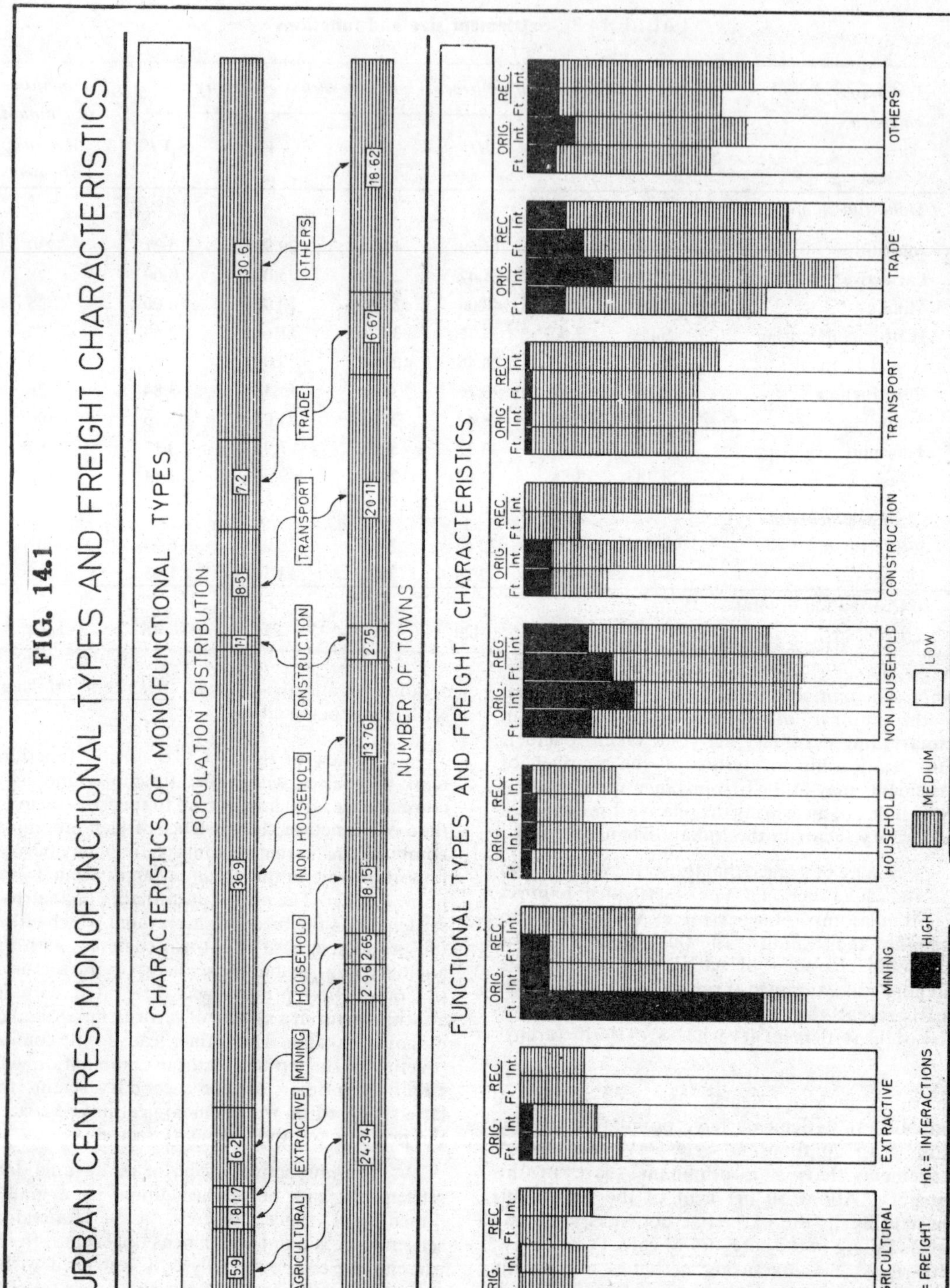

FIG. 14.1

URBAN CENTRES: MONOFUNCTIONAL TYPES AND FREIGHT CHARACTERISTICS services as one of their functions; and this non-productive sector tends to coalesce with another non-productive sector that is 'trade' in the case of 35 per cent of the total bi-functional settlements. While the share of bi-functional settlements where non-productive sectors come together is quite large, the proportion of settlements which eithercombine the productive sectors or a productive sector with its ancillary non-productive sector is very small. The existence of large number of be-functional settlements in non-productive sectors in comparison to their share in technologically linked production-distribution cycle is definitely not a healthy sign of the be-functional segment of the Indian urban system.

The foregoing analysis of the urban economic base and their functional character clearly brings out the dysfunctional character of the Indian urban system, which goes on becoming more and more acute as one goes lower down the hierarchy of these settlements. It appears that the characteristics of the colonial organisation of space are so deeply embedded in the spatial structure of under development that the massive efforts undertaken since independence to correct these distortions have been able to make only marginal dent.

TABLE 14.4 : **Distribution of bi-functional settlements**

	Other Services	*Trade*	*Manufacturing*	*Household manf.*	*Transport*	*Other fns.*
Agriculture	6	8	4	10	1	2
Extractive	—	—	—	—	—	—
Mining	4	—	1	—	—	—
Household manf.	2	5	5	—	—	—
Manufacturing	8	7	—	—	1	—
Construction	—	—	—	—	—	—
Trade	37	—	—	—	4	—
Transport	2	—	—	—	—	—
Other services	—	—	—	—	—	—

ECONOMIC BASE AND COMMODITY FLOW CHARACTERISTICS

Let us now examine the commodity flow characteristics in relation to the economic base and the functional attributes of the urban settlements. A preliminary exploration into the nature of the relationship was attempted in the following manner.

i With a view to consider the nature of correspondence or association between the indicators of economic base (X) and commodity flows (Y), a correlation matrix was generated and is presented in Table 14.5

ii Each function has been examined in relation to its commodity flow characteristics and the results are presented in Fig. 14.1 and Table 14.6.

The significant relationships between economic base and the fuctional attributes, on the one hand, and commodity flow characteristics, on the other, are discussed below :

i The inter-correlations amongst the commodity flow indicators are all positive and highly significant. In general, shipments, receipts and the number of spatial linkages are positively correlated. It indicates that the Indian home market is tending to become integrated through bi-directional interactions in a system of varying critical ranges of flows and differing indices of spatial dispersion of demand of diverse commodities. The identification and explanation of differentials in the range and the rate of distance decay in the flows of different type of commodities has been examined separately.

ii Population also has significant positive relationship with total tonnage and the number of spatial linkages both for originating as well as for terminating freight. This emphasises the crucial role being played by the cities and large towns in the organisation of space through the mechanism of commodity flows.

iii It may be noted that population size has a greater degree of correspondence with receipts than with shipments. This is indicative of the fact the urban settlements continue to be the centres of consumption rather than of production. Receipts are, by and large, linked with the former; and shipments with the latter. There is a very high degree of correspondence between population size and the strength of the workforce (.98). Both are homogeneous in terms of consumption reflected in receipts; but are differentiated between the productive and the non-productive in terms of production reflected in shipments. It would therefore, be appropriate to undertake an in-depth analysis of the relationships between commodity flow characteristics and the economic base of the urban system as reflected in the distribution of the work-force therein and their functional character.

iv The proportion of agricultural workers in a settlement is significantly and negatively related to the volume and the number of spatial linkages. It shows that the settlements which have relatively large share of agricultural work-force have low level of commodity flows as well as that of spatial linkages and *vice-versa.* The relative self sufficiency and the lack of backward and forward linkages of agricultural centres is also evident if one considers the proportion of settlements falling in different categories of shipments, receipts and the number of interactions. In view of the small volume of surplus and low level of economic activity at these centres, the receipts and shipments are of low magnitude. 80-88 per cent of such settlements interact with less than 100 settlements each and 80-85 per cent of the agricultural settlements have shipments and receipts of less than 1 lakh quintals.

v A similar type of association has been observed in the case of household industries wherein all the four indicators of commodity flows are negatively related with the percentage share of workers in this sector. The freight characteristics of urban centres predominantly engaged in household industries show relative self-sufficiency and limited interactions with other settlements of the urban system. Thus, the essential characteristics of urban settlements engaged in household industries are similar to those of urban settlements specialising in agriculture.

vi The reversal of this tendency can be observed in the case of manufacturing centres where the proportion of workers in manufacturing sector are positively related with all the commodity flow indicators. From Table 14.6 it is evident that the larger the share of workers in manufacturing activities, the larger is the volume of shipments, receipts, and the number of spatial linkages. The manufacturing centres send and receive larger amount of freight and interact with larger number of nodes as compared to other categories of urban settlements. Nearly 50 per cent of these have shipments and receipts ranging from 1 lakh to 16 lakh quintals, and more than 50 per cent interact with 100—500 settlements. The commodity flow characteristics of the agricultural and household industrial centres are thus in sharp contrast to those of manufacturing nodes. The urban settlements based on agriculture and household industry show relative self-sufficiency and are, by and large, inert and passive in the interactive mechanism wherein the manufacturing nodes emerge as effective instruments of integrating the dynamic system of inter-depdendencies constituting the national home market.

vii Mining areas have a very large originating tonnage because of the bulky nature of their output. This has been shown by a positive correspondence between the volume of shipments and the proportion of employment in mining. Over 65 per cent of mining settlements send more than 16 lakh quintals each. The terminating freight does not, however, show this characteristic and over 90 per cent of the

TABLE 14.5 : **Correlation matrix between urban attributes and freight characteristics**

	X_1	X_2	X_3	X_4	X_5	X_6	X_7	X_8	X_9	X_{10}	Y_1	Y_2	Y_3	Y_4
Y_1	+0.47	–0.14	0.02	+0.33	–0.07	+0.09	+0.03	–0.09	+0.06	+0.01	+1.00			
Y_2	+0.65	–0.28	0.07	+0.01	0.10	+0.30	+0.05	+0.03	+0.20	+0.08	+0.45	+1.00		
Y_3	+0.65	–0.14	–0.03	+0.02	0.06	+0.20	+0.06	–0.04	+0.06	+0.02	+0.50	+0.58	1.00	
Y_4	+0.72	–0.34	–0.10	–0.05	0.11	+0.27	0.00	+0.10	+0.18	+0.16	+0.37	+0.80	+0.58	1.00

Note : A comparison of the computed 't' values with tabulated 't' values shows that all coefficients above 0.07 are significant at 99% level and a coefficient of 0.06 is only significant at 95% level.

TABLE 14.6 Urban Centres: Functional types and Freight Characteristics

Town types based on Nelson's Method	*Total freight (Ori.) % of towns sending*			*Total freight (termi.) % of towns receiving*			*No. of interaction % of towns sending commodities (Shipments)*			*No. of interactions (Receipts) % of towns receiving commodities*		
	Less than 1 lakh quint.	*1 lakh 1.6 mill. quint.*	*above 1.6 mill. quint.*	*less than 1 lakh quint.*	*1 lakh 1.6 mill. quint.*	*above 1.6 mill. quint.*	*Less than 100*	*100 to 500*	*above 500*	*Less than 100*	*100 to 500*	*above 500*
Agriculture	85.21	14.77	0	80.86	19.10	0.43	87.81	12.15	0	79.55	20.42	0
Entractive activity (other than mining)	71.41	24.99	3.57	78.56	17.85	3.57	82.13	17.85	0	82.17	17.85	0
Mining	20.00	12.00	68.00	52.00	40.00	8.00	60.00	32.00	8.00	68.00	32.00	0
Household Manufacturing	77.91	19.46	2.59	77.91	18.16	3.88	83.11	12.96	3.87	74.02	23.36	2.58
Manuf. (Other than household)	29.98	49.21	19.12	23.06	46.14	30.75	22.29	53.06	24.57	31.52	50.75	17.63
Construction	76.90	19.12	7.69	57.67	34.61	7.68	84.59	15.38	0	53.84	46.15	0
Transport	33.32	55.54	11.10	14.27	61.90	23.79	25.38	58.71	15.84	26.98	61.88	11.10
Trade	53.14	45.24	1.57	52.09	46.29	1.58	52.10	46.30	1.56	46.30	52.62	1.05
Other Services	48.85	43.16	7.93	39.20	47.72	13.05	46.01	45.44	8.45	37.49	53.96	8.49

mining settlements receive less than 16 lakh quintals each. The mining centres are thus characterised by large shipments, low receipts and low level of spatial linkages. This is indicative of the absence or weakness of the links between extraction and secondary production within this subset of urban settlements which are mere raw material and fuel appendages of larger agglomerations specialising in manufacturing.

viii Tertiary activities by their very nature are expected to be more associated with the level of spatial linkages rather than with the volume of freight. This phenomenon has been found to be true in the case of trade, transport and other tertiary activities. The increase in the share of employment in the tertiary sector leads to a corresponding increase in the level of spatial linkages both for shipments and receipts. Urban settlements specialising in *'trade'* and *'other services'* have low volume of shipments and receipts as compared to the settlements sepcialising in transport activities wherein both the volume of commodity flows and the level of spatial linkages tend to be large.

The above analysis has thus shown that while the urban settlements engaged in the primary and household manufacturing activities are mainly self-sufficient and have a tendency for low level of spatial linkages, the urban settlements engaged in industrial activities have large volume of commodity flows and interact with a large number of nodes. The tertiary towns show more association with the level of spatial linkages rather than with the volume of flows.

URBAN ATTRIBUTES AND COMMODITY FLOWS: CAUSAL RELATIONSHIPS

In the foregoing analysis, we have considered only the associational type or relationships. On the basis of its findings, it was considered desirable to examine the causal relationships between freight characteristics and urban attributes. The essential purpose of this exercise is to identify the influence of various urban attributes on the freight characteristics of an urban settlement. This has been attempted through the application of the technique of stepwise regression analysis. The variables relating to urban attributes constitute the set of independent variables and the commodity flow indicators as a dependent variable being taken one at a time. The results are discussed below:

Total shipments : The vairables which significantly expalin total shipments are population (X_1) and mining (X_4). These two variables taken together explain nearly 35 per cent vairation in the originating freight. The positive sign of the regression coefficient of X_1 and X_4 shows that the volume of total shipments is an increasing function of population size and the proportion of workers engaged in mining. The estimated regression equation is an under :

$$Y_1 = 79334.7 + \underset{(22.8)}{8.7\ X_1} + \underset{(16.3)}{21846.5\ X_4}$$

$$F\ Value = 387.25 \qquad R^2 = .347$$

Number of spatial linkages (shipments) : The findings of the associational analysis thus get corroborated by the more rigorous regression analysis as well. The variables which are significant in explaining the number of spatial linkages or interactions (shipments) are population size and the share of manufacturing and transport sectors in the total work-force. Thus the number of originating interactions are an increasing function of X_1, X_6 and X_9. The regression coefficients of all the these variables are positive. It follows that larger size towns normally interact with a larger number of nodes and urban settlements which specialise in manufacturing and ship products to many more places than towns specialising in other activities. The estimated regression equation is :

$$Y_2 = -2.92 + \underset{(32.020)}{0.001\ X_1} + \underset{(10.411)}{4.583\ X_6} + \underset{(8.543)}{5.471\ X_9}$$

$$F\ Value = 466.598 \qquad R^2 = .490$$

Total receipts : It is quite interesting to observe that the only variable which is significant in explaining the terminating flow is the size of the town or its population, and the share of the explained variance is 42.4 per cent. Other urban attributes have failed to explain any significant proportion of variations in the volume of terminating freight. From the regression equation given below it is evident that, the larger a town is, the greater is the demand for various products for intermediate and final demand consumption. The requirements of food products increase in direct proportion to the increase in population size. In addition, the urban centres also require a large variety of weight reducing raw materials and industrial products for the manufacturing sector. It is because of this fact that the regression coefficient and the intercept is much higher in the case of receipts as compared to shipments. The estimated regression equation is :

$$Y_3 = 111917 + 13.69\ X_1$$
$$(32.8)$$
F Value = 1075.8 $R^2 = .424$

Spatial linkages (receipts) : Population size and the proportion of agricultural workers are the only two variables that explain nearly 58 per cent of variation in the number of spatial linkages fro receipts However, it may be noted that the regression coefficient of population size is positive, while that of the proportion of workers engaged in agriculture is negative. This indicates the mutual exclusivity of large size and agricultural specialisation and corroborates the earlier finding that the larger size settlements with their strong economic base tend to play a potent role in the organisation of the economic space and the small size towns with agricultural specialisation tend to be semi-closed self-suffieient entities. The estimated regression equation is :

$$Y_4 = 173.6 + .001\ X_1 - 2.847\ X_2$$
$$(39.69) \quad (13.04)$$
F Value = 996.678
$R^2 = .577$

SUMMARY

From the foregoing discussion, we can conclude the following :

i The reorganisation of space accompanying the urbanisation process is based, firstly, on the transformation of a uniform surface of settlements into the multi-layered surfaces; and secondly, on the strengthening of the interactive mechanism operating both horizontally among settlements at the same level and vertically among settlements at different levels. The analysis of commodity flows acquires socio-economic meaning within such analytical frame.

ii The current fragmentation of the urban-rural continuum in India is the direct consequence of the historical hiatus between the twin processes of industrialisation and urbanisation, between vertical shifts and horizontal mobility.

iii The essential weakness of the Indian urban system lies in its economic base, which is characterised by a significant primary, a weak secondary and a bloated tertiary sector. The large non-productive surperstructure of the Indian urban system rests on a weak productive base. The intensity of this infirmity goes on becoming more and more acute as we go down the hierarchy in the system.

iv The distribution of settlements in functional categories indicates the dominance of the settlements specialising in non-household industries and the concentration of manufacturing settlements in the large size categories. While the share of bi-functional settlements, where the non-productive sectors come together is large, the proportion of settlements which either combine the productive sectors or a productive sector with its ancillary non-productive sector is very small.

v From among the urban attributes only population size shows a high degree of correlation with commodity flow indicators. It may, however, be noted that it has a higher degree of correspondence with receipts than with shipments. This is indicative of the fact that the urban settlements continue to be the centres of consumption rather than of production; as the receipts are, by and large, linked with the former and the shipments with the latter.

vi While the urban settlements based on agriculture and household industries show relative self-sufficiency and are, by and large, inert and passive in the interactive mechanism; the manufacturing towns emerge as an effective instrument of integrating a dynamic system of interdependencies constituting the national home market.

vii Mining centres tend to have large shipments and low receipts, indicating the absence or weakness of the links between extraction and secondary production within this subset of towns which are mere raw material and fuel appendages of large agglomeration specialising in manufacturing.

viii Urban settlements specialising in tertiary activity tend to have larger number of spatial linkages but a smaller volume of commodity flows.

ix The examination of causal relationships through stepwise regression corroborates the finding that the population size exerts a strong impact on commodity flows; and that the share of the manufacturing and transport sectors alongwith the population size strongly influences the level of spatial linkages.

It follows from the above that in the Indian context, any strategy of urban development which does not aim at transforming the distorted economic base of the Indian urban system would be futile. It is only by strengthening the secondary sector and bringing the tertiary activities in relation to it, that the Indian urban system can be made to play its crucial role in organising the space economy of the country in such a manner that it corresponds with and contributes to basic socio-economic transformation.

15

METROPOLITAN COMMODITY FLOWS AND THE SPATIAL ORGANISATION OF THE INDIAN ECONOMY

METROPOLITAN centres constituting the apex of the hierarchical system of settlements, play a crucial role in the integration of the home market through the processes of upward, downward and lateral interactions. Their ability to play this role effectively is essentially derived from the nature and strength of their bi-directional links with the rest of the system of settlements. Viewed thus, the metropolitan centres in India are greatly constrained by their legacy, inherited from the period of colonial rule.

Let us recaptulate the socio-economic context in which, the metropolitan ports emerged on the Indian scene. They were established on the virgin land and acted as counter magnets against the system of centripetal pulls exerted by the inter-settlement linkages, which had traditionally evolved over time. The new port towns and the port oriented railway network established by the British in India was a potent instrument of implementing the policy of transforming colonial economy into a source of raw material and a market for the manufactured goods of the metropolitan Britain. The orientation of the internal commodity flows towards these newly developed ports led to the emergence and strengthening of centrifugal pulls operationalising the suction mechanism. The substitution of an essentially interactive and symbiotic by a one-sided and an exploitative relationship led to fragmentation of the urban-rural continuum.

Since they played a crucial role in tne colonial economy, the new ports, in a short time developed into primate cities, which devoured like cannibals the other towns of the hinterland. Since the framework within which the primate cities emerged and 'thrived' in India was deeply embedded in the colonial set up, their characteristics were fundamentally different from the primates of the developed countries. While the emergence ot the latter reflected the consolidation and integration of the national market, the emergence of the former reflected its fragmentation; while the latter emerged as poles in the national field of centripetal forces; the former became effective instruments for operationalising the centrifugality of the colonial economy; while the latter were autonomous nodes for the diffusion of development impluses, the former were the foci of the exploitative mechanism; they were primates, no doubt, but they were satellitic primates (Raza and Habeeb, 1976). The spatial model incorporating the basic elements and characteristics of a regional structure of the economy of the Colonial India which provides the spatial framework within which evolved the relationship between the 'enclave of dysfunctional development' at the port conurbation and the various elements of the hinterland has already been discussed in Chapter 5.

During the last three decades of planned development, efforts have been made to alter this structure through massive public investments in resource rich regions most of which happen to be away from the metropolitan ports. This was also followed by the rationalisation of the freight structure so that some of the infirmities of the colonial freight rate structure are modified. However, the inherited regional structure of underdevelopment continues to inhibit the development of productive forces even after nearly thirty years of independence. The hierarchy of the system of settlements still continues to be lopsided as is evident from the data presented in chapter 13.

As we go up the hierarchy of urban settlements[2] the process of concentration tend to become sharper still. Table 15.1 presents the distribution of population in different types of settlements structures. It may be observed from Table 15.1 that the proportion of urban population in the metropolitan cities (with population above one milliön) has been consistently increasing since 1901. In 1971 the metropolitan cities in India accounted for 5.00 per cent of the total population and 25.13 per cent of the country's urban population. In 1901 their shares were .62 per cent and 5.76 per cent respectively. When we consider the share of metropolitan cities[3], the process of concentration can be further witnessed within the system of metropolitan cities themselves, in which the share of the first four metropolitan centres (Calcutta, Bombay, Delhi and Madras) is as large as 72.28 per cent. For a detailed discussion on the process of urbanisation in India, a reference may be made to Raza *at. el.* (1980).

This excessive concentration or urban population in a few traditional nodes can be further explained in terms of urban primacy and rank-size rule. The primate city growth pattern can be observed in all the first four metropolitan systems of India mentioned above. It is, however, most pronounced in the Calcutta metropolitan system as indicated in Table 15.2. Calcutta alone claims 25.53 per cent of the total metropolitan population. The rank-size relationship of the four metropolitan systems also reveals the distortion in the urban systems of India. These distortions are again most marked in the Calcutta system where all class I cities have lower populations than the expected population. This indicates that there is a wide gap between the lower and higher order settlements and an absence of middle order settlements.

It is evident from the above analysis that the nine million cities are the heavy weight components of the top heavy system of urban settlements in India. Their role in the commodity flows of the

TABLE 15.1 : **National metropoles : population size and growth (1901—1971)**

(Population in '000')

Metropole	1971	1961	1951	1941	1931	1921	1911	1901
1. Calcutta	7031	5737	4589	3578	2108	1851	1718	1488
2. Bombay	5971	4152	2967	1686	1268	1245	1018	812
3. Delhi	4066	2359	1437	696	447	304	238	214
4. Madras	2469	1729	1416	856	713	579	556	541
5. Total (1 to 4)	19537	13977	10409	6816	4534	3979	3330	3055
6. Population of Class I towns	60911	38177	26426	16004	9498	7593	6472	6225
7. Total Urban Population	109114	78937	62444	44153	33456	28086	25942	25852
8. Total Population	547950	439073	360950	318539	278867	251239	252005	238337
9. %of Met. population to total population of Class I towns (5/6)	32.07	36.61	39.38	42.58	47.74	52.40	54.54	49.07
10. %of Met. population to total urban population (5/7)	17.91	17.70	16.66	15.44	13.55	14.16	13.60	11.81
11. %of Met. population to total population in India (5/8)	3.57	3.18	2.88	2.16	1.63	1.58	1.40	1.28

Source : 1. General Population Tables—1971 Part II-a(i)
2. Statistical Abstract of India—1974

TABLE 15.2-a : **Index of primacy 1971**

Metropolitan system	*Index of primacy*	*Primate city population as % to total urban population of the system*
Calcutta	6.4	35.27
Bombay	1.7	21.70
Madras	1.3	15.68
Delhi	1.7	16.09

TABLE 15.2-b : **Changing metropolitan characteristics (1901-1971)**

Year	*No. of Urban settlement*	*No. of Metrop. cities*	*Metrop. cities as % of total urban setts.*	*%of total pop. in Metrop. cities*	*%of Urban pop. in Metrop. cities*
1901	1851	1	.05	.62	5.76
1971	2626	9	.34	5.00	25.12

Source : Census of India : General Population Tables 1971

country is a reflection of the spatial imbalances, of which they are the product and which, in their turn, they sustain.

It is unfortunate that this crucial relationship has not attracted the attention of many scholars for long. It is only recently that some attempts have been made in this direction. In the Indian context, the relationship between the urban economic base and their commodity flow patterns has already been examined. The study has clearly shown that the large non-productive superstructure of the Indian urban system rests on a weak productive base, which is characterised by a significant primary, a weak secondary and a bloated tertiary sector. The distorted role played by them in the organisation of national economic space is a function of their essential infirmity. Berry (1966) in his pioneering study of commodity flows in India, was not primarily concerned with and did not focus his attention on the role of urban commodity flows in the organisation of the space economy. In spite of this even he could not escape the conclusion that four metropolitan centres—three of them being the colonial ports—continue to be the main hinges on which the system of commodity flows rests in India. Chakraborty (1979) focused his attention on the relationship between urbanisation and economic processes for the metropolitan centres of India. It is clear from the above that the relationship between metropolitan base and commodity flows has not above that the relationship between metropolitan economic base and commodity flows has not been so far examined. It is our endeavour in this Chapter to examine the role of the metropolitan centres in the spatial organisation of the Indian economy. Within this framework the following relationships are formulated :

i Indian metropoles continue to suffer from the persistence of a primary sector; the weakness, the inadequacies, and distortions of the secondary sector; and a large unproductive tertiary sector;

ii Metropolitan dominance is reflected in a relatively large share of the metropolitan centres in commodity flows of the country as well as in the strong lateral integration at this level;

iii The inequities of metropolitan hinterland relationships are reflected in strong upward and weak downward flows; and

iv The metropolitan centres continue to be the major centres of consumption and distribution rather than of production; and this weakness of their economic base is reflected in the diversified nature of its shipments and receipts.

The study of commodity flow characteristics in relation to economic base and the functional attributes of the Indian metropolitan system presupposes the availability of a huge volume of data, for each metropolitan centre, both on commodity flows and on the occupational distribution of the work-force. Besides the commodity flow data used in the present study, the data on the attributes of the metropolitan centres relating to their economic base have been derived from the Census of India, 1961 and 1971. Table B IV—Part C, gives the number of workers in each of major and minor groups of the various divisions identified in the Indian Standard Industrial Classification, 1961 and National Industrial Classification, 1971. Division 2 and 3 give details of the manufacturing sector. The industrial data for the metropolitan centres was aggregated in terms of the 16 industrial categories. In order to examine the distribution of workers in different types of productive sectors, the data was further aggregated into 3 major productive sectors in the following manner :

Consumption Goods : Food products manufacturing, beverage manufacturing, tobacco manufacturing, textile manufacturing, footwear, clothing and other wearing apparel, furniture and fixtures, paper and paper products.

Intermediate Goods : Wood and cork products, rubber products, industrial chemicals, products of petroleum and coal, non-metallic mineral products. (all consumption goods within these major categories have been excluded from this category for example furniture of wood).

Capital Goods : All types of machinery including electrical and transport equipment (the consumer oriented products have been excluded from this category, for example, refrigerators and airconditioners).

The data on tertiary sector is given in division 6, 7, 8 and 9 of the Indian Standard Industrial Classification—1961, and National Industrial Classification—1971. The activities in the tertiary sector have been divided into 33 major groups and 124 sub-groups. For the purpose of the present analysis, 124 minor-groups were aggregated into the following 7 groups :

1. Social and economic overhead services
2. Professional and non-professional personal services
3. Community services
4. Financial activities
5. Distributive services in wholesale trade
6. Distributive services in retail trade
7. Unspecified services

In order to study the concentration and diversification of different tertiary functions in different metropolitan cities in India, the method of location quotient was used. The nature of dominant tertiary functions of the metropolitan cities for 1961 and 1971 has been examined by using the technique of factor analysis.

In order to fully understand the variations in the spatial linkage pattern of the nine million cities, the following variables have been generated using the information on metropolitan flows :

I Flow variables :
- i. volume of shipments—commodity-wise and total
- ii. volume of receipts—commodity-wise and total

II Spatial linkage variables :
- i. number of interactions—shipments
- ii. number of interactions—receipts

III Spatial dispersion variables :
- i. average distance of shipments
- ii. average distance of receipts

ECONOMIC BASE OF THE METROPOLITAN CENTRES IN INDIA

The urbanisation process in India has been essentially constrained by the anaemic agricultural base and the weak and the disarticulated process of industrialisation in the country. Indian urban system continues to be by the large, stultified and dysfunctional—mainly concerned with services rather than with production. Efforts were, no doubt, made in the post independence period to alter this structure through massive investments in public sector undertakings and through the system of controls imposed on the private sector. The end product of these efforts, spread over the last thirty years, is the persistence of a weak and stagnant secondary sector and a bloated tertiary sector. The continued existence of such a phenomenon in the metropolitan economies is revealed by the analysis of the sectoral distribution of the work-force in India.

Sectoral distribution of workers

The number of workers engaged in production other than primary (which includes mining, qarrying, household and non-household manufacture and construction) was only 10.9 per cent of the total work-force in 1951. This clearly shows that the secondary sector, inherited from colonial rule, was far too small to sustain any major development effort. This share had risen to 13.4 per cent in 1971, only marginally higher than in 1951. Even this figure is an over-estimation in the light of the changed definition of workers in the 1971 Census.

TABLE 15.3 : **Economic base of Indian urban centres 1971**

Industrial categories	*Number employed in the cetegory as percentage of the total*
Primary sector :	12.8
(a) Cultivators	5.1
(b) Agricultural labourers	6.0
(c) Livestock, forestry, fishing, hunting, plantations and orchards and related activities	1.7
Secondary sector :	28.7
(d) Manufacturing, processing, servicing and repairs	22.8
(e) Mining and quarrying	1.0
(f) Household industry	4.9
Tertiary sector :	58.5
(g) Transport, storage and communication	10.0
(h) Trade and commerce	20.1
(i) Other services	24.9
(j) Construction	3.5

This stagnation is clearly indicative of the essential inadequacy of the strategy of industrial development.

If one looks at the Indian urban system, the picture is even more disappointing. It is distressing to note that the Indian urban system continues to be, by and large, stultified and dysfunctional-mainly concerned with services rather than with production. The existence of such a phenomenon is revealed in Table 15.3

The metropolitan centres, which constitute the apex of the urban system do not show a significantly different pattern as compared to the rest of the urban system. The characteristics of under development which manifest themselves in the urban economy of the country, are seen in a pronounced form in the metropolitan centres of India. These four national metropoles grew as outposts of the colonial power to serve as points from where manufacture products could be fed into the country and raw materials sucked out. Attendant on these processes was the development of a large tertiary sector since poeple from an improverished country-side cam to the metropolises and were 'absorbed' in this sector.

The most significant characteristic of the occupational structure of the four national metropolitan cities, as brought out in Table 15.4 is the proliferation of the tertiary sector, a phenomenon which stands in contrast to that of the advanced countries. Manufacturing sector accounts for a relatively small share in the total work force as compared to the tertiary sector. They also have a significant number of primary workers in their workforce. The share of tertiary sector ranges from 53 per cent in the case of Bombay to 69 per cent in Delhi, while the corresponding values for the sedondary sector range from 29 per cent in the case of Delhi to about 45 per cent in the case of Bombay. A comparison of the 1971 and 1961 figures however, reveals that the percentage share of workers employed in the secondary sector of Calcutta increased by over 12 per cent.

Thus, the available evidence points to the persistence of the characteristics of underdevelopment in the Indian metropolitan system. Such a weak and lop-sided economic base of the Indian metropoles warrants a closer examination of their secondary and tertiary sectors.

The manufacturing sector

The manufacturing sector accounts for a relative small proportion of the work—force and this too is highly concentrated in the consumer goods sector as can be seen from Table 15.5 and 15.6. A close examination of these tables reveals the following :

i Delhi and Madras have only a small proportion of their population engaged in manufacturing.

ii Between 1961 and 1971, there has been a rise in the share of the manufacturing sector in all the four centres with Calcutta exhibiting an increase of about 12 per cent.

iii Consumer goods industries form the

TABLE 15.4 : **Sectoral distribution of workers in the metropolitan cities (1961—1971)**

Metropole		*Primary*	*Secondary*	*Tertiary*	*Percentage of tertiary in*		
					Skilled	*Semi-skilled*	*Unskilled*
Calcutta	1961	0.27	29.17	70.55	27.13	38.76	33.29
	1971	1.52	41.22	57.24	35.59	39.95	24.46
Bombay	1961	1.89	43.50	54.61	28.80	41.29	29.48
	1971	1.25	45.33	53.40	34.94	35.44	29.28
Delhi	1961	1.60	26.82	71.57	43.54	25.01	30.58
	1971	1.60	29.48	68.91	42.34	30.42	27.24
Madras	1961	1.50	31.23	67.35	29.61	35.42	34.81
	1971	4.00	34.20	61.78	48.62	20.97	30.41

bulk of manufacturing activity with all the four metropoles having more than 50 per cent of their manufacturing workers engaged in such activities, with the percentage being the highest in Bombay at both time periods. Comparing the figures of 1961 with those of 1971, one notes that the proportion of workers in consumer goods industries has decreased except in Delhi where the percentage share increased by 10 per cent.

iv While the percentage share of workers in intermediate goods industries has remained constant in Calcutta between 1961 and 1971, it had increased by about 4-5 per cent in Bombay and Madras and has decreased in Delhi by 10 per cent.

v Madras has the highest percentage of workers in capital goods industries—22.13 and 27.01 in 1961 and 1971 respectively. In all the 4 cities, the share of workers engaged in capital goods industries has increased especially in Calcutta where it has risen from about 8 per cent to 16 per cent.

vi Among the consumer goods industries, it is textiles, wood, paper products and publishing which have the bulk of industrial workers. Miscellaneous industries account for 5—10 per cent of the workers in those cities.

vii Basic metals and their products form the largest component of the intermediate goods industry.

viii Transport equipment forms a large share of the capital goods industry especially in Madras where it employs 20 per cent of the workers in manufacturing. Machinery and electrical equipment show an appreciable increase between 1961 and 1971 except in Delhi where it accounts for just over 1 per cent.

The foregoing analysis of the manufacturing sector of the four super metropolitan centres evidently shows that :

i Of the four super metropoles only Bombay and Calcutta can be classified as being industrial centres.

ii All of them exhibit a highly consumer oriented manufacturing sector.

iii Over the decade 1961—1971 there has been a slight increase in the share of intermediate and capital industries.

iv The increase in the percentage of workers in machine building indicates healthy trend.

Tertiary sector

The earlier analysis has brought out that the most significant characteristic of the occuptional structure of Indian metropolitan cities is the proliferation of the tertiary sector. Since, most of the tertiary sector activities fall under the informal sector which is not conducive to economic development of a country, an indepth analysis of the role of the tertiary activities would be warranted. The structure of the teritary sector in the metropolitan centre in terms of the seven subdivisions is presented in Table 15.7. The following points emerge from the analysis of Table 15.7

Table 15.5 : **The metropolitan manufacturing sector (1961 and 1971)**

	Food Industries	*Tobacco and Beverages*	*Cotton Textile*	*Jute Textile*	*Wollen and silk textile*	*Misc laneous textiles*	*Wood*	*Paper, paper products, and printing publishing*	*Leather and Leather products*	*Rubber, Petroleum and coal*	*Chemical*	*Non-metallic minerals*	*Basic metals and chemical products*	*Machinery and electrical equip.*	*Transport*	*Miscelleanous*
1	2	3	4	5	6	7	8	9	10	11	12	13	14	15	16	17
Delhi																
1961	5.02	0.89	14.66	0.11	.29	11.96	7.80	9.42	5.63	0.80	4.23	4.14	14.64	4.21	7.77	8.41
1971	5.46	1.08	11.37	0.09	.20	11.10	6.38	9.83	5.02	3.29	2.64	3.35	9.84	5.31	16.30	9.30
Bombay																
1961	3.50	1.96	36.00	0.09	2.29	5.41	3.66	4.24	1.88	2.47	6.28	3.32	7.78	5.62	7.53	7.95
1971	3.63	1.10	27.65	0.07	2.13	5.99	3.65	4.48	1.76	4.56	7.52	2.64	8.90	13.40	6.69	5.81
Madras																
1961	5.18	8.19	14.40	0.01	.10	7.54	6.70	10.30	2.03	0.73	2.80	2.27	8.37	2.65	19.48	9.23
1971	5.18	5.27	9.57	0.21	.01	8.86	6.90	9.41	1.86	3.01	4.40	1.76	7.76	10.57	19.18	6.03
Calcutta																
1961	6.83	5.43	2.18	4.52	.61	7.40	7.08	9.51	5.68	2.98	6.04	4.28	13.50	7.44	5.15	11.00
1971	7.79	2.31	0.82	3.79	.06	8.57	6.41	9.12	7.44	5.01	5.87	3.83	9.54	15.14	7.97	6.33

TABLE 15.6: Sectoral distribution of workers in manufacturing industries in the metropoles (1961 and 1971)

Metropole	*Year*	*Consumption goods industries*	*Intermediate goods industries*	*Capital goods industries*	*Manufacturing as percentage of total workforce*
1	*2*	*3*	*4*	*5*	*6*
Delhi	1961	54.31	30.12	15.48	22.66
	1971	64.38	19.57	16.04	23.98
Bombay	1961	75.74	12.87	11.39	40.98
	1971	67.69	17.59	14.71	42.29
Madras	1961	61.93	15.94	22.13	26.94
	1971	54.94	18.04	27.01	29.64
Calcutta	1961	73.02	19.05	7.93	25.98
	1971	64.22	19.72	16.05	39.07

TABLE 15.7 : **Percentage of workers engaged in different activities of tertiary sector in the metropolitan cities of India (percentage in terms of total tertiary workers)**

Metropole	*Social and overhead*	*Personal profes-sional (2a)*	*Services non-profes-sional (2b)*	*Community services*	*Financial activities*	*Distributive services in whole-sale services trade*	*Retail trade*	*Unspecified workers**
1961								
Calcutta	35.5	3.1	22.3	2.5	4.6	4.6	21.7	5.6
Bombay	37.5	3.4	22.2	2.3	5.5	3.6	22.2	3.2
Delhi	44.9	2.9	13.3	2.5	2.9	3.4	20.6	9.3
Madras	36.3	3.7	15.3	4.1	7.1	2.4	17.4	13.4
1971								
Calcutta	35.4	3.1	21.3	2.0	7.5	6.3	24.3	
Bombay	37.8	3.6	19.3	3.7	10.0	3.5	22.6	0.35
Delhi	46.0	3.5	20.4	2.4	4.5	2.8	21.3	
Madras	57.0	2.5	12.7	3.4	3.5	1.5	19.0	

*Because of definitional changes, the figures for 1961 and 1971 are not comparable for unspecified services.

i A significant proportion of the sector workers are unskilled or semi-skilled and are engaged in activities which are labour intensive such as retail trade and non-professional personal services.

ii The social and economic overhead services continue to account for a major share of the tertiary sector.

iii The share of personal services, the second largest component of the tertiarv sector, has decreased in all the metropoles except Delhi. The increase in the case of Delhi is largely due to non-professional personal services.

vi In all the metropoles the share of distributive activities, the third largest component of the tertiary sector, has increased. This increase is mainly confined to the retail trade.

v The share of workers in financial activities, which are mainly city functions, has almost doubled in all the metropoles, except in the case of Madras.

The growth of the tertiary sector to a position of dominance within the economy of the Indian metropolitan cities is neither a symptom of nor an inducement to economic development. On the contrary this proliferation is a symptom of economic stagnation and under-development.

One may conclude from this study that the deep seated disequilibrium and asymmetrical growth of the tertiary sector, which characterise the economy of Indian metropolises during the last two decades, are displayed in the characteristics and processes of contemporary urbanisation in the country. The tertiary sector of the metropolitan cities may be characterised as a parasite feeding on the host of a distorted, imbalanced and inefficient urban economy. Its growth remains dysfunctional in relation to the process of economic development and in fact, it further reinforces the crisis of metropolitan cities of India.

METROPOLITAN DOMINANCE IN COMMODITY FLOWS

In this section, we bring out some of the important characteristics of metropolitan freight, with a view to validate our hypotheses relating to metropolitan dominance in commodity flows. The preliminary base is provided by the consideration of freight characteristics of nine million cities. These characteristics have been presented in Table 15.8 and Table 15.9.

The dominance of nine million cities in the total freight is quite clear from Table 15.8. Although there are 6775 nodes served by the railways, the share of originating and terminating freight of the nine million cities in the national freight is nearly 7.5 per cent and 18.6 per cent respectively. This is so inspite of the fact that only 5 per cent of the total population lives in these metropoles.

Among the nine million cities, the dominance of the four largest metropolises of Bombay. Calcutta, Madras and Delhi is evident. Except for Delhi, the remaining three nodes are port towns, which were developed into satellitic primate cities during the British regime in India. Nearly 61 per cent of the total shipments from the metropoles originate from Bombay and Calcutta.

The nature of spatial linkages is strongly related to the size of the metropole. It has been observed that the larger the size of the metropole, the larger is the number of interactions both in terms of originating and terminating freight. Calcutta, the largest among the metropoles has the highest number of interactions in terms of shipments and receipts. Out of 6775 nodes in India, it interacts with as many as 3076 for shipments and with 2442 for receipts. The correlation between the size of the metropole and the number of spatial linkages is as high as 0.91 for orignating 0.92 for terminating freight. These correlations are significant at 99 per cent level of confidence.

The degree of forward linkages measured in terms of originating interactions are much larger than the degree of backward linkages measured in terms of receiving interactions. This phenomenon is particularly true for the four largest metropoles

TABLE 15.8 : **Metropolitan Commodity flow characteristics**

S. No.	Name of metropole	*% share of freight in Metropoles*		*All India*		*Interactions*		*Average Distance*		*Average flow per interaction (100 tonnes)*	
		Orig	*Term*	*Orig*	*Term*	*Orig*	*Term*	*Orig*	*Term*	*Orig*	*Term*
1.	Calcutta	18.57	27.89	1.38	5.19	3076	2442	804	528	0.81	3.96
2.	Bombay	42.53	18.22	3.16	3.39	2998	2347	764	883	1.92	2.62
3.	Delhi	4.98	15.91	0.37	2.96	2414	2065	893	882	0.28	2.62
4.	Madras	18.57	14.24	1.38	2.65	1809	1567	574	630	1.38	3.11
5.	Kanpur	7.94	5.10	0.59	0.95	1782	1510	506	650	0.60	1.14
6.	Ahmedabad	0.96	3.28	0.07	0.61	788	932	709	834	0.16	1.19
7.	Hyderabad	3.23	5.00	0.24	0.93	1260	1221	374	458	0.35	1.38
8.	Bangalore	2.14	3.65	0.15	0.68	1301	1091	680	677	0.21	1.12
9.	Pune	1.08	6.74	0.08	1.26	1114	1185	647	489	0.14	1.93

Table 15.9 : **Commodity-wise distribution of metropolitan and non-metropolitan flows (1973-74)**

S. No.	Commodity group		Metropole flows as a percentage of national flows										
			Calcutta	*Bombay*	*Delhi*	*Madras*	*Kanpur*	*Ahmedabad*	*Hyderabad*	*Bangalore*	*Pune*	*% all metropoles (Col. 13-11)*	*% non-metropolitan flows*
1	*2*		*3*	*4*	*5*	*6*	*7*	*8*	*9*	*10*	*11*	*12*	*13*
1.	Food products	(O)	1.49	4.37	1.38	2.50	0.24	0.10	0.66	0.30	0.18	11.22	88.78
1.	—do—	(R)	8.38	5.48	3.88	1.59	0.69	0.49	1.55	1.51	1.07	24.63	75.37
3.	Raw materials	(O)	0.20	0.22	1.07	0.11	0.05	0.12	0.07	0.04	0.001	0.88	99.12
4.	—do—	(R)	5.50	2.14	0.62	5.87	0.38	0.21	0.18	0.11	3.38	18.39	81.61
5.	Coal fuel	(O)	0.49	2.26	0.003	1.35	0.73	0.002	0.001	0.11	0.001	4.95	95.05
6.	—do—	(R)	3.95	0.96	3.76	1.37	1.18	0.84	1.01	0.60	0.36	13.66	86.34
7.	Inputs into agri.	(O)	2.36	7.42	0.76	3.63	2.21	0.11	0.39	0.17	0.07	17.12	82.88
8.	—do—	(R)	1.05	4.62	0.69	0.49	0.45	0.14	0.37	0.37	0.30	8.49	91.51
9.	Cons. materials	(O)	0.55	4.59	0.17	1.53	0.01	0.03	0.57	0.002	0.01	7.46	92.54
10.	—do—	(R)	5.54	4.54	4.08	2.51	1.06	0.88	1.46	1.28	1.03	22.37	77.63
11.	Ind. product	(O)	8.95	5.56	0.76	1.69	0.24	0.09	0.35	0.42	0.13	18.18	81.82
12.	—do—	(R)	9.26	7.59	5.15	3.47	2.14	1.17	1.74	1.35	0.56	32.43	67.57
13.	Total originating		1.38	3.16	0.37	1.38	0.59	0.07	0.24	0.15	0.08	7.43	92.57
14.	Total terminating		5.19	3.39	2.96	2.65	0.95	0.61	0.93	0.68	1.26	18.61	81.39

O=Originating
R=Receipts

that is Delhi, Calcutta, Bombay and Madras. The reversal of this trend is significant only in the case of Ahmedabad, where interactions for receipts tend to be significantly larger as compared to those of shipments.

The dominance of metropolitan flows in the various commodities is also quite evident. The metropolitan share in the national freight is disproportionately high. 32.4 per cent of industrial products, 24.6 per cent of food products and 22 per cent of construction materials terminate in the million cities. The only exception is provided by the shipments of raw materials and fuels which are mainly the produce of the hinterland.

The relative location of metropolitan centres with reference to localised distribution of fuels, minerals and other primary raw material is reflected in the average distance of movement. In general, the spatial dispersion of metropolitan receipts is larger than that of the shipments. This is so because the raw materials and other primary goods are usually received from a large catchment area. Calcutta and Pune are the only exceptions where the average distance of receipts is significantly lower than the average distance of shipments. While the former is located close to the fuel and resource rich regions, the flow patterns of the latter are modified by the shadow of Bombay.

As has been observed earlier, the interaction variables are a function of the size of the metropole. The larger the size of the metropole, the larger would be the number of linkages. What becomes crucially important in the analysis of metropole-hinterland flows is the differentials in the average receipts and average shipments. The average receipts are consistently larger as compared to average shipments. While the average shipments per interaction indicate the extent of the diffusion process, the average receipts per interactions are a measure of pull exerted by different metropoles on their respective hinterlands. In the present context, it is interesting to note that as the size of the metropole increase the intensity of pull towards the metropole also increases. The correlation coefficient between city size and the average receipts per node is as high as 0.88—significant at 99 per cent level. This, is, however, not true of the degree of diffusion which does not appear to be strongly responsive to metropolitan size. The existence of such a phenomenon essentially shows the dichotomy in the bi-directional role of the metropolitan cities. While, on the one hand, the primate cities of India continue to appropriate large surpluses from the hinterland, they fail to act as generators or channels for transmission of growth impluses.

The inter-metropolitan exchange dominates the commodity flow patterns of the metropolitan centres inspite of the large distance separating them. It is interesting to note that 12.8 per cent of the shipments from the metropoles terminate in metropolitan centres themselves. In the case of industrial products, the share of inter-metropolitan flows is as high as 21.6 per cent of the total industrial products originating from the metropolitan cities. Commodity-wise share of 'lateral' or metropole to metropole flows in the total shipments of metropolitan centres is shown in Table 15.10 :

The dominance of the metropolitan cities in the Indian economic space is thus evident from the above discussion. It has also been shown that at the metropolitan level there is a strong tendency for lateral flows, that is, flows at the same level of the hierarchy.

TABLE 15.10 : **Share of metropolitan-metropolitan flows to total metropolitan shipments**

Commodity group	*Originating freight from metropoles ('000 tonnes)*	*Metropole to metropole flows ('000 tonnes)*	*Metropole flow as proportions of total metropole originating*
Total freight	13496	1731	12.83
Food products	2307	372	16.16
Raw materials	373	77	20.64
Fuels	3634	276	7.59
Inputs into agriculture	2227	80	3.59
Construction materials	1015	80	7.89
Industrial products	2229	482	21.62

Following the gross features emerging from the analysis of commodity composition of metropolitan freight, we now proceed to examine the magnitude and the direction of individual flows from and to the metropoles. Such an analysis assumes greater significance since the preceding analysis has shown that the strength of spatial linkages not only varies from one metropole to another, but it also widely differs for shipments and receipts for the same metropole. One of the simplest methods to examine the intensity and the direction of the individual flows is to represent them with the cartographic line symbols in the form of flow maps. On the basis of dominant spatial linkages of different nodes with various metropoles, the flow maps for shipments from and

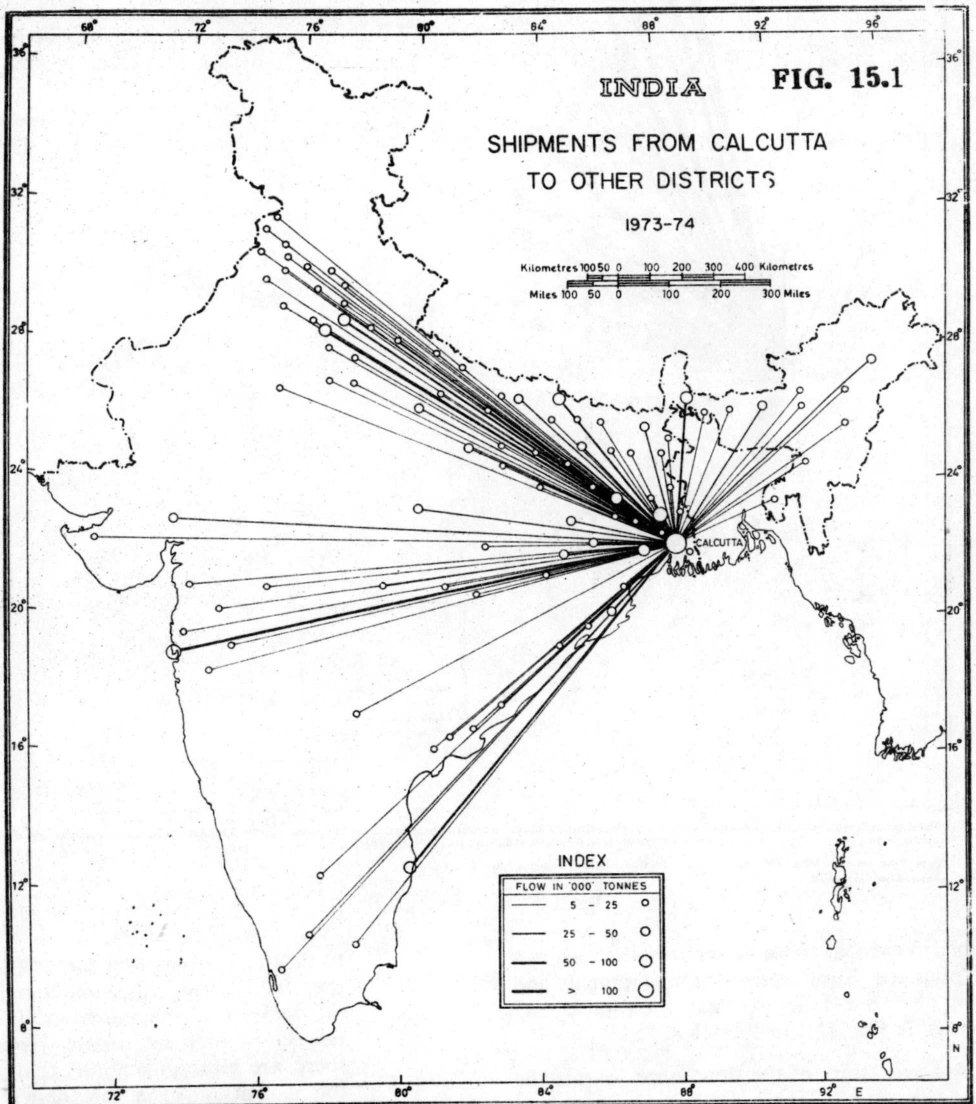

The territorial waters of India extend into the sea to a distance of twelve nautical miles measured from appropriate base line.

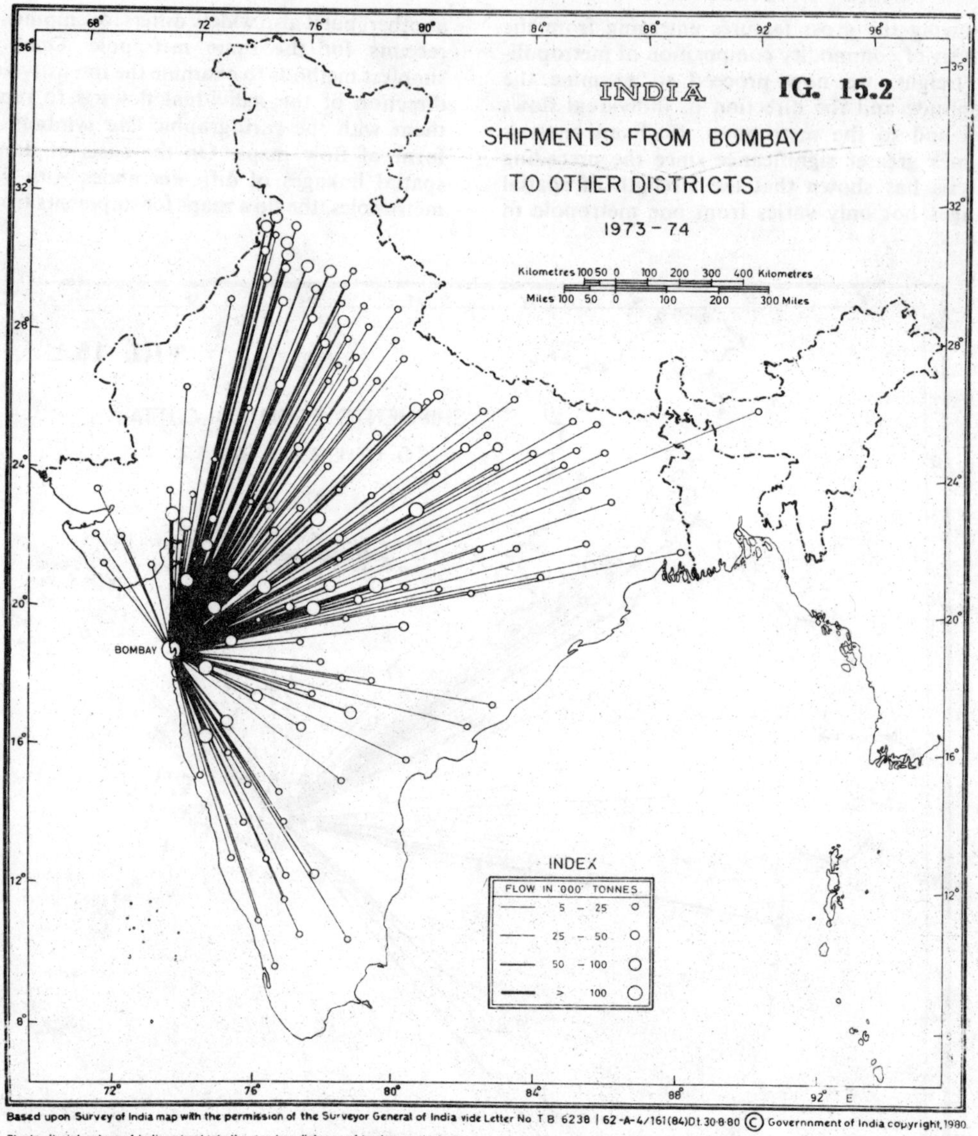

Based upon Survey of India map with the permission of the Surveyor General of India vide Letter No T B 6238 | 62-A-4/161(84)Dt.30-8-80

The territorial waters of India extend into the sea to a distance of twelve nautical miles measured from appropriate base line.

receipts to each of the nine metropolitan centres were prepared. Flow maps for the shipments and receipts for the four national metropoles are presented in Fig. 15.1 to Fig. 15.8.

A Close study of the flow maps reveals the following :

i These maps, by themselves, do not lead to the delineation of the hinterlands, as they fail to bring out dominant spatial linkages of all the areal units with respect to each metropole. However, there are clear indications that with the exception of a few nodes each metropole has its own hinterland with which it mostly interacts.

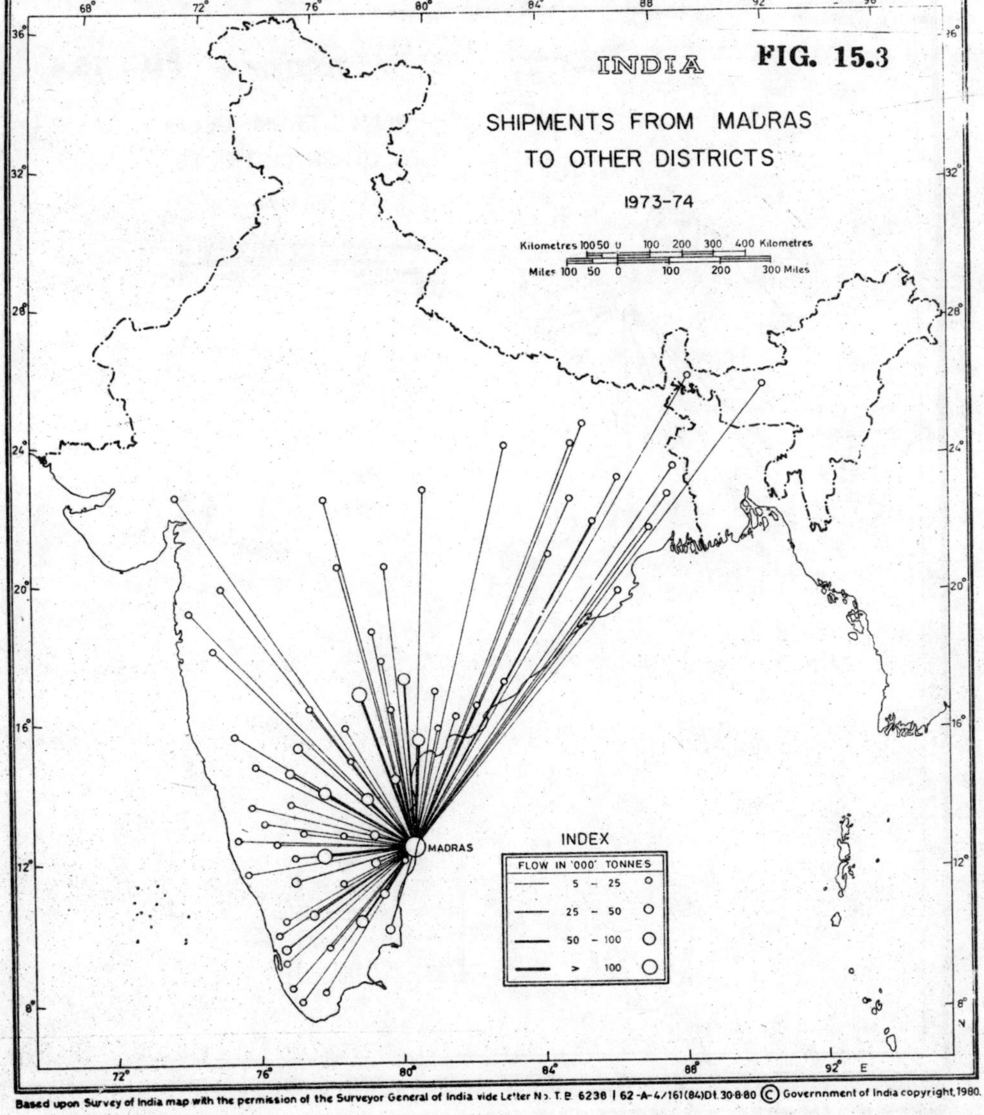

Based upon Survey of India map with the permission of the Surveyor General of India vide Letter No. T.B. 6238 / 62-A-4/161(84)Dt.30-8-80 © Government of India copyright,1980.

The territorial waters of India extend into the sea to a distance of twelve nautical miles measured from appropriate base line.

ii The differentials in the pattern, magnitude and the direction of flows are not only marked for different metropoles but also vary for shipments and receipts of the same metropole. Thus, it can be argued that different metropoles are selective about the pattern of their shipments and receipts. A detailed analysis of the pattern of interaction of shipments and receipts with different areal units would show the manner in which the space economy is organised in terms of the 'upward', 'downward' and 'lateral' flows.

iii In view of the fact that there is a strong tendency for metropolitan centres to interact with a different set of nodes for

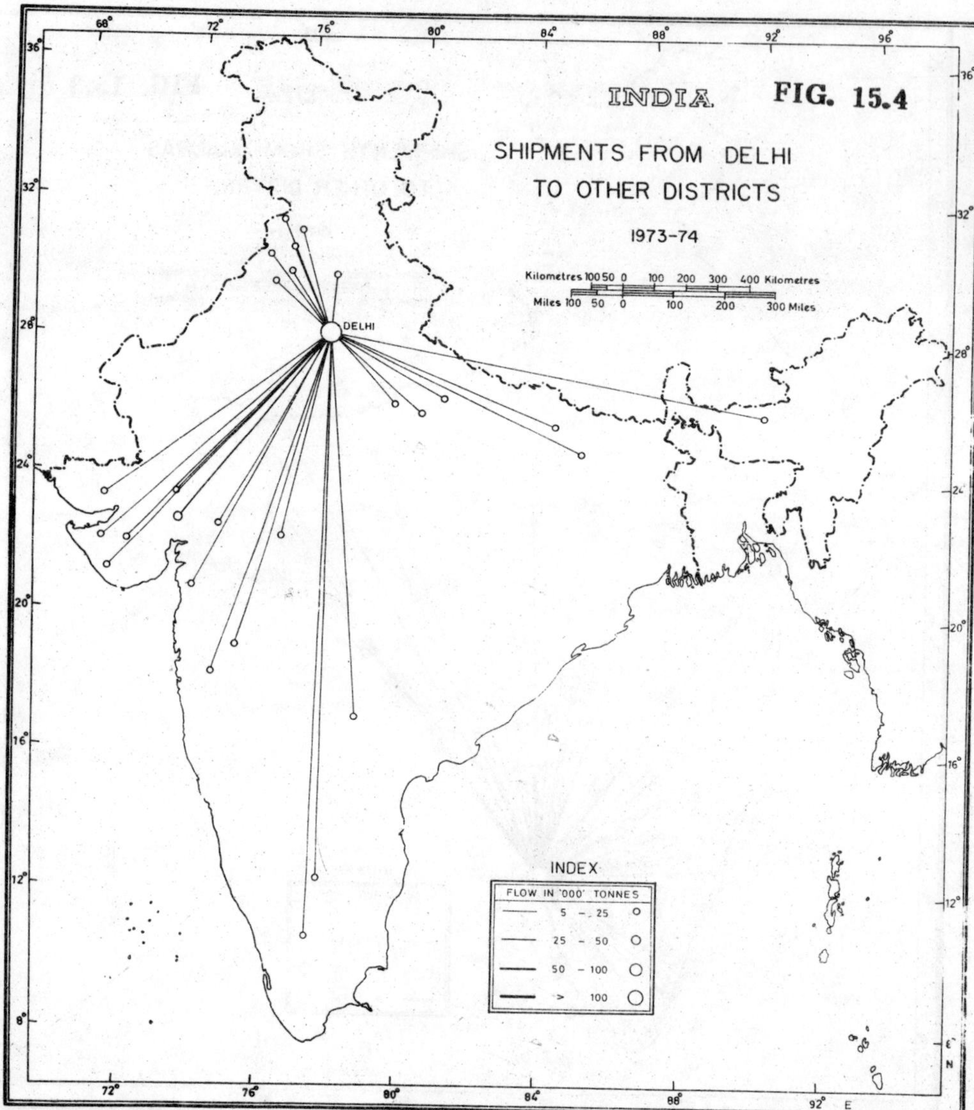

Based upon Survey of India map with the permission of the Surveyor General of India vide Letter No. T. B. 6238 | 62-A-4/161(84)Dt. 30-8-80 © Government of India copyright, 198
The territorial waters of India extend into the sea to a distance of twelve nautical miles measured from appropriate base line.

shipments and receipts, it can be argued that each metropole has its own area of catchment as well as of influence. The range and rates of distance decay would, therefore, be different not only for different metropoles but also for shipment and receipts of the same metropole. However, what is crucially important from the view point of this study is the shape of the distance-freight curve for shipments and receipts. Since the superimposition of one on the other would bring out the tendency of metropolitan centres to receive from and ship to different areal units.

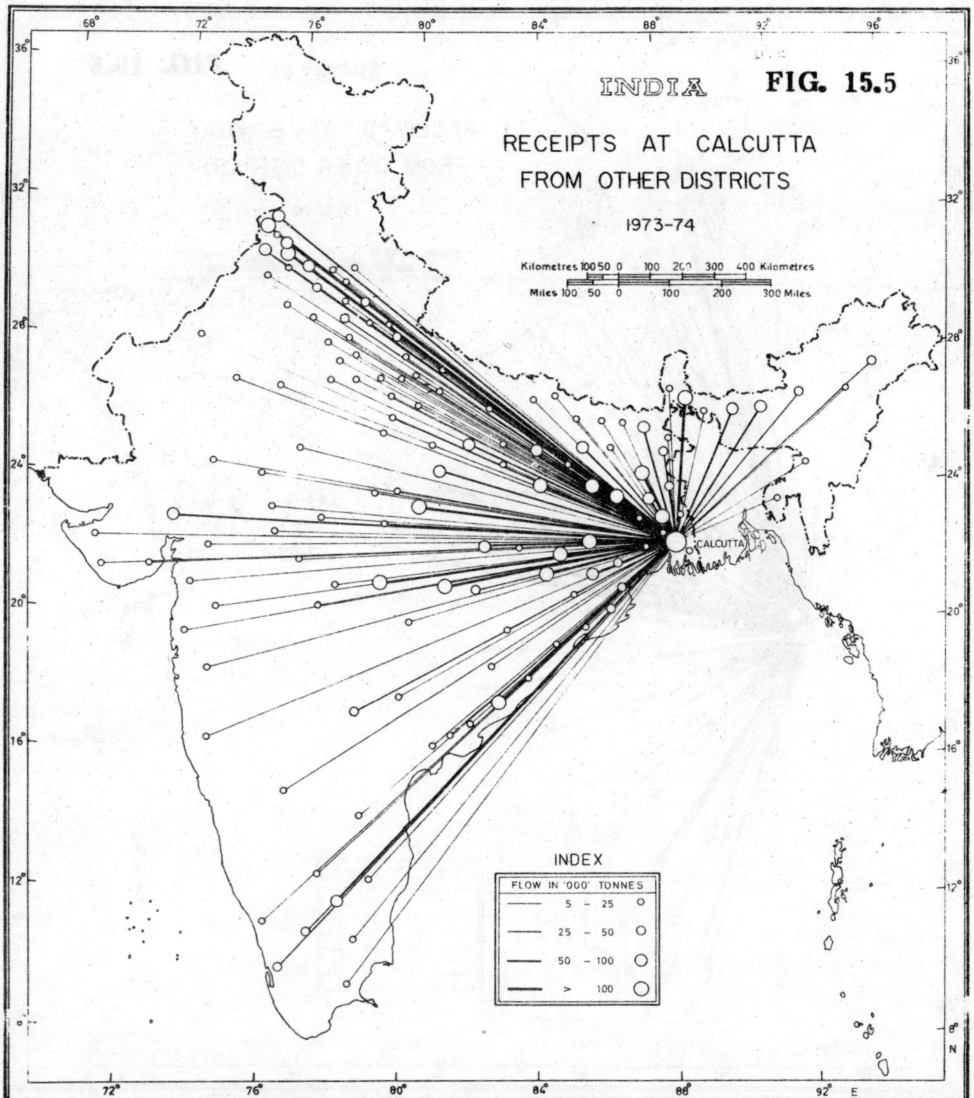

Based upon Survey of India map with the permission of the Surveyor General of India vide Letter No. T.B. 6238 | 62-A-4/161(84)D1.30-8-80 © Government of India copyright, 1980.

The territorial waters of India extend into the sea to a distance of twelve nautical miles measured from appropriate base line.

The above analysis of flow maps has evidently brought out some major characteristics of commodity flows, which need to be examined in detail so as to unravel the role of metropolitan centres in the spatial organisation of the Indian economy. The foregoing analysis is a step in this direction.

METROPOLES AND THEIR HINTERLANDS

The flow maps have clearly shown that there is a tendency, exhibited by some nodes, to channel their interactions in such a manner that they fall under the orbit of influence of two or more metropoles. For a meaningful analysis of the inter-metropolitan and metropole-hinterland flows with

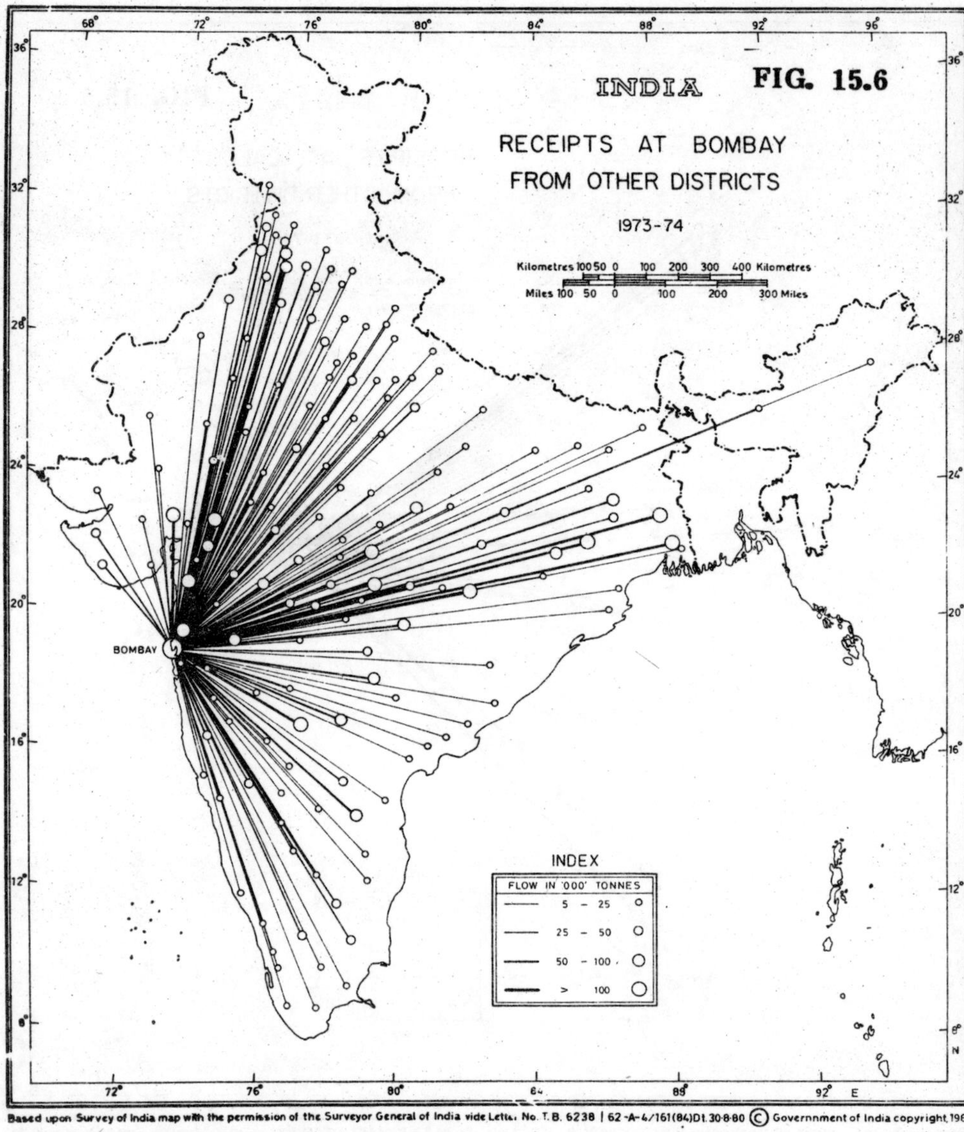

respect to the composition of the freight exchange, it is necessary to delineate the hinterlands of various metropoles. This has been achieved in the following manner

A specific symbol was allotted to each metropole and all stations having dominant linkages in terms of the volume of commodity flows were plotted with that symbol. It may, however, be noted that for the purpose of delineating the hinterlands, stations having a total flow of 5000 tonnes or less were not considered. The hinterlands were then delineated by drawing a line connecting the midpoints of two sets of symbols.

A close study of the map revealed that while, Delhi and Kanpur have common shippers and receivers and thus may be considered to have a common bi-nodal metropolitan hinterland, the

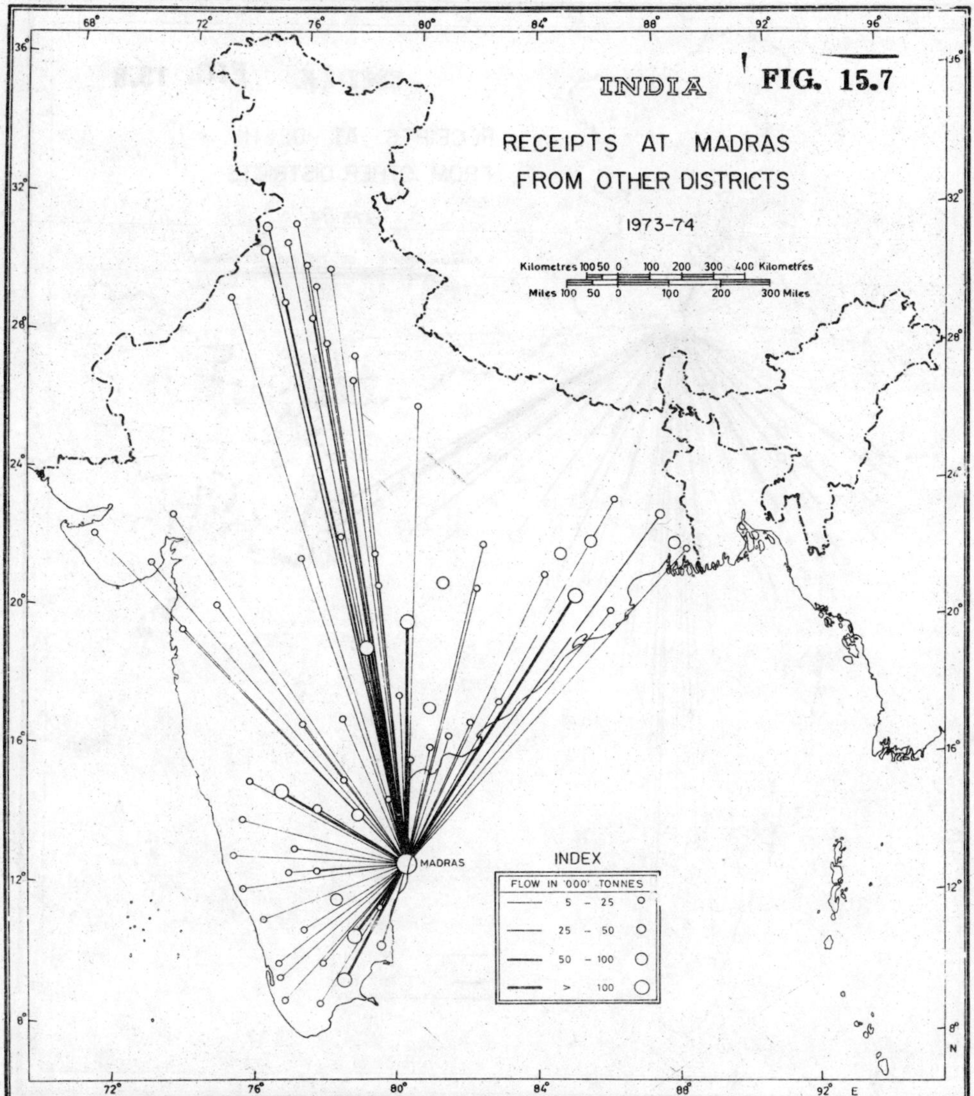

Based upon Survey of India map with the permission of the Surveyor General of India vide Letter No. T. B. 6238 | 62-A-4/161(84)Dt 30-8-80 © Government of India copyright, 1980.

The territorial waters of India extend into the sea to a distance of twelve nautical miles measured from appropriate base line.

four metropolitan centres of Ahmedabad, Pune, Hyderabad and Bangalore, are in reality assimilated within the hinterland of the four major metropoles. As a consequence, Ahmedabad and Pune got linked to Bombay, while Bangalore and Hyderabad were linked to the metropole of Madras.

The line of demarcation was then adjusted to the district boundaries. Finally we were left with four metropolitan centres : Bombay Calcutta, Madras and Delhi and their mutually exclusive hinterlands. The metropoles and their respective boundaries are shown in Fig. 15.9. The demographic as well as other characteristics within the different hinterlands as delineated above, have

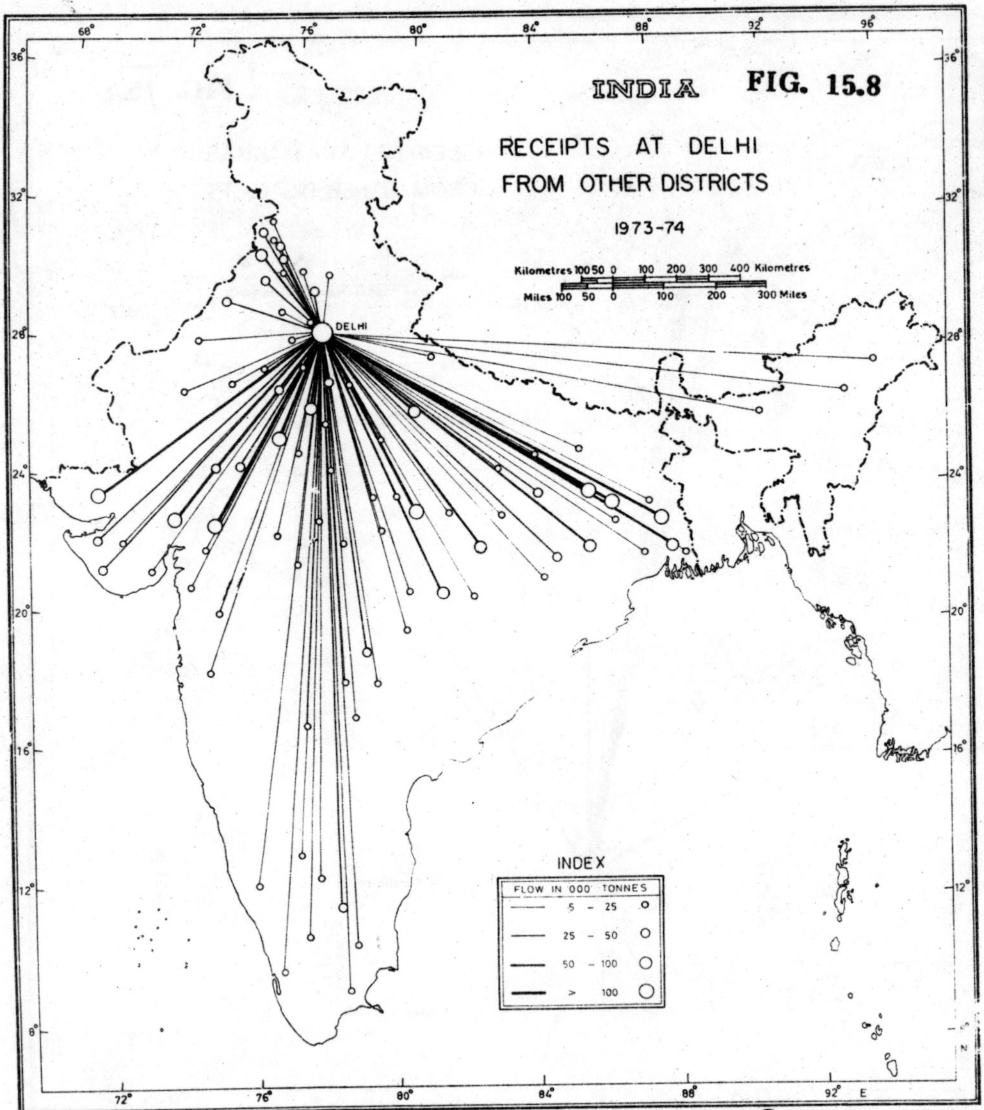

Based upon Survey of India map with the permission of the Surveyor General of India vide Letter No. T. B. 6238 / 62-A-4/161(84)Dt 30-8-80

The territorial waters of India extend into the sea to a distance of twelve nautical miles measured from appropriate base line.

been examined through Table 15.11, wherein the settlement distribution, population, area and other major characteristics of the four hinterlands are presented.

METROPOLITAN FREIGHT AND SPATIAL LINKAGES

In order to unravel the ways in which the various units interact, an analysis of the pattern of spatial interaction for shipments and receipts of freight from and to the metropolitan centres has been undertaken. In the first instance only those flows have been considered which individually exceed a thousand tonnes annually between a metropolitan centre and the various districts of the country The districts have been classified according to their levels of development.[5]

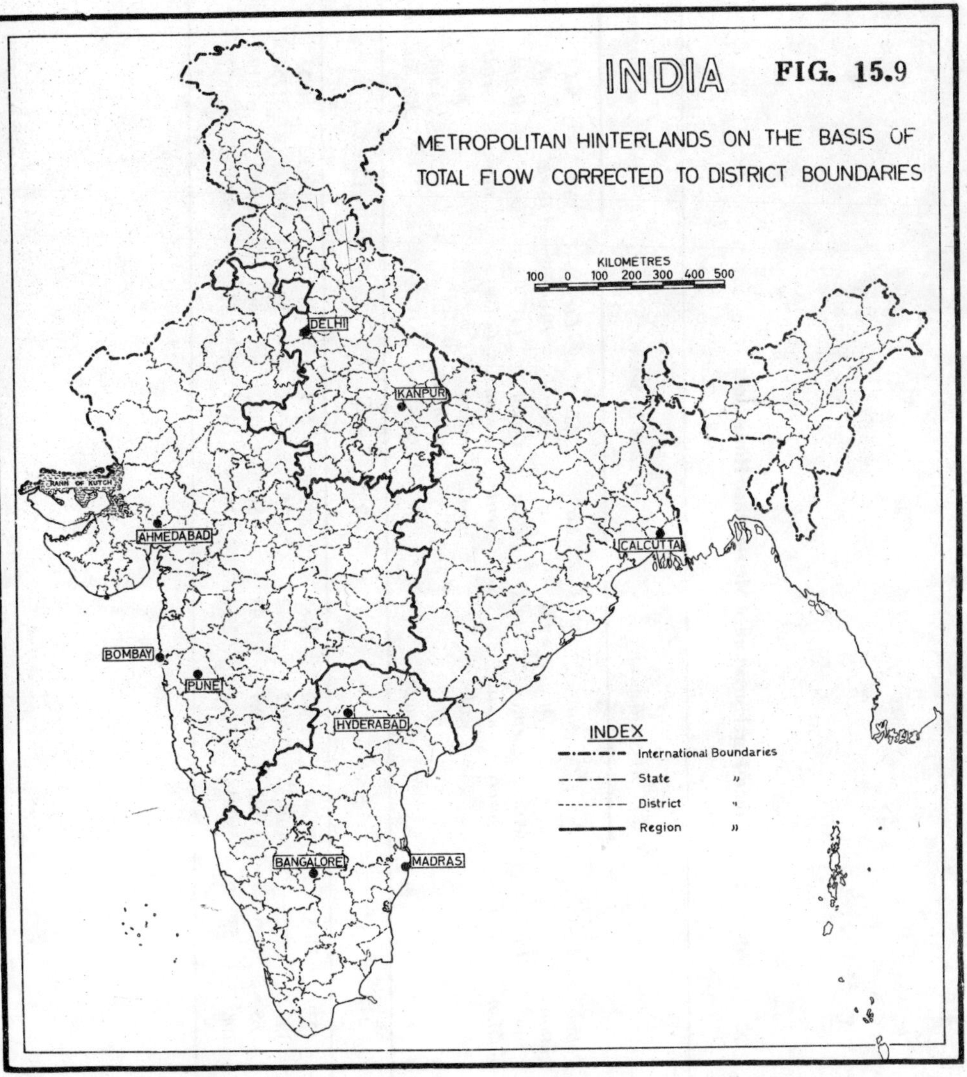

FIG. 15.9

METROPOLITAN HINTERLANDS ON THE BASIS OF TOTAL FLOW CORRECTED TO DISTRICT BOUNDARIES

In an aggregated manner the flows originating from the four metropolitan places, and terminating in different districts in the four categories of development were tabulated. In a similar manner, the flows terminating in the metropolitan centres and originating from different districts were tabulated for all the categories (refer Appendix XIII). The districts, on the basis of their levels of development were classified into four categories. The proportion of excess of receipts over shipments for each metropolitan centre and for the four categories of districts were calculated by combining these two tables[5] (see Table 15.12).

The Table 15.12 evidently brings out the high degree of capillary movement in the space economy wherein commodity exchanges occur through upward movement from poorly developed areas to metropolitan centres. One cannot fail to notice the excess of receipts over shipments, at each successive lower levels of development in the districts. This is indicative of the pattern where the

TABLE 15.11 : **Urban-Rural Structure of Metropolitan Hinterlands**

S. No.	Hinterland	Total area in Sq. Kms.	Population in (million)	No. of Districts	All Settlements			Total U. Settle.			Total Rural Settlements		
					No. of settlements	No. of settlements with Rly Station	% of Col. 7 to 6	No. of Urban settlement.	No. of Urban settlements with Rly Station	Col. 10 as % to Col. 9	No. of Rural settlements	No of Rural settlement with Rly. Station	% of Col. 13 to 12
1	2	3	4	5	6	7	8	9	10	11	12	13	14
1.	Bombay	1147023	123	105	129242	2362	1.83	879	509	58	128363	1853	1.44
2.	Calcutta	874270	199	92	270162	2125	0.78	623	367	59	270339	1758	0.65
3.	Delhi–Kanpur	625975	85	80	117502	1089	0.93	451	272	60	117051	817	0.70
4.	Madras	511041	108	53	55095	1194	2.17	576	317	55	54519	877	1.61

TABLE 15.12 : **Proportion of excess of receipts over shipments to the shipments**

Districts in Development Level	*Bombay*	*Delhi*	*Calcutta*	*Madras*
Low	0.44	22.15	4.44	3.93
Medium	1.77	27.48	2.76	3.11
High	—0.18	10.23	7.97	0.34
Very high	—0.42	1.50	0.83	—0.83

metropolitan centres tend to receive proportionally more freight from the areas in lower levels of development than they do from the areas in the higher level of development. Delhi and Calcutta present the unique case where the excess of receipts decrease successively with increase in the levels of development of the various districts with which it interacts. In the case of Bombay and Madras shipments to highly developed districts exceed the respective receipts. Thus the pattern of shipments and receipts is an indication of the suction mechanism embedded in the process of spatial integration of the metropolitan centres.

METROPOLITAN FREIGHT AND DISTANCE CHARACTERISTICS

The foregoing analysis has shown that the pattern of interaction of metropolitan centres is selective. There is an evidently strong tendency for metropoli-tan centres to receive freight from poorly developed areas and ship their (metropolitan centres) freight to areas in the higher levels of development. Since the better developed areas occur in pockets surrounded by large areas of poor development, the distance-freight relationship cannot be one of a smooth distance-decay pattern, but one where the shipments and receipts of metropolitan centres when plotted against distance must reveal a series of 'troughs' and 'peaks' Consequently, the 'troughs' of metropolitan shipments would be juxtaposed by the peaks of metropolitan receipts and vice-versa. To verify this relationship between freight and distance, average shipments and receipts of each of the four metropolitan centres to various districts falling in different distance bands were plotted and are shown in Figs. 15.10 to 15.13. The graphs thus plotted clearly validate the expected 'troughs' and 'peaks' pattern of distance decay of the metropolitan freight. It is also clear that generally the tendency is towards a juxtaposition of 'troughs' of shipments on 'peaks' of receipts and vice-versa.

Although this pattern is valid generally for all metropolitan centres, the peaks appear at different distances for each of the four metropolitan centres. This has largely to do with the type of commodities that dominate their receipts and shipments. For example, dominance of fuel (a localised product) occurring in the distance range of 900 to 1200 kms. (Fig. 15.11). Conversely, since Calcutta is located near the industrial region of south-eastern India and because its receipts are dominated by industrial products, the highest 'peak' occur within 200 kms. (Fig. 15.12). On the other hand, Madras and Bombay tend to reveal a series of well defined 'peaks' and 'troughs' of shipments and receipts throughout various distance ranges. The higher peaks both in the case of Bombay and Madras are to be found within 500 kms. (Figs. 15.10 and 15.13).

Thus the dominant pattern of spatial links in the Indian economy is best described by flows originating from poorly developed areas and terminating at metropolitan centres and exchange of goods between metropolitan centres and freight originating at metropolitan centres and terminating at areas of higher development. Thus within the nodal hierarchy, the movements are upward from the hinterland nodes at the lower levels and lateral at higher levels.

INEQUITIES OF METROPOLIS-HINTERLAND COMMODITY FLOWS

Following the analysis of commodity composition of metropolitan freight, we now proceed a step further in our analysis and try to identify the level at which the 'upward' and 'downward' flows in the hierarchy of settlements deviate from the normative system. We are restricting this analysis firstly, to the four largest metropolises of Bombay, Calcutta, Delhi and Madras, whose dominance in the metropolitan flows has already been brought out and secondly, to the originating and terminating flows in terms of only two commodity groups, that is, raw materials from primary sources

FIG. 15.10

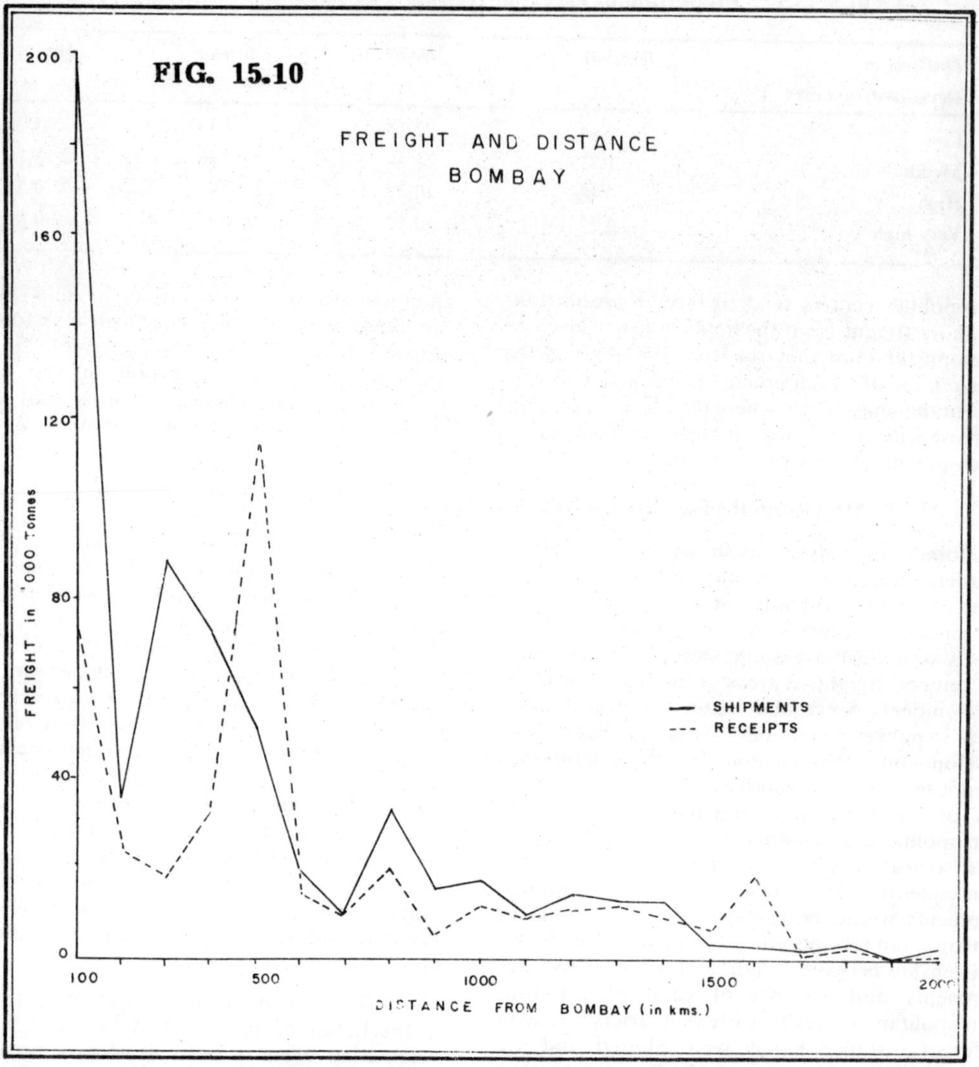

and industrial products, which bring out inter-sectoral relationships most effectively. The first commodity is generated predominantly from the hinterland, while the latter is produced in the urban segment. If the rural-urban interactions are symbiotic and not exploitative, the products of the primary sector would be shipped from the rural to the urban sector in the form of food and raw materials in exchange for wage goods, which would be shipped from urban centres to the rural areas. In the context of such a model, it should be possible to assess the empirical evidence. With this end in view, we have examined the flows from each of the our metropolitan centres to the nodes at various levels of the settlement hierarchy and vice-versa. The results are presented in Table 15.13. The classification of nodes is as under :

	Type of settlement	*Population*
i	Rural (R)	All rural population
ii	Urban class I cities (U_1)	1,00,000 and above
iii	Urban class II towns (U_2)	50,000—99,999

FIG. 15.11

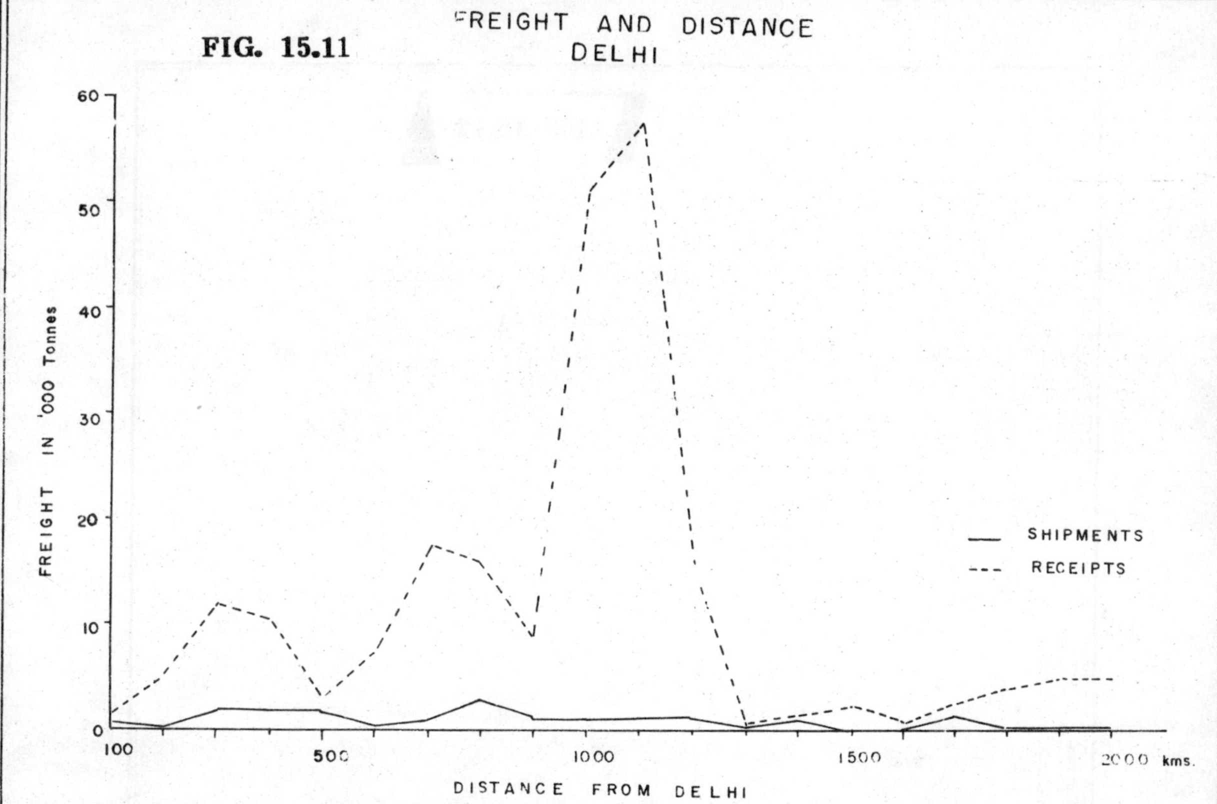

iv	Urban class III towns (U_3)	20,000—49,999
v	Urban class IV and lower order towns ($U_4+U_5+U_6$)	<20,000

While there is a strong tendency for upward flows of raw materials and the four largest metropoles receive nearly 67 per cent of raw materials from rural and small urban settlements, the flow of industrial products remains restricted to a large extent within the urban sector itself. The shipments from these centres are restricted to high order urban nodes, only a small proportion trickling down to the lower order nodes. As much as 57.53 per cent of total shipments of industrial products from the metropolitan towns terminate in large (U_1) urban nodes and only 6.61 per cent terminate in medium size (U_2) urban areas and only 18 per cent in the vast rural hinterland accounting for about 80 per cent of the population of the country. The strength of downward flow from the metropolitan centres to the lower order settlements is thus very weak and anaemic as compared to upward flows which tend to be quite strong.

There are significant inter-metropole variations in this respect. Delhi, for example, has a weak industrial base and share of its shipments of raw materials to its satellite industrial towns in its total shipments is as high as 27.8 per cent. The variations in the nature of the strong upward flows is influenced by the differentials in the economic base of the metropoles, their relative location and the nature of their hinterland. While Calcutta receives most of its raw materials from small towns (49.6 per cent) and the rural periphery (24.2 per cent), Madras receives its largest share from the rural periphery only that is 67.4 per cent. In view of the lack of feedbacks to the lower order centres, the influence of these factors is not marked the case of lateral and downward movement.

Inequities of metropolitan-hinterland relationships in terms of commodity flows are thus evident from the analysis presented above. Though there are significant inter-metropole variations in commodity flow patterns, the rural-urban flows indicate a fragmentation of the national market. While there is a strong tendency for upward low, the downward flows are weak and anaemic. —

FIG. 15.12

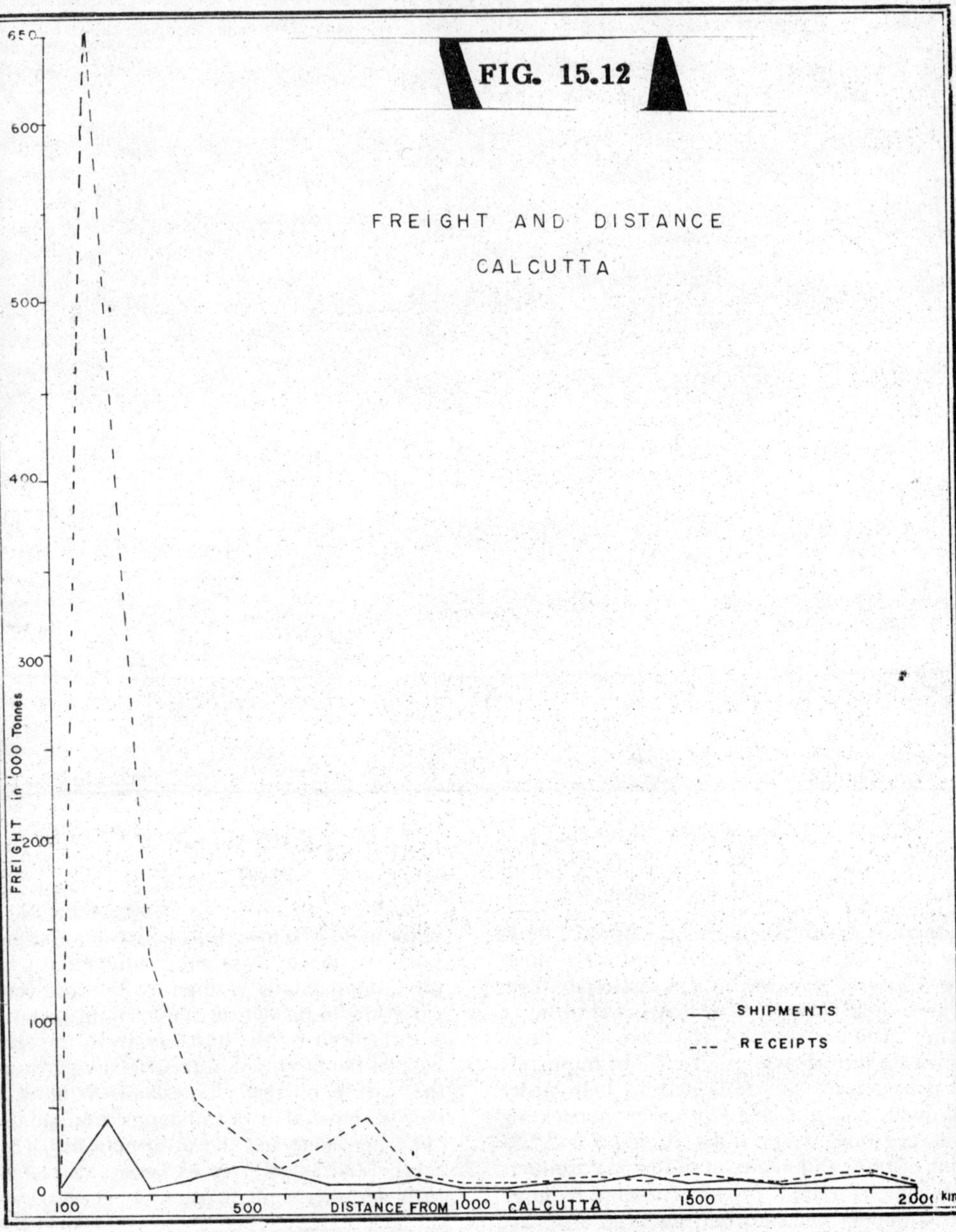

CONSUMPTION ORIENTED NATURE OF METROPOLITAN CENTRES

The analysis of commodity-wise shipments and receipts provides us with a meaningful tool to validate our hypothesis related to the consumption oriented nature of the metropolitan economies. The share of the metropolitan shipments to total originating and terminating freight is shown in col. 12 of Table 15.9. Except for inputs into agriculture (which receives greater proportion of originating tonnage because of high imports of fertilizers), receipts dominate over shipments in all other commodity groups. Bombay provides an exception to the general receipt dominant pattern in the

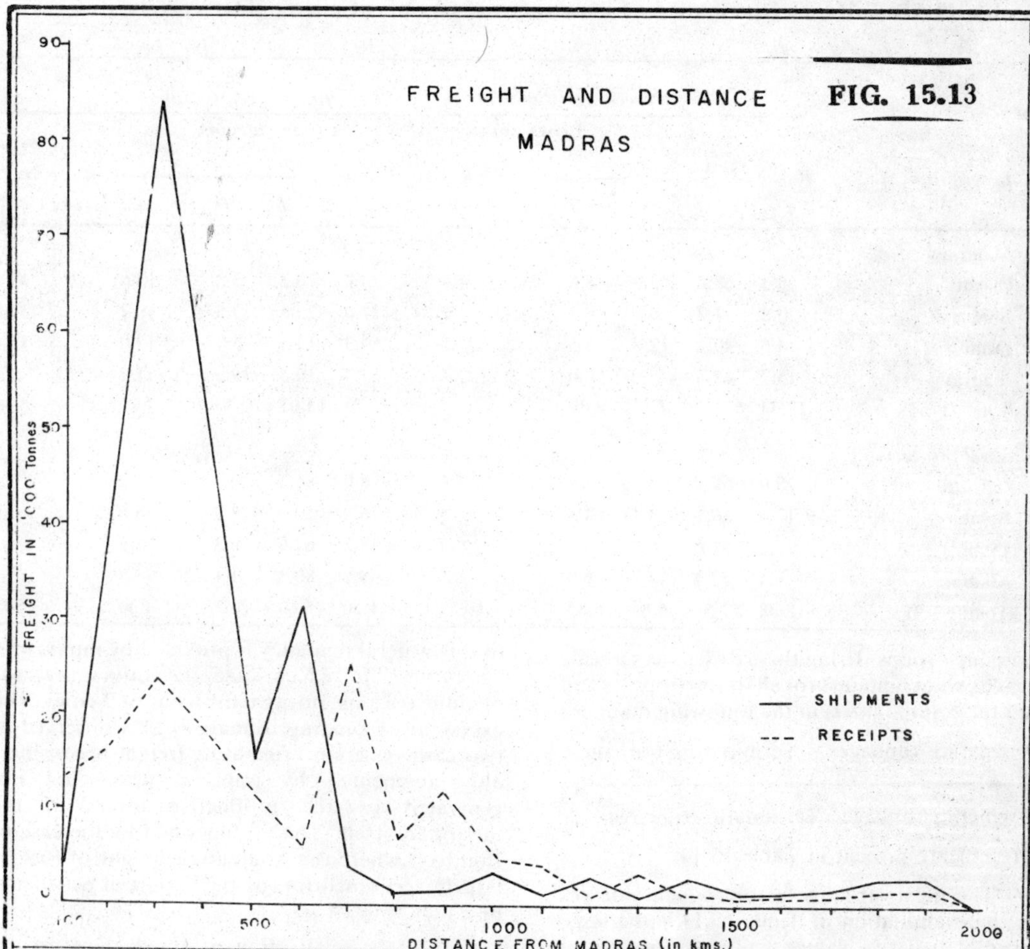

FIG. 15.13

case of fuels, as the originating tonnage is bloated due to imported petroleum products.

The most striking feature that emerges from the study of the table is the consistent dominance of receipts over shipments irrespective of the nature of the product, be it a hinterland produce (like food products and raw materials) or metropolitan urban products (industrial products and construction materials). A reversal of the pattern is noticed only in the case of inputs into agriculture which has to be ultimately consumed in the rural hinterland and of which the metropolitan centres have little use. The fact that industrial products account for the largest share of the metropolitan shipments (18%) as compared to other commodity groups is easily offset by the highest share of the same group in their receipts (32%)

Since cities are not the producers of food and raw materials from primary sources, the metropolitan receipts of these two commodities are for obvious reasons, much larger than their shipments. However, many of these cities also ship food products on a significant scale. This indicates that side by side with being large consumers of food, they also act as import, collection and distribution centres for this commodity group. Madras is the only centre where shipments are larger than receipts in the case of food products. In the light of this, the role of other modes of transport needs to be further examined.

The weakness of the economic base of the metropoles and their character as centres of consumption is clearly reflected in the difference between shipments and receipts of different

TABLE 15.13 : **Distribution of shipments and receipts of metropolitan centres**

S. No.	Description	Percentage shipments to: Rural	Urban category: I	II	III	Others (IV+V+VI)	Percentage receipts from: Rural	Urban category: I	II	III	Others (IV+V+VI)
I	Raw Materials										
1.	Calcutta	15.3	68.7	2.9	8.6	4.4	24.2	10.2	5.3	10.6	49.6
2.	Bombay	20.8	57.2	8.8	6.7	3.5	27.0	25.8	13.5	16.2	17.5
3.	Delhi	14.6	40.1	12.8	4.6	27.8	50.3	17.5	4.8	12.0	15.4
4.	Madras	15.7	63.3	7.6	10.0	3.4	67.4	10.5	19.3	1.7	1.1
5.	Total (1—4)	17.32	60.11	7.13	8.79	5.65	43.72	13.01	12.39	7.81	23.09
II	*Industrial products*										
6.	Calcutta	20.9	55.1	5.7	8.6	9.6	6.0	86.3	0.7	3.2	3.8
7.	Bombay	17.5	56.3	8.7	4.1	13.4	15.4	70.0	3.3	3.6	7.9
8.	Delhi	17.2	61.6	6.3	8.2	6.7	17.2	61.6	6.3	8.2	6.7
9.	Madras	8.4	72.4	4.7	6.0	8.5	9.2	80.1	1.1	3.7	5.8
10.	Total(6—9)	18.38	57.53	6.61	6.85	10.61	11.50	75.60	2.57	4.40	5.88

commodity groups. Using these differences a scale free index was computed for all the metropoles and for all the commodities, in the following manner :

$$\frac{\text{Originating tonnage} - \text{Terminating tonnage}}{\text{Originating tonnage} + \text{Terminating tonnage}}$$

The results are present in Table 15.14.

The most striking feature which emerges from the examination of Table 15.14 is the large number of negative values, indicating excess of receipts over shipments. This is also true for the commodity group like industrial goods, which are by and large, urban products. The only exception to this general tendency is provided by inputs into agriculture, in which case the values are, for obvious reasons, positive for 6 out of 9 cities. The excess of originating tonnage is also observed in two cases wherein originating freight is considerably augmented by imports, which are not generated by the productive forces of the metropole itself. This is illustrated by the case of Bombay, where the originating freight of fuel, is largely accounted for, by the import of petroleum products.

Thus the relatively weak involvement of the metropoles in the production system of the country gives them the character of centres of consumption rather than of production.

TABLE 15.14 : **Trade in the economy of nine metropolitan centres**

S. No.	Name of commodity groups	Ahmeda-bad	Bangalore	Bombay	Calcutta	Delhi	Hedera-bad	Kanpur	Madras	Pune
1	2	3	4	5	6	7	8	9	10	11
1.	Total freight	—.79	—.63	—.03	—.58	—.78	—.59	—.24	—.32	—.88
2.	Food products	—.65	—.67	—.11	—.70	—.48	—.40	—.48	+.22	—.71
3.	Raw materials from primary sources	—.26	—.50	—.82	—.93	—.79	—.44	—.77	—.96	—1.00
4.	Coal/fuel	—1.00	—.50	+.40	—.78	—1.00	—.99	—.24	—.01	—.99
5.	Inputs into agriculture	—.12	—.38	+.23	+.38	+.05	+.03	+.66	+.76	—.62
6.	Construction materials	—.94	—1.00	+.01	—.82	—.92	—.44	—.99	—.24	—.98
7	Industrial products	—.86	—.53	—.15	—.11	—.74	—.66	—.80	—.35	—.62

SUMMARY

The examination of the role played by the commodity flows from and to the metropoles in the organisation of the Indian economic space and the consequent integration of the national home market has clearly brought out that this role is greatly constrained by the inherited characteristics of the regional structure of under-development and the anaemia characterising the development process in the country. The imbalances of the space economy have generated the distorted role of the metropoles and have been themselves sustained by these distortions.

The following broad conclusions emerge from the preceding analysis of economic base and the freight characteristics of the metropolitan centres in India :

i The persistence of the primary sector, the weakness, inadequacies and distortions of the secondary sector and a huge intensity of tertiary activities are symptoms of the chronic analogy from which the Indian metropoles continue to suffer in spite of a quarter century of planned development in the country.

ii The national market operationalised by commodity flows generated through the metropoles continues to be top heavy wherein metropolitan dominance does not lead to the development of the national market as a whole.

iii Not only is the phenomenon of the distorted dominance of the metropoles well marked but even within the limited system of the metropoles themselves also, the four super metropoles, recognised by Berry in 1966, continue to play their distorting role even in the middle seventies.

iv The strength of spatial linkages and the ability to appropriate surpluses from the rest of the economy appears to be a function of the size of the city rather than of its economic base.

v Within the nodal hierarchy, the commodity flows are upward from poorly developed areas and lateral for areas with higher levels of development.

vi The strong lateral inter-metropolitan flows and the disproportionately large share of the same in the system of national flows indicates a partial fragmentation of the vertical continuum of the national market, whereby the metropolitan system is fast acquiring the character of an encapsulated world in itself. The strength of this tendency is further evidenced by the fact that lateral flows are able to overcome strong friction of distance.

vii The adverse consequences of the fragmentation mentioned above become exceptionally strong in the context of strong upward and weak downward movements in the system of flows pivoted on the metropoles.

viii The essential weakness of the Indian metropoles, which substantially contributes to the distorting role played by them in the organisation of the national economic space, lies in their economic base. Their relatively weak involvement in the production system of the country gives them the character of centres of consumption rather than of production.

It follows from the above that the role of the Indian metropoles continue to be embedded in the inherited regional structure of under-development; and its inadequacies and limitations can be removed only by transforming the essential character of the regional structure.

NOTES

1. The concept of primate cities was first put forward by Marx Jefferson in 1939 in an article entitled 'The Law of the Primate Cities, published in *Geographical Review*, Vol. 29. pp. 226-32. The concept primarily referred to the relationship in size between the largest city and other cities in a country. It was stated that there were many reasons why a city exceeds its neighbours in size but once it did, 'this mere fact gives it an impetus to grow...and it draws away from all (other cities) in character as well as in size...it becomes the primate city'. The development of the concept has been reviewed by S.K. Mehta, 'Some Demographic and Economic Correlates of Primary Cities : A case for revolution', *Demography*, 1 (1964), pp. 136-47.

2. The settlements have been classified into various categories in the following manner :—

Type of classification	*Population size*
Metropolitan cities	10,00,00 and above
Class I	1,00,000 and above
Class II	50,000—99.999
Class III	20,000—49,999
Class IV	10,000—19,999
Class V	5,000—9,999
Class VI	less than 5,000

3. According to 1971 Census, there were nine cities falling in the category of million cities, with their population greater than one million. These were Calcutta, Bombay, Madras, Hyderabad, Kanpur, Ahmedabad, Bangalore and Pune.

4. The concepts and methods of distance decay in commodity flows have been examined in a separate study by the authors. Interested readers may see : Raza Moonis and Aggarwal Y.P., Distance Decay and Railway Freight Flows in India : A Preliminary Enquiry, *Indian Journal of Regional Science*, Volume XII, Number I, 1980.

5. The levels of development of various districts are based on the work of M.N. Pal, Regional Disparities in the Levels of Development in India, *Indian Journal of Regional Science*-Vol. VII, 1975, pp 35—52.

16

NODAL HIERARCHY AND THE REGIONAL ORGANISATION OF THE ECONOMY

IT has alrady been noted that as the economy of a region grows, the loosely knit and weakly connected settlements increase their interactions through the exchange of surplus production. Consequently, some locations acquire greater significance as compared to others. These locations further get differentiated by virtue of their functional character and their ability to interact with the remaining settlements, which is sometimes constrained by the absence of adequate infrastructure. Looked at in this frame of reference, for a given space economy, we may be able to identify three types of sub-spaces—homogeneous, polarised and planned. Of these the polarised space, with its hierarchy of nodes is propelled by a set of linkages between the nodes that aid the organisation of the space economy. In the process of ecônomic development there is a progressive replacement of highly polarised primate centre-periphery structure with a single system of nodes extending throughout the space economy (Friedman, 1966).

The concept of spatial organisation may thus be approached by considering the economy as a system where a set of nodes of different hierarchical orders are interlinked by sets of relationships within each as well as between the different levels of the hierarchy. The hierarchical arrangement of the nodes in such system is axiomatic. The theoretical- contributions by Christaller (1966) through the study of market centres provided the framework for the analysis of the spatial organisation of the entire economy. However, it is important to acknowledge the later contributions of others such as I osch (1950), Berry (1959) and Garrison (1958). The theory is based on the relationship between a set of suppliers of goods and services and a large set of consumers. It may be noted that the central place and allied models do not provide for links within each hierarchic order whereas the modern approach based on the systems analysis considers links within the hierarchic order as well as those between hierarchic orders. In the central place models the links within a hierarchic order are unwarranted because they essentially deal with the tertiary sector of the space economy. It is also apparent that the concept of hierarchy and its validity is unmarred even if one does include the secondary sector. "There is, however, evidence to suggest that manufacturing shows fairly close accordance with general distribution of population, implying that not all specialised activities are located in centres outside the regularities of the central place hierarchy" (Hagget, 1977). Whereas the validity of the hierarchic arrangement explicitly stated in central place model, the hierarchic links between settlements get distorted. This is mainly because tertiary functions at a given hierarchic order are ubiquitous but many manufacturing functions are not. Thus, regional specialities of the manufacturing sectors have to be exchanged within each hierarchic order also. The focus of enquiry along these lines would be two-fold. First, texonomic—the identification and classification of nodes into different orders and secondly the analysis of links between different order of nodes. Although the concepts of hierarchy and spatial organisation form the basis, none of the earlier models is directly applicable for our analysis. The non-applicability stems from several characteristics associated with this study.

Firstly, a study of spatial organisation through a set of linkages presupposes an economy within which demands and supplies are in equilibrium through price mechanisms. The validity of such an assumption has been questioned in the case of large under-developed countries like India. It is argued that regional elements in such countries are not sufficiently related and are composed of regional islands (Friedman, 1964). Consequent upon this, the integration of the home-market is weak, whereas the nesting of the local in the regional market and the regional in the national market is weaker still.

Secondly, in a closed economic system, the models of Christaller and others envisage that the changes in the hierarchy emanate from lower order nodes, whereas in a country like India the impulses for change and growth till the recent past came from higher order metropolitan nodes. We have already discussed such a model of spatial organisation in Chapter 5.

CLASSIFICATION OF NODES

In the study of hierarchy in the nodal system, a variety of criteria and a number of techniques may be used. While some studies utilise infrastructural facilities available at the nodes and their population size, the others strive to base the identification of hierarchic levels on the magnitude and nature of interactions of the nodes. A close correspondence of the population size of the nodes to their hierarchic level cannot go unnoticed. The principle of any type of classification warrants, that the items within a group be more similar and close (in terms of the selected criteria) to other items in the same group than to the items of other groups, and also all items should be classified into groups which are mutually exclusive and no item falls in more than one group. Within the framework of our analysis it was considered to identify three types of nodes--metropolitan, satellite and hinterland nodes. In view of the above classification, the purpose of the exercise would be to identify the metropolitan centres and the satellite centres whereas the remaining nodes would fall in the third group, that is the hinterland.

Method of classification

It may be noted that we require certain criterion on the basis of which different nodes could be assigned to any of the three groups. One such variable may be the volume of shipments and receipts of different nodes or the number of nodes with which each of them interacts. A third dimension could be introduced with the inclusion of distance/range of interaction to indicate the field of each node. A node characterised by large shipments and receipts, a large number of interactions and large distance of commodity exchange would together warrant its classification in the higher order of the hierarchic scale and vice-versa. The selected variables are as under :

Volume of shipments (tonnage)
Number of interactions (shipments)
Average distance (shipments)
Volume of receipts (tonnage)
Number of interactions (receipts)
Average distance (receipts)

The ranking of these variables for all the nodes may produce an ordering of the nodes and would not include the principle of nesting which is the major focus of the present study. We, therefore, add another criteria based on the principle of nestin that in addition to satisfying the thresholds of the six variables, a first order centre must have dominant links with some of the satellite/second order centres and the satellite centres must have dominant association with the third order/hinterland nodes.

The method as outlined above, has been followed for classification of nodes and can be best presented with the help of some elementary concepts of the set theory. The universe consists of 6,775 nodes and the purpose is to classify them into three mutually exclusive groups.

If there are distinct groupings or break points in the distribution of these attributes of nodes, than a hierarchical ordering in them might be based on such break points. Thus the scatter of the data itself may reveal threshold values which may be extremely useful for the classification. It may not be possible to use the data for all the nodes to arrive at the cut off points. In the present exercise, a random stratified sample of 2 per cent from the 6,775 nodes was drawn to seek the two

FIG. 16.1 RANK-VALUE GRAPHS OF FREIGHT CHARACTERISTICS (136 SAMPLE STATIONS)

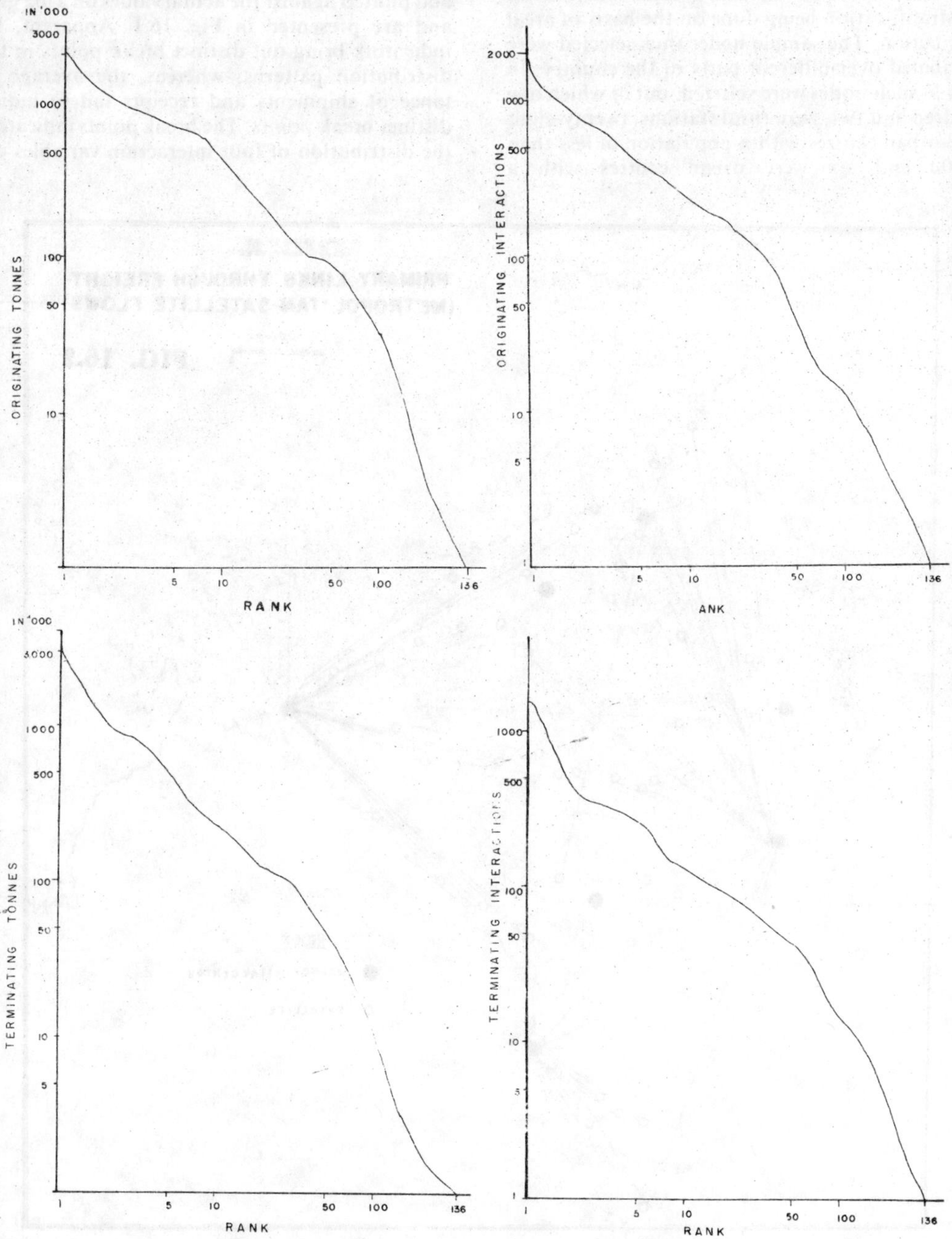

critical limits for each of the six variables. Firstly, the nine million cities were considered separately and one out of them was randomly selected as a sample. From the rest of the 6,766 centres, a systematic stratified random sample was drawn, the stratifi-cation being done on the basis of areal distribution. The sample nodes thus selected were distributed over different parts of the country. In all, 136 such nodes were selected, out of which one hundred and two were rural stations, twenty-eight were urban centres with a population of less than 50,000 and six were urban centres with a population of more than 50,000 including one metropolitan city.

The values of the six indicators for each of 136 sample points were then ranked individually and plotted against the actual values on a log graph and are presented in Fig. 16.1. Apparent, four indicators bring out distinct break points in their distribution patterns, whereas, the average distance of shipments and receipts fail to indicate distinct break points. The break points indicated in the distribution of four interaction variables were

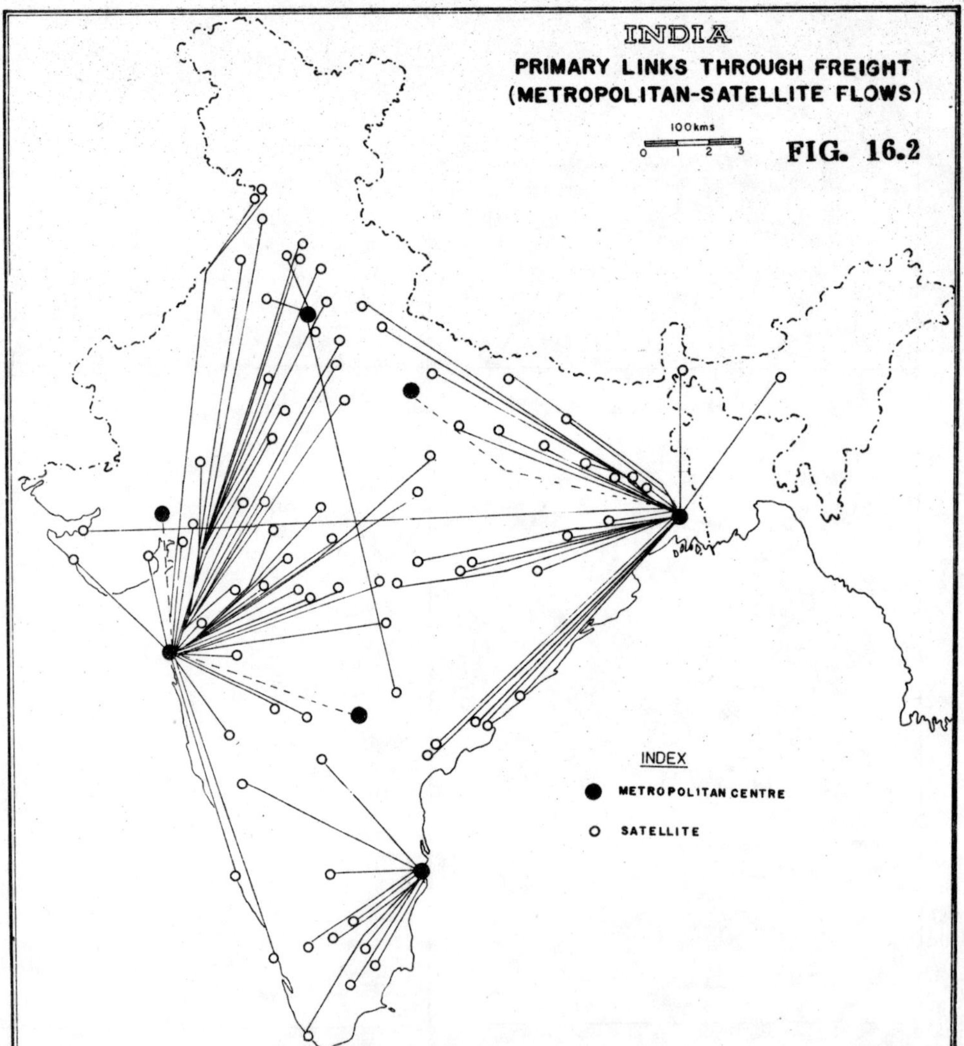

FIG. 16.2

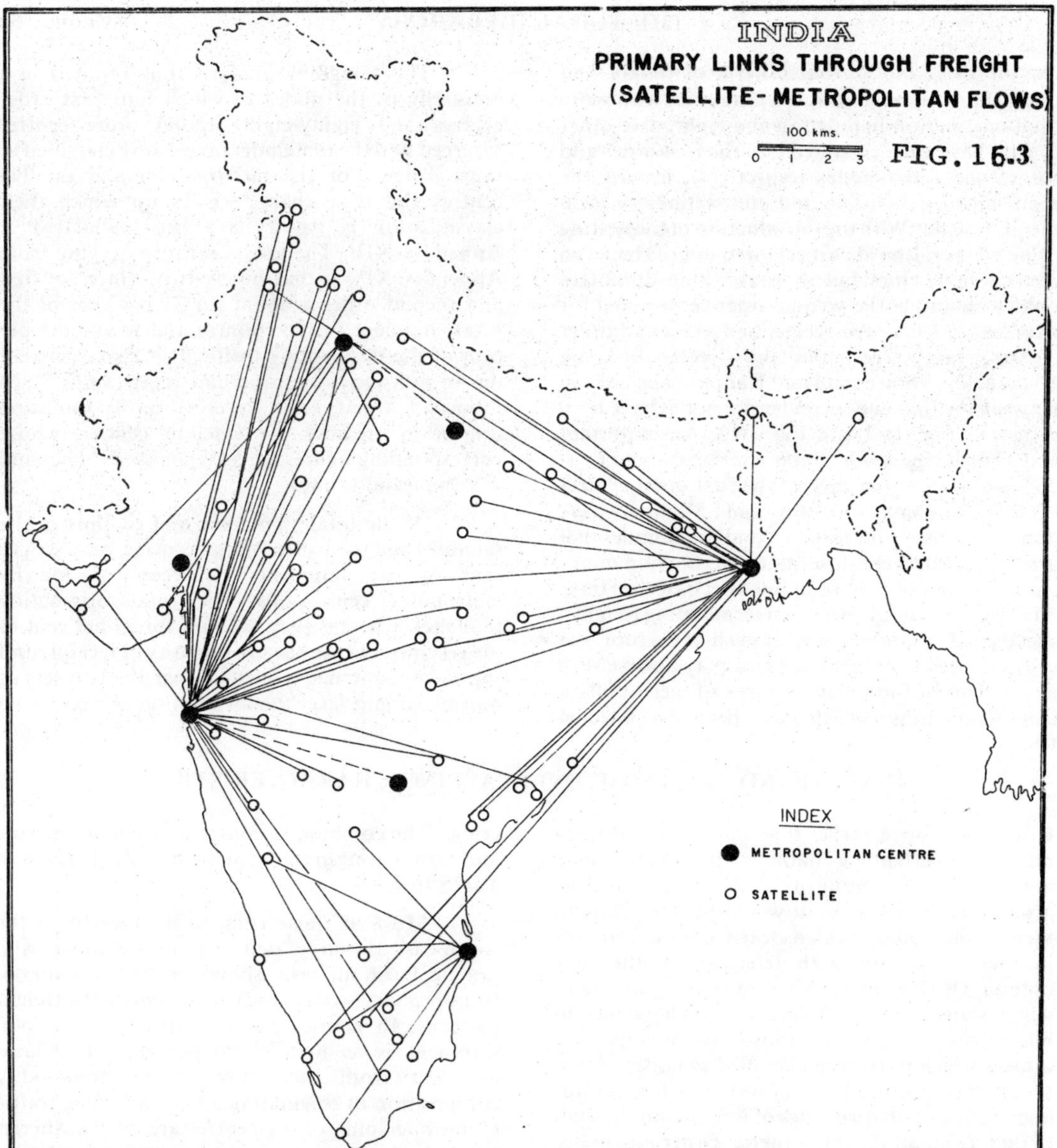

FIG. 16.3

used for classification. Thus a decision to drop the two distance indicators for the purposes of classificaion was necessitated, as the break points could not be identified for them.

The procedure of introducing the principle of nesting was as follows. The first stage related to the ranking of the nodes and classifying them into the three categories as per the above criterion. The second stage defined the dominant flows from and to each of the first order centres, with reference to the second order centres. The links between the first and second order nodes is thus established. Such linkages are evident from the examination of Fig. 16.2 and Fig. 16.3. Theoretically speaking, the range may vary from a simple dominance of all centres by one centre through an integrated hierarchy in which case only one centre dominates all other centres directly or indirectly to an absence of hierarchy in which a number of independent centres may be left loosely connected.

THE NODAL HIERARCHY

On the basis of the four criteria of freight and interactions, seven out of the nine cities with more than one million population and eighty-five other centres have been classified into the first order and the second order nodes respectively, leaving the remaining six thousand and odd stations to form the hinterland. With the introduction of the nesting principle as outlined earlier, three out of the seven metropolitan cities fail in establishing dominant links with any of the second order centres and for that reason have been reclassified as second order centres. The three cities thus reclassified are Hyderabad, Ahmedabad and Kanpur. The linkage between the first and second order nodes have been shown in Fig. 16.2 and Fig. 16.3. An important feature that emerges from the examination of Figs 16.2 and 16.3 is that each of the first order centres (Delhi, Bombay, Calcutta and Madras) have dominance over only those second order nodes that are found relatively closer to them. Barring minor variations in the pattern of linkages based on links established by originating and terminating freight a specific field of interaction for each of the four first order centres is discernible. This may also be seen in the light of the broad features of metropolitan commodity flows which have been discussed in Chapter 15.

The foregoing analysis thus resulted in a hierarchy of the nodes in which four first order centres and eighty-eight second order centres emerged and the remainder nodes were classified as third order. For the metropolitan and satellite centres the four characteristics on which their classification is based have been tabulated in Appendix XIV. The gross feature emerging from Appendix XIV is that ninety-two centres of first and second order account for 31 per cent of the total shipment in the country and forty-nine per cent of the terminating traffic. It is also clear that on an average a metropolitan centre ships 2,874 thousand tonnes and receives 6,640 thousand tonnes as against the satellite centres whose corresponding figures are 543 thousand tonnes and 773 thousand tonnes.

Of the total shipments and receipts of the satellites and the metropolitan centres, only six per cent of the shipments is accounted for by metropoles centres (of the total originating tonnage), whereas they account for 27 per cent of the receipts. On the basis of quantity of receipts and shipments, one may conclude that the two sets of centres remain largely consumption centres.

HINTERLAND NODES OF OVERLAPPING CHARACTERISTICS

It was mentioned earlier that a number of centres may have overlapping characteristics. While it may not be necessary to bring out all the centres which lie around the border lines, it would be interesting to identify those nodes which clearly show differences in their behaviour with reference to the four criteria. Of this nature the most striking are those which show a very high quantity of shipments, in many cases exceeding those of metropolitan centres which have been classified as nodes of first order, their shipments confined to a few centres and receive small quantities of freight and thus fail to qualify on all the four criteria. Other possibility is that of nodes with large receipts and very small shipments and interactions. Such cases are, however, only marginal.

A list of centres with high shipments, few interactions and very small receipts are given in Table 16.1 alongwith the values of originating tonnage, originating interactions, terminating tonnage and terminating interactions. In all, twenty-six centres of such type have been identified. Almost all these centres are located in the mineral belt except for a few which are again based on some resources like refineries of imported crude. The commodity composition of originating and terminating freight for such nodes is given in Table 16.2.

Most of those centres are located in the south-east resource rich regions of India, and practically in all cases shipments of raw material from primary sources or fuels dominate the freight patterns. In many cases their share in the total shipment is as high as 90 per cent. It is also apparent from the study of the commodity composition of originating and terminating traffic that while some of the centres are coal washeries where both the incoming and outgoing product is only coal, in other cases the products shipped are raw material and fuel and the small amount of receipts are those of food products, industrial products and construction materials. In all these cases the number of originating interactions is around 100 or less. The terminating interactions are equally few.

Such nodes tend to behave like captive raw material suppliers to either satellite centres or metropolitan centres. This feature could be partly brought out by simply analysing the interaction

TABLE 16.1 : **Shipments, receipts and interactions of hinterland nodes with pronounced overlapping characteristics**

Sl. No.	*Hinterland Nodes*	*Originating tannage (in '000 tonnes)*	*Interactions originating*	*Terminating tannage ('000 tonnes)*	*Terminating Interactions*
1.	Andal	7382	594	96	63
2.	Kirandul	3967	3	1	8
3.	Bhalli Rajhara	3885	92	4	63
3.	Chandrapura	2813	84	5	67
5.	Naomundi	2464	33	2	39
6.	Bajuva	2221	90	66	10
7.	Kusunda	2161	618	8	72
8.	Bellan palli	1975	138	11	71
9.	Birmitrapur	1817	474	37	137
10.	Bolanikadan	1457	74	2	19
11.	Sitarampur	1445	42	3	69
12.	Ikhora	1417	252	1	11
13.	Chirmisi	1374	132	8	71
14.	Mohuda	1293	276	14	48
15.	Ray	1277	156	1	13
16.	Dugda	1270	6	2	5
17.	Jorapukur	1114	11	457	4
18	Katrasgarh	1100	552	23	106
19.	Banspani	1070	43	1	16
20.	Khasi Rohar Rd.	1053	98	15	19
21.	Barsuan	1027	10	1	11

pattern of such centres. As an illustration of this phenomenon two such stations are considered, one solely supplying coal (Kargali) and another solely supplying raw material for manufacturing (Noamundi), both located in the mineral belt. The former supplies about 1,800 thousand tonnes of coal to 54 other places, of which about 60 per cent is accounted for by receipts at Bhilai, Bokaro and Varanasi. Similarly from Noamundi, about 2,464 thousand tonnes of minerals move to 33 other places of which about 90 per cent is accounted for by Tatanagar and Bokaro. Apparently, the same situation is likely to be encountered in all such cases.

THE NODAL HIERARCHY AND THE SPATIAL ORGANISATION

It is clear, therefore, that the selected centres in the first two orders are oriented towards organising the space economy, each of them characterised by a large number of interactions, receipts and supplies and their hinterland is composed of large number of centres with small shipments and smaller receipts with a few centres of bulk supply of raw materials and fuel to specific satellite centres and metropolitan centres, and these in turn receive small quantities of food products and other commodities for their survival. We may, therefore, view of spatial organisation of the economy, as manifested in the commodity movements as a system composed of few metropolitan centres with a set of satellite centres rooted to the large base of a hinterland of mineral resources and to a lesser extent to food products. We shall examine the commodity flow characteristics for the second order nodes in the following section. We have already undertaken such an analysis of the metropolitan freight flows in Chapter 15.

THE SATELLITE CENTRES : SOME ATTRIBUTES OF INTERACTION

After having identified the second order nodes, it was considered necessary to examine their flow

TABLE 16.2 : **Commodity composition of hinterlands nodes of pronounced overlapping characteristics**

S. No.	Nodes	*% Shipments to total shipments*			*% Receipts to total receipts*					
		Raw materials	*Fuel*	*Others*	*Food products*	*Raw materials*	*Fuel*	*Consturc-tion materials*	*Industrial products*	*Others*
1	2	3	4	5	6	7	8	9	10	11
1.	Umreli	0	100	0	—	—	—	—	—	—
2.	Gaya	77	0	23	36	2	46	3	5	8
3.	Ray	0	100	0	8	3	2	65	9	14
4.	Patrata	1	99	0	0	0	95	3	2	0
5.	Chandrapura	0	100	0	0	0	99	0	1	0
6.	Kargali	0	100	0	0	84	0	8	7	1
7.	Palsaur	100	0	0	50	11	4	16	9	10
8.	Kariganaru	100	0	0	70	76	0	0	0	24
9.	Karwar	100	0	0	11	27	0	16	28	18
10.	Talcher	1	99	0	5	2	3	14	58	17
11.	Kirandul	100	0	0	0	0	7	3	36	54
12.	Radhanagar	0	99	1	0	62	4	2	14	8
13.	Dugda	0	100	0	0	0	100	0	0	0
14.	Jorapukur	0	100	0	0	0	100	0	0	0
15.	Normundi	100	0	0	1	3	76	4	4	12
16.	Banspani	97	0	3	2	39	53	2	4	10
17.	Bolanikadan	100	0	0	0	0	37	0	57	6
18.	Bimargarh	100	0	0	52	35	4	0	6	3
19.	Berman	100	0	0	3	0	14	12	51	20
20.	Birmitrapur	100	0	0	55	8	8	14	2	13
21.	Kiriburu	100	0	0	0	0	0	14	76	10
22.	Chirmiri	0	100	0	9	26	1	25	24	15
23.	Bishrampur	4	95	1	54	1	14	15	3	13
24.	Dallirajhara	100	0	0	0	5	78	5	10	2
25.	Gervra Road	0	100	0	0	4	92	0	3	1
26.	Bajuvagurjat	0	98	2	0	53	34	0	10	3

characteristics, which to a large extent would be related to their economic base characteristics. We have attempted to examine their freight characteristics by examining the distribution of various commodities in a centre.

The proportion of commodity shipments of different group of commodities, along with their specialisation has been given in Table 16.3. All the centres which record values of mean plus one standard deviation and above in different commodity groups has been taken to be specialising in that group. In case, the centre does not specialise in any commodity, it has been classified as diversified centre.

An examination of Table 16.3 reveals that out of 88 second order nodes only 13 centres have been identified as diversified. Most of these are large urban centres with a population of 1,00,000 and above. Bangalore, Agra, Tiruchirapalli and Jaipur and so on fall in this group. Some of these nodes are also characterised by locational attributes with reference to the railway network (important railway centres like Gorakhpur, Itarsi, Agra etc.) while others are minor ports and Mangalore and Cochin.

Eight centres show specialisation in the shipments of industrial products. Five of these are centres of public investment—the steel plant centres, Durgapur (75%), Rourkela (74%), Tatanagar (93%), Bhilai (89%), and Bokaro (75%). The other three are represented by Asansol (in the eastern industrial belt), Bhopal (51%) and Varanasi (37%). This group of nodes therefore represents the planners emphasis on the heavy industries and the consequent new large industrial complexes and the deliberate introduction of manufacturing activities in the existing urban agglomerations.

In all 17 centres specialise in the shipment of food products. These represent the wheat producing region of the Punjab and western U.P (Ambala, Jalandhar, Patiala, Bhatinda, Kotkapura, Saharanpur, Meerut, Bareily etc.), the rice and dry millet areas of the south (Kakinada, Vijayawada, Erode, Ahmadnagar). The absence of centres of food shipments in central India and eastern and north-eastern India are noticeable.

Specialisation in the shipments of raw materials from primary sources must necessarily involve some resource base of agriculture, minerals, forests, plantation and so on to which certain satellites are rooted. Consequently, the plantation products of north-eastern India and south India are funnelled through Gauhati and Hubli-Dharwar respectively; mineral centres are Gondia, Kota and Ballabgarh; Itwari and Akola ship cotton that is produced in their hinterland; Madurai, Ahmedabad and Godhra deal with semi processed materials; and Trivandrum ships imported raw material, Pathankot acts as the entry point for products originating from Jammu and Kashmir and Himachal Pradesh. Consequent upon the dispersed distribution of such resources, the satellites specialising in the shipments of raw materials are also spatially dispersed.

Ten centres indicate large shipments of fuel. These are of three types, the refinery based centres of Baroda, Jalpaiguri and Kanpur, the railway fuel collection/distribution centres of Hyderabad, Chandrapur and Patna, and the coal mining centres represented by Durgapur, Dhanbad and Gondia.

Inputs into agriculture are shipped in large quantities from nine centres. All these represent the fertilizer plant location at Raichur, Dhulia, Khamgaon, Khandwa, Amravati, Indore, Gulbarga, Kanpur and Nangal. Similarly, construction materials are represented by large shipments of cement from Salem, Coimbatore, Virudhunagar, Hirakund, Satna, Katni, Allahabad and Dehri-on-son. These centres have a tendency to record a very large proportion of shipments in construction material (Virudhunagar 95 per cent, Salem 72 per cent, Sawai Madhopur 94 per cent, Dehri-on-son 75 per cent). The dominance of miscellaneous commodities are indicated by eight centres most of which are found to be defence cantonments (Nasik, Jalgaon, Dehu, Udaipur, Gwalior and so on).

Commodity composition of receipts

Table 16.4 records the proportion of different commodities received by these centres, the different mean receipts and the functional type of classification of each based on the mean and standard deviation. Fuel receipts, in general, is the dominant feature brought out by the table. The average receipts of fuel by the satellite centres amount to 41 per cent followed by food products, raw materials and then industrial products.

Consequent upon this high average values of fuel receipts, although a large number of centres receive significant proportions of fuel, they tend to be classified as diversified centres. The centres are spatially well distributed. Of these, five centres are satellites of Madras, nine of Bombay, six of Delhi and four of Calcutta. Out of these twenty-four centres eight are found to be common to those which emerged as diversified centres of shipments. The remaining sixteen centres were earlier classified as shippers of specialised commodities, the food product shippers (Erode, Bareilly and Saharanpur), the cement shippers (Salem, Coimbatore and Hirakud), and the raw material shippers (Madurai, Ahmedabad, Nagda and Kota). None of the centres whose shipments are dominated by industrial products receive diversified commodities. A comparison of the commodity composition of receipts and shipments also indicates some of the satellite centres which have developed manufacturing activity, particularly Salem, Coimbatore, Ahmedabad, Kota, Hirakud and so on.

Receipts of industrial products are dominant in some centres (Baroda, Hissar, Jaito, Jalandhar, Gondia, Allahabad and Patna). Three of these indicate dominant food shipments matched by dominant receipts of industrial products. Obviously, whereas much of the industrial products are likely to be consumed at these centres, the food products shipped by them are not produced by the centres themselves but by their hinterlands.

Food product receipts are dominant in fourteen centres, most of which are the satellites of Bombay (ten) and two each of Madras and Calcutta. Raw

TABLE 16.3 : **Commodity composition of shipments of satellites**

Sl. No.	*Satellite centres*	*Total originating freight ('000 tonnes)*	*% Food product*	*% Raw materials*	*% Fuel*	*% Agricultural inputs*	*% Construction materials*	*% Industrial Product*	*% Others*	*Average distance of shipments in kms.*	*Specialisation in commodity shipments*
1	2	3	4	5	6	7	8	9	10	11	12
1.	Nasik	48	3	3	0	6	1	7	79	836	Misc.
2.	Dhulia	37	18	3	0	71	0	4	4	337	A. inp.
3.	Jalgaon	46	18	4	5	21	1	5	46	708	Misc.
4.	Khandwa	92	42	19	0	30	0	1	9	709	Ag. inp.
5.	Khamgaon	46	12	22	0	61	0	2	2	548	Ag. inp.
6.	Akola	54	41	36	0	17	0	4	2	671	Raw mat.
7.	Amravati	81	23	9	0	59	0	2	7	516	Ag. inp.
8.	Ahmadnager	92	63	12	0	2	0	4	18	509	Food prod.
9.	Dehu	151	25	1	1	[illegible]	1	11	56	647	Misc.
10.	Jamnagar	565	24	0	0	3	57	0	8	525	Const. mat.
11.	Porbandar	179	1	6	1	0	68	0	10	423	Const. mat
12.	Bhavnagar	338	38	2	0	15	1	36	8	1078	Ind. pord.
13.	Udaipur	126	2	7	0	21	1	0	68	878	Misc.
14.	Ahmedabad	576	17	40	0	11	3	9	19	709	Raw mat.
15.	Godhra	17	40	38	0	10	7	2	3	517	Raw mat.
16.	Baroda	21	1	0	96	0	0	2	1	1695	Fuel
17.	Gwalior	60	45	4	1	3	0	3	44	818	Misc.
18.	Bhopal	80	35	3	0	2	1	51	10	773	Ind. prod.
19.	Itarsi	35	43	31	11	3	0	1	11	657	D
20.	Ratlam	31	29	28	0	5	4	12	22	640	D
21.	Nagda	63	1	45	1	0	0	22	31	774	Raw mat.
22.	Indore	132	37	13	0	38	0	7	5	689	Ag. inp.
23.	Nagpur	656	6	10	2	8	1	7	67	493	Misc.
24.	Itwari	208	18	62	0	12	0	4	4	786	Raw mat.
25.	Chandrapur	266	11	2	76	5	3	2	0	545	Fuel
26.	Miraj	76	68	1	0	12	1	3	14	610	Food prod.
27.	Sholapur	32	50	3	23	13	1	5	5	551	D
28.	Hyderabad	7096	2	0	94	1	1	1	1	373	Fuel
29.	Warangal	36	47	16	17	17	0	2	1	662	D
30.	Gulbarga	59	46	8	0	42	0	1	4	517	Ag. inp.
31.	Ujjain	25									
32.	Ballabgarh	117	15	44	0	2	18	17	4	626	Raw mat.
33.	Meerut	112	86	1	0	3	1	2	8	924	Food prod.
34.	Hissar	96	61	7	1	7	0	20	5	1094	Food prod.
35.	Kota	206	19	57	0	5	9	3	7	396	Raw mat.
36.	Sawai Madhopur	639	5	0	0	0	94	0	1	406	Const. mat.
37.	Jaipur	50	39	3	1	22	2	19	15	826	D
38	Kanpur	994	5	2	54	29	0	3	7	506	Fuel/ag. inp
39	Agra	247	53	2	0	11	0	8	26	877	D

	2	3	4	5	6	7	8	9	10	11	12
40.	Aligarh	73	79	2	0	14	0	4	1	915	Food prod.
41.	Lucknow	124	21	24	0	5	2	7	41	741	Misc.
42.	Moradabad	119	37	2	0	1	0	5	37	550	D
43.	Barelly	128	85	3	0	5	1	1	2	894	Food prod.
44.	Saharanpur	84	65	2	0	3	0	23	8	917	Food prod.
45.	Ambala	95	68	0	1	3	0	20	7	977	Food prod
46.	Chandigarh	245	2	4	0	88	0	2	4	267	Ag. inp.
47.	Jaito	178	82	2	0	4	0	8	3	1379	Food prod.
48.	Jalandhar	142	69	2	0	1	0	13	13	1179	Food prod.
49.	Pathankot	60	21	60	1	1	0	2	15	690	Raw mat.
50.	Kotkapura	80	80	16	0	3	0	0	1	821	Food prod.
51.	Bhatinda	82	59	10	0	11	0	1	20	668	Food prod
52.	Patiala	226	96	0	0	1	0	0	2	1285	Food prod.
53.	Durgapur	2570	1	0	40	1	1	55	2	643	Ind. prod./fuel
54.	Dhanbad	7650	0	0	96	3	1	0	0	394	Fuel
55.	Jalpaiguri	233	5	28	61	1	1	1	3	443	Fuel
56.	Tatanagar	1341	0	2	2	1	1	93	1	765	Ind. prod.
57.	Rourkela	1170	0	10	9	1	4	74	1		Ind. prod.
58.	Hirakund	823	13	6	28	2	3	15	4	479	Const. mat
59.	Gauhati	207	21	44	2	4	3	6	20	695	Raw mat
60.	Vishakapatnam	1607	22	1	39	21	7	3	7	600	Fuel
61.	Vijayawada	91	76	6	0	2	2	2	2	659	Food
62.	Guntur	70	46	32	0	16	0	4	1	654	Raw mat.
63.	Rajamundri	108	41	7	3	1	0	41	7	708	Ind. prod.
64.	Kakinada	114	70	0	0	28	0	90	0	523	Food prod.
65.	Satna	1066	0	32	0	0	64	1	0	451	Const. mat.
66.	Katni	1538	4	21	1	0	65	0	9	517	Const. mat.
67.	Gondia	58	6	42	39	3	5	5	2	726	Food prod.
68.	Bhilai	2254	1	1	5	2	1	89	1	1499	Ind. prod.
69.	Raipur	203	47	29	0	15	0	1	7	710	D
70.	Varanasi	16	33	3	0	21	1	37	3	633	Ind. prod.
71.	Allahabad	166	9	17	8	8	3	10	9	432	Const. mat.
72.	Patna	600	1	1	94	0	0	2	2	410	Fuel
73.	Gorakhpur	21	47	22	2	15	1	8	5	403	D
74.	Dehri-on-son	236	1	9	0	0	75	13	483	481	Const. mat.
75.	Bokaro	946									
76.	Asansol	1622									Raw mat
77.	Bangalore	1227	25	4	36	4	14	13	4	677	D
78.	Hubli-Dharwar	562	11	73	1	4	6	3	1	266	Raw mat
79.	Raichur	260	8	2	78	7	3	1	1	433	Fuel
80.	Salem	258	23	7	53	4	5	7	1	595	D
81.	Erode	177	16	8	60	7	3	3	3	536	D
82.	Coimbatore	497	19	5	48	9	3	14	2	688	D
83.	Mangalore	212	5	11	44	13	17	8	2	501	Ag. inp.
84.	Cochin	254	63	7	2	2	2	23	2		Food prod.
85.	Trivanduram	241	68	2	8	3	14	4	1	994	Food prod.

1	2	3	4	5	6	7	8	9	10	11	12
86.	Tiruchirapalli	374	19	4	37	12	6	19	3	566	Ag. inp/ind.
87.	Madurai	284	29	5	36	8	13	6	2		D
88.	Virudhunagar	160	16	3	76	1	1	1	2	1131	Fuel

D = Diversified

TABLE 16.4 : **Commodity composition of receipts of satellites**

Sl. No.	*Satellite centres*	*Total terminating tonnage ('000 tonnes)*	*% Food products*	*% Raw materials*	*% Fuel*	*% Agricultural inputs*	*% Construction materials*	*% Industrial products*	*Others*	*Average distance of receipts in kms.*	*Specialisation in commodity receipts*
1	2	3	4	5	6	7	8	9	10	11	12
1.	Nasik	1053	6	2	80	2	6	3	2	558	Fuel
2.	Dhulia	137	10	8	43	21	12	4	2	550	Ag. inp
3.	Jalgaon	178	35	4	22	22	9	4	5	596	Ag. inp.
4.	Khandwa	119	38	9	29	9	8	4	3	522	Food prod.
5.	Khamgaon	265	36	21	17	12	8	5	1	504	Ag. inp.
6.	Akola	248	37	8	34	7	8	4	3	569	Food prod.
7.	Amravati	182	43	8	20	12	9	6	2	639	Food prod.
8.	Ahmadnager	191	54	6	7	11	11	3	9	716	Food prod.
9.	Dehu	2286	10	63	11	2	6	3	5	490	Food prod.
10.	Jamnagar	878	8	43	26	17	2	2	1	513	Raw mat/ Fuel
11.	Porbandar	142	8	10	71	4	2	3	3	814	Fuel
12.	Bhavnagar	324	15	11	50	8	7	7	2	910	D
13.	Udaipur	144	54	5	23	3	8	3	4	521	Food prod.
14.	Ahmedabad	2850	9	8	56	2	15	13	2	834	D
15.	Godhra	130	75	3	13	2	5	1	1	407	Food prod.
16.	Baroda	328	33	9	16	4	14	18	5	1445	Ind. prod.
17.	Gwalior	154	13	5	54	5	8	9	5	755	D
18.	Bhopal	236	8	2	45	3	13	20	8	596	Ind. prod.
19.	Itarsi	215	7	0	87	1	2	1	2	480	Fuel
20.	Ratlam	170	17	9	48	6	12	3	6	376	D
21.	Nagda	379	16	4	57	1	1	13	9	529	D
22.	Indore	391	33	16	20	10	6	9	5	496	D
23.	Nagpur	390	45	31	26	2	7	11	7	716	Food prod.
24.	Itwari	113	50	21	12	2	1	10	4	545	Food prod.
25.	Chandrapur	97	27	5	16	7	36	6	4	489	Const. mat
26.	Miraj	327	38	5	17	10	20	5	5	540	Food prod
27.	Sholapur	327	31	10	36	4	14	4	1	536	D
28.	Hyderabad	1682	19	5	44	3	12	13	5	458	D
29.	Warangal	138	24	11	46	9	7	2	1	465	D
30.	Gulbarga	154	58	4	20	12	4	2	1	661	Food. prod. Ag.inp

1	2	3	4	5	6	7	8	9	10	11	12
31.	Ujjain	1512									
32.	Ballabgarh	202	1	12	28	4	42	6	7	806	Const. mat.
33.	Meerut	472	5	4	45	16	17	8	5	852	Ag. inp.
34.	Hissar	325	5	4	60	2	9	17	1	901	Ind. prod.
35.	Kota	254	13	4	52	4	11	12	4	541	D
36.	Sawai Madhopur	1045	3	75	20	0	1	0	0	221	Raw. mat.
37.	Jaipur	160	23	8	10	4	27	20	8	679	Const. mat Ind. prod.
38.	Kanpur	1728	8	9	50	3	8	15	5	661	Ind. prod.
39.	Agra	1351	11	4	62	2	8	10	3	830	D
40.	Aligarh	144	5	15	29	14	22	14	3	741	Const. mat./ Ind. prod.
41.	Lucknow	854	13	10	38	4	17	9	10	542	D
42.	Moradabad	197	12	4	56	9	14	3	2	801	D
43.	Bareilly	517	4	25	46	7	10	3	5	692	D
44.	Saharanpur	347	9	10	53	8	10	3	7	805	D
45.	Ambala	271	2	1	67	4	5	8	12	871	Fuel
46.	Chandigarg	400	3	7	30	3	37	14	6	751	Const. mat. Ind. prod.
47.	Jaito	387	9	4	46	5	13	18	6	1270	Ind. prod.
48.	Jalandhar	539	3	3	59	4	10	15	6	1085	Ind. prod.
49.	Pathankot	392	11	0	55	1	20	3	8	939	Const. mat.
50.	Kotkapura	182	2	0	68	19	9	0	2	753	Fuel/Ag. inp
51.	Bhatinda	163	3	2	20	25	23	12	14	981	Ag. inp./ const. mat.
52.	Patiala	262	2	3	71	6	12	4	3	860	Fuel
53.	Durgapur	5688	1	37	56	0	3	2	1	169	Raw mat.
54.	Dhanbad	2181	33	19	1	30	2	7	8	255	Ag. inp.
55.	Jalpaiguri	332	59	1	24	2	11	2	1	826	Food prod.
56.	Tatanagar	6489	1	49	42	0	2	4	1	142	Raw mat.
57.	Rourkela	1280	5	69	16	1	1	3	2		Raw mat.
58.	Hirakund	711	10	17	36	6	13	7	11	399	D
59.	Gauhati	446	64	2	15	1	5	10	3	1100	Food prod.
60.	Vishakapatnam	180	2	0	0	15	3	3	77	523	Misc./Ag..
61.	Vijayawada	449	2	2	82	5	0	9	1	490	Fuel
62.	Guntur	144	12	9	46	17	6	3	7	561	Ag. inp.
63.	Rajamundri	251	4	15	54	4	13	3	7	556	D
64.	Kakinada	413	2	52	1	19	1	26	8	554	Raw mat. Ind. prod.
65.	Satna	370	14	7	69	2	2	3	3	442	Fuel
66.	Katni	903	2	6	88	0	1	1	2	274	Fuel
67.	Gondia	83	28	12	34	4	4	18	2	401	Ind. prod.
68.	Bhilia	8613	0	50	43	0	1	2	3	745	Raw mat.
69.	Raipur	195	29	4	27	14	6	13	7	509	D
70.	Varanasi	3135	3	0	92	2	2	1	1	457	Fuel.
71.	Allahabad	405	20	3	26	8	13	18	12	586	Ind. prod.

1	2	3	4	5	6	7	8	9	10	11	12
72.	Patna	280	15	12	41	2	8	14	7	652	Ind. prod.
73.	Gorakhpur	202	19	14	42	6	10	6	2	598	D
74.	Dehri-on-son	490	5	10	57	1	9	4	14	434	Misc. Raw mat.
75.	Bokaro	2939									
76.	Asansol	1622									
77.	Bangalore	1227	25	4	36	4	14	13	4	677	D
78.	Hubli-Dharwar	562	11	73	1	4	6	3	1	266	Raw mat.
79.	Raichur	260	8	2	78	7	3	1	1	433	Fuel
80.	Salem	258	23	7	53	4	5	7	1	595	D
81.	Erode	177	16	8	60	7	4	3	2	536	D
82.	Coimbatore	497	19	5	48	9	3	14	2	688	D
83.	Mangalore	212	5	11	44	13	17	8	2	501	Ag. inp.
84.	Cochin	254	63	7	2	2	2	23	2		Food prod.
85.	Trivanduram	241	68	2	8	3	14	5	1	994	Food prod.
86.	Tiruchirapalli	374	19	4	37	12	6	19	3	566	Ag. inp/ind
87.	Madurai	284	29	5	36	8	13	6	2		D
88.	Virudhunagar	160	16	3	76	1	1	1	2	1131	Fuel

D = Diversified

Material receipts are dominant in ten centres, of which except for Hubli-Dharwar (which collects and distributes raw materials) the rest of the nine centres are industrial centres (their shipments being dominated by industrial products and construction materials).

As indicated earlier, fuel receipts of the satellite centres are large, thus the threshold limits for the centres to be classified as dominant receivers of fuel are high. Yet, twelve centres show specialisation in fuel receipts. Of these, two are satellites of Madras, three of Bombay, three of Delhi and four of Calcutta. Most of these centres' shipments are dominated by construction materials except for the railway centres of Itarsi and Vijayawada and the port centre of Porbandar.

Receipts of agricutural inputs are generally low, the mean being about 6 per cent. Consequently, fifteen centres indicate specialisation in this commodity. The major feature of the distribution of dominant receivers of agricultural inputs is the fact that a number of centres shipping food products from the Punjab and western Uttar Pradesh record high values of receipt of inputs into agriculture (more than two or three standard deviations above mean). Eight centres indicate specialisation in the receipt of construction materials six of which are Delhi's satellites.

The distance range of shipments and receipts

In general, one would notice from the data presented in earlier Tables that the average distance of receipts of the satellite centres is lower than the distance of shipments. Of the eighty-eight satellites only twenty-two record values where distances of shipments are less than distances of receipts. As indicated above, the receipts of the hinterland which are processed, the manufactured products being marketed to farther off places and other satellites and metropolitan centres. This is supported by the distance characteristics of the shipments and receipts of the satellite centres. The twenty-two centres which record contrary values may be explained by their relative locations and the commodities dominating their shipments and receipts. One can clearly notice certain trends by a comparison of these twenty-two centres as regards the composition of their shipments and receipts. Where the shipments are dominated by raw materials or by inputs into agriculture, the originating freight's average distance tends to be low, and when the receipts of those centres are dominated by industrial products or fuel (because of its localised distribution and supply point) average distances of terminating freight tend to be larger. Thus the nature of commodities shipped and received are to some extent responsible for the reversal of distance values in the twenty-two centres that occur in the tables.

A typology of satellites

The foregoing analysis clearly indicates the distinct

TABLE 16.5 : **Typology of satellite centres**

S. No.	*Type*		*Nodes*
I	Old satellites of tertiary activities	(a)	Tiruchirappalli, Madurai, Nasik, Jalgaon, Khandwa, Akol, Udaipur, Gwalior, Itarsi, Ratlam, Nagda, Indore, Ujjain, Nagpur, Miraj, Sholapur, Warangal, Gulburga, Jaipur, Agra, Lucknow, Moradabad, Varanasi, Patna.
	Old satellites	(b)	Ahmedabad, Baroda, Bhopal, Kanpur, Hyderabad, Coimbatore, Dhulia, Virudhnagar, Salem, Allahabad, Jalandhar, Raichur, Amravathi, Bangalore, Dehu, Rajamundri, Trivandrum.
	Old satellites of tertiary activity	(c)	Ahmadnagar, Godhra, Itwari, Meerut, Hissar, Aligarh, Barreily, Saharanpur, Ambala, Jaito, Pathankot, Bhatinda, Patiala, Dhanbad, Jalpaiguri, Gauhati, Vijayawada, Guntur, Raipur, Gorakhpur, Hubli-Dharwar, Erode, Chandrapur, Kotkapura.
II	New satellites of industrial activity		Durgapur, Tatanagar, Rourkela, Hirakund, Satna, Katni, Asansol, Bokaro, Dehri-on-son, Khamgaon, Gondia, Ballabgarh, Kota, Swai-Madhopur, Bhilai, Chandigarh.
III	Minor ports		Mangalore, Cochin, Kakinada, Jamnagar, Porbandar, Bhavnagar, Vishakapattnam.

types of satellite centres that may be grouped into categories suggested in the model outlined.

The new satellite centres based on industrial enterprises and characterised by shipments of manufactured products, and receipts of raw materials, the former involving larger distances and the latter involving comparatively very small distances. Sixteen centres of this type can be identified. A list of the centres falling under different types are tabulated in Tables 16.5

Of these sixteen centres, classified as new satellites of industrial activity five are the steel plant centres of Durgapur, Tatanagar, Rourkela, Bokaro and Bhilai. Fertilizer plants are represented by Khamgaon and Nangal near Chandigarh. Cement plants also emerge in this category represented by Dehri-on-son, Kota, Sawai-Madhopur, Hirakund and so on.

The old satellite centres may further be subdivided into those which still continue to be trading centres of diverse products, and those where manufacturing activity has been introduced in the post-independence period in addition to their existing base of the tertiary and secondary sector. Of the former type a large number of centres may be identified. Most of these places are large urban centres mainly dealing with shipments and receipts of a variety of commodities. Of the latter type are centres like Ahmedabad, Bhopal, Jalandhar, Hyderabad and Coimbatore, which generally are characterised by diverse commodity shipments and receipts with a slight dominance of manufactured products.

A larger number of centres are also to be seen in the food surplus areas and plantation which receive and ship food products and raw materials from primary sources which constitute an appreciable proportion of their freight. These centres are also well distributed over the country. Centres like Bhatinda, Pathankot, Ahmadnagar, Meerut, Vijayawada, Jalpaiguri, Gauhati, Rajpur, Hubli-Dharwar etc. fall in this group. Their distance characteristics tend to be mixed up without consistency which is affected by the commodity mix in their receipts and shipments.

We are also in a position to identify another set of centres which, though they may otherwise fall in some other category mentioned above, are yet differentiated by being ports which disturbs some feature or other of the above categories and may warrant therefore a separate grouping.

It is very clear from the above analysis that the satellites have a well marked regional base from where products are gathered, and simply exchanged for other products or processed and then shipped to other places. The distance characteristics clearly bring out that their links are regional when considering their receipts and spatial when their shipments are considered.

17

STRUCTURAL ANALYSIS OF INTER-REGIONAL COMMODITY FLOWS

INTRODUCTION

IN our discussion on commodity flows as a spatial process, the emphasis has so far been placed, within the framework of analysis, upon the spatial patterns associated with the aggregate shipments and receipts. No doubt, such an analysis is useful in defining the broad characteristics of the movement phenomenon, but they tell us very little about the nature of specific interactions between the origins and destinations. Since, in practice, the flows are never independent of direction, the basic configuration of the commodity flows takes the form of bilateral interactions which may be adequately represented in the form of inter-regional commodity flow matrices.

It may be recalled from our earlier discussion that the basis for such interactions are provided by the inter-dependencies of the various sectors of the economic system. The density of inter-regional flow matrix not only depends upon the realisation of economies of scale and agglomeration as revealed through inter-sectoral transaction matrix, but is also considerably influence by the level of regional specialisation, the pattern of spatial demand, transport costs and the time taken during transhipments, on the one hand, and the existence of political and social barriers, on the other. As a consequence certain regions acquire relatively more importance than others as they play a decisive role in the subsequent organisation of space.

Thus, there is a tendency among some regions to interact more often with certain specific regions as compared to others. Our analysis of aggregate shipment and receipt patterns in the second part of this book has shown that there is a strong tendency for certain commodities to be traded inter-regionally as compared to others. The existence of the regional specialisation in the production processes and concentration of demand in certain regions evidently shows that all regions do not participate in the exchange process on an equal basis. The existence of such a phenomenon is also suggested by the wide differences in the average lead of different commodities. These features of concentration of flows, however, do suggest, that in a large country like India, there will exist economic sub-systems—a group of regions having strong links mutually within the groups than with other regions outside the group.

Within the framework of the present study the identification of such groups of origins, or of groups of destinations, or of groups of origins and destinations that are functionally bound together by a high degree of interaction, would add yet another dimension to our understanding of the inter-regional commodity flow phenomenon. In view of the fact that regional development planners are essentially concerned with the strategy for location of economic activities in space, the knowledge of the patterns of spatial interdependence and the nature of such functional regions, as may exist in the national system, may provide a very useful framework for the analysis of these problems. The purpose of the present chapter, therefore, is to identify the basic structural features of the bi-lateral and multi-lateral interaction processes through the manipulation of commodity flow matrices.

The casual inspection of commodity flow matrices, however, may not lead to the identification of such cluster of regions. In our endeavour to examine the dominance-dependence patterns of origins and destinations, the multi-variate inferential techniques have been used by suitable manipulation of flow matrices. In the past, a number of attempts have been made to examine the basic anatomy of flows. The structure of the shipment into and out of the Hong Kong port has been examined by Boxer through a correlation matrix for 37 flow characteristics. However, the most promising approach to this problem involves the use of R & Q modes of factor analysis. A detailed discussion on the application of these techniques to the structural analysis of commodity flow matrices has already been undertaken in Chapter 3.

The limitations of the studies undertaken in the Indian context have already been examined in detail in the first Chapter. However, it may be recalled that in view of the non-availability of data on intra-regional flows, the role of commodity flows in the integration of national economy could not be properly brought out. Some of the most promising studies conducted by Berry (1966) and Hashim (1971) fall in this category. The magnitude of this inadequacy for such studies may be gauged from the fact that some of the regions were as big as states in India. The present set of data allows us for the first time, to undertake a complete structural analysis of the commodity flow matrices which include intra-regional flows as well.

The present chapter is, thus, essentially an enquiry into the structural aspects of the Indian economic space and is intended to serve two basic objectives; firstly to see if as a result of 25 years of planned development, the colonial character of the Indian economy has undergone a change; and secondly, to probe into some aspects of commodity flows, which for a variety of reasons have remained unexplored so far.

It may be mentioned here that the choice of regions would invariably influence the structural patterns of commodity flows as well as the level of intra and inter-regional flows. It is with this end in view, that a reasonably homogenous areal unit has been selected for such an analysis. We have considered NSS regions as defined earlier for the purpose of analysis in this chapter. More specifically, the present study has the following aims :

i to examine the level and magnitude of intra and of inter-regional flows and linkages for different commodities;

ii to examine the phenomenon of multi-lateral interactions by mapping and suitably defining the structural regions on the basis of similarities in their flow profiles.

INTRA/INTER-STATE FLOWS AND SPATIAL LINKAGES

The patterns of intra and inter state flows and spatial linkages have been examined through Table 17.1. The table reveals the following:—

(i) It may be observed that nearly 34% of the total originating freight terminates within the originating state itself. Thus, intra-state flows account for a significant share of the total flow system.

The proportion of intra-state flows vary from one commodity to other and to a large extent would depend upon its production—consumption cycle. The proportion of intra-regional flows may also tend to be large, if there are statutory restriction on the inter-state movement of certain commodities. It may be noted that from Table 17.1, that for some commodities, the proportion of intra-state flows is very large. In the case of sugarcane nearly 93 per cent of its flows are intra-state only. Similarly, more than the 40 per cent of the movement of some types of foodgrains, limestone, iron ore, coal & fuels, manure and cement is intra-state. Commodities with very little intra-state flows are fruits and vegetables, tea, cotton, tabacoo, edible oils, textiles, glassware and agricultural implements.

(ii) Similarly, in the case of spatial linkages our analysis has shown that nearly 27 per cent of the spatial linkages are established within the state only. The commodities with large proportion of

TABLE 17.1 : Intensity of Intra/Inter-state Flows

Sl. No.	Commodity Description	Freight (000 tonnes) Total	Intra State	% Intra to total (4/3)	No. of Spatial Linkages Total	Intra State	% Intra to total (7/6)	Freight Per Intra Linkage (5/4)	Inter State (8/7)
1	2	3	4	5	6	7	8	9	10
1	Rice	3577	1172	34.76	12493	8449	67.63	.1387	.5947
2	Wheat	6241	1488	23.84	9118	4340	47.60	.3428	.9948
3	Gram & Pulses	2351	210	8.93	28051	5817	20.73	.0361	.0963
4	Other Foodgrains	2369	966	40.78	20187	8297	41.10	.1164	.1180
5	Sugarcane	1692	1573	92.97	416	360	86.54	4.3694	2.0178
6	Fruits & Vegetables	450	12	2.67	3540	431	12.18	.0278	.1408
7	Fish	14	4	28.57	411	53	12.90	.0754	.0279
8	Tea	216	11	5.09	4473	717	16.03	.0153	.0545
9	Oil Seeds	1069	143	13.38	20542	4961	24.15	.0288	.0588
10	Cotton	539	39	7.24	12987	2974	22.90	.0131	.0499
11	Jute	678	192	28.32	9575	1532	16.00	.0671	.0604
12	Sugar	2341	432	18.45	17465	2862	16.39	.1509	.1307
13	Tobacco	87	5	5.74	4026	987	24.52	.0051	.0269
14	Salt Spices	2960	295	9.97	31713	6299	19.86	.0468	.1049
15	Hides & Skins	260	30	11.54	6525	2223	34.07	.0135	.0534
16	Plantation	232	22	9.48	8069	1864	23.10	.0118	.0338
17	Forestry	3110	750	24.12	31451	8327	26.79	.0890	.1025
18	Edible Oils	417	28	6.71	7388	1700	23.01	.0165	.0688
19	Limestone	11838	5515	46.58	17484	5557	31.78	.9924	.5301
20	Iron Ore	20112	8937	44.43	365	102	27.94	87.6175	42.49
21	Manganose Ore	2102	462	22.02	1507	241	15.99	1.9212	1.2946
22	Non-Ferrous Metals	135	12	8.89	10444	1990	19.05	.0006	.0145
23	Iron & Steel	9176	1326	14.45	62807	15099	24.04	.0878	.1645
24	Metal Scrap	348	54	15.51	3623	963	26.58	.0561	.1105
25	Coal & Fuels	62659	25404	40.54	12922	2390	18.50	10.6292	3.5373
26	Mineral Oils	10248	1992	19.44	7617	2795	36.69	.7127	1.7122
27	Firewood	1177	449	17.66	4592	1871	40.74	.2399	.2675
28	Fodder	2542	793	31.20	24979	8150	29.12	.0973	.1039
29	Manure	335	145	43.28	2127	562	26.42	.2580	.1214
30	Fertilizers	5194	1417	27.28	16646	5274	31.68	.2687	.3321
31	Pr. Bldg. Materials	1320	324	24.54	4572	1523	53.31	.2127	.3267
32	coal Tar	1063	116	10.91	2908	586	20.15	.1980	.4078
33	Cement	10257	4175	40.70	13897	5702	41.03	.5094	.7422
34	Bricks	561	82	14.62	2696	455	16.88	.1802	.2137
35	Textiles	624	38	6.08	33106	8469	24.12	.0045	.0220
36	Electrical Goods	332	53	10.25	21139	4032	19.07	.0082	.0169
37	Glassware	234	14	5.98	10906	12692	24.68	.0052	.0268
38	Paper	879	102	11.60	16496	5388	32.66	.0189	.0699
39	Rubber & Leather	195	20	10.26	12378	40277	32.53	.0049	.0209
40	Chemicals	708	114	16.10	28841	7891	27.36	.0144	.0284
41	Agricultural Implements	34	3	8.82	4289	1049	24.46	.0028	.0096
42	Transport Equipments	28	6	21.43	3203	642	20.04	.0093	.0086
43	Miscelleneous	5135	962	18.74	170121	52206	30.69	.0184	.0354

intra-state linkages are rice, wheat, sugarcane, other foodgrains, limestone and diesel.

(iii) Another interesting feature of the intra & inter-state flows is that normally the freight per interaction tends to be high for inter-state flows as compared to intra-state flows. The explanation lies in the fact that on the average the long distance interactions, though less in number, tend to be of bulk character as compared to the short distance interactions. The only exceptions are sugarcane, jute, limestone, iron ore, manganese ore, manure and miscellaneous commodities. For these commodities, the intra-state movements tend to be large.

The above analysis has clearly shown that for most of the commodities intra-regional flows and spatial inter-actions tend to be significant as compared to the total freight and any attempt to analyse the commodity flow matrices without considering the intra-regional flows would not properly bring out the complexities of the intra-regional flow phenomenon. It is this end in view, that the structural analysis of commodity flow matrices has been attempted in the following sections.

COMMODITY FLOWS AND THE REGIONAL STRUCTURE OF THE INDIAN ECONOMY:

To this point, the study was mainly concerned with the analysis of aggregate flows, omitting the inter-regional interdependencies. However, we now extend our area of enquiry to the strucural interdependence of various regions on one another. Analytical technique selected for this purpose is again Factor Analysis, using the non-symmetrical form of inter-regional flow matrices. Two different decompositions are performed-R-mode and Q-mode. The applicability and usefulness of these techniques in the decomposition of origin-destination matrices has been discussed earlier.

It may be recalled that through the application of R-mode factor analysis, the principal consuming regions (receivers) get linked to the major producting regions (origins). Following this method the regionwise commodity flow matrix was subjected to R-mode of factor analysis. The factoring process was halted after 10 factors, which explained about 78.5 per cent of the variance. However, we shall be discussing the results of only seven factors which taken together account for about 63 per cent. The contribution of other factors was less that 5 per cent. The communalities as shown in Column 11 of Tablè 172, range from 0.38 to 0.99. It may be noted that 36 out of a total of 61 regions have communalities greater than 0.90. The lower values of communalities represent the places where the competition among the neighboruing regions clouds the emerging pattern. One of such region is Coastal Gujarat which happens to be under the influence of Inland Gujarat as well as that of Coastal Maharastra. Therefore, the variations explained for this particular region is quite small.

The factor loadings and the corresponding prominent source of supply are depicted in Table 17.2. In most of the cases, the factor loadings are quite strong for the regions having high scores. This testifies the importance of intra-regional flows. The emerging patterns are depicted in Fig. 17.1. A number of sub-systems having strong interaction among themselves are easily discermable from the map. With a view to make comparisons between different sub-systems, only one composite map has been prepared.

The first factor accounts for about 16 per cent of the variance and designates the eastern portion (under the dominant influence of the port of Calcutta) of the country as a major generator of the railway freight traffic. The whole of North-West India and Gangetic plains have common receipt patterns and are linked to the Calcutta region. The dominent position of this region is partly a reflection of a colonial past in which import export requirements were the principal determinants of commdity flows. It may be noted that more than 10 per cent of the total national freight originates from the Calcutta metropolitan centre belonging to Central West Bengal region.

The second factor represents the Inland Gujarat as the major generator of freight traffic meant for Rajasthan, Delhi, Punjab and parts of Haryana. The port of Kandla influences considerably the receipt patterns of these regions. The share of Inland Gujarat to total originating freight in the country is about 5 per cent.

The third factor represents the receipts in the

TABLE : 17.2 **Factor loadings and destinations**

Region Code	*FACTOR* I	II	III	IV	V	VI	VII	VIII	IX	Commun-alities
1	2	3	4	5	6	7	8	9	10	11
1	—	—	—	—	—	—	—	—	—	.720
2	—	—	—	—	—	—	—	—	—	.649
3	.60966	—	—	—	—.54421	—	—	—	—	.969
4	.67398	.52111	—	—	—	—	—	—	—	.890
5	.56063	.60495	—	—	—	—	—	—	—	.966
6	.51528	.65321	—	—	—	—	—	—	—	.843
7	.87051	—	—	—	—	—	—	—	—	.923
8	—	.75183	—	—	—	—	—	—	—	.870
9	—	.54799	—	—	—	—.65408	—	—	—	.971
10	—	.87538	—	—	—	—	—	—	—	.828
11	—	.70589	—	—	—	—	—	—	—	.673
12	—	.94448	—	—	—	—	—	—	—	.957
13	—	.51248	—	—	—	—	—	—	—	.905
14	—	—	—	—	—	—	—	—	—	.953
15	.76937	—	—	—	—	—	—	—	—	.981
16	—	—	—	—	—	—	—	—	—	.644
17	.60404	—	—	—	—	—.69021	—	—	—	.887
18	—	—	—	—	—	—	—	—	—	.954
19	—	—	—	—	—.87135*	—	—	—	—	.989
20	—	—	—	—	—.60140	—	—	—	—	.897
21	—	—	—	.77806	—	—	—	—	—	.965
22	—	—	—	—	—.91121	—	—	—	—	.981
23	.60853	—	—	—	—	—	—	—	—	.560
24	—	.78507*	—	—	—	—	—	—	—	.868
25	—	—	—	—	—	—	—	—	—	.379
26	—	.58985	—	*	—	—	—	—	—	.887
27	—	—	—	.84373	—	—	—	—	—	.961
28	—	—	—	.81842	—	—	—	—	—	.975
29	—	—	—	—	—	—	—	—	—	.827
30	—	—	—	.61928	—	—	.73564	—	—	.981
31	—	—	—	—	—	—	—	—	—	.966
32	—	—	—	—	—	—	—	.83579	—	.821
33	.56022	—	—	—	—	—	—	—	—	.857
34	—	—	—	—	—	—	—	—	—	.874
35	—	—	—	—	—	—	.66758*	—	—	.971
36	—	—	—	—	—	—	—	.84146	—	.890
37	—	—	—	—	—	—	—	.64817*	—	.756
38	—	—	—	—	—	—	.95324	—	—	.965
39	—	—	—	—	—	—	—	.69569	—	.655
40	—	—	—	—	—	—	—	.93986	—	.913

1	2	3	4	5	6	7	8	9	10	11
41	—	—	—	—	—.93583	—	—	—	—	.971
42	—	—	—	—	—	—	—	—	—	.889
43	—	—	—	—	—	—	—	—	—	.868
44	—	—	—	—	—	—	—	—	.93784	.907
45	—	—	—	—	—	—	—	—	.86958	.835
46	—	—	—	—	—	—.57035	—	—	.75136*	.974
47	—	—	—	—	—	—.88150*	—	—	—	.980
48	.74482	—	—	—	—	—	—	—	—	.611
49	.93321	—	—	—	—	—	—	—	—	.966
50	.63491	—	.69511	—	—	—	—	—	—	.970
51	.93098	—	—	—	—	—	—	—	—	.968
52	.81151*	—	—	—	—	—	—	—	—	.984
53	.91938	—	—	—	—	—	—	—	—	.962
54	—	—	.97819*	—	—	—	—	—	—	.996
55	—	—	.97253	—	—	—	—	—	—	.981
56	—	—	.97439	—	—	—	—	—	—	.977
57	—	—	.97912	—	—	—	—	—	—	.991
58	—	—	—	—	—	—	—	—	.79616	.843
59	—	—	—	—	—	—	.97619	—	—	.974
60	—	—	—	—	—	—	—	—	—	.974
61	—	—	—	—	—	—	—	—	—	.979
Eigen velus										
	9.4675	5.9752	5.1200	3.9184	3.9063	3.7736	3.7154	3.4180	3.31	
Cumulative %										
	15.52	25.32	33.64	40.06	46.46	52.65	58.74	64.34	69.75	

*Indicates the prominent source of shipments for the factor.

North-Eastern regions with Assam as tne major generator of freight traffic for this region.

The Eastern Madhya Pradesh representing fifth factor emerges as a leading traffic generator for Coastal Andhra and Western Madhya Pradesh.

The sixth factor accounts for intra-state flows only.

The seventh factor accounts for nearly 10 per cent of the variance and designates the Inland Northern Karnatka as the second largest generator of the railway freight traffic. It's major shipments are those of iron ore.

Similarities in the receipt patterns of Kerala, parts of Tamil Nadu and Karnataka are represented through the sixth factor which accounts for 5.66 per cent of the total variance and designates the Southern Kerala as one of the leading traffic generators.

The above analysis has revealed some interesting features of the regional structure of the Indian economy. it is interesting to abserve that a number of nodal regions are associated with the port towns which act as the major originator of freight traffic.

In a similar fashion, the similarities in the shipments were examined through the application of Q-mode of factor analysis of the total inter-regional freight flow matrix. The Q-mode of factor analysis produces factors where loadings identify common origins and the factor scores represent a common origins and the factor scores represent a common destination. In all 14 factors have been obtained accounting for more than 85 per cent of the total variance. The communalities vary from 0.50 to 0.98 and in most of the cases are

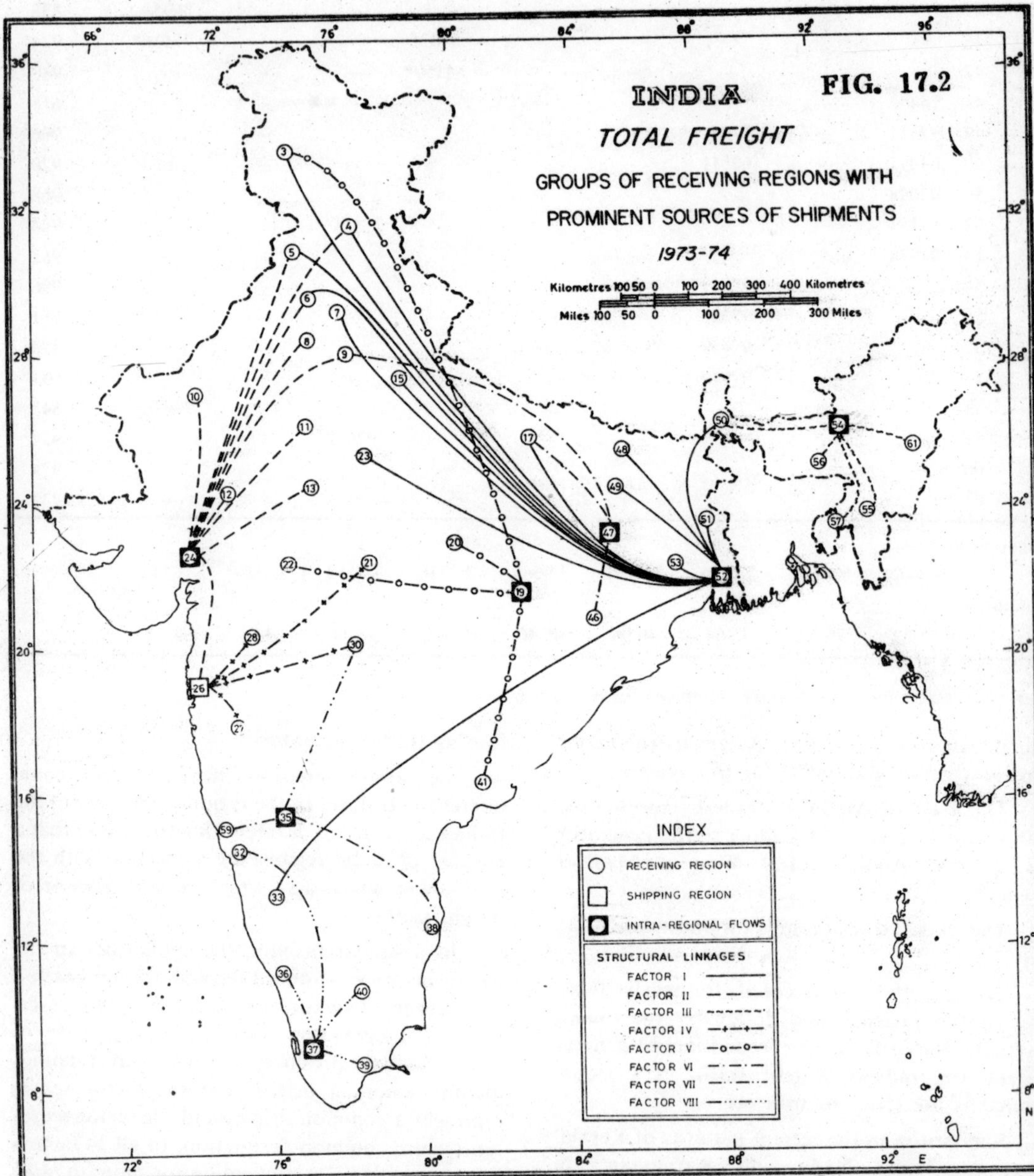

The territorial waters of India extend into the sea to a distance of twelve nautical miles measured from appropriate base line.

greater than 0.90. The factor loadings and the corresponding prominent receiving region based on the Q-mode of factor analysis of the inter-regional flow matrix are depicted in Table 17.3, Fig. 17.2 depicts the decomposed structure of the inter-regional flow matrix.

The first factor accounts for nearly 24 per cent of the total variance and depicts the orientation of the flows towards coastal Maharashtra. The reason for such a strong orientation of flows towards this region can be the relative importance of the port of Bombay and the consumption oriented nature of the metropolitan cities. Low factor loadings for this region on first factor points to the fact that most of the inflows are from other regions and intra-regional flows are not significant in this case. Most of the shipments from Gujarat, Rajasthan, Punjab, Haryana, parts of Madhya Pradesh and Delhi are to coastal Maharashtra. Coastal Maharashtra receives 3.88 per cent of the total national freight. It has also been observed that 91.81 per cent of the total receipts in Coastal Maharashtra are in Class and Class II cities only. The foregoing analysis thus clearly shows that the hinterland of Bombay extends to western and north-western India.

TABLE 17.3 : **Factor loading and sources of supply**

Region Code	*FACTOR* I	*II*	*III*	*IV*	*V*	*VI*	*VII*	*VIII*	*IX*	*Communalities*
1	2	3	4	5	6	7	8	9	10	11
1	.97181	—	—	—	—	—	—	—	—	.972
2	—	—	—	—	—	—	—	.75396	—	.710
3	—	.92403	—	—	—	—	—	—	—	.948
4	—	—	—	—	—	—	—	—	—	.813
5	.57162	.70918	—	—	—	—	—	—	—	.902
6	.84334	—	—	—	—	—	—	—	—	.954
7	.75183	—	—	—	—	—	—	—	—	.947
8	.57715	—	—	—	—	.51864	—	—	—	.695
9	.80726	—	—	—	—	—	—	*	—	.948
10	—	—	—	—	—	—	—	.73442*	—	.887
11	—	—	—	—	—	—	—	.70988*	—	.712
12	.70909	—	—	—	—	—	—	.61057	—	.939
13	—	—	—	—	—	.54700	—	.53614	—	.917
14	—	—	—	.82246	—	—	—	—	—	.888
15	—	—	—	.92684	—	—	—	—	—	.887
16	—	—	—	.95314*	—	—	—	—	—	.947
17	—	—	—	—	—	—	—	—	—	.598
18	—	—	—	.96735	—	—	—	—	—	.962
19	—	—	—	—	—	—	—	—	.79551	.767
20	—	—	—	—	—	—	—	—	—	.701
21	.59194	—	—	—	—	—	—	—	—	.874
22	.88405	—	—	—	—	—	—	—	—	.964
23	—	—	—	—	—	—	—	—	—	.567
24	-	—	—	—	—	.83254	—	—	—	.837
25	—	—	—	—	—	.84165*	—	—	—	.783
26	*	—	—	—	—	.59990	—	—	—	.850
27	.78667	—	—	—	—	—	—	—	—	.867
28	.96429	—	—	—	—	—	—	—	—	.963

1	2	3	4	5	6	7	8	9	10	11
29	.87724	—	—	—	—	—	—	—	—	.958
30	.97415	—	—	—	—	—	—	—	—	.968
31	.51585	—	—	—	—	—	—	—	—	.806
32	—	—	.59145	—	.54667	—	—	—	—	.849
33	—	—	—	—	.94847	—	—	—	—	.955
34	—	—	—	—	.73994*	—	—	—	—	.944
35	—	—	—	—	—	—	—	—	—	.744
36	—	—	.81880	—	—	—	—	—	—	.899
37	—	—	.85083	—	—	—	—	—	—	.783
38	—	—	—	.76039	—	—	—	—	—	.897
39	—	—	.87895	—	—	—	—	—	—	.818
40	—	—	.63261*	—	—	—	—	—	—	.766
41	—	—	—	—	—	—	—	—	.88411*	.888
42	—	—	—	—	—	—	—	—	.57841	.805
43	.50294	—	—	—	—	—	—	—	—	.857
44	—	.81973	—	—	—	—	—	—	—	.883
45	—	—	—	—	—	—	—	—	—	.505
46	—	.66745	—	—	—	—	—	—	—	.862
47	—	—	—	—	—	—	—	—	—	.801
48	—	—	—	—	—	—	—	—	—	.548
49	—	.62275	—	—	—	—	—	—	—	.876
50	—	.94652	—	—	—	—	—	—	—	.966
51	—	.96785	—	—	—	—	—	—	—	.972
52	—	.92133*	—	—	—	—	—	—	—	.964
53	—	.75886	—	—	—	—	—	—	—	.813
54	—	—	—	—	—	—	.93864*	—	—	.990
55	—	—	—	—	—	—	.85406	—	—	.931
56	—	.97767	—	—	—	—	—	—	—	.973
57	—	.91674	—	—	—	—	—	—	—	.975
58	.97891	—	—	—	—	—	—	—	—	.979
59	—	—	—	—	.61598	—	—	—	—	.759
60	—	—	.95807	—	—	—	—	—	—	.954
61	—	—	—	—	—	—	.95364	—	—	.932
Eigen values										
	10.8149	9.4639	4.5186	3.9575	3.5655	2.9723	2.8500	2.6295	2.4960	
Cumulative %										
	17.73	33.24	40.65	47.14	52.99	57.86	62.53	66.84	70.93	

*Indicates the prominent destination for the factor.

The second factor accounts for nearly 15 per cent of the variance and also represents the orientation of flows towards another metropolitan city of Calcutta (Central West Bengal). It has been observed that 82 per cent of the receipts of this region are in again class I and class II cities only and it receives nearly 11% of the total freight in India. The regions falling in this group are from Orissa, Bihar and North-Eastern Hills. All those regions have similar shipment patterns with a common destination as Calcutta based Central West Bengal. The hinterland of Calcutta is this restricted to neighbouring regions only and is much small in area as compared to that of Bombay hinterland. Inspite of this, the share of commodities received in the Central West Bengal

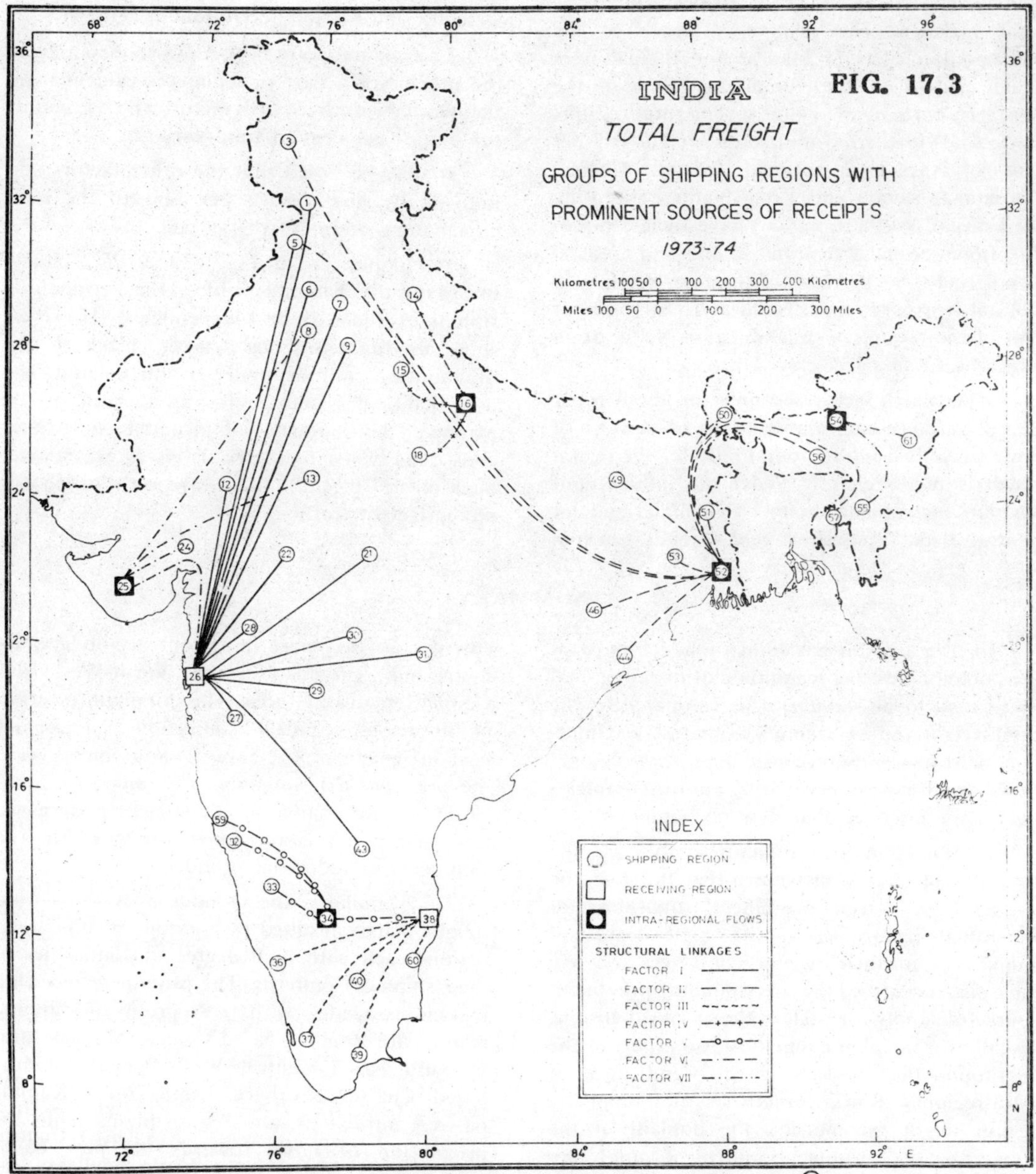

INDIA
FIG. 17.3
TOTAL FREIGHT
GROUPS OF SHIPPING REGIONS WITH
PROMINENT SOURCES OF RECEIPTS
1973-74
Kilometres 100 50 0 100 200 300 400 Kilometres
Miles 100 50 0 100 200 300 Miles
INDEX
SHIPPING REGION
RECEIVING REGION
INTRA-REGIONAL FLOWS
STRUCTURAL LINKAGES
FACTOR I
FACTOR II
FACTOR III
FACTOR IV
FACTOR V
FACTOR VI
FACTOR VII

are nearly 3 times that of coastal Maharashtra having Bombay as an prominent city.

The third factor represents the orientation of flows in the Southern India. These flows take place towards inland and coastak norther Tamil Nadu and account for about 10 per cent of the total variance. The relative influence of the metropolitan cities of Madras and Bangalore is again evident in the commodity flow in the Southern parts of the country. The total receipts at Coastal Northern Tamil Nadu are about 3 per cent of the total national freight. Coastal Karnataka, Kerala and Tamil Nadu (excepting the Coastal Northern region) have their commodity flows oriented towards Inland and Coastal Tamil Nadu. 95 per cent of the total receipts in Coastal Northern Tamil Nadu and nearly 74 per cent of the receipts in Inland Tamil Nadu are in large cities (class I & class II).

The fourth factor accounts for about 6 per cent of variance and represents the orientation of flows towards Central Uttar Pradesh—the region which is predominantly under the influence of Kanpur metropolitan city. The hinterland of Central Uttar Pradesh largely extends towards West, since there is no other major competing region influencing overlapping with its area of influence. However, on the eastern side, the Eastern Uttar Pradesh fails to get sufficiently high loadings for any of the factors. This clearly represent the area of common influence of Calcutta and Kanpur metropolitan centres.

The orientation of flows towards Assam from the other North-Eastern regions is evident from the factor loadings of fifth factor, which accounts for only 5 per cent of total variance.

It may be noted that the other factors add individually less than 5 per cent to the total explanatory power of the system.

A comparison of Fig. 17.1 & 17.2 clearly brings out the changing profile of the metropolitan system in India since Independence. However, some modifications have taken place in the organisation. For example, Inland Gujarat, has now acquired a new status as a result of the planned development of Kandla port and consequently led to the relatively weak involvement of the Coastal Maharashtra as the originator of the freight traffic.

SUMMARY

(i) The analysis has shown that for most of the commodities, the magnitude of intra-regional flows tend to be significant as compared to the total freight and an attempts to analysis the inter-regional flows without considering intra-regional flows would not properly bring out the complexities of the inter-regional flow phenomenon.

(ii) The R-mode of factor analysis of the total freight matrix has shown that India can be divided into seven prominent subgroups of functional regions each with high degree of similarities in their receipt characteristics. We have also indentified the corresponding prominent source of supply for each of the seven subgroups. Usually the supplying region is also a part of the subgroups thus underlying the significance of intra-regional flows, otherwise the supplying region might fall outside the domain of the subgroup The prominent sources of supply are Calcutta based central West Bengal, Inland Gujarat Assam, Coastal Maharashtra, Northern Madhya Pradesh, Southern Bihar and Inland Northern Karnataka. Calcutta based West Bengal emerges as the most important region and its hinterland extends to the North-West and Gangatic plains of India. The dominant position of this region is partly a reflection of a colonial past in which import export requirements were the principal determinants of commodity flows. From our earlier analysis of aggregate patterns we find that this region mainly specialises in the shipments of industrial products.

(iii) Similarly, the Q-mode analysis of total freight matrix resulted in 5 groups of functional regions each with high degree of similarities in their shipment patterns. The prominent receiving regions associated with these group of shipping regions are Bombay based Coastal Maharashtra, Calcutta based Central West Bengal, Madras based Coastal Northern Tamil Nadu, Kanpur based Central U.P. and Assam plains. Thus the orientation of flows towards the port based metropolitan cities is quite strong. The results of aggregate commodity flow patterns show that these regions receive large quantities of freight.

18

SOME CONCLUDING OBSERVATIONS

AS a conclusion to the study, it would be appropriate to review the implications of our empirical results. Such a review will serve a number of imporant purposes. First, it would permit us to evaluate the success of our own analysis using empirical evidence as a frame of reference. Second, it would allow us to re-evaluate some of the existing notions about the complexities of inter-regional flows in the light of the new evidence brought out by the present study. Third, it would allow us to identify the weaknesses of the present study in answering some questions and also permit us to speculate on future lines of research so as to further extend the frontiers of analysis of inter-regional commodity flows.

Recognising the fact that our knowledge of the composition, magnitude and direction of the inter-regional trade, by and large, is meagre, the present study is designed to fill this gap through the empirical analysis of point to point commodity flow matrices in respect of the freight carried by the Indian Railways for the year 1973-74. The importance of the railway freight in the economy is evident from the fact that more than 90 per cent of the total production of raw materials need transportation and the Indian Railways account for bulk of the movement of intermediate inputs like coal, cement, fertilizers, iron and steel ores and cotton.

To begin with, an analysis of the transport network structure is essential in order to understand the pattern of flows in the economic system. The analysis of transport network has indicated the concentration of flows towards large metropolitan centres. The overpowering pull of the metropolitan centres in shaping the regional pattern of network becomes apparent from the gauge composition of the railway network. It has been observed that the spatial variations in the network density of different order settlements is a function of their relative location with respect to the higher order centres and the alignment of trunk routes. The patterns of regional inter-dependencies and the relationships among flows have been identified and analysed in the light of current theoretical understanding of inter-connections embracing multi-lateral commodity flows. The analysis is primarly based on the assumption that the movement of a particular commodity from one region to the other reflects the gross inter-connection of an economy's sectoral as well as territorial components. Thus, the structure of the economy, manifests itself in the level and pattern of inter-regional commodity flows and it is in this context that the commodity flows acquire socio-economic meaning. The analysis of inter-regional commodity flows has, therefore, been considered to be a valid and useful tool for probing in to the pattern of regional inter-dependencies within the national economy.

The Indian experience is particularly valuable for a study of multi-lateral commodity flows since the port oriented railway network established by the British in India was a potent instrument of implementing the policy of trans froming the colonial economy into a source of raw materials and a market for the manufactured goods of British origin. Thus, the associated freight policies were evolved to operationalise the centrifugality of commodity flows over the vast tracts of the country.

Though India achieved independence more than three decades ago, the nature of the port oriented flows has only been marginally modified and the present day problems of lopsided development can be traced back to the colonial era. Berry's analysis of commodity flow data for the early sixties has shown that the four functional regions of India have continued to gravitate towards the super metropolitan centres of the country. These are Calcutta, Bombay, Delhi and Madras. It has been observed that the essential weakness of the Indian economic space lies in its economic base, which is characterised by a significant primary, a weak secondary and a bloated tertiary sector and the current fragmentation of the urban-rural continuum in India is a direct consequence of the historical hiatus between the twin processes of industrialisation and urbanisation between vartical shifts and horizontal mobility.

In the light of these specificities of the Indian situation, which it shares, in its essential characteristics, with the entire colonial world, it was considered worthwhile to examine whether the regional structure of the Indian economy has undergone a qualitative change after thirty year's of planned development.

It is paradoxical to observe that while in the Indian context, the planners have recognised the balanced regional development as one of the policy objectives and in practice, the effective national economic planning is being persued without detailed statistical information on the nature and pattern of the interactions and the structure of the inter-regional inter-dependencies. The planners have been unconcerned about the linkages and perhaps unaware of the patterns of regional inter-dependencies. The present study intends to provide inputs which in conjuction with other factors should assist in the recognition of spatial and non-spatial problems associated with regional inter-dependencies.

To begin with, an analysis of the transportation network structure is essential in order to understand the flow patterns. Such an analysis of the Indian railway network indicates the concentration of well connected centres in a few pockets of the Indian space economy which are usually associated with large metropolitan and city centres, wherein the controlling role of the metropolitan centres in shaping the regional pattern of network efficiency also becomes apparent. Such linkages are further accentuated by the gauge composition of the railway network. It is observed that the spatial variation in the network density of different order settlements is a function of their relative location with respect to the bigger order centres and the alignment of trunk routes. Thus, the settlements have a high density along the Gangetic plains and around the metropolitan and bigger order urban centres. Low density is observed in Central and South-Central railway zone.

Given the imbalances in the railway network structure, an attempt is then made to examine the inter-regional exchange patterns and its relationship with the patterns of development.

The commodity composition of the railway freight has shown that bulk commodities continue to dominate the freight flows in India. Their share in the total freight has moved from 52.8 per cent in 1950-51 to 84.5 per cent in 1977-78. These commodities are basic raw materials, coal, fuels, cement, and iron and steel which are mainly used as intermediate inputs in many productive sectors of the economy and consequently have very high forward linkages.

The role of Indian railways in the national development process has been studied by considering the relationship between the indices of railway freight and other economic indicators. A very high correspondence between the index of rail freight, on the one hand and indices of national income and of industrial, mining and agricultural production, on the other strengthens the hypothesis that increase in the level of economic activity leads to increase in the interdependence among regions and hence to increases in the railway freight.

The analysis of the average lead presents an interesting picture. While it increased during the period 1950-51 to 1974-75, a declining trend has been observed since 1974-75. Rising average lead generally suggests that geographically compact production complexes, with strong input-output links within, have not been formed. The declining trend in the average lead, however, does suggest a reversal of this phenomenon. The trend of the falling average lead has not, however, been stabilized and it is quite possible that the fall in the Average lead during the last two or three years may well turn out to be quite enphemeral in character. Average lead of all the important commodities has increased over the years except for coal and fuel.

Wide regional variations in the volume of originating freight have been observed. All the regions of the economic system do not necessarilly participate in the exchange process to the same extent or in the same manner. Out of a total of 335 districts in India, 18 do not participate in the exchange process at all. The spatial distribution of the total originating and terminating freight brings out the relative concentration of the production and consumption centres. On the basis of the distribution of the total originating and terminating freight, three broad categories of spatial arrangements have been identified. These are:

i areas like Dhanbad, Burdwan, Hazaribagh, Singhbhum and Bhilai specialising in mineral and basic manufacturing industries;

ii important ports like Calcutta, Bombay, Madras, Kandla and Visakhapatnam, which act as transhipment points for imports and exports; and

iii industrially advanced nodes like Kanpur, Baroda, Ahmedabad, Pune and jamnagar.

That the consumption centres are more dispersed in space as compared to the production centres is evident from the fact that the pattern of receipts is more evenly distributed as compared to that of the shipments. On the basis of the total shipments and receipts from and to a particular region, a classification of the districts based on the following criterion was developed and was illustrated with suitable maps. The classification is as under:

i high originating and high receipt areas
ii high originating and low receipt areas
iii low originating and high receipt areas
iv low originating and low receipt areas

It is interesting to note that out of a total 317 districts, 225 fall in the category of low shipments and low receipts. 57 districts have total shipments more than the national average and 67 have receipts more than the corresponding national average. Only a few districs account for a large share of shipments and receipts. It has been observed that the 8 top ranking districts account for 35 per cent of the total shipments and 31 per cent of the total receipts, while the lowest 100 districts account for only 0.50 per cent of shipments and 70 per cent of the total receipts. It is clear from the above that the pattern of inter-regional trade is dominated by a relatively few areas. The inequalities in the production and consumption processes of various commodities have been measured by coefficient of variation and Lorenz curve analysis. The value of Gini coefficient has also been calculated for shipments and receipts for each commodity separately.

The distribution of shipments is more skewed as compared to the distribution of receipts. This shows that the production centres are relatively more concentrated in space as compared to the consumption centres. The highly skewed distribution pattern of certain commodities like ores, raw materials, mineral oils and resource based products can be a healthy sign of modernisation and industrial development. Location of natural resources, economies of scale and technological constraints in the production processes would result in the skewed distribution of these commodities. However, the highly skewed distribution of commodities like iron and steel, cement, fertilizers, and other industrial products, show that the disparities exist between the few top consumers and the remaining areas of the economic system. Wide regional disparities in their consumption and production processes have been observed in spite of the fact that balanced regional development has been one of the major policy objective of Indian planning.

In any economic system actively engaged in the production and consumption activities, the movement of any particular commodity will be related to the movement of other commodities either in the same or in the opposite direction. For example, raw materials and fuels which are complimentary to each other in the production process are expected to be received at similar nodes. While the movement of raw materials and industrial products is expected to be negatively related with each other. Receipts of one would be associated with the shipments of the other. In this study an attempt was made to capture the inter-relationships between the movement of various commodities. The analysis has shown that the primary and resource based industries are efficiently located in space. Dominance of a few regions in the inter-regional trade of industrial products has been clearly brought out by a significantly high correlation between the originating and terminating freight of the industrial products. It has also been observed that areas which receive industrial products also receive construction material, fuels and raw materials. Areas specialising in the production of fuels are generally backward in agriculture and depend on other regions of the system for their requirements of food products. A high correlation has been observed between the shipments and receipts of fuels and raw materials showing that these commodities move over shorter distance and their movement is of an intra-regional type.

Another meaningful dimension of the commodity flow analysis pertains to the study of spatial distribution of areas with similar flow characteristics. The analysis has shown that similarities in the freight pattern are more pronounced in the receipts than in the case of originating freight. Three groups of shippers have been identified on the basis of commodity flows for originating freight:

- i areas specialising in industrial activity;
- ii areas specialising in the agricultural activity; and
- iii areas specialising in the shipments of coal and fuels.

Well defined areal clusters have been identified for industrially active regions and these are:

- i spatial clusters specialising in industrial activity around mining areas;
- ii spatial clusters specialising in industrial activity around principal port towns; and
- iii other important nodes of industrial activity.

Similarly, the spatial clusters in terms of the shipments of coal and fuel and agricultural activity have been shown cartographically in a series of maps. It has also been shown that agriculturally advanced areas do not have strong industrial base thus leading to huge imports of cement, fertilizers, iron and steel and other industrial goods into these areas. Thus the development of industry and agriculture in space appears to be mutually exclusive, have in general low level of agricultural activity and vice-versa.

Areas having similar receipt characteristics have also been identified. Since the areas which receive food products also receive large quantities of raw materials, fuels, construction material and industrial products, the impact of industrial characterstics is more pronounced in receipts. Composite index has been developed for the level of industrial activity in each district and three distinct type of regions have been identified and these are:

- i port towns which act as traditional outle of imports and exports;
- ii industrially advanced areas receiving mainly raw materials and fuels; and
- iii areas specialising in the production of agriculture but receiving large quantities of non-agricultural products.

Relationships between the freight characteristics and the levels of development of a district have also been studied in detail. It has been observed that the indices of development are better related to the receipts than to shipments. This leads us to conclude that consumption patterns reflect the level of development of a district more effectively. Index of urban development has the highest correlation with the receipts thus showing that urban centres are the major consumers of food products, raw materials, construction material and industrial products. Trends in the level of urban development and the level of industrial activity also show positive correspondence. The analysis also show that most of the manufacturing is being done at urban centres which continue to dominate the Indian space economy.

The existence of numerous spatially separated nodes of consumption as well as competing sources of supply suggest the existence of distance decay effect. Practically no empirical evidence is available about the nature of distance decay function for commodity flows in India.

The existence of distance-freight relationship for the commodity flows in India has been demonstrated by plotting the variables on graph paper on a linear scale and the degree of association between the two variables has been measured by finding out the coefficient of determination. The analysis has shown that the distance decay rates vary from one commodity to another depending upon its nature and utility. Low rated commodities like ores, raw materials and coal have a very sharp rate of decay, while for high rated commodities like iron and steel, the distance effect is smaller though significant.

Simple linear and log linear regression models were tested to explain the distance decay for various commodities. Log linear regession model has been found to be a good fit for low rated commodities like raw materials, coal and fuels. These commodities move in bulk over short distances and hence the decay is fast and the intercept is large. Simple linear regression model has been found suitable for all the other commodities. The bulk movement of construction materials is over shorter distances. The distance decay rate has been found to be very high for construction materials. Based on the value of the two parameters of the regression equation, market accessibility of each commodity has been calculated. Industrial products have the highest value of the market accessibility followed by food products, miscellaneous commodities, coal and fuel, inputs into agriculture, construction material and raw materials, in that order. The highest and the lowest value of market accessibility for industrial products and raw materials reveal that the manufacturing industries tend to be located near the sources of raw materials rather than the market centres. The above analysis also establishes that the intervening distance is a major determinant of the inter-regional trade and the intensity of movement falls as the distance increases.

It has been recognised that the effect of any transportation system upon regional specialisation is necessarily transmitted through the freight rate policy as the transportation costs which get reflected through the freight rate structure play a definitive role in motivating location decisions. Freight rate policy is one of the instruments which may be operated differentially across the regions to achieve the desired pattern of industrialisation and may be manipulated to overcome the effect of the friction of distance to the advantage or disadvantage of a given region. This can be operationalised either by grouping the commodities in different classes and/or by suitably tapering the freight rates.

Freight equalisation is another instrument which may be operated differentially for fostering the industrialisation along the desired lines. However, the analysis has shown that freight equalisation by itself is not an optimal policy for achieving the objectives of balanced regional development.

The available evidence has shown that the expansion of railway network in India was definitely not governed by the requirements of the internal economy but was manipulated to the advantage of the British empire and the freight rates were successfully manipulated as an effective instrument to regulate the magnitude and direction of the commodity flows. The port oriented traffic was highly subsidised at the cost of the inland traffic. However, efforts have been made during the recent past to rationalise the freight structure in the light of specific task which the railways have been assigned in the development process.

The analysis of the existing freight rate structure has shown that wide differentials in the basic rates of different commodities still continue to exist and the approach to rate fixation has more or less remained unchanged. It is more related to the principle of 'what the traffic will bear' rather than the 'cost of service'. In view of the monopolistic position of the Indian railways, the cross-subsidisation of the unremunerative by remunerative traffic was possible. This is evident from the fact that the impact of distance is considerably neurtalised by suitably tapering the freight rates. In this context, it may be noted that for most of the bulk commodities, the exponential model fits well between distance and freight rates and such commodities are carried at below rates in view of public policy considerations. Such a situation has resulted in operational losses for the railways.

With the recent expansion and liberalising of policies relating to road transport, the railways are no longer able to maintain their monopoly position and are consequently losing a considerable volume of high rated traffic in favour of road transport and this has further aggrevated the financial situation of the railways leading to high operational losses. The analysis has shown that nearly 60 per cent of the total losses were incurred on the movement of foodgrains only.

The analysis has further shown that there is a little scope for railways to eliminate their losses by following the policy of cross-subsidisation since the freight rates for nearly 80 per cent of traffc are fixed on public policy considerations. For the remaining commodities there is already stiff competition from the road hauliers and any increase in their rates may have only marginal impact. Thus the only alternative is to adjust the freight rates on the basis of cost of service principole. It is unfortunate to observe that inspite of its crucial importance, precise data on movement costs of different commodities is not available and hence it becomes difficult to find out the incidence of cost oriented freight rates on prices. It is expected that the railways in their own interest would evolve suitable costing techniques.

It is evident from the above findings that all regions do not participate in the exchange process to an equal extent. The ability of a particular settlement to participate in the exchange process would depend upon its location in terms of accessibility and connectivity, on one hand and upon its functional nature, on the other. It is in this context that the analysis of urban-rural interactions acquires added significance. Urban-rural interactions reflect inter-sectoral realtions and are essentially derived from the latter. In a normative frame of reference, the product of the primary sector would be shipped from the rural to the urban sector in the form of food products and raw materials in exchange for wage goods and technological inputs into agriculture which would be shipped from the urban to rural areas. The upward, downward and lateral commodity flows are thus expected to reinforce and provide the necessary inputs for the balanced development of all types of settlements. However, the empirical reality is much different. The analysis of such flows between villages, towns and cities has shown the persistence of uni-directional rather than bi-directional linkages. It has been observed that the small towns instead of becoming the nodes of diffusion of growth impulses have become weak and anaemic. The analysis has shown that while upward flows (from lower order to higher order settlements) are quite strong, the corresponding intensity of downward flows is very weak. It has also been shown that the intensity of the inter-city exchange for the industrial products is very strong. The cities with 13 per cent of total population account for more than 70 per cent of receipts of industrial products.

In view of the uni-directional nature of urban-rural flows, it was considered necessary that an exploratory analysis of the relationships between the economic base of the Indian urban settlements and their freight characteristics would provide a meaningful insight into the nature of inter-dependencies generated through the organisation of economic activities in space. It has been observed that the Indian urban settlements are characterised by the persistence of a weak secondary and a bloated tertiary sector and has consequently led to distortions in the nature and magnitude of their commodity flows also. The intensity of this infirmity goes on becoming more and more acute as we go down the hierarchy in the system.

This assessment of the Indian urban system also gets corraborated by the analysis of the functional characteristics of urban settlements. The distribution of settlements in functional categories indicates the dominance of the settlements specialising in non-household industries and the concentration of manufacturing settlements in the large size categories. It is interesting to observe that the bi-functional characteristics of the urban settlements show the combination of non-productive sectors rather than the productive sector with its ancillary non-productive sector.

The commodity flow characteristics of the urban settlements have shown that the towns with agriculture and household industries show relative self-sufficiency and are, by and large, inert and passive in the interactive mechanism. Mining centres tend to have large shipments and low receipts and also indicate the absence or weak nature of the links between extraction and secondary production within this subset of towns which have emerged as fuel and raw material appendages of large agglomerations specialising in manufacturing. The urban centres specialising in tertiary activities tend to have large spatial linkages but a small volume of flows. It is, therefore, evident that any strategy of urban development which does not aim at transforming the distorted economic base of the Indian urban system would be futile. Such a developmental strategy should be based on the strengthening of the secondary sector and bringing the tertiary sector to a reasonable proportion.

It has also been observed that the metropolitan centres constituting the apex of the hierarchical system of settlements have played a crucial role in the integration of the home market through the process of upward, downward and lateral interactions. There were nine metropolitan cities in India in 1971. These are Calcutta, Bombay, Delhi, Madras, Hyderabad, Bangalore, Kanpur, Ahmedabad and Pune. The Indian metropoles were established on the virgin land and acted as counter magnets against the system of centrifigal pulls exerted by the historically evolved inter-settlement linkages. During the colonial period, the orientation of the internal commodity flows towards these newly developed ports led to the emergence and strengthening of the centrifugal pulls operationalising the suction mechanism. In view of their crucial importance, the metropolitan port towns developed into 'primate' cities which devoured like cannibals the other towns of the hinterland. The examination of the commodity flow data for the metropolitan cities clearly brings out their dominant role in the spatial organisation of the Indian economic space. The analysis has shown that the imbalances in the space economy have generated the distorted role of the metropoles and have been themselves sustained by these distortions.

The analysis of commodity flow data has shown that not only the phenomenon of distorted dominance of the metropoles is well marked but even within the limited system of the metropoles (Bombay, Calcutta, Delhi and Madras) have continued to play their distorting role even in the seventies. There is also a tendency for strong lateral inter-metropolitan flows and the disproportionately large share of the same in the system of national flows indicates a partial fragmentation of the vertical continnum of the national market, whereby the metropolitan system is fast acquiring the character of an encapsulated world in itself.

It is evident from the foregoing findings that the economy is organised as a system where a set of nodes at different hiearchical levels are inter-linked by sets of relationships with each as well as between the different levels of hierarchy. Within the framework of our analysis it was considered to identify three types of nodes metropolitan, satellite and the hinterland nodes. For analysis of hierarchy in the nodal system a variety of techniques are available. We have used the indicators corresponding to the volume of flows, spatial linkages and the average lead. To identify the nodes falling in each category, the principle of nesting was also introduced.

The analysis of data for all 6775 nodes resulted in a hierarchy of nodes in which four first order centres and eight second order centres emerged and the remaining nodes were classified as the nodes of third order. Some nodes having overlapping characteristics were also identified. The nodes included in this group were those which could not qualify on all the selected criterion. For example, it has been shown that all nodes falling in the mineral producing belt are characterised by high originating flows but low receipts and low average distance.

An attempt was also made to develop a typology of satellite centres on the basis of their commodity flow characteristics. Three major groups have been identified. The first group of nodes consists of old satellites of tertiary activities. This group includes towns like Baroda, Ahmedabad Sholapur, Gwalior and Itarsi etc. The second group of nodes corresponds to new satellites of industrial activity. Prominent amongthese are towns like Durgapur, Tatanagar and Rourkela etc. The third group of satellite towns consists of ports like Mangalore, Cochin, Kandla, and Visakhapatnam.

It is clear from the analysis of satellite towns that they have a very well marked regional base from where the commodities are gathered and exchanged with other nodes. The distance characteristics clearly bring out the nature of their links with the neighbouring regions. These features of concentration of flows, however, do suggest that in a large country like India, there would exist economic sub-systems i.e., a group of regions having strong links mutually within the group than with other regions outside the group. Within the framework of the present study, the identification of such groups of origins or of groups of destinations or of groups of origins and destinations, that are functionally bound together by a high degree of interaction has been undertaken through the application of R and Q modes of factor analysis to the inter-regional commodity flow matrices.

Before proceeding with the identification of different sub-groups, the intensity of intra-regional flows was examined for different commodities and the analysis has shown that for most of the commodities, the intra-state flows and the number of spatial linkages tend to be significant as compared to the national freight and the corresponding number of spatial linkages. Thus, because of the non-availability of data on intra-regional flows the earlier studies on commodity flows in the Indian context could not bring out properly the role of commodity flows in integrating the national economy.

It is interesting to observe that for some

commodities, the proportion of intra-state flows to total flows is very large. For example, more than 93 per cent of the sugarcane movement through the railways is intra-state. More than 40 per cent of the movement of other foodgrains, limestone, iron ore, coal and fuels, manure and cement is intra-state. Another important feature of the intra and inter-state flows is that normally the freight per interaction tends to be very high for inter-state flows as compared to the intra-state flows.

The R-mode of factor analysis of the total freight matrix has resulted in a scheme of regionalisation which shows that India can be divided into seven prominent sub-groups of functional regions, each with high degree of similarities in their receipt characteristics. The prominent sources of supply corresponding to each of these seven sub-groups have also been identified through the analysis of factor scores. It is interesting to note that normally the supplying region is also a part of the sub-group thus underlying the importance of intra-regional flows and the system in such cases would appear to be a closed sub-system.

The overshadowing influence of Calcutta based West Bengal on its hinterl and extending to the North-West and Gangetic plains is partly a reflection of the colonial past in which the import export requirements were the principal determinants of commodity flows.

The analysis has also shown that Bombay based Coastal Maharashtra is relatively less involved in the originating freight as compared to Inland Gujarat, which has now acquired a new status as a result of development planning during the successive Five Year Plans. As a part of the planning strategy it was decided to modernise the port of Kandla for handling the incoming freight so as to relieve the Bombay port of the excessive congestion. The other metropolitan centres of Delhi and Madras are also losing their importance as the major originators of freight. In its place some new centres of public investment have emerged as the leading suppliers of industrial and other items of mass consumption. These trends are indicative of the successful implementation of India's strategy for self-reliance. Apart from old satellite centres, a new set of satellite centres of public investment have thus emerged to serve the main agglometrations.

The Q mode of factor analysis of total freight matrix resulted in 5 sub-groups of supplying regions, the flows from which are directed to the following prominent receiving regions :

i Bombay based Coastal Maharashtra;
ii Calcutta based West Bengal;
iii Madras based Coastal Northern Tamil Nadu;
iv Kanpur based Central Uttar Pradesh; and
v Assam plains.

The analysis has thus clearly shown that the direction of flows still continues to be metropolitan oriented. Curiously enough, most of the commodities terminate in large cities only. For example, while class I and class II cities receive more than 82 per cent of the receipts in Calcutta based West Bengal, the corresponding figure for Bombay based Coastal Maharashtra is nearly 92 per cent. A similar trend also emerges through the analysis of the number of spatial linkages.

In the present study we have broached upon a subject, which can only be described as enormous, and which lies at the interface of Economics and Geography. The results comprise in their own right, an important contribution that this study makes to the understanding of the commodity flow phenomenon. The approach that we have adopted has emphasised the need for commodity flow analysis not only at a highly aggregated level but also looking at it from the disaggregated point of view as well. The level of aggregation that we have used varies from the highly aggregate that is the nation to that of individual node in the system of interactive process. In spite of this, further work needs to be done in understanding the nature and patterns of commodity flows at the micro-level. Directly arising from this study is the need, firstly, to extend the analysis to other modes of transport and secondly to examine the temporal shifts in commodity flows and the spatial organisation of the space economy. One gap that still remains in the field of freight flows is to provide reliable and precise estimates of the movement costs associated with different commodities by different modes. Such an analysis would be highly useful in formulating a sound national transport policy. Finally, an area which we have not touched upon at all is to make use of this data for the projection purposes. However, a meaningful investigation in these areas would require much bigger efforts and is expected that the results of this study would provide useful inputs for a series of exercises along the suggested lines.

APPENDICES

APPENDIX I

SOURCES OF COMMODITY FLOW DATA IN SOME SELECTED COUNTRIES

AUSTRALIA

A review of literature reveals that there is no systematic mechanism by which commodity flow data is collected periodically in Australia. However, number of studies based on commodity flow data have been reported for the Australian economy. Earlier works such as that of Rimmer (1970) have focused on particular sectors of the freight industry, sometimes in selected areas. Later attempts by Holsman (1975, 1980) used aggregate state data for an analysis of interaction patterns, or Smith (1963, 1970a, 1970b)has used commodity flow data for ascertaining regional spheres of influence in selected areas of the Australian economy.

For effective national economic planning, like other developing economies, the Australian economy was also faced with the lack of detailed information on spatial and industrial linkages that existed between its various regions. To overcome this weakness in the national economic data base, a national freight study was undertaken by the Commonwealth Government during 1972. It ascertained the tonnage of freight flows by road rail, sea, air and pipeline between different regions of Australia for the year 1971. Such data was published for the first time in 1976. Road and rail transport are predominantly used for non-bulk freight. Road transport in Australia, as elsewhere, is predominantly involved in short distance haulages only. The pipeline are exclusively involved in inter-state movement of crude oil gas liquids in Victoria.

The commodity flow matrices for the Australian economy have been published by the Bureau of Transport as 'Estimates of Australian Inter-regional Freight Movement—1971-72.' The survey covered the following modes :

- i Road;
- ii Railways;
- iii Sea; and
- iv Air.

In addition, the total freight was again divided in to 3 categories and the data on individual commodities has not been published. These categories are :

- i Bulk liquids;
- ii Bulk solids; and
- iii Non-bulk freight.

Flow data were recorded between regions which are basically the statistical sub-divisions as defined by Australian Bureau. of Statistics. In all, 84 regional sub-divisions of Australia were considered for this survey. The absolute accuracy of the data is unknown and it also varies from one mode to another. Some studies have reported that the most accurate data related to sea freight movement.

GREAT BRITAIN

Until the last decade, no comprehensive data was available for Great Britain on the freight movement. The basic reason for the lack of information is that there is no statutory cause for any government agency to collect it on regular basis. The gap in the knowledge of commodity flows, has been filled up, to some extent by undertaking special surveys. In the following paragraphs, we present a brief review of the available data on commodity flows for the British economy.

1962 commodity flow data

A special road traffic survey was conducted in 1962-on a sample of 1 per cent of all 'C' licensed vehicles exceeding three tons unloaden. A stratified random sampling design was adopted to account for regional variations in the sample. A weekly survey was conducted in four stages to account for seasonal variations in the nature of freight traffic. The vehicles undertook about 7 lakh journeys during the survey period. The data was collected for 107 zones, each zone being the sub-division of the Ministry of Transport for the purposes of traffic management. In terms of commodities, the coverage was restricted to 15 groups only.

Some of the information compiled from the 1962 survey has been published by the Ministry of Transport. The full tabulation of the 107 × 107 matrices have not been published, though they have been made available to some researchers. It may be noted that since the data were obtained from a survey of the operators of the road haulage industry, the origin and destination of goods means the origin and destination for that particular movement only. It is possible, that the same commodity may appear again as a seperate movement.

One important feature of the 1962 data is that there are some inevitable sampling errors and no formal estimate of their magnitude could be made. However, it has been stated that errors are greater for small flows and least for the largest.

1964 commodity flow data (railways)

It has been reported that in 1964, the British Railway Board had collected some data on the commodity flows through the railways. The survey was undertaken independently of the 1962 road survey and there are inevitable problems in matching the two sets of data. No details are known on the way in which the 1964 data were collected.

In the first place, a compromise set of 78 regions was used. These were mostly the aggregations over the earlier 107 zones but in some cases sub-divisions were also considered. The second problem of reconciliation related to the aggregation of commodities. Fifteen commodities of the 1962 survey were compressed into 13 groups for the 1964 survey.

Surprisingly, no estimates of commodity flows either through road or through railways have been reported after the 1964 survey.

UNITED STATES OF AMERICA

Like India, USA is also one of those countries where the commodity flow data is collected periodically. The coverage, however, being on sample basis. The inter-state Commerce Commission of USA collects the 1 per cent selective sample of the carload waybill termination for Class I railroads only. The data is published annually in the from of state-to-state rail freight traffic measured in tons and classifed by type of commodity. The commodity classicication is based on the 'Freight Commodity Statistics Classifications' of the Association of American Railroads. The commodity flows through ports are reported in Water Borne Commerce of the United States. A number of commodity flow studies have been undertaken based on state-to-state ICC data.

JAPAN

There are four major sources of commodity flow data in Japan, and these are : Japanese Ministry of Transport, Japan National Railways, Department of Ports and Harbours. The distribution of originating inter-regional freight in Japan shows that nearly 50 per cent of the total freight is carried by ships, followed by railways, which account for nearly 40 per cent of the freight and the remaining is carried by trucks.

Prior to 1963, the publication of data by different departments was based not only on different areal units, but the commodity group classification also varied from one source to another. The existence of non-comparable data has thus created serious problem for researchers engaged in research associated with commodity flows.

However, in 1963, the Ministry of Transpor complied for the first time the data which was based on standardised areas and standardised commodity groups by railways, ships and trucks. In all 32 commodity groups and 46 perfectures were considered.

CANADA

Canada is one of the those fortunate countries where adequate data on commodity flow through railways and roads is available. While, the railroad data is provided by the Board of Transport Commissioners, the data for truck transportation is provided through Special Motor Transportation Surveys conducted by the Dominion Bureau of Statistics.

The railroad data is based on the waybill sample and provides information on stations of origin and destination, distance, weight carried and freight cost. Such data are the only data available in Canada for rail commodity traffic. However, it is unfortunate that it excludes traffic of less than car-load lots originating outside Canada, as well as for highways, air and water traffic. Such exclusions would naturally introduce biases that have to be kept in mind while using such data.

The road data is based on returns received each quarter on all trips made during the survey weak by a sample of 12 per cent of all the registered trucks. The returns are divided into two classes, highway traffic and intra-city and farm traffic. The estimats of road traffic are accurate for shorter distance bands and become less representative for long distances, for which the sample size is small.

It is evident from the foregoing review that in spite of its crucial importance, a comprehensive set of commodity flow data is not available for a very large number of countries.

APPENDIX II

COMMODITY LIST AND CODE FOR MONTHLY AND ANNUAL RAILWAY GOODS ZONAL STATISTICS AND INLAND TRADE STATISTIC (1973-74)

Commodity	*Code*	*Group Code*
A REVENUE EARNING TRAFFIC		
I. Products of agriculture		
1. Rice		
a Rice in husk	011	01
i Rice not in husk	021	01
ii Rice flour	022	01
iii Rice parched	023	01
2. Gram and Pulses		
a i Gram including gram products except flour	031	03
ii Pulses other than gram and gram products	032	03
b Gram Flour	041	03
3. Wheat		
a Wheat	051	02
b Wheat Flour	061	02
4. Jowar and Bajra(Including Flour)		
a Jowar	071	04
b Jowar Flour	072	04
c Bajra	073	04
d Bajra Flour	074	04

Commodity	Code	Group Code
5. Other Grains		
a Maize	081	04
b Millet	082	04
c Barley	083	04
d Ragi	084	04
e Other grains	085	04
f Flour other than rice, wheat, gram, jowar and bajra flour	086	04
6. Oil Seeds		
a i Groundnuts with shells	091	15
ii Groundnuts without shells	092	15
b i Caster seeds	101	15
ii Cotton seeds	102	15
iii Linseed	103	15
iv Rape mustard seeds	104	15
v Till or jinjilli seeds	105	15
vi Copra (coconut kernal)	106	15
vii Mohwa seeds	107	15
viii Other oil seeds	108	15
7. Cotton Raw		
a Pressed		
i Cotton raw full pressed (Indian)	111	16
ii Cotton raw full pressed (Foreign)	112	16
iii Cotton raw, ginned half-pressed (Indian)	113	16
iv Cotton raw, ginned half-pressed (Foreign)	114	16
b Cotton raw, unpressed		
i Loose ginned (Indian)	121	16
ii Loose ginned (Foreign)	122	16
iii Loose unginned (Indian)	123	16
iv Loose unginned (Foreign)	124	16
v Cotton waste full pressed	120	16
vi Cotton waste half pressed	125	16
vii Cotton waste loose	126	16
8. Jute Raw		
a i Full pressed	131	17
ii Half pressed	122	17
b i Unpressed	141	17
ii Waste and cuttings unpressed	140	17
9. Fruits and Vegetables—Fresh		
i Mango	151	12
ii Plantains	152	12
iii Oranges	153	12
iv Other fruits fresh	154	12
v Vegetables fresh	155	12
vi Coconuts fresh (Green or tender)	156	12

Commodity	Code	Group Code
10. Sugarcane	160	11
11. Fodder		
a Fodder booked under famine fodder-concession rates	171	61
b Bran	172	61
c Husks of grains and pulses other than bran	173	61
d Grass dry and grass green	174	61
e Other fodder excluding oil cakes and items 11(a) to 11(d)	175	61
f Oil Cake		
i Coconut oil cake	181	61
ii Groundnut oil cake	182	61
iii Cottonseed oil cake	183	61
iv Linseed oil cake	184	61
v Sesamum oil cake	185	61
vi Mustard oil cake	186	61
vii Castor oil cake	187	61
viii Other oil cakes	188	61
12. Tobacco country unmanufactured	191	25
II Animals and products of animals		
1. Livestock		
i Calves or suckling carried free with parent animals	200	91
ii Calves or sucklings	201	91
iii Cattle excluding horned cattle	202	91
iv Horned cattle	203	91
v Horses, ponies and mules	204	91
vi Wild animals	205	91
vii Sheep and goats	206	91
viii Other sorts	207	91
ix Elephants	208	91
x Camels	209	91
2. Hides and skin		
i Hides common dry	211	24
ii Hides common wet	212	24
iii Skin or pelts common dry	213	24
iv Skin or pelts common wet	214	24
3. Bones		
i Bones raw	221	24
ii Bones meal	220	24
III. Products of mines		
1A Coal, Coke and patent fuel for public and non-governmental railways		
a Booked from collieries		
I For steel plants		
i Bhilai	231	51

Commodity	Code	Group Code
ii Rourkela	232	51
iii Durgapur	233	51
iv Tisco	234	51
v IISCO	235	51
vi Bhadravathy	236	51
vii Bokaro	237	51
II For washeries	241	51
III For other users		
i Coking plants	251	51
ii Thermal power houses	252	51
iii Cement factories	253	51
iv Textile mills	254	51
v For Pakistan	255	51
vi For other exports	256	51
vii To ports for movement by sea to other ports in India	257	51
viii Others	258	51
b Booked from other points		
1B To steel plants from washeries		
i Bhilai	261	51
ii Rourkela	262	51
iii Durgapur	263	51
iv Tisco	264	51
v IISCO	265	51
vi Bhadravathy	266	51
vii Bokaro	267	51
2. To steel plants from other points (from points other than collieries and washeries)		
i Bhilai	271	51
ii Rourkela	272	51
iii Durgapur	273	51
iv Tisco	274	51
v IISCO	275	51
vi Bhadravathy	276	51
vii Bokaro	277	51
3. To other users		
i Coking plants	281	51
ii Thermal power houses	282	51
iii Cement factories	283	51
iv Textile mills	284	51
v For Pakistan	285	51
vi For other exports	286	51
vii To ports for movement by sea to other ports in India	287	51
viii Others	288	51

Commodity	Code	Group Code
2. Marble and stones		
a Marble		
i Marble tiles	**301**	71
ii Marble powder, flour etc.	**302**	71
iii Marble excluding marble tiles, chips etc.	**303**	71
iv Marble (including Baroda green) ballast and chips	**304**	71
v Marble (including Baroda Green) carved, monuments, tables (memorial) NOC	**305**	71
vi Marble (including Baroda Green) in Blocks, dressed	**306**	71
vii Marble (including Baroda Green) in block, rough or undressed, powder, slabs or tiles	**307**	71
b Lime stone and dolomite		
1. Lime stone booked for steel plants		
i Bhilai	311	31
ii Rourkela	312	31
iii Durgapur	313	31
iv Tisco	314	31
v IISCO	315	31
vi Bhadravathy	316	31
vii Bokaro	317	31
2. Dolomite booked for steel plants		
i Bhilai	321	31
ii Rourkela	322	31
iii Durgapur	323	31
iv Tisco	324	31
v IISCO	325	31
vi Bhadravathy	326	31
vii Bokaro	327	31
3. Booked for other users		
a Dolomite		
i For glass factories	331	31
ii For other users	332	31
b Lime stone		
i For glass factories	334	31
ii For other users	335	31
c Gypsum		
i To cement factories	341	31
ii To fertilizer factories	342	31
iii Other to others	343	31
d Other stones		
i Ballast	351	31
ii Grind stone including wheat stone, stone pumies etc.	352	31
iii Stone roller	353	31
iv Other stone (NOC)	351	31

Commodity	Code	Group Code
v Stone-ware pipes	355	31
vi Other-stone ware (NOC)	356	31
4. Metallic orec		
a Manganese ores		
i Booked for export	361	31
ii Booked for steel plants		
a Bhilai	371	33
b Rourkela	372	33
c Durgapur	373	33
d Tisco	374	33
e IISCO	375	33
f Bhadravathy	376	33
g Bokaro	377	33
iii Booked for other users	381	33
b Iron ore		
i Booked for export	391	32
ii Booked for steel plants		
a Bhilai	401	32
b Rourkela	402	32
c Durgapur	403	32
d Tisco	404	32
e IISCO	405	32
f Bhadravathy	406	32
g Bokaro	407	32
iii Booked for other users	411	32
a Other ores	421	33
4. Mica	431	33
5. Sand	441	71
IV Mineral oils		
1. Oil fuel		
a Diesel oil		
i in bulk	451	52
ii in tins	452	52
b Crued oil		
i in bulk	453	52
ii in tins	454	52
c Liquid fuel		
i in bulk	455	52
ii in tins	456	52
d Other fuel oils		
i in bulk	457	52
ii in tins	458	52

Commodity	Code	Group Code
2. Kerosene		
i In bulk	461	52
ii In tins	471	52
iii In drums	472	52
iv In cases	473	52
3. Petrol		
i In bulk	481	52
ii In tins	491	52
4. Other mineral oils		
a Dangerous	501	52
b Non-dangerous	502	52
V. Production of forests		
1. Fire wood and other fuel		
a Charcoal	510	53
b Fire wood	520	53
c Other fuel	521	53
2. Wood unwrought		
a Bamboo		
i Bamboo	522	26
ii Bamboo chips, cut splints and other splints	523	26
b Other wood		
i Teak wood	524	26
ii Other timber	525	26
3. Lac		
a Refined in shellac	526	26
b Unrefined	527	26
4. Bidi leave	528	25
VI. Manufactures		
1. a Sugar		
i Sugar excluding sugar candy and glucose	537	21
ii Sugar candy	538	21
iii Glucose	539	21
b Khandsari sugar	540	21
c Gur, jagree and gurshkhar	541	21
d Molasses		
i in bulk	542	21
ii in tins	543	21
2. Salt		
a Salt NOC	544	23
b Other salt	545	23
3. Tea	546	14
4. Soap	547	83

Commodity	Code	Group Code
5. Matches		
a Safety	548	83
b Non-safety	549	83
6 Tobacco manufactures		
i Tobacco country manufactured	550	22
ii Cigerattes	551	22
iii Bidies	552	22
7. Vegetable oil and other edible oils		
a Hydrogenated oils	554	27
b Non-hydrogenated oils		
i Groundnut oils		
a in bulk	555	27
b in tins	556	27
ii Mustard oil		
a in bulk	557	27
b in tins	558	27
iii Coconut oil	559	27
iv Other edible oils		
a Linsed oil		
i in bottles	560	27
ii NOC	561	27
b Sesamum oil	562	27
c Cotton seed oil	563	27
d Castor oil		
i in bottles	564	27
ii NOC	565	27
e Other edible oils excluding above mentioned oils		
Divn. A	566	27
Divn. B	567	27
Divn. C	568	27
Divn. D	569	27
8. Cotton manufactured and other piece goods		
i Cotton twist and yarn foreign, press packed	570	81
ii Cotton twist and yarn foreign, not press packed	571	81
iii Cotton twist and yarn Indian, press packed	572	81
iv Cotton twist and yarn Indian, not press packed	573	81
v Cotton piece goods, foreign, press packed	574	81
vi Cotton piece goods, foreign, not press packed	575	81
vii Cotton piece goods, Indian, press packed	576	81
viii Cotton piece goods, Indian, not press packed	577	81
ix Other cotton manufactured press packed	578	81
x Other cotton manufactured not press packed	579	81
9. Jute manufactured		
a Gunnies		

Commodity	Code	Group Code
i Gunnies sack	586	81
ii Hessian cloth	587	81
iii Other gunnies	588	81
iv Other manufactures	589	81
10. Leather and leather manufactures		
i Hide and skin tanned	591	85
ii Other leather manufactures	592	85
iii Leather scrap	595	85
11. Rubber		
i Rubber tubes and tyres	600	85
ii Rubber or synthetic rubber manufactured	601	85
iii Rubber goods (unservicable)	602	85
12. i Woolen piece goods press packed in boxes or in bales	603	81
ii Woolen piece goods not press packed in boxes or cases	604	81
iii Artificial silk piece goods press packed in boxes or bales	605	81
iv Artificial silk piece goods not press packed in boxes or bales	606	81
v Silk piece goods	607	81
vi Coir rope string	608	17
vii Other coir	609	17
13. Cement		
a Cement		
i in b gs	617	73
ii in casks	618	73
iii in bulk	619	73
b Cement manufactured		
i Asbestos cement products excluding cement tiles	620	73
ii Cement tiles excluding asbestos cement tiles	621	73
iii Other cement manufactures	622	73
14. i Bricks, common	623	74
ii Bricks refractory	624	74
iii Tiles common flooring	625	74
iv Tiles common roofing earthen	626	74
v Tiles glassed and ornamental	627	74
vi Tiles glassed not ornamental	628	74
vii China ware (potteries)	629	83
15. Iron and steel wrought :		
a Division 'A' (Booked form steel plants)		
i Bhilai	631	42
ii Rourkela	632	42
iii Durgapur	633	42
iv Tisco	634	42
v IISCO	635	42
vi Bhadravathy	636	42

Commodity	Code	Group Code
vii Bokaro	637	42
b Division 'B' (Booked from steel plants)		
i Bhilai	641	42
ii Rourkela	642	42
iii Durgapur	643	42
iv Tisco	644	42
v IISCO	645	42
vi Bhadravathy	646	42
vii Bokaro	647	42
c Division 'C' (Booked from steel plants)		
i Bhilai	651	42
ii Rourkela	652	42
iii Durgapur	653	42
iv Tisco	654	42
v IISCO	655	42
vi Bhadravathy	656	42
vii Bokaro	657	42
d Pig iron (Booked from steel plants)		
i Bhilai	661	42
ii Rourkela	662	42
iii Durgapur	663	42
iv Tisco	664	42
v IISCO	665	42
vi Bhadravathy	666	42
vii Bokaro	667	42
e Other iron and steel wrought (Booked from steel plants)		
i Bhilai	671	42
ii Rourkela	672	42
iii Durgapur	673	42
iv Tisco	674	42
v IISCO	675	42
vi Bhadravathy	676	42
vii Bokaro	677	42
f Booked from other points		
i Division 'A'	681	42
ii Division 'B'	682	42
iii Division 'C'	683	42
iv Pig iron	684	42
v Other iron and steel		
1. Agricultural implements	685	87
2. Cycle and cycle parts	686	88
3 Motor cars including taxi cars	687	88
4. Motor cars including taxi cars booked in covered wagons	690	88
5. Iron and steel scrap	688	43
6. Others	689	42

Commodity	*Code*	*Group Code*
16. Electrical goods		
a Electrical fans	692	82
b Electrical motors (all sorts) and parts	693	82
c Bulbs	694	82
d Balteries	695	82
e Division 'A'	696	82
f Division 'B'	697	82
g Division 'C'	698	82
17. Glassware		
i Glass heavy division 'A'	705	83
ii Glass heavy division 'B'	706	83
iii Glass heavy division 'C'	707	83
iv Glass tiles division 'C'	708	83
v Glass light division 'C'	709	83
18. Non-ferrous metals		
a i Tin in the form of pellets, rods, plates, sheets etc.	711	41
ii Tin wares	712	41
iii Tin scrap	713	43
b i Brass ingots	714	41
ii Brass rods, sheets etc.	710	41
iii Brass ware	715	41
iv Brass scrap	716	43
c i Bell metal ware	717	41
ii Bell metal, ingots, sheets or slabs	718	41
iii Bell metal scrap	719	41
d i Copper in the form of pellets, rods, plates, sheets etc.	720	41
ii Copper ware	721	41
iii Copper scrap	722	43
e i Zink ingots or slabs	723	41
ii Zinc ware	724	41
iii Zink scrap	725	41
f i Lead ingots or slabs	726	41
ii Lead ware	727	41
iii Lead scrap	728	41
g Other non-ferrous metals	729	41
h Aluminium		
i Aluminium ingots, or slabs	731	41
ii Aluminium ware	732	41
iii Aluminium scrap	733	43
iv Aluminium sheets	734	41
19. Paper		
i Paper NOC in cases	740	84
ii Paper NOC in rolls or reels	741	84
iii Paper ware (other than stationery) NOC	742	84
iv Paper waste and cuttings	743	84

Commodity	Code	Group Code
v Pulp and pulp sheet	744	84
iv Pulp board in bales	745	84
vii Pulp board in cases	746	84
viii Paper or card board cones, cores, spools and tubes	747	84
ix Newsprint	748	84
x Other including stationery	749	84
20. Paints and varnishes		
i Paints and varnishes (removers inflammable nitrocellucose etc.)	750	86
ii Paints and varnishes division 'A'	751	86
iii Paints and varnishes division 'B'	752	86
iv Paints, thinners having a flash point below 24.4	753	86
v Paints partly composed of inflammable liquids	754	86
21. Colours and dyes		
i Division 'A'	755	86
ii Division 'B'	756	86
iii Tanning extract of all kinds	757	86
v Tanstuff NOC	758	86
22. Fireworks	759	86
23. i Soda caustic including caustic soda liquor	760	86
ii Soda ash	761	86
24. Medicines	762	86
25. Alcohol		
i Industrial	763	86
ii Power	764	86
iii Absolute	765	86
iv Others	766	86
26. Acids		
i Sulphuric acid including diuted	767	86
ii Other acids		
a Acid picric	768	86
b Acid chromic, creslic hydrofluouric, percheloric, diluted and sulphurous (solution)	769	86
c Acid citric, medicinal vegetable NOC tannie and terteric	770	86
d Acid acetic, carbolic, hydrobromic diluted and phospheric	771	86
e Acid boric	772	86
f Acid calcium, phosphate and steoric	773	86
g Citric acid	774	86
h Acid hydrochloirc including diluted	775	86
i Acid lactic	776	86
j Acid oxclic	777	86
k Acid sludge	778	86
l Acid phosphoric	779	86

VII. Miscellaneous

1. Manure

Commodity	Code	Group Code
a Chemical manure		
i Ammonium sulphate	806	63
ii Superphosphates	807	63
iii Other division 'A'	808	63
iv Other division 'B'	809	63
b organic manure oil cake		
i Coconut oil cake	810	62
ii Groundnut oil cake	811	62
iii Cotton oil cake	812	62
iv Linseed oil cake	813	62
v Sesamum oil cake	814	62
vi Mustard oil cake	815	62
vii Castor oil cake	816	62
viii Other oil cake	817	62
c Fish dry (Manure)	818	62
d Other organic manure	819	62
2. Provision		
i Coffee	820	14
ii Fruits dried	821	23
iii Ghee	822	2[illegible]
iv Meat	823	13
v Meat products (other than meat manures)	824	13
vi Eggs	825	13
vii Fish fresh	826	13
viii Fish dry	827	13
ix Pepper	828	23
x Turmeric	829	23
xi Chillies	830	23
xii Cardamom	831	23
xiii Ginger dry	832	23
xiv Other spices	833	23
xv Coconut dry	834	23
xvi Betal nut	835	23
xvii a Seeds other than oil seeds (common)	836	23
b Seed NOC	837	23
xviii Groceries	838	23
xix Other provisions	839	23
3. Milirey reddix	840	92
4. i Liquid petroleum gas (commercial butane of propane)	841	92
ii Compressed gas (Methane, nitrogen, air compressed)	841	52
ii Oxygen compressed	843	86
iv Liquid gas	844	86
5. i Coal tar	845	72
ii Bitumen	846	72
6. Other commodities		
i Wool raw (full pressed)	850	16

Commodity	Code	Group Code
ii Wool raw (half pressed)	851	16
iii Wool raw (loose,	852	16
iv Silk raw	853	16
v Silk waste	854	16
vi Hamp and fibre full pressed	855	17
vii Hamp and fibre half pressed	856	17
viii Hamp and fibre unpressed	857	17
ix Rubber crude, raw	858	85
x Rubber scrap	859	85
xi Dry grass including saboi grass (other than those included under fodder)	860	26
xii Myrobalam	861	26
xiii Mowha flowers	862	26
xiv Opium	863	25
xv Narcotic and narcotic drugs	864	86
xvi Drugs (crude or raw)	865	86
xvii Lime	866	71
xviii Petroleum cake	867	52
xix China clay	868	31
xx Timber wrought	869	26
xxi Cinematograph films		
a inflammable	870	17
b non-inflammable	871	17
7. Other commodities (not included above)		
Container service	910	90
Freight forwarding service		
8. Non-revenue traffic		
VII. Railway coal and diesel oil		
1. From collieries		
a For home line	960	51
b For other government railways and manufacturing units like CLW, ICP, etc.	961	51
2. Sea-borne coal moved from ports		
a For home lines	962	51
b For other government railways and manufacturing units like CLW, ICP	963	51
3. From other points		
a For home line	964	51
b For other government railways and manufacturing units like CLW, ICP, etc.	965	51
Diesel oil		
a Diesel oil booked by companies for railway purposes in bulk	966	52
b Diesel oil booked by companies for railway purpose in tins	967	52

Commodity	Code	Group Code
IX General stores and materials		
1. Carried on other than departmental wagons and ballast trains		
a For home line		
i Iron and steel	971	42
ii Cement	972	73
iii Bricks	973	74
iv Tiles	974	74
v Lime and limestone	975	71
vi Teak wood	976	26
vii Other wood	977	26
viii Kerosene oil	978	52
ix Diesel oil	979	52
x Other stores	980	83
b For other government railways and manufacturing units like CLW, ICF, etc.		
i Iron and steel	981	42
ii Cement	982	73
iii Bricks	983	74
iv Tiles	984	74
v Lime and limestone	985	71
vi Teak wood	986	26
vii Other wood	987	26
viii Kerosene oil	988	52
ix Diesel oil	989	52
x Other stores	980	83
2. Carried by departmental wagons and ballast trains		
a For home line	990	83
b For other government railways and manufacturing units like CLW, ICF, etc.	991	83

APPENDIX III

FORMATS OF GOODS SUMMARY TAPES

NORTHERN RAILWAY
TAPE FORMAT : ANNUAL GOODS MOVEMENT FOR 1973-74

S. No.	*Description*	*Length*	*Field*
1.	Year	2	1,2
2.	Zone	1	3,3
3.	Distance	4	4,7
4.	Gauge	1	8,8
5.	Commodity code	3	9,11
6.	Station to	5	12,16
6.	Station from	5	17,21
7.	No. of wagons	6	22,27
8.	Actual weight	10	28,37
10.	Weight full	10	38,47
11.	Weight small	10	48,57
12.	Freight full	10	58,67
13.	Freight small	10	68,77
14.	Tonne kms full	15	78,92
15.	Tonne kms small	15	93,107
16.	Full invoices	6	108,113
17.	Small invoices	6	114,119
18.	Record mark	1	120,120 (+)

Notes :

1. Weight in quintals 2. Freight in rupees 3. Block size : 120×21 (2520) 4. Tape density : 556 b.p.i.

NORTH EASTERN RAILWAY
TAPE FORMAT : ANNUAL GOODS MOVEMENT—1973-74

S. No.	Description	Length	Field
1.	Card code	1	1,1
2.	Month	2	2,3
3.	Zone	1	4,4
4.	Gauge	1	5,5
5.	Station from	5	6,10
6.	Station to	5	11,15
7.	Blank	3	16,18
8.	Commodity code	3	19,21
9.	Blank	11	22,32
10.	Charged weight (full)	6	33,38
11.	Charged weight (small)	6	39,44
12.	Freight (full)	7	45,51
13.	Freight (small)	6	52,57
14.	Blank	17	58,74
15.	Charged distance	4	75,78
16.	Blank	1	79,79
17	Record mark	1	80,80

Notes :

1. Weight in quintals 2. Freight in Rupees 3. Block size : 80×30 (2400) 4. Tape density : 556 b.p.i.

CENTRAL RAILWAY
FORMAT OF GOODS ANNUAL TAPE—1973-74

S. No.	Description	Length	Field
1.	Station from	5	1,5
2.	Station to	5	6,10
3.	Commodity	3	11,13
4.	Charged weight (full)	10	14,23
5.	Charged weight (small)	10	24,33
6.	Calculated freight (full)	10	34,43
7.	Calculated freight (small)	10	44,53
8.	Blank	1	54,54
9.	Record mark	1	55,55

Notes :

1. Weight in quintals 2. Freight in rupees 3. Block size : 55×21 (1155) 4. Tape density : 556 b.p.i.

SOUTHERN RAILWAY
TAPE FORMAT : ANNUAL GOODS MOVEMENT—1973-74

S. No.	Description	Length	Field
1.	Station from	5	1,5
2.	Station to	5	6,10
3.	Commodity	3	11,13
4.	Wagons	2	14,21
5.	Weight (full)	10	22,31
6.	Weight (small)	10	32,41
7.	Freight (full)	10	42,51
8.	Freight (small)	10	52,61
9.	Tonne kilometres (full)	13	62,75
10.	Tonne kilometres (small)	14	76,89
11.	Record mark	11	90,100

Notes :

1. Block size : (100×12) = 1200 2. Freight in rupees 3. Weight in quintals 4. Density : 556 b.p.i.

SOUTH CENTRAL RAILWAY
TAPF FORMAT OF GOODS SUMMARY TAPE 1973-74

S. No	Description	Length	Field
1.	Card code	1	1,1
2.	Month	2	2,3
3.	Zone	1	4,4
4.	Originating gauge	1	5,5
5.	Station from	5	6,10
6.	Station to	5	11,15
7.	Blank	3	16,18
8.	Commodity code	3	19,21
9.	No of wagons	4	22,25
10.	Actual weight	7	26,32
11.	Charged weight (full)	6	33,38
12.	Charged weight (small)	6	39,44
13.	Calculated freight (full)	7	45,51
14.	Calculated freight (small)	6	52,57
15.	Tonne kilometres (full)	10	58,67
16.	Tonne kilometres (small)	7	68,74
17.	Number of invoice	5	75,79
18.	Record mark	1	80,80

Notes :

1 Weight in quintals 2. Freight in rupees 3. Record length=80 4. Tape density=556 b.p.i.

SOUTH EASTERN RAILWAY
TAPE FORMAT : ANNUAL GOODS MOVEMENT—1973-74

S. No.	*Description*	*Length*	*Field*
1.	Card code	1	1,1
2.	Month	2	2,3
3.	Zone	1	4,4
4.	Originating gauge	1	5,5
5.	Station from	5	6,10
6.	Station to	5	11,15
7.	Blanks	3	16,18
8.	Commodity code	3	19,21
9.	Blanks	11	22,32
10.	Charged weight (full)	6	33,38
11.	Charged weight (small)	6	39,44
12.	Calculated freight (full)	7	45,51
13.	Calculated freight (small)	6	52,57
14.	Blanks	17	58,74
15.	Charged distance	4	75,38
16.	Record mark	2	79,80

Notes :

1. Weight in quintals 2. Freight in rupees 3. Block size : 80×24 =(1920) 4. Density=556 b.p.i.

WESTERN RAILWAY
TAPE FORMAT OF GOODS ANNUAL SUMMARY—1973-74

S. No.	*Description*	*Length*	*Field*
1.	Code	1	1,1
2.	Zone	1	2,2
3.	Orginating gauge	1	3,3
4.	Station from	5	4,8
5.	Station to	5	9,13
6.	Commodity code	6	14,19
7.	No. of wagons	5	20,24
8.	Actual weight	8	25,32
9.	Charged weight (full)	8	33,40
10.	Charged weight (small)	8	41,48
11.	Freight full	9	49,57
12.	Freight small	7	58,64
13.	Tonne kilometres (full)	11	65,75
14.	Tonne kilometres (small)	8	76,83
15.	Year	4	84,87
16.	Record mark	1	88,88

Notes :

1. Weight in quintals 2. Freight in rupees 3. Block size=88 4. Tape density=556 b.p.i.

NORTH EAST FRONTIER RAILWAY
MERGED SUMMARY TAPE—MONTHWISE (1973-74)

S. No.	Description	Length	Field
1	Card code	1	1,1
2.	Month	2	2,3
3.	Zone	1	4,4
4.	Originating gauge	1	5,5
5.	Station from	5	6,10
6.	Station to	5	11,15
7.	Blank	3	16,18
8.	Commodity code	3	19,21
9.	Blank	11	22,32
10.	Charged quintals (full)	6	33,38
11.	Charged quintals (small)	6	39,44
12.	Calculated freight (full)	7	45,51
13.	Calculated freight (small)	6	52,57
14.	Tonne kilometres (full)	10	58,67
15.	Tonne kilometres (small)	7	68,74
16.	Charged distance	4	75,78
17.	Record mark	2	79,80

Notes :

1. Weight is in quintals 2. Freight in rupees 3. Block size=80×18 (1440) 4. Density=556 b.p.i.

EASTERN RAILWAY
TAPE FORMAT : ANNUAL GOODS MOVEMENT—1973-74

S. No.	Description	Length	Field
1.	Card code	1	1,1
2.	Month	2	2,3
3.	Zone	1	4,4
4.	Originating gauge	1	5,5
5.	Station from	5	6,10
6.	Station to	5	11,15
7.	Blank	3	16,18
8.	Commodity code	3	19,21
9.	Blank	11	22,32
10.	Charged weight (full)	6	33,38
11.	Charged weight (small)	6	39,44
12.	Calculated freight (full)	7	45,51
13.	Calculated freight (small)	6	52,57
14.	Blank	17	58,74
15.	Charged distance	4	75,78
16.	Record mark	2	79,80

Notes :

1. Weight in tonnes 2. Freight in rupees 3. Block size=80×24 (1920) 4. Density=556 b.p.i.

APPENDIX IV

FORMAT OF MASTER DATA FILES

S. No.	Description	Length	Field
1.	Station from	5	1,5
2.	Rural urban classification	2	6,7
3.	Blank	1	8
4.	District code (Originating)	3	9,11
5.	Blank	3	12,14
6.	Levels of development of originating district	6	15,20
7.	Station to	5	21,25
8.	Rural/urban classification	2	26,27
9.	Blank	1	28
10.	District code (Receiving)	3	29,31
11.	Blanks	3	32,34
12.	Levels of development of receiving district	6	35,40
13.	Blanks	6	41,46
14.	Commodity code	3	47,49
15.	Blanks	10	50,59
16.	Originating wt. (Qts.)	10	60,69
17.	Blanks	30	70,99
18.	Charged freight (Rs.)	10	100,109
19.	Blanks	11	110,120

Tape density = 800 b.p.i.

Record length = 120

Blocking foctor =˚100 records

APPENDIX V

DESCRIPTION OF NATIONAL SAMPLE SURVEY REGIONS (ADJUSTED)

Region code	Description	Districts
	Jammu & Kashmir	
01	Mountainous	Jammu and Kathua
02	Outer Hills	Doda, Udhampur, Punch, Rajauri and Ladakh
03	Jhelum Valley	Baramula, Srinagar and Anantnag
	Himachal Pradesh	
04	Himachal Pradesh	Chamba, Mandi, Bilaspur, Mahasu, Kinnaur, Simla, Kangra, Lahaul & Spiti, Kulu and Sirmaur
	Punjab	
05	Northern	Gurdaspur, Amritsar. Kapurthala, Jullundur, Ludhiana, Hoshiarpur and Ropar
06	Southern	Patiala, Sangrur, Firozpur and Bhatinda
	Haryana	
07	Eastern	Karnal, Ambala, Rohtak and Gurgaon
08	Western	Mahendragarh, Jind and Hissar
	Delhi	
09	Delhi	Delhi
	Rajasthan	
10	Western	Jhunjhunu, Sikar, Churu, Bikaner, Nagaur, Jodhpur, Jaisalmer, Barmer and Jalor
11	Norht-Eastern	Ganganagar, Alwar, Bharatpur, Sawai Madhopur, Jaipur, Tonk, Bhilwara, Ajmer and Pali
12	Southern	Banswara, Dungarpur, Udaipur and Sirohi
13	South-Eastern	Jhalawar, Kota, Bundi and Chittorgarh
	Uttar Pradesh	
14	Himalayan	Pithoragarh, Chamoli, Uttarkashi, Dehra Dun, Tehri Garhwal, Garhwal, Almora and Nanital
15	Western	Saharanpur, Muzaffarnagar, Bijnor, Meerut, Moradabad, Bulandshahr, Rampur, Bareilly, Pillibhit, Shahjahanpur, Budaun, Aligarh, Mathura, Etawa and Agra
16	Central	Kheri, Sitapur, Hardoi, Lucknow, Bara Banki, Rae Bareli, Unnao, Fatehpur and Kanpur
17	Eastern	Bahraich, Gonda, Basti, Gorakhpur, Deoria, Ballia, Azamgarh, Faizabad, Sultanpur, Jaunpur, Ghazipur, Varanasi, Mirzapur, Allahabad and Paratapgarh
18	Southern	Banda, Hamirpur, Jalaun and Jhansi
	Madhya Pradesh	
19	Eastern	Surguja, Raigarh, Bilaspur, Raipur, Durg, Balaghat and Baster

Region code	Description	Districts
20	Inland-Eastern	Sidhi, Rewa, Satna Panna, Jabalpur, Shahdol, Mandla and Seoni
21	Inland-Western	Damoh, Sagar, Vidisha, Sehore, Raison, Narsimhapur, Chhindwara, Hoshangabad and Betul
22	Western	Mandsaur, Rajgarh, Shajapur, Ujjain, Ratlam, Jhabua, Dhar, Indore, Dewas, Khargone (West Nimar) and Khandwa (East Nimar)
23	Northern	Chhatarpur, Tikamgarh, Bhind, Gwalior, Morena, Shivpuri and Guna
	Gujarat	
24	Inland	Banas Kantha, Sabar Kantha, Panch Mahals, Vadodara, Bharuch, Dangs, Valsad, Mahesana, Ahmedabad, Ghandhinagar, Khera, Kutch and Surendranagar
25	Coastal	Bhavnagar, Amreli, Junagadh, Jamnagar
	Maharashtra	
26	Coastal	Thana, Greater Bombay, Kolaba and Ratnagiri
27	Inland-Western	Ahmadnagar, Poona, Sholapur, Satara, Sangali and Kolhapur
28	Inland-Northern	Jalgaon, Dhulia and Nasik
29	Inland-Central	Aurangabad, Bhir, Parbhani, Nanded and Osmanabad
30	Inland	Nagpur, Wardha, Amravati, Buldhana, Akola and Yeotmal
31	Eastern	Bhandara and Chandrapur
	Karnataka	
32	Coastal & Ghats	North Kanara and South Kanara
33	Inland-Eastern	Shimoga, Chikmagalur, Hassan and Coorg
34	Inland-Southern	Kolar, Tumkur, Bangalore, Mandya and Mysore
35	Inland-Northern	Bidar, Gulbarga, Bijapur, Belgaum, Dharwar, Raichur, Bellary and Chitradurga
	Kerala	
36	Northern	Cannore, Koshikode, Malappuram and Palaghat
37	Southern	Trichur, Ernakulam, Kottayam, Alleppey, Quilon and Trivandrum
	Tamil Nadu	
38	Coastal-Northern	Madras, Chinglepur, North Arcot and South Arcot
39	Coastal-Southern	Thanjavur, Ramanathapuram, Tirunelveli, Kanya Kumari
40	Inland	Salem, Dharmapuri, Madhurai, Trichuchirapall, Coimbatore and Nilgiris
	Andhra Pradesh	
41	Coastal	Srikakulam, Visakapatnam, East Godavari, West Godavari, Krishna, Ongole, Guntur and Nellore
42	Inland-Northern	Adilabad, Karimnagar, Nizamabad, Medak, Warangal, Khammam, Nalgonda, Hyderabad and Mahbubnagar
43	Inland-Southern	Kurnool, Anantapur, Cuddapah, and Chittoor

Region code	Description	Districts
	Orissa	
44	Coastal	Balasore, Cuttack, Puri, and Gunjam
45	Southern	Baudh Khondmals, Kalahandi and Korapur
46	Northern	Mayurbhanj, Keonjhar, Sundergarh, Sambalpur, Dhenkanal and Bolangir
	Bihar	
47	Southern	Santal Parganas, Dhanbad, Hazaribagh. Palamau, Ranchi and Singhbhum
48	Northern	Purnea, Darbhanga, Muzaffarpur, Champaran and Saran
49	Central	Bhagalpur, Monghyr, Saharsa, Patna, Gaya and Shahabad
	West Bengal	
50	Himalayan	Darjeeling, Jalpaiguri and Cooch Behar
51	Eastern-Plains	West Dinajpur, Malda, Murshidabad, Nadi and Birbhum
52	Central-Plains	24-Parganas, Calcutta, Howrah, Hoogly and Burdwan
53	Western-plains	Bankura, Purullia and Midnapore
	Assam	
54	Plains	Lakhimpur, Sibsagar, Darrang, Nowgong, Kamrup, Goalpara, and Cachar
55	Hills	Mikir Hills, North Cachar Hills Mizo Hills
56	**Meghalaya**	
57	**Tripura**	
58	**Manipur**	
59	**Goa**	
60	**Pondichery**	
61	**Nagaland**	

Note : The district spellings in some cases have been changed after 1981 Census.

APPENDIX VI

FORMAT OF AGGREGATED BASIC DATA FILES

S. No.	*Description*	*Length*	*Field*
1.	Station from	5	1—5
2.	Rural/urban classification	2	6—7
3.	Blank	1	8
4.	District code (Originating)	3	9—11
5.	Blanks	3	12—14
6.	Levels of development of originating district	6	15—20
7.	Station to	5	21—25
8.	Rural/urban classification	2	26—27
9.	Blank	1	28
10.	District code (Receiving)	3	29—31
11.	Blanks	3	35—40
12.	Levels of development of receiving district	6	35—40
13.	Blanks	6	41—46
14.	Weight of commodity group I	10	47—56
15.	Weight of commodity group II	10	57—66
16.	Weight of commodity group III	10	67—76
17.	Weight of commodity group IV	10	77—86
18.	Weight of commodity group V	10	87—97
19.	Wright of commodity group VI	10	97—106
20.	Weight of commodity group VII	10	107—116
21.	Weight of commodity group VIII	10	117—126
22.	Weight of commodity group IX	10	127—136

Tape density = 800 b.p.i.

Record lenght = 136

Blocking factor = 100

APPENDIX VII

STATION TO STATION FLOWS : ORIGINATING

Code for originating station			R/U classification				District code					Level of Development
S. No.	Code for receiving station	Dist. code & levels of dev.	Commodity Code									
			food prod.	Raw mat.	Coal/fuel	Inputs in agri-culture	Const mat	Industrial prod.	Defence good	Livestock	Miscellaneou	Total
1	2	3	4	5	6	7	8	9	10	11	12	13

APPENDIX VIII

STATION TO STATION FLOWS : TERMINATING

Code for receiving station | *R/U classification* | *District code* | *Level of development*

S. No.	*Code for originating station*	*Dist. code & levels*	*Commodity Code*									
			Food prd.	*Raw mat.*	*Cool/fuel*	*Inputs in agriculture*	*Const mat*	*Industrial prod.*	*Defence good*	*Livestock*	*Miscellaneous*	*Total*
1	*2*	*3*	*4*	*5*	*6*	*7*	*8*	*9*	*10*	*11*	*12*	*13*

APPENDIX IX

CHARACTERISTICS OF COMMODITY FLOWS (STATION-WISE)

Code of the districts

Station code	Name Dist.	State Station	Rural classification	Total originating tonnage	Total receiving tonnage	Each commodity as % of: Originating tonnage	Each commodity as % of: Receiving tonnage	No. of inter-actions: Originating	No. of inter-actions: Receiving	Average Distance: Originating	Average Distance: Receiving
						1 2 3 4 5 6 7	1 2 3 4 5 6 7				

APPENDIX X

FORMAT OF DISTRICTWISE/REGION-WISE URBAN RURAL DATA TABULATION

District Code (Originating/Terminating) *Commodity Code*

Term. Orig.	*R*			*U1*			*U2*			*U3*			*U4*			*Total Orig.*		
	W	*I*	*AD*	*W*	*I*	*AD*	*W*	*I*	*AD*	*W*	*I*	*AD*	*W*	*I*	*AD*	*W*	*I*	*AD*
R																		
U1																		
U2																		
U3																		
U4																		
Total Term.																		

Notes :

R = Rural
U1 = Class I urban towns
U2 = Class II urban towns
U3 = Class III urban towns
U4 = Glass (IV + V + VI) urban towns
W = Weight (qts)
I = No. of Interactions
AD = Average Distance

APPENDIX XI

AVAILABILITY OF RAILWAY NETWORK FACILITY

Sr.No.	District Name	Number of Railway stations in Villages	Town	Cities	Total	Number of stations per 100 Villages	Town	City	Number of stations per 100 kms. of Village	Town	City
1	2	3	4	5	6	7	8	9	10	11	12
1	Srikakulum	27	12	—	39	0.94	0.75	—	0.28	6.7	—
2	Visakhapatnam	23	4	33	60	0.55	0.33	11.0	0.17	4.0	25.0
3	E. Godavari	16	6	3	25	1.19	0.55	1.5	0.15	3.7	4.0
4	W. Godavari	27	7	3	37	3.21	0.88	1.5	0.35	7.1	7.7
5	Krishna	21	4	18	33	2.24	0.31	2.7	0.25	2.5	8.3
6	Guntur	38	14	4	56	5.52	1.0	2.0	0.34	9.1	10.0
7	Nellore	32	16	6	54	3.04	2.70	8.0	02.5	25.0	50.0
8	Chittoor	24	7	3	34	1.88	0.60	1.5	0.15	4.8	10.0
9	Cuddapah	17	2	2	21	1.90	0.33	1.0	0.11	1.8	14.3
10	Anantpur	27	9	4	40	2.90	1.00	2.0	0.14	3.0	5.6
11	Kurnool	29	4	6	39	3.23	0.60	2.0	0.16	10.0	10.0
12	Mahboobnagar	12	5	1	18	0.82	0.50	1.0	0.07	3.6	10.0
13	Hyderabad	13	3	59	95	1.37	0.19	59.0	0.18	8.3	20.0
14	Medak	7	1	—	8	0.57	0.13	—	0.07	1.4	—
15	Nizamabad	11	4	2	17	1.27	0.80	2.0	0.14	6.7	5.7
16	Adilabad	10	13	—	23	0.64	1.18	—	0.10	8.3	—
17	Karimnagar	6	3	—	9	0.57	0.27	—	0.05	1.5	—
18	Warangal	11	3	1	15	1.12	1.0	1.0	0.09	9.1	1.8
19	Khammam	17	2	1	19	1.55	0.5	0.5	0.11	1.6	2.9
20	Nalgonda	3	1	—	4	0.27	0.17	—	0.02	1.5	—
21	Goalpara	29	6	—	35	0.76	0.50	—	0.28	11.1	—
22	Kamrup	19	8	4	31	0.60	0.50	4.0	0.19	14.3	9.1
23	Darrang	28	5	—	33	1.10	0.72	—	0.32	12.5	—
24	Lakhimpar	44	8	5	57	1.14	0.73	2.5	0.35	14.3	25.0
25	Nowgong	31	4	1	36	1.58	1.3	1.0	0.56	25.0	16.7
26	Sibsagar	46	66	—	52	1.96	0.66	—	0.52	16.7	—
27	Cochar	28	4	1	33	1.16	0.57	1.0	0.40	14.3	10.0
28	Garo Hill	—	—	—	—	—	—	—	—	—	—
29	United Khasi & Jaintia Hills	2	—	2	4	—	—	—	—	—	—
30	United Mikir & N. Cochar Hills	24	3	—	27	1.26	—	—	0.16	—	—
31	Mizo Hills	—	1	—	1	—	0.5	—	—	—	—
32	Patna	31	8	10	49	1.34	0.73	3.3	0.58	8.3	9.1
33	Gaya	34	7	2	43	0.55	0.64	2.0	0.28	7.1	6.7
34	Shahabad	23	6	1	30	0.48	0.55	1.0	0.21	5.5	3.2
35	Saran	35	7	—	42	0.79	1.0	—	0.51	16.7	

1	2	3	4	5	6	7	8	9	10	11	12
36	Champaran	36	8	1	45	1.36	0.89	1.0	0.40	9.1	12.5
37	Muzaffarpur	30	5	2	37	0.73	0.71	2.0	0.39	8.3	12.5
38	Darbhanga	40	5	1	46	1.26	1.0	1.0	0.46	50.0	5.3
39	Monghyr	23	11	5	39	0.69	0.73	2.5	0.24	5.9	16.6
40	Bhagalpur	14	4	4	22	0.55	1.0	4.0	0.25	11.1	12.5
41	Saharsa	49	5	—	54	3.36	0.71	—	0.85	5.3	—
42	Purnea	19	6	13	38	0.51	1.0	6.5	0.18	6.7	16.7
43	Santal-Parganas	21	10	—	31	0.21	0.91	—	0.15	10.0	—
44	Palamau	22	4	—	26	0.68	0.8	—	0.17	6.7	—
45	Hazaribagh	32	17	13	62	0.52	0.85	6.6	0.18	5.6	12.5
46	Ranchi	38	4	5	47	0.99	0.36	5.0	0.21	3.3	8.0
47	Dhanbad	32	6	15	53	2.34	0.25	7.5	1.25	2.8	7.1
48	Singhbhum	29	12	14	55	0.67	0.63	14.0	0.22	7.7	10.0
49	Jamnagar	29	9	13	51	4.11	0.92	13.0	0.21	2.3	33.3
50	Rajkot	46	11	10	67	5.36	1.38	2.5	0.42	7.1	11.1
51	Surendrangagar	34	4	3	41	5.25	0.4	3.0	0.34	1.2	9.1
52	Bhavnagar	36	17	8	63	4.32	1.31	8.0	0.35	5.9	9.1
53	Amroli	22	11	—	33	3.70	0.92	—	0.04	3.7	
54	Junagarh	29	14	7	50	2.66	0.78	2.3	0.29	3.1	9.1
55	Kutch	20	13	1	34	2.22	1.3	1.0	0.34	3.7	10.0
56	Banskantha	34	4	—	36	2.52	0.5	—	0.27	2.6	
57	Sabarkantha	9	4	—	13	0.65	0.57	—	0.12	2.9	—
58	Mehsana	60	9	2	71	5.54	0.9	0.7	0.68	4.2	4.5
59	Ahmedabad	50	7	13	70	6.90	0.33	33.0	0.57	2.2	11.1
60	Kairo	41	12	4	57	3.28	0.86	1.3	0.60	5.9	3.3
61	Panch Mahals	36	5	7	48	1.89	0.71	3.5	0.41	5.9	25.0
62	Baroda	68	7	5	90	4.65	0.64	5.0	1.0	6.7	6.3
63	Broach	36	6	6	48	3.17	1.0	6.0	0.4	6.7	50.0
64	Surat	50	12	5	67	4.11	1.2	5.0	0.7	14.3	10.0
65	Dangs	—	—	—	—	—	—	—	—	—	—
66	Anantnag	—	1	—	1	—	0.11	—	—	2.5	—
67	Srinagar	—	—	1	1	—	—	0.5	—	—	3.3
68	Baramulla	—	—	—	—	—	—	—	—	—	—
69	Ladakh	—	—	—	—	—	—	—	—	—	—
70	Doda	—	—	—	—	—	—	—	—	—	—
71	Udhampur	—	1	—	1	—	0.2	—	—	1.9	—
72	Jammu	5	1	2	8	0.47	0.17	2.0	0.20	1.3	2.8
73	Kathua	—	1	—	1	—	0.25	—	—	1.7	—
74	Poonch-Rajouri	1	1	—	2	0.63	0.5	—	0.26	3.3	—
75	Cannanore	14	9	4	27	7.87	0.82	2.0	0.31	5.9	14.3
76	Kozhikode	19	4	3	26	17.43	0.50	1.5	0.52	4.2	2.9
77	Palaghat	17	4	2	23	11.56	0.57	1.0	0.30	6.0	7.1
78	Trichur	8	6	1	15	2.39	0.75	1.0	0.30	3.2	7.7
79	Ernakulum	4	4	14	22	3.88	0.36	14.0	0.13	3.1	14.3
80	Kottayam	3	3	2	8	2.97	0.38	2.0	0.05	3.1	12.5
81	Allepey	2	3	2		2.04	0.50	1.0	0.10	4.2	2.9

1	2	3	4	5	6	7	8	9	10	11	12
82	Quilon	13	3	1	17	13.26	1.00	1.0	0.31	14.3	5.3
83	Trivandrum	4	3	5	12	4.55	0.33	5.0	0.21	3.7	6.7
84	Morena	25	2	—	27	2.00	0.33	—	0.20	4.2	—
85	Bhind	6	2	—	8	0.67	0.50	—	0.13	20.0	—
86	Gwalior	12	1	4	17	1.59	0.33	4.0	0.24	33.3	3.6
87	Datia	4	1	—	5	0.99	1.00	—	0.20	20.0	—
88	Shivpuri	4	—	1	5	0.31	—	0.3	0.40	—	2.2
89	Guna	6	3	—	9	0.30	0.5	—	0.05	5.3	—
90	Tikamgarh	3	1	—	4	0.34	1.9	—	0.06	6.3	—
91	Chhatarpur	1	1	—	2	0.09	0.14	—	0.01	1.8	—
92	Panna	—	—	—	—	—	—	—	—	—	—
93	Satna	5	2	6	13	0.28	0.67	6.0	0.07	2.5	12.4
94	Rewa	1	—	1	2	0.04	—	1.0	0.02	—	1.9
95	Shahdol	19	4	—	23	0.96	0.4	—	0.14	3.2	—
96	Sidhi	—	—	—	—	—	—	—	—	—	—
97	Mandsaur	8	5	1	14	0.51	0.45	1.0	0.08	20.0	14.3
98	Ratlam	15	1	2	18	0.14	0.24	2.0	0.31	16.7	12.5
99	Ujjain	24	7	7	38	2.19	1.4	7.0	0.40	20.0	9.1
100	Jhabua	7	—	—	7	0.53	—	—	0.10	—	—
101	Dhar	1	1	—	2	0.07	—	—	0.01	5.6	—
102	Indore	14	—	—	21	2.18	—	1.4	0.37	—	10.0
103	Dewas	—		1	1	—	—	7.0	—	—	6.7
104	W. Nimar	1	3	—	4	0.06	0.23	—	0.01	7.1	—
105	Shajapur	11	3	—	14	1.03	0.5	—	0.18	11.1	—
106	E. Nimar	24	2	4	30	2.19	1.0	2.0	0.23	33.3	—
107	Rajgarh	—	—				—	—	—	—	—
108	Vidisha	6	3	—	9	0.40	0.75	—	0.08	33.3	—
109	Sehore	16	1	5	22	1.03	0.17	5.0	0.18	6.7	3.7
110	Raisen	6	—	—	6	0.42	—	—	0.07	—	—
111	Hoshiangabad	22	8	—	30	1.57	0.73	—	0.22	6.3	—
112	Betul	9	3	—	12	0.69	0.75	—	0.09	10.0	—
113	Sagar	20	5	1	26	1.10	0.63	1.0	0.20	12.5	1.9
114	Damoh	7	1	1	9	0.61	0.5	1.0	0.10	16.7	6.3
115	Jabalpur	35	15	10	60	1.55	1.5	5.0	0.36	14.3	3.2
116	Narsimhpur	8	2	—	10	0.80	0.5	—	0.16	4.0	—
117	Mandla	5	2	—	7	0.24	0.67	—	0.04	6.7	—
118	Chindwara	26	7	1	34	1.37	0.58	1.0	0.22	5.0	9.1
119	Seoni	13	1	—	14	0.82	0.5	—	0.15	11.1	—
120	Balaghat	9	4	—	13	0.69	1.0	—	0.10	11.1	—
121	Sarguja	10	4	—	14	0.42	0.44	—	0.04	9.1	—
122	Bilaspur	26	5	2	33	0.74	0.5	2.0	0.13	4.2	4.1
123	Raigarh	6	2	—	8	0.27	0.5	—	0.05	10.0	—
124	Durg	12	2	7	21	0.29	0.22	3.5	0.06	4.3	3.7
125.	Raipur	28	4	5	37	0.73	0.57	5.0	0.13	7.7	14.3
126.	Bastar	1	1	—	2	0.03	0.33	—	0.00	1.3	—

1	2	3	4	5	6	7	8	9	10	11	12
127.	Madras	—	—	72	72	—	—	45.1	—	—	14.3
128.	Chingleput	27	4	1	32	1.52	0.05	1.0	0.37	3.7	2.5
129.	N. Arcot	30	8	8	46	1.61	0.31	1.3	0.25	5.9	7.7
130.	S. Arcot	39	9	6	54	1.67	0.9	1.5	0.37	5.9	6.7
131.	Salem	35	7	12	54	3.65	0.17	6.0	0.42	3.1	10.0
132.	Coimbatore	21	5	23	49	2.25	0.09	5.8	0.14	2.0	3.7
133.	Nilgiri	7	1	4	12	16.7	0.07	2.0	0.43	0.4	4.2
134.	Madurai	27	5	1	43	2.66	0.15	2.8	0.22	1.6	7.7
135.	Tiruchirapalli	40	8	14	62	3.04	0.28	4.7	0.29	2.9	12.5
136.	Thanjavur	73	13	9	95	3.64	0.46	2.3	0.78	5.0	12.5
137.	Ramanathapuram	24	15	11	50	1.70	0.54	1.8	0.20	5.6	9.1
138.	Tirunelvali	29	9	10	48	1.60	0.19	2.5	0.27	2.4	2.6
139.	Kanyakumari	—	—	—	—	—	—	—	—	—	—
140.	Bombay	—	—	156	156	—	—	52.1	—	—	25.9
141.	Thana	23	4	16	43	1.45	0.19	5.3	0.25	3.6	16.9
142.	Kolaba	9	12	—	21	0.53	0.86	—	0.13	7.7	—
143.	Ratnagiri	—	—	—	—	—	—	—	—	—	—
144.	Nasik	17	9	7	33	1.04	0.5	3.5	0.11	3.7	4.8
145.	Dhulia	13	3	2	18	0.94	0.6	1.0	0.10	5.6	5.3
146.	Jalgeon	25	9	7	41	1.76	0.75	2.3	0.22	4.0	14.3
147.	Ahmednagar	20	1	1	22	1.52	0.2	1.0	0.12	1.2	5.1
148.	Poona	25	9	34	38	1.59	0.43	34.0	0.17	3.6	10.0
149.	Satna	15	—	1	16	1.31	—	1.0	0.15	—	12.5
150.	Sangli	18	—	6	24	3.34	—	6.0	0.22	—	9.1
151.	Sholapur	34	6	7	47	3.59	0.86	2.3	0.23	1.8	10.0
152.	Kolhapur	7	2	6	15	0.65	0.22	3.00	0.09	2.0	6.7
153.	Aurangabad	14	–	3	17	0.75	—	1.5	0.09	—	4.0
154.	Parbhani	24	9	1	34	1.59	0.82	1.0	0.20	5.3	2.2
155.	Bhir	3	4	—	7	0.29	0.57	—	0.03	1.2	—
156.	Nanded	15	3	1	19	1.13	0.3	1.0	0.15	1.2	8.3
157.	Osmanabad	9	3	3	15	0.65	0.25	3.0	0.07	0.8	25.0
158.	Buldhana	5	3	1	9	0.41	0.38	1.0	0.05	16.7	7.7
159.	Akola	27	6	2	35	1.81	0.75	2.0	0.26	6.7	10.0
160.	Amravati	8	3	2	13	0.49	0.27	1.0	0.07	2.9	3.8
161.	Yeotmal	3	4	1	8	0.18	0.57	1.0	0.02	4.8	12.5
162.	Wardha	15	6	1	22	1.56	1.2	1.0	0.24	25.0	12.5
163.	Nagpur	36	9	15	60	2.22	0.75	15.0	0.38	9.1	6.3
164.	Bhandra	22	6	2	30	1.47	1.5	2.0	0.24	12.5	11.1
165.	Chanda	21	3	4	28	0.74	0.5	4.0	0.08	3.8	14.3
166.	Bangalore	34	4	22	60	1.38	0.19	22.0	0.44	5.6	12.5
167.	Tumkur	9	4	1	14	0.36	0.36	1.0	0.09	8.3	7.7
168.	Chitradurg	9	4	1	17	0.72	0.4	2.0	0.08	14.3	14.3
169.	Kilar	8	7	—	15	0.28	0.54	—	0.10	20.0	—
170.	Bellary	25	1	6	32	4.25	0.11	3.0	0.26	0.5	14.3
171.	Mysore	14	4	3	21	0.88	0.33	3.0	0.12	3.0	9.3
172.	S. Kanara	—	1	2	3	—	0.06	2.0	—	4.2	4.5
173.	Coorg	—	1	—	1	—	0.09	—	—	—	—
174.	Hassan	5	3	1	9	0.22	0.3	1.0	0.07	9.1	7.1
175.	Shimoga	10	1	4	15	0.57	0.09	2.0	0.10	2.9	25.0
176.	Chikmagalur	4	6	—	10	0.40	0.66	—	0.06	14.3	—
177.	Mandya	6	3	1	10	0.44	0.34	1.0	0.12	5.9	5.9

1	2	3	4	5	6	7	8	9	10	11	12
178.	Belgaum	14	8	2	24	1.21	0.44	2.0	0.11	2.1	5.9
179.	Bijapur	13	8	3	24	1.05	0.53	1.5	0.08	1.5	8.3
180.	N. Kanara	3	6	—	9	0.23	0.75	—	0.03	25.0	—
181.	Dharwar	30	7	9	46	2.24	0.41	9.0	0.23	2.0	4.5
182.	Gulbarga	13	7	2	22	1.00	0.58	2.0	0.08	14.3	14.3
183.	Bidar	6	1	—	7	1.01	0.2	—	0.11	2.4	—
184.	Raichur	5	2	2	9	0.36	0.2	2.0	0.04	3.0	9.1
185.	Kalahandi	5	3	—	8	0.19	0.6	—	0.04	3.7	—
186.	Koraput	9	2	—	11	0.16	0.2	—	0.03	0.7	—
187.	Sambalpur	16	1	41	58	0.47	0.1	41.0	0.09	0.6	50.0
188.	Bolangir	7	2	2	11	0.27	0.3	—	0.08	2.0	—
189.	B. Khondmals	—	1	—	1	—	0.50	—	—	2.8	—
190.	Ganjam	11	5	1	17	0.26	0.36	1.0	0.09	5.0	3.4
191.	Sundergarh	19	3	5	27	1.17	0.75	5.0	0.20	3.8	4.2
192.	Dhenkanal	5	1	—	6	0.19	0.25	—	0.05	2.3	—
193.	Puri	15	2	3	20	0.35	0.67	1.5	0.15	3.6	3.7
194.	Keonjhar	3	1	—	4	0.14	0.25	—	0.04	1.1	—
195.	Cuttack	20	2	4	26	0.33	0.29	4.0	0.18	1.7	5.6
196.	Mayurbhanj	13	2	—	15	0.35	1.0	—	0.13	9.1	—
197.	Balasore	17	3	—	20	0.45	0.75	—	0.27	4.3	—
198.	Hissar	26	10	6	42	2.46	1.0	3.0	0.19	25.0	14.3
199.	Gurgaon	13	13	1	27	0.88	1.1	0.5	0.21	25.0	3.6
200	Rohtak	11	2	2	15	1.43	0.33	1.0	0.18	9.1	6.3
201.	Karnal	12	9	3	24	0.88	1.0	1.5	0.15	16.7	11.1
202	Ambala	15	10	22	47	1.23	1.4	7.3	0.40	25.0	33.3
203.	Simla	14	4	2	20	1.0	0.8	2.0	1.01	15.2	—
204.	Kangra	14	8	—	22	0.17	0.9	—	0.17	2.1	—
205.	Lahul & Spiti	—	—	—	—	—	—	—	—	—	—
206.	Hoshiarpur	25	7	2	34	1.58	0.9	2.0	0.65	25.0	20.0
207.	Jullundhur	25	9	4	38	2.07	0.82	4.0	0.76	20.0	6.3
208.	Ludhiana	15	3	6	24	1.55	0.6	6.0	0.40	7.7	14.3
209.	Ferozepur	34	6	6	46	2.29	0.55	2.0	0.34	16.7	20.0
210.	Amritsar	21	6	8	35	1.78	0.75	8.0	0.42	16.7	20.0
211.	Gurdaspur	8	6	5	19	0.52	0.75	5.0	0.23	20.0	20.0
212.	Kapurthala	6	2	1	9	1.08	1.0	1.0	0.38	6.7	9.1
213.	Bhatinda	15	11	3	29	2.19	0.85	3.0	0.22	20.0	14.3
214.	Sangrur	28	13	—	41	3.94	0.92	—	0.56	50.0	—
215.	Patiala	16	6	2	24	1.12	0.54	2.0	0.35	12.5	7.7
216.	Mahendragarh	8	6	—	14	1.48	1.2	—	0.23	25.0	—
217.	Ganganagar	43	11	9	63	1.80	1.0	9.0	0.28	14.3	100.0
218.	Bikaner	26	2	3	31	4.82	0.4	3.0	0.10	1.8	5.0
219.	Churu	24	5	2	31	2.82	0.5	2.0	0.14	3.1	3.2
220.	Jhunjhunu	9	4	—	13	1.30	0.3	—	0.15	5.0	—
212.	Alwar	12	3	1	16	0.64	1.0	1.0	0.14	11.1	2.4
222.	Bharatpur	21	5	8	34	1.12	0.63	8.0	0.26	4.0	33.3
223.	Sawai-Madhopur	12	7	—	19	0.78	1.2	—	0.11	8.3	—
224.	Jaipur	41	9	4	54	1.53	0.9	4.0	0.30	7.1	1.5
225.	Sikar	19	4	1	24	2.35	0.67	1.0	0.25	11.1	4.1
226.	Ajmer	19	5	5	29	1.99	0.83	2.5	0.23	10.0	9.1
227.	Tonk	8	2	1	11	0.80	0.4	1.0	0.11	1.2	6.7
228.	Jaiselmer	6	3		9	1.39	1.5	—	0.02	0.9	—

1	2	3	4	5	6	7	8	9	10	11	12
229.	Jodhpur	29	5	4	38	4.31	1.67	4.0	0.13	2.2	1.7
230.	Nagaur	33	13	—	46	2.71	1.6	—	0.19	5.6	—
231.	Pali	32	1	—	33	3.88	0.17	—	0.26	0.5	—
232.	Barmer	26	2	—	28	3.11	1.0	—	0.09	5.9	—
233.	Jalor	13	1	—	14	2.18	0.5	—	0.12	9.1	—
234.	Sirohi	7	5	—	12	1.65	1.0	—	0.14	8.3	—
235.	Bhilwara	8	2	1	11	0.53	0.67	1.0	0.08	2.9	0.8
236.	Udaipur	28	4	2	34	0.90	0.80	2.0	0.16	5.0	3.3
237.	Chitorgarh	12	6	—	18	0.57	0.86	—	0.11	4.8	—
238.	Durgapur	5	1	—	6	0.61	0.50	—	0.13	4.8	—
239.	Banswara	—	1	—	1	—	0.50	—	)	4.8	—
240.	Bundi	6	3	—	9	0.42	0.75	—	0.11	4.0	—
241.	Kota	18	4	4	26	0.94	0.80	4.0	0.15	6.3	—
242.	Jhalwar	3	2	—	5	0.21	0.40	—	0.05	2.7	—
243.	Uttar Kashi	—	1	—	1	—	1.0	—	—	8.3	—
244.	Chamoli	2	3	—	5	0.13	1.0	—	0.02	10.0	—
245.	Pithorgarh	2	1	—	3	0.13	1.0	—	0.03	16.7.	—
246.	Tehri Garhwal	1	2	—	1	—	0.25	—	—	2.1	—
247.	Garhwal	3	3	—	6	0.09	0.50	—	0.06	4.8	—
248.	Almora	—	3	—	3	—	0.75	—	—	11.1	—
249.	Nanital	19	5	1	25	1.07	0.63	1.0	0.28	14.3	9.1
250.	Bijnore	20	8	—	28	0.95	0.73	—	0.42	14.3	—
251.	Moradabad	29	3	7	39	1.18	0.38	1.8	0.50	7.7	12.5
252.	Budaun	10	1	1	12	0.55	0.2	1.0	0.19	6.7	50.0
253.	Rampur	8	—	4	12	0.73	—	2.0	0.34	—	20.0
254.	Barailly	22	2	17	41	1.14	0.33	17.0	0.54	14.3	33.3
255.	Pilibhit	10	2	1	13	0.87	1.0	1.0	0.29	33.3	33.3
256.	Shajahanpur	16	2	6	24	0.77	0.5	6.0	0.35	20.0	25.0
257.	Dehradun	6	6	1	13	0.78	0.75	1.0	0.20	5.6	1.8
258.	Saharanpur	24	2	10	36	1.42	0.29	3.3	0.44	4.5	16.7
259.	Muzaffarnagar	7	3	3	13	0.76	0.5	3.0	0.17	16.7	25.0
260.	Meerut	20	8	13	41	1.33	0.42	4.3	0.35	11.1	12.5
261.	Bulandshahr	9	3	4	16	0.59	0.27	2.0	0.19	11.1	33.3
262.	Aligarh	11	4	7	22	0.64	1.0	3.5	0.22	100.0	16.7
263.	Mathura	12	4	7	23	1.36	0.67	7.0	0.32	33.3	33.3
264.	Agra	25	3	25	53	2.12	0.27	12.5	0.53	16.7	25.0
265.	Etah	16	6	—	22	1.05	0.86	—	0.36	25.0	—
266.	Mainpuri	7	4	—	11	0.51	0.57	—	0.17	20.0	—
267.	Farkhabad	13	4	3	20	0.80	1.0	3.0	0.30	33.3	20.0
268.	Etawah	77	3	2	12	0.47	0.75	2.0	0.16	33.3	20.0
269.	Kanpur	29	—	85	144	1.53	—	77.0	0.50	—	25.0
270.	Fatehpur	10	2	1	13	0.74	2.0	1.0	0.24	20.0	1.0
271.	Allahabad	45	3	1	49	1.27	0.6	1.0	0.63	25.0	1.2
272.	Jhansi	20	6	3	29	1.38	0.55	3.0	0.20	12.5	5.0
273.	Jalaun	3	3	—	6	0.31	0.75	—	0.07	12.5	—
274.	Hamirpur	15	5	—	20	1.61	1.0	—	0.21	20.0	—
275.	Banda	9	4	1	14	0.75	1.0	1.0	0.12	20.0	33.3
276.	Kheri	23	2	—	25	1.38	0.5	—	0.30	20.0	—
277.	Sitapur	19	3	5	27	0.82	0.6	5.0	0.33	10.0	12.5
278.	Hardoi	17	4	—	21	0.90	0.57	—	0.28	11.1	—
279.	Unnao	22	3	—	25	1.29	3.0	—	0.48	50.0	14.3
280.	Lucknow	20	1	18	39	2.21	0.3	18.0	0.83	50.0	—
281.	Rae Bareli	15	4	—	19	0.86	2.0	—	0.33	33.3	—
282.	Bahraich	17	1	1	19	0.90	0.5	1.0	0.25	25.0	8.3

1	2	3	4	5	6	7	8	9	10	11	12
283.	Gonda	22	3	4	29	0.78	0.6	4.0	0.30	16.7	33.3
284.	Bara Banki	16	5	—	21	0.78	0.83	—	0.36	20.0	—
285.	Faizabad	17	3	3	23	0.64	0.6	3.0	0.39	50.0	5.9
286.	Sultanpur	19	1	—	20	0.76	1.0	—	0.43	14.3	—
287.	Partapgarh	16	—	—	16	0.73	—	—	0.43	—	—
288.	Bastar	12	2	—	14	0.17	0.67	—	0.17	5.9	—
289.	Gorakhpur	28	—	4	32	0.68	2.0	—	0.45	10.0	—
290.	Deoria	25	3	—	28	0.70	0.75		0.47	10.0	—
291.	Azamgarh	15	5	—	20	0.30	1.0	—	0.26	16.7	—
292.	Jaunpur	19	3	4	26	0.59	0.6	4.0	0.47	25.0	16.7
293.	Ballia	14	3	—	17	0.73	0.0	—	0.44	12.5	—
294.	Ghazipur	22	2	—	24	0.88	0.67	—	0.65	14.3	—
295.	Varanasi	34	4	13	51	0.93	0.33	13.0	0.68	9.1	14.3
296.	Mirzapur	21	16	2	39	0.70	1.45	12.0	0.19	25.0	5.0
297.	Darjeeling	22	3	3	28	4.34	1.0	3.0	0.72	12.5	20.0
298.	Jalpaiguri	56	3	2	61	7.53	0.5	1.0	0.91	50.0	2.8
299.	Cooch Bihar	12	3	2	17	1.04	0.5	2.0	0.36	33.3	14.3
300.	West Dinajpur	21	3	1	25	0.66	0.5	1.0	0.41	6.3	16.7
301.	Malda	13	—	3	16	0.81	—	1.5	0.35	—	33.3
302.	Murashidabad	25	9	—	34	1.30	0.9	—	0.48	12.5	—
303.	Nadia	22	6	4	32	1.73	0.55	2.0	0.58	12.5	7.7
304.	24-Paraganas	46	4	6	56	1.21	0.06	1.2	0.35	1.0	5.9
305.	Calcutta	—	—	140	140	—	—	61.7	—	—	25.0
306.	Howrah	9	3	—	12	1.16	0.11	—	0.68	2.0	—
307.	Hoogly	40	3	—	43	2.10	0.18	—	1.32	2.5	—
308.	Burdwan	54	10	24	88	2.07	0.53	8.0	0.81	9.1	12.5
309.	Birbhum	24	7	—	31	1.07	1.2	—	0.53	16.7	—
310.	Bankura	4	1	1	6	0.11	0.25	1.0	0.06	4.8	5.6
311.	Midnapore	26	11	5	42	0.25	0.79	2.5	0.19	7.2	11.1
312.	Purulia	27	3	1	31	1.10	0.5	1.0	0.43	9.1	7.1
313.	Andaman-Hicobar	—	—	—	—	—	—	—	—	—	—
314.	Delhi	—	—	113	113	—	—	45.93	—	—	8.75
315.	Chamba	1	2	—	3	—	—	—	0.01	—	—
316.	Mandi	3	4	—	7	—	—	—	0.08	—	—
317.	Bilaspur	—	2	—	2	—	—	—	—	—	—
318.	Mahasu	—	1	—	1	—	—	—	—	—	—
319.	Sirmur	—	2	—	2	—	—	—	—	—	—
320.	Kinnaur	—	—	—	—	—	—	—	—	—	—
321.	Laccadive Minicoy	—	—	—	—	—	—	—	—	—	—
322.	Manipur	—	—	1	1	—	—	—	—	—	3.2
323.	Tripura	8	—	—	8	0.17	—	—	0.08	—	—
324.	Dadar and Nagar Haveli	—	—	—	—	—	—	—	—	—	—
325.	Goa	16	1	—	17	4.02	01	—	0.45	7.3	—
326.	Daman	—	—	—	—	—	—	—	—	—	—
327.	Diu	—	—	—	—	—	—	—	—	—	—
328.	Pondicharry	—	—	2	2	—	—	0.92	—	—	0.69
329.	Karaikal	1	1	—	2	—	—	—	—	—	—
330.	Mahe	—	1	—	1	—	—	—	—	—	—
331.	Yaman	—	—	—	—	—	—	—	—	—	—
332.	Kohima	3	3	—	6	—	—	—	—	2.8	—
333.	Mokuk Chung	—	—	—	—	—	—	—	—	—	—
334.	Tuensang	—	—	—	—	—	—	—	—	—	—
335.	Sikir	—	—	—	—	—	—	—	—	—	—

APPENDIX XII

DISTRICT WISE FACTOR SCORES FOR SHIPMENTS AND RECEIPTS

Distt. code	District	Shipments 1st Factor	Shipments 2nd Factor	Shipments 3rd Factor	Receipts 1st Factor
1	2	3	4	5	6
001	Srikakulam	—0.16421	0.32152	—0.03002	—0.70408
002	Vishakhapatnam	1.80854	3.48943	—1.45813	12.27488
003	East Godavari	—0.44746	0.24901	—0.09967	0.76741
004	West Godavari	—0.64111	1.02600	—0.78100	—1.26206
005	Krishna	—0.32349	0.59621	—0.65978	—0.44358
006	Guntur	0.53089	0.09945	—1.21980	—0.38992
007	Nellore	—0.58843	0.13653	—0.06424	0.09495
008	Chittoor	—0.80377	—0.14870	0.10886	—1.11073
009	Cuddapah	—0.60104	—0.43743	0.14620	—1.40585
010	Anantapur	—0.64971	—0.16951	0.10812	—0.99253
011	Kurnool	0.96245	0.16262	—0.82549	—1.23337
012	Mahbubnagar	—0.80950	—0.35082	0.30513	—1.54982
013	Hyderabad	3.37443	1.32450	0.71340	4.95620
014	Medak	—0.77236	—0.31230	0.31050	—1.61281
015	Nizamabad	—0.79786	—0.14653	0.14971	—1.41876
016	Adilabad	1.08620	—0.06307	0.65833	—0.52886
017	Karimnagar	1.24418	0.39698	0.19051	—0.93737
018	Warangal	—0.79406	—0.22669	0.21647	—1.10756
019	Khamman	—0.09410	—0.18396	0.96390	—0.28000
020	Nalgonda	—0.83085	—0.35899	0.31490	—1.54257
021	Golapara	—0.60906	—0.31165	0.09232	—1.12451
022	Kamrup	—0.04459	0.15655	0.02358	—0.36986
023	Darrang	—0.68310	—0.22819	0.20767	—0.45698
024	Lakhimpur	—0.28750	0.01355	0.25079	0.05358
025	Nowgong	—0.75215	—0.13707	0.07168	—1.41283
026	Sibsagar	—0.73643	—0.25259	—0.21433	—0.82569
027	Cachar	—0.19512	0.06951	0.14223	—0.14069
028	United Khasi & Jaintia Hills	—0.83556	—0.36380	0.31631	—1.62189
029	United Mikir & N.C Hills	—0.79921	—0.36987	0.29339	—1.46279
030	Mizo Hills	—0.83557	—0.36530	0.31765	—1.62230
031	Patna	—0.30025	0.01457	0.37950	0.59664
032	Gaya	—0.57655	—0.39942	0.09358	—1.00499
033	Shahabad	2.15658	—0.30006	—0.54073	1.11983
034	Saran	—0.62105	—0.15688	0.00423	1.24136
035	Champaran	—0.30995	—0.23089	—0.24992	0.08591
036	Muzaffarpur	—0.70283	—0.25669	0.15057	—0.48461

1	2	3	4	5	6
037	Darbhanga	—0.59754	—0.20701	0.01634	—0.24893
038	Monghyr	—0.36147	—0.40647	0.07307	—0.44413
039	Bhagalpur	—0.79986	—0.33000	0.28770	—1.06165
040	Saharsa	—0.73058	—0.34095	0.19835	—1.25409
041	Purnea	—0.49200	—0.18428	—0.06457	—0.73404
042	Santal Parganas	0.91473	—1.26142	—0.97189	—1.24183
043	Palaman	1.24615	—0.08284	—0.73289	0.01654
044	Hazaribagh	3.91365	0.22251	5.15834	3.18000
045	Ranchi	0.66307	—0.05348	—0.08290	0.30235
046	Dhanbad	10.38770	—0.63504	7.42453	10.43067
047	Sighbhum	11.04298	—5.37929	—3.64933	11.12752
048	Jamnagar	2.93841	0.79622	—1.84267	0.76079
049	Rajkot	—0.45295	—0.04139	—0.14155	—0.40135
050	Surendranagar	—0.68767	1.15819	—0.93803	—1.23414
051	Bhavnagar	0.10917	0.46454	—0.19879	—0.45168
052	Amreli	—0.81647	—0.31695	0.29030	—0.36344
053	Junagarh	1.69742	0.25841	—1.18855	—0.79725
054	Kutch	0.88780	5.38812	—2.68188	—0.59176
055	Banaskantha	—0.79652	—0.24100	0.19041	—1.15098
056	Sabarkantha	—0.79803	—0.33252	0.30933	—0.96852
057	Mehesane	—0.71616	—0.21074	0.16252	1.59145
058	Ahmedabad	0.70884	0.47159	—0.03731	7-40808
059	Kheda	—0.42894	0.95305	—0.80165	0.12451
060	Panchmahals	0.86868	0.17580	1.06479	—0.86249
061	Baroda	1.05572	0.15123	0.99935	0.94141
062	Bharuch	—0.75602	—0.34205	0.27744	—0.95153
063	Surat	—0.33603	0.58074	—0.10936	3.06102
064	Anantnag	—0.83557	—0.36539	0.31765	—1.62291
065	Srinagar	—0.83190	—0.36318	0.31782	—1.41576
066	Udhampur	—0.82714	—0.36182	0.31813	—1.61806
067	Jammu	—0.77878	—0.34654	0.30861	—0.28362
068	Kathua	—0.82801	—0.36503	0.31610	—1.47440
069	Poonch-Rajauri	—0.83557	—0.30532	0.31765	—1.62300
070	Cannanore	—0.72480	—0.35933	0.24895	—1.15190
071	Kozhikode	—0.44860	—0.01933	—0.06057	—0.44218
072	Palghat	—0.78696	—0.35339	0.28339	—1.17214
073	Trichur	—0.47187	—0.25206	0.07142	—1.08240
074	Ernakulam	0.67825	0.59202	0.30613	2.45279
075	Kottayam	—0.74417	—0.35098	0.26978	—1.26008
076	Alleppey	—0.89175	—0.36459	0.30476	—1.27760
077	Quillon	—0.64120	—0.40300	0.24557	—1.01652
078	Trivandrum	—0.79476	—0.36667	0.31021	—1.00420
079	Morena	—0.49037	—0.17106	—0.06298	—1.20052
080	Bhind	—0.83002	—0.26189	0.22797	—1.56929
081	Gwalior	—0.48767	—0 07435	0.25059	—0.70520

1	2	3	4	5	6
082	Datia	—0.83055	—0.33939	—0.22527	—1.58449
083	Shivpuri	—0.52040	—0.33528	0.29749	—1.58271
084	Guna	—0.78598	-0.22236	0.20775	—1.43125
085	Tikamgarh	—0.81873	—0.29573	0.26416	—1.61149
086	Chatarpur	—0.82924	—0.35528	0.30904	—1.56511
087	Satna	2.81229	0.17965	—2.23592	—0.96054
088	Rewa	—0.81787	—0.36146	0.30927	—1.62156
089	Shahdol	0.01767	—0.29549	1.05718	—1.23961
090	Mandsaur	—0.68545	—0.15979	0.19715	—1.30425
091	Ratlam	—0.70091	—0.23969	0.24127	—0.92954
092	Ujjain	—0.27282	—0.20984	0.27909	1.98119
093	Jhabua	—0.82362	—0.35911	0.31105	—1.55346
094	Dhar	—0.83523	—0.36552	0.31746	—1.61995
095	Indoor	—0.58793	0.12272	0.04642	—0.24169
096	Dewas	—0.83347	—0.36487	0.31775	—1.38773
097	West Nimar	—0.83132	—0.36843	0.31504	—1.55350
098	East Nimar	—0.46091	—0.12004	0.15866	—0.07540
099	Shajapur	—0.82570	—0.31836	0.28236	—1.40148
100	Vidhisha	—0.79442	—0.10862	0.12656	—1.42786
101	Sehare	—0.52360	—0.12070	0.12445	—0.00623
102	Raisen	—0.80812	—0.33645	0.30962	—1.43279
103	Hoshangabad	—0.40902	0.08278	0.07273	—0.42264
104	Betul	—0.63086	—0.29119	0.28905	—1.09302
105	Sagar	—0.37907	0.14018	—0.15146	—1.09486
106	Demoh	—0.80574	—0.30077	0.27199	—1.49895
107	Jabalpur	6.54310	2.40444	—3.32433	3.31336
108	Narsimhapur	—0.81286	—0.14059	0.11754	—1.53713
109	Mandla	—0.79860	—0.34745	0.27956	—1.53767
110	Chindwara	0.39475	—0.30486	1.77381	—1.38892
111	Seoni	—0.81632	—0.32625	0.28732	—1.55549
112	Balaghat	—0.55909	—0.42377	0.06092	—1.55375
113	Surguga	0.86772	—0.15888	1.96717	—1:35086
114	Bilaspur	2.70554	0.08971	—0.95705	2.13146
115	Raigarh	—0.73600	—0.27554	0.21380	—1.50181
116	Durg	13.28987	—6.10645	—2.57606	16.77606
117	Raipur	4.43952	—3.05205	—4.50513	—0.50027
118	Bastar	—0.83252	—0.36779	0.31519	—1.61219
119	Madras	2.36139	0.94283	0.33180	13.57362
120	Chingleput	—0.74858	—0.28406	0.28754	—0.80355
121	North Aroot	—0.69420	0.04330	—0.01637	—0.32891
122	South Arrot	—0.58667	—0.03101	0.14728	—0.67338
123	Salem	1.56269	0.76883	—1.68440	—0.44587
124	Coimbatore	0.06370	0.39041	—0.63589	0.53478
125	The Nilgiris	—0.81014	—0.35029	0.31516	—1.37558
126	Madurai	—0.75061	—0.24670	0.19846	—0.16397

1	2	3	4	5	6
127	Tiruchirappali	0.82425	0.43445	—0.98019	0.20496
128	Thanjavur	—0.74910	1.44104	—1.10183	—0.73473
129	Ramanathapuram	2.34480	0.57460	—1.80219	—0.69063
130	Tiruneveli	—0.35006	1.09906	—0.98404	—0.05353
131	Kanyakumari	—0.83335	—0.36506	0.31773	—1.61462
132	G. Bombay	15.08648	7.25077	0.05438	25.85329
133	Thana	0.53849	1.36870	—0.25870	2.70408
134	Koleba	—0.42670	0.09703	0.13687	—0.64673
135	Nasik	0.24030	0.64385	0.09882	1.39710
136	Dhulia	—0.74992	—0.12709	0.20212	—0.96128
137	Jalgaon	—0.44260	0.13424	0.20595	0.17293
138	Ahmednagar	—0.65525	0.39981	—0.23950	—0.40079
139	Poona	0.27454	0.67337	0.06509	6.43497
140	Satara	—0.78445	—0.18839	0.19004	—0.68230
141	Sangli	—0.67016	—0.00753	0.11276	6.28307
142	Sholapur	—0.77561	—0.18042	0.19445	—0.24601
143	Kolhapur	—0.73448	0.16801	—0.09971	—0.77789
144	Aurangabad	—0.82222	—0.34941	0.30508	—0.53339
145	Parbhani	—0.79532	—0.27354	0.24334	0.90375
146	Bhir	—0.81272	—0.34128	0.31113	—1.18045
147	Nanded	—0.79637	—0.26305	0.23149	—1.28054
148	Osmanabad	—0.82618	—0.24486	0.22915	—1.46575
149	Buldhana	—0.75899	—0.23552	0.25854	—1.40237
150	Akola	—0.71968	—0.14169	0.16738	—0.56565
151	Amravati	—0.59980	0.01055	0.19995	—1.08016
152	Yeotmal	—0.72915	—0.32246	0.22872	—1.45849
153	Wardha	—0.63499	—0.21647	0.28971	—0.89956
154	Nagpur	—0.04977	—0.15210	0.30879	2.27904
155	Bhandara	0.27219	0.07145	0.04769	—0.76987
156	Chandrapur	0.77860	0.13636	0.08364	0.05500
157	Bangalore	0.19953	0.33561	0.11152	4.21134
158	Tumkur	0.36965	—0.02317	—0.48006	—1.36557
159	Chitradurg	—0.53574	—0.32608	0.16349	—1.14912
160	Kolar	—0.81609	—0.27073	0.24172	—1.46085
161	Bellary	3.53452	—3.35805	—3.14076	—0.47057
162	Mysore	—0.75612	—0.27062	0.22804	—0.68064
163	S. Kanara	—0.67150	—0.05887	0.04541	—0.85298
164	Coorg	—0.83529	—0.36544	0.31768	—1.59828
165	Hassan	—0.68851	—0.21948	0.25892	—1.18123
166	Shimoga	0.36916	—0.02995	0.08372	—0.64840
167	Chikmagalur	—0.76586	—0.34275	0.29384	—1.52935
168	Mandya	—0.79097	—0.25076	0.22884	—1.01551
169	Balgaum	—0.38575	—0.13228	0.13664	—0.67384
170	Bajapur	—0.22250	—0.17779	—0.09002	—0.61802
171	N. Kanara	1.00642	—1.59240	—0.93659	—1.03551

1	2	3	4	5	6
172	Dharwar	—0.47483	—0.11440	0.20034	—0.04575
173	Gulburga	2.76353	0.64850	—2.06984	—0.61621
174	Bidar	—0.82928	—0.29240	0.25609	—1.52841
175	Raichur	—0.77929	—0.27591	0.27443	—1.07021
176	Kalahandi	—0.63316	—0.18442	0.05530	—1.48968
177	Koraput	—0.49304	—0.23660	0.26452	—0.26192
178	Sambalpur	2.98123	—0.45907	—1.93793	1.96937
179	Bolangir	—0.77521	—0.3224	0.26102	—1.55709
180	Baudh—Khondamals	—0.83550	—0.36537	0.31760	—1.62294
181	Ganjam	—0.57543	—0.26686	0.16736	—0.96079
182	Sundergarh	8.56639	—3.86328	—3.32732	7.61373
183	Dhen-Kanal	—0.43404	—0.28555	0.52637	—1.18904
184	Puri	—0.52505	—0.12498	0.24160	—0.69730
185	Keoujhar	2.59511	—2.83897	—2.28002	—1.46489
186	Cuttack	—0.41696	—0.35623	0.20734	1.17710
187	Mayurbhanj	—0.66379	—0.32234	0.28083	—1.57570
188	Belasore	—0.62103	—0.16866	0.16040	—1.24145
189	Hissar	—0.58268	0.74405	—0.62091	0.55834
190	Rohtak	—0.45471	—0.04068	0.08861	0.45848
191	Gurgaon	—0.03024	0.28206	—0.24862	1.85668
192	Karnal	—0.58426	2.17755	—1.08183	—0.52824
193	Ambala	0.67475	1.11886	—0.65168	4.08277
194	Simla	—0.68868	—0.16048	0.20088	—1.41859
195	Kangra	—0.83082	—0.35771	0.31354	—1.32008
196	Hoshiarpur	—0.30608	0.91017	—0.45811	—0.50224
197	Jullundur	—0.38281	1.73368	—1.24746	1.80161
198	Ludhiana	—0.61087	2.14791	—1.73579	0.73566
199	Ferozpur	—0.48971	2.79986	—2.28644	0.18913
200	Amritsar	—0.54208	2.45086	—1.69010	0.54113
201	Gurdaspur	—0.57988	0.93531	—0.73441	3.05226
202	Kapurthala	—0.76947	0.69340	—0.55645	—1.33380
203	Bhatinda	—0.56008	1.30585	—1.03298	0.15749
204	Sangraur	—0.74673	2.24480	—1.85354	—0.72581
205	Patiala	—0.53587	1.94500	—1.53751	0.30292
206	Mahendagarh	—0.31115	—0.01474	—0.20863	—1.33730
207	Ganganagar	—0.36994	0.57992	—0.83908	—0.21790
208	Bikaner	—0.01860	—0.22837	—0.00680	—0.26800
209	Churu	—0.78333	—0.19299	0.15021	—1.30723
210	Jhun jhunu	—0.79238	—0.29706	0.24402	—1.06288
211	Alwar	—0.73201	—0.17112	0.16915	—1.22715
212	Bharatpur	—0.60953	—0.18167	0.07669	—0.48215
213	Sawai Madhopur	2.68614	—0.31105	—2.15613	—0.04390
214	Jaipur	—0.37502	0.68846	0.46717	0.27462
215	Sikar	—0.74127	—0.33550	0.26753	—1.36340
216	Ajmer	—0.55259	—0.16707	0.26803	—0.93380

1	2	3	4	5	6
217	Tonk	—0.82310	0.35263	0.31463	—1.58355
218	Jaisalmer	—0.59916	—0.44706	0.14737	—1.37211
219	Jodhpur	—0.45564	0.07248	—0.18627	—0.33977
220	Nagaur	—0.38899	0.10039	—0.44165	—1.06585
221	Pali	—0.70723	—0.32852	0.24047	—1.49956
222	Barmer	—0.53774	—0.18410	0.14856	—1.39562
223	Jalor	—0.82530	—0.35009	0.30181	—1.49107
224	Sirohi	—0.76119	—0.32337	0.328813	—1.43332
225	Bhilwara	—0.61522	—0.22560	0.29022	—1.45254
226	Udaipur	0.95815	0.71149	0.04201	—1.07616
227	Chitragarh	0.23680	—0.07753	—0.39643	—1.40885
228	Durgapur	—0.71334	—0.28822	0.31955	—1.54631
229	Banswara	—0.85048	—0.36106	0.31782	—1.62267
230	Bundi	—0.23268	—0.03932	—0.40060	—1.39002
231	Kota	0.12409	0.19584	—0.33072	—0.10514
232	Jhalawar	—0.81897	—0.34778	0.29882	—1.53794
233	Uttar Kashi	—0.83557	—0.36539	0.31765	—1.62188
234	Chamoli	—0.83374	—0.36416	0.31772	—1.62184
235	Pithoragarh	—0.83482	—0.56496	0.31769	—1.61168
236	Tehri Garhwal	—0.83557	—0.36539	0.31765	—1.62287
237	Garhwal	—0.79828	—0.33855	0.30786	—1.46902
238	Almora	—0.83431	—0.36447	0.31763	—1.60862
239	Nainital	—0.48697	—0.05499	—0.11557	—0.76791
240	Bijnor	—0.52986	0.04662	—0.15134	—0.80106
241	Moradabad	—0.15656	0.42586	—0.17610	—0.41329
242	Budaur	—0.81651	—0.30650	0.25640	—1.44388
243	Rampur	—0.74228	0.18263	—0.13398	—1.23348
244	Bareilly	—0.47002	0.71709	—0.47780	0.41131
245	Pillibhit	—0.68850	—0.19583	0.09851	—1.47952
246	Shahjanpur	—0.57541	00.10054	0.00312	—0.82166
247	Dehra Dun	—0.43514	—0.39381	0.13549	0.42385
248	Saharanpur	—0.52321	0.10357	—0.13929	0.51544
249	Muzaffarnagar	—0.74064	0.27072	—0.17312	—0.91723
250	Meerut	—0.31855	0.69440	—0.41212	4.19832
251	Bhulandshahr	—0.81291	0.52069	—0.42350	—1.04629
252	Aligarh	—0.71542	0.27528	—0.18173	0.85791
253	Mathura	—0.61003	0.00210	0.10243	—0.64356
254	Agra	0.01296	0.79415	—0.23411	3.29955
255	Etah	—0.81478	—0.11990	0.11367	—1.33070
256	Mainpuri	—0.80671	—0.11711	0.62230	—1.11737
257	Farrukhabad	—0.80591	0.20468	—0.15751	—1.21070
258	Etawah	—0.82087	—0.09526	0.10238	—1.13351
259	Kanpur	0.59744	1.25005	0.16823	5.10280
260	Fatehpur	—0.82015	—0.30956	0.27918	—1.41737
261	Allahabad	0.66760	0.10625	—0.38970	1.13981
262	Jhansi	—0.28783	—0.10258	—0.15583	—0.47742

1	2	3	4	5	6
263	Jalaur	—0.80907	—0.21266	0.20630	—1.23023
264	Hamirpur	—0.71873	—0.16335	0.09618	—1.30912
265	Banda	—0.60319	0.02704	—0.09540	—1.26925
266	Kheri	—0.09944	—0.48413	—0.56001	—0.83323
267	Sitapur	—0.64077	—0.07722	—0.01934	0.00196
268	Hardoi	—0.71169	—0.30435	0.11404	—1.29213
269	Unnao	—0.79174	—0.29106	0.27447	—0.99750
270	Lucknow	—0.16329	0.15133	0.15106	3.11760
271	Rai Bareli	—0.82606	—0.34957	0.30742	—1.20382
272	Bahraich	—0 67919	—0.22620	0.14608	—1.14553
273	Gonda	—0.59713	—0.26077	—0.05879	—1.06322
274	Bara Banki	—0.72794	—0.26993	0.25274	—0.90698
275	Faizabad	—0.65937	—0.22521	0.12427	—0.97088
276	Sultanpur	—0.82419	—0.35014	0.30351	—1.44302
277	Pratapgarh	—0.82842	—0.35657	0.31220	—1.48993
278	Basti	—0.76678	—0.25498	0.13958	—1.21693
279	Gorakhpur	—0.60090	—0.12556	0.10930	—0.38624
280	Deoria	—0.65688	—0.03316	—0.14498	—0.81282
281	Azamgarh	0.06309	0.25614	0.32056	—1.37990
282	Jaunpur	—0.82904	—0.34101	0.29661	—1.13397
283	Ballia	—0.80728	—0.24448	0.19496	—1.35602
284	Ghazipur	—0.82576	—0.30618	0.26796	—1.43004
285	Varanasi	—0.69562	—0.22747	0.20485	3.29516
286	Mirzapur	1.46853	0.00645	—0.30933	0.21517
287	Darjeeling	—0.67428	—0.25632	0.27052	—0.87451
288	Jalpaiguri	—0.34859	—0.23430	0.14105	0.12548
289	Cooch Behar	—0.77952	—0.32105	0.25680	—1.42296
290	West Dinajpur	—0.81429	—0.34420	0.27419	—1.42408
291	Malda	—0.75473	—0.34060	0.25285	—1.17108
292	Murshidabad	—0.77449	—0.38156	0.26824	—1.23779
293	Nandia	—0.80383	—0.37300	0.28086	—1.32789
294	24 Parganas	0.04965	—0.41713	0.37339	2.85960
295	Calcutta	7.77205	0.77537	0.87113	31.49599
296	Howrah	—0.77283	—0.36760	0.31836	—1.33121
297	Hoogly	—0.69980	—0.36088	0.32076	0.09460
298	Burdwan	14.22988	—0.69608	7.71024	14.60618
299	Birbhum	—0.41415	0.00251	0.06159	—1.33748
300	Bankura	—0.81357	—0.34615	0.30038	—1.37608
301	Midnapur	—0.60577	—0.19599	0.22015	0.14877
302	Purulia	—0.61542	—0.33850	0.53384	—1.16900
303	Delhi	1.31510	0.73291	0.34015	18.31844
304	Chamba	—0.83492	—0.36540	0.31771	—1.62004
305	Mandi	—0.83543	—0.36533	0.31766	—1.62071
306	Bilaspur	—0.83556	—0.36539	0.31765	—1.62113
307	Mahasu	—0.83557	—0.36540	0.31765	—1.62299

1	2	3	4	5	6
308	Sirmaur	—0.83548	—0.36534	0.31766	—1.62208
309	Manipur	—0.83399	—0.36486	0.31775	—1.52204
310	Tripura	—0.77214	—0.33130	0.24884	—1.14667
311	Goa, Daman, Diu	—0.55164	0.17822	0.09369	0.49308
312	Pondicherry	—0.76435	—0.23330	0.32347	—1.38070
313	Karaikal	—0.83503	—0.36555	0.31763	—1.56297
314	Mahe	—0.83279	—0.36599	0.31798	—1.61645
315	Kohima	—0.66815	—0.14830	0.31320	—0.67385
316	Sikkim	—0.83557	—0.36539	0.31765	—1.62299

RECEIPTS AT METROPOLITAN CENTRES

Dist. from	Hyderabad	Ahmedabad	Madras	Bombay	Puna	Bangalore	Kanpur	Calcutta	Delhi
1	2	3	4	5	6	7	8	9	10
1	3	1	25	0	1	5	1	110	19
2	68	50	56	73	21	0	0	722	19
3	121	34	155	240	24	15	12	173	32
4	488	66	74	92	11	11	3	130	4
5	215	0	125	97	9	9	0	237	0
6	317	9	51	88	13	31	27	30	26
7	133	15	145	73	10	27	0	44	0
8	20	6	4	123	9	7	0	11	0
9	18	29	686	551	12	1	0	51	42
10	27	10	321	82	8	20	2	14	9
11	153	23	90	482	208	132	4	45	16
12	2	0	5	10	2	1	0	1	0
13	205	72	134	912	215	105	39	260	144
14	0	0	0	4	0	0	0	0	0
15	74	15	5	27	2	4	0	10	65
16	2139	40	4827	307	33	22	45	25	443
17	3181	2	41	800	40	20	1	23	215
18	58	4	107	53	2	5	1	59	30
19	231	0	667	14	0	66	0	15	11
20	0	0	0	4	0	0	0	0	0
21	0	2	6	27	3	0	6	615	16
22	4	110	14	83	4	22	21	701	57
23	3	6	0	13	1	0	2	302	7
24	12	22	11	120	6	9	21	316	142
25	0	1	0	2	0	0	5	29	10
26	0	10	7	0	1	0	2	120	51
27	0	3	0	4	1	0	6	224	16
28	0	0	0	0	0	0	0	0	0
29	0	0	0	0	0	0	0	6	0
30	0	6	4	5	0	3	0	0	0
31	0	0	0	0	0	0	0	0	0
32	12	11	4	83	2	32	152	726	54
33	0	3	3	25	0	0	9	81	2
34	34	13	32	184	54	13	7	815	74
35	0	13	0	3	0	0	13	25	1
36	6	27	0	3	0	0	26	186	11
37	0	2	0	3	0	0	6	107	2
38	10	6	0	23	0	0	15	94	16

1	2	3	4	5	6	7	8	9	10
39	0	1	2	54	0	0	7	156	14
40	0	0	0	6	0	0	3	43	29
41	0	0	0	0	0	0	7	230	1
42	0	40	0	56	0	3	58	880	15
43	0	0	1	2	1	0	0	8840	48
44	0	0	13	11	0	0	17	1099	382
45	32	27	16	106	1	44	3290	2173	3311
46	2	2	8	47	2	1	11	16	40
47	222	865	204	872	187	179	788	4184	11211
48	238	348	678	1224	60	326	446	4174	774
49	59	1899	82	374	26	43	36	175	346
50	2	11	2	46	3	1	7	5	155
51	1	14	0	80	6	0	55	14	24
52	24	180	54	214	19	30	77	149	192
53	0	0	0	0	0	0	0	0	7
54	11	839	18	264	12	3	19	85	326
55	2	1177	16	95	6	1	152	44	5506
56	3	1	1	84	1	0	8	23	30
57	0	0	0	46	0	1	0	2	8
58	6	3	40	41	2	9	28	29	47
59	26	115	83	997	57	23	33	718	1251
60	15	9	31	152	16	14	0	0	0
61	0	2228	40	1209	22	2	11	28	2357
62	33	60	38	930	209	48	22	89	216
63	2	7	2	71	7	0	10	4	3
64	7	184	40	1176	58	7	0	50	51
65	0	0	0	0	0	0	0	0	0
66	0	0	0	0	0	0	0	0	0
67	0	0	0	0	0	0	0	0	0
68	0	0	0	0	0	0	0	0	0
69	0	0	0	0	0	0	0	0	0
70	0	0	0	0	0	0	0	0	0
71	0	0	0	0	0	0	0	0	0
72	0	17	0	88	12	0	0	0	0
73	0	0	0	0	0	0	0	0	0
74	0	0	0	0	0	0	0	0	0
75	1	2	141	105	60	14	0	25	10
76	11	6	86	165	62	100	8	49	15
77	0	4	30	36	9	1	0	0	0
78	91	7	29	149	101	36	0	32	5
79	183	40	174	244	128	119	33	304	86
80	8	0	117	26	15	22	2	0	32
81	1	0	17	1	0	1	1	9	1
82	15	22	151	77	15	12	2	24	16
83	0	0	6	0	0	0	0	4	3

1	2	3	4	5	6	7	8	9	10
84	8	0	20	68	1	14	68	32	52
85	0	0	7	11	0	0	1	0	5
86	4	1	27	63	26	12	6	29	42
87	0	0	0	3	0	0	0	0	5
88	0	0	0	1	0	0	0	1	0
89	1	2	1	72	9	12	0	8	90
90	0	5	0	5	0	7	6	3	2
91	5	0	0	12	0	16	3	20	36
92	0	0	0	0	0	0	0	0	0
93	0	0	0	173	7	6	418	563	32
94	0	0	0	0	0	0	0	0	0
95	0	1865	6	72	343	0	8	14	98
96	0	0	0	0	0	0	0	0	0
97	16	6	37	60	4	21	4	68	47
98	10	8	12	82	3	1	0	27	25
99	4	37	3	130	15	19	3	89	18
100	0	7	0	2	0	0	0	1	0
101	0	0	0	0	0	0	0	0	0
102	5	28	8	425	18	18	14	123	97
103	0	0	0	0	0	0	0	0	0
104	0	1	0	1	0	0	0	2	0
105	10	36	68	368	20	87	20	127	118
106	0	0	0	10	0	1	0	0	0
107	0	0	0	0	0	0	0	0	0
108	2	4	2	76	2	14	5	40	16
109	23	22	30	156	8	28	6	91	93
110	1	1	0	6	0	0	0	3	5
111	12	58	72	166	13	10	2	47	80
112	0	51	8	81	17	4	3	2	37
113	8	12	11	113	71	23	98	99	156
114	0	0	0	17	0	0	12	50	110
115	120	72	44	586	71	40	531	1810	1267
116	0	42	10	157	3	10	3	129	56
117	0	1	0	10	0	0	10	14	19
118	28	1261	65	1225	628	3	2	23	38
119	0	0	4	3	1	0	0	11	0
120	0	19	0	4	1	0	0	0	0
121	0	2281	7	479	66	0	29	14	243
122	112	531	81	465	8	22	101	622	502
123	0	0	3	42	0	1	0	62	10
124	491	561	682	97	108	297	603	2468	685
125	17	53	53	1403	28	20	6	438	116
126	0	0	0	0	0	0	0	1	7
127	2687	96	0	0	85	4512	0	0	0
128	2	0	1	7	0	0	0	7	0
129	31	4	18	205	45	12	3	108	11
130	30	0	123	32	15	21	0	7	2
131	70	269	715	333	62	457	47	513	332
132	20	86	199	259	14	199	15	329	115

1	2	3	4	5	6	7	8	9	10
133	0	0	1	0	4	0	0	0	0
134	23	10	54	134	8	15	0	24	3
135	18	0	1059	441	18	187	96	148	221
136	32	1	271	6	2	133	0	22	15
137	12	13	1780	213	17	3	3	111	227
138	105	19	254	99	5	304	17	32	35
139	0	0	0	0	0	0	0	0	0
140	690	1424	0	0	3312	272	785	0	0
141	101	56	51	1211	109	42	12	66	47
142	54	10	33	75	97	5	0	26	16
143	—	—	—	—	—	—	—	—	—
144	4	8	50	225	25	14	41	250	123
145	1	95	12	443	24	0	4	16	23
146	2	16	23	690	29	6	4	45	32
147	5	13	16	518	41	6	20	21	32
148	34	48	46	244	151	17	24	57	64
149	0	26	0	148	1	6	2	26	35
150	1	8	3	67	17	2	9	18	14
151	0	31	15	58	65	7	0	12	7
152	0	59	1	262	9	4	4	82	3
153	0	6	7	46	0	11	0	22	17
154	2	1	7	70	0	9	0	15	20
155	1	0	0	16	0	0	0	1	0
156	3	1	6	45	3	30	0	8	15
157	0	3	12	120	0	7	0	4	1
158	3	17	3	343	28	0	10	21	8
159	3	15	24	335	6	14	5	56	36
160	9	35	10	401	26	8	16	49	18
161	0	28	21	219	7	10	1	11	7
162	1	17	6	141	27	4	3	25	4
163	38	39	117	1620	38	31	19	1329	27
164	0	126	12	294	11	3	8	15	65
165	191	203	1996	989	93	146	4	60	119
166	37	32	130	219	43	26	9	102	71
167	0	3	232	69	99	690	19	1	57
168	3	5	11	79	12	33	1	11	4
169	3	8	7	28	9	0	0	17	0
170	14	19	22045	121	29	73	0	62	5
171	7	22	29	31	13	38	1	10	10
172	0	0	153	15	3	181	2	0	0
173	0	0	0	0	0	0	0	0	215
174	4	0	0	0	0	0	9	0	0
175	46	2	161	0	0	214	0	0	0
176	0	0	45	2	1	84	0	0	5
177	5	28	60	33	4	32	0	22	9
178	4	11	11	43	41	120	2	19	4
179	4	0	0	101	133	89	0	7	1

1	2	3	4	5	6	7	8	9	10
180	23	7	30	179	13354	39	1	12	30
181	15	19	93	268	52	176	4	9	17
182	1226	5	68	2222	1317	105	87	7	61
183	0	2	29	0	0	10	0	2	1
184	7	8	30	242	10	30	0	12	5
185	1	3	32	2	2	1	3	89	3
186	8	16	45	51	5	12	3	71	27
187	18	45	65	163	19	16	6	1497	95
188	0	1	15	9	3	0	1	21	1
189	—	—	—	—	—	—	—	—	—
190	2	1	6	15	3	2	4	121	16
191	217	338	638	852	29	147	274	2977	489
192	0	0	1061	2	1	89	0	136	0
193	15	0	6	22	0	1	4	73	12
194	0	0	1	7	0	15	0	569	0
195	6	0	58	84	17	16	17	403	39
196	2	0	3	48	2	1	0	359	4
197	9	0	2	97	2	0	2	256	11
198	43	181	148	433	46	103	7	107	166
199	0	29	57	406	23	20	4	66	71
200	66	117	86	259	38	73	129	228	27
201	9	225	242	473	154	88	3	597	316
202	17	46	63	186	48	23	25	184	170
203	2	5	2	71	5	36	2	5	23
204	0	0	0	3	3	0	0	0	1
205									
206	43	1	67	165	27	0	0	0	0
207	46	85	159	469	127	0	0	548	444
208	58	337	25	566	51	0	3	1038	334
209	46	263	335	825	175	73	20	573	657
210	49	54	251	343	61	19	1	1311	282
211	53	11	29	181	35	9	7	513	198
212	1	35	33	128	63	75	12	255	222
213	25	76	2	350	60	68	10	160	271
214	3	173	4	803	216	310	3	180	230
215	51	160	64	416	106	75	2	855	183
216	11	53	20	31	6	28	0	41	76
217	6	62	57	313	2	38	40	4	277
218	0	15	21	75	0	7	1	87	54
219	0	12	0	74	0	2	1	10	12
220	0	4	7	0	4	0	8	10	6
221	0	10	4	9	1	8	31	32	50
222	2	5	7	51	3	2	43	51	276
223	1	21	0	199	0	0	26	10	760
224	5	27	10	146	12	27	69	86	258
225	1	3	2	11	1	0	5	21	52

1	2	3	4	5	6	7	8	9	10
226	5	35	2	69	13	1	2	6	6
227	0	0	0	5	0	0	0	0	0
228	0	1	0	1	0	0	3	0	31
229	4	52	14	47	6	3	16	23	123
230	4	46	29	159	26	20	83	67	92
231	0	22	6	89	1	9	0	15	13
232	0	59	5	74	1	2	1	16	35
233	0	0	0	0	0	0	0	2	17
234	0	17	8	46	4	0	0	11	10
235	1	0	0	95	0	0	0	0	4
236	10	15	21	267	8	16	10	117	261
237	0	2	2	29	0	2	0	5	347
238	0	0	0	42	0	0	0	0	0
239	0	0	0	0	0	0	0	0	0
240	0	0	0	34	0	0	0	0	1033
241	0	623	6	381	15	7	20	64	191
242	0	4	0	8	0	0	1	8	10
243	—	—	—	—	—	—	—	—	—
244	0	0	0	0	0	0	0	0	1
245	—	—	—	—	—	—	—	—	—
246	—	—	—	—	—	—	—	—	—
247	0	0	0	0	0	0	2	0	2
248	—	—	—	—	—	—	—	—	—
249	0	64	3	57	0	0	16	44	12
250	0	2	0	10	0	0	12	343	11
251	6	31	7	140	13	1	7	141	20
252	1	12	3	1	0	0	28	7	2
253	6	5	2	112	9	0	29	199	0
254	13	19	27	67	3	7	32	384	12
255	18	11	0	26	0	0	2	2	3
256	5	5	18	34	1	1	66	62	8
257	4	18	7	90	14	4	31	110	22
258	1	15	12	150	8	3	62	140	23
259	0	74	0	34	9	0	0	138	7
260	14	89	30	64	39	4	72	444	34
261	4	20	16	29	8	4	272	144	0
262	6	19	57	171	10	25	113	252	6
263	13	6	15	56	15	43	19	58	14
264	54	58	89	427	43	57	35	136	53
265	1	15	17	15	17	5	15	13	0
266	6	10	19	74	3	9	23	56	2
267	4	70	35	83	1	1	7	67	0
268	0	3	37	76	2	0	110	119	13
269	31	7	101	321	32	23	126	222	525
270	2	15	5	0	2	10	16	0	0
271	17	7	2	158	0	14	41	610	35

1	2	3	4	5	6	7	8	9	10
272	26	4	3	82	14	47	762	78	232
273	3	2	2	30	1	7	114	66	4
274	1	1	1	43	1	9	109	39	11
275	3	8	9	46	5	11	148	126	2
276	0	25	0	50	1	0	51	23	196
277	0	16	0	62	0	0	21	151	8
278	12	0	11	59	6	0	0	63	13
279	0	1	—	—	—	—	—	—	—
280	171	5	—	1	14	18	38	81	34
281	1	0	0	3	0	0	4	7	21
282	0	21	3	17	0	0	81	19	12
283	21	8	7	23	0	0	173	13	2
284	8	0	4	2	0	1	3	28	1
285	29	0	12	176	0	0	19	84	5
286	5	0	2	18	0	0	3	6	4
287	1	0	0	0	0	0	1	1	6
288	0	7	0	2	0	0	32	7	0
289	0	16	0	14	1	0	72	13	4
290	0	6	0	24	0	0	40	60	7
291	0	0	0	0	0	0	1	8	0
292	0	0	0	0	0	0	0	13	0
293	0	1	0	0	0	0	2	17	0
294	4	0	0	0	0	0	0	14	0
295	8	3	8	24	2	1	1	137	9
296	3	1	8	30	1	2	210	94	57
297	0	5	0	3	3	0	2	117	4
298	1	12	1	29	4	1	14	1717	17
299	0	3	0	0	0	0	14	136	8
300	0	0	0	0	0	0	1	122	9
301	0	0	0	2	0	1	0	417	8
302	0	0	2	0	0	0	0	285	3
303	0	0	1	0	0	0	0	197	0
304	0	18	65	128	4	13	36	148	86
305	199	285	883	1386	117	172	459	625	978
306	0	1	4	0	0	0	1	7	5
307	1	15	0	21	9	5	3	65	29
308	158	450	425	1580	203	323	4602	2758	3323
309	0	1	3	27	0	0	14	765	59
310	0	0	0	1	0	0	0	63	29
311	0	27	4	10	0	0	16	127	109
312	0	0	0	428	0	0	1	21	158
313	92	354	0	0	90	90	77	0	0
314	—	—	—	—	—	—	—	—	1
315	—	—	—	—	—	—	—	—	—
316	0	3	0	0	0	0	1	206	11
317	71	0	8	67	386	16	0	1	0

APPENDIX XIV

SHIPMENTS, RECEIPTS AND INTERACTIONS OF METROPOLITAN AND SATELLITE CENTRES

Sl. No.	*Centres*	*Originating Tonnage ('000 tonnes)*	*Terminating Tonnage ('000 tonnes)*	*Number of originating Interation*	*Number of Terminating Interactions*
1	2	3	4	5	6
1.	Bombay	5746	5565	2748	1733
2.	Nasik	48	1053	490	803
3.	Dhulia	37	137	300	428
4.	Jalgaon	46	178	396	696
5.	Khandwa	92	119	478	516
6.	Khangaon	46	65	201	413
7.	Ahola	54	248	531	749
8.	Amravathi	71	182	794	605
9.	Ahmadnagar	92	191	194	644
10.	Dehu	151	2286	1059	1140
11.	Jamnagar	565	878	637	853
12.	Porbandar	179	142	594	394
13.	Bhavnagar	338	324	1004	904
14.	Udaipur	126	144	460	513
15.	Ahmedabad	1024	2850	220	924
16.	Godhra	17	130	261	369
17.	Baroda	21	328	879	1643
18.	Gwalior	60	154	471	540
19.	Bhopal	80	236	603	642
20.	Itarsi	35	215	251	331
21.	Ratlam	31	170	553	490
22.	Nagda	63	379	175	204
23.	Indor	132	391	1066	973
24.	Ujjain	25	1512	654	536
25.	Nagpur	656	390	838	789
26.	Itwari	208	113	579	551
27.	Chandrepur	266	97	334	287
28.	Miraj	76	327	465	603
29.	Sholapur	32	327	564	772
30.	Hyderabad	7096	1682	1199	1216
31.	Warangal	36	138	247	266
32.	Gulburga	59	154	318	385
33.	Delhi	735	5650	2284	2042
34.	Ballabgarh	117	202	296	304
35	Meerut	112	472	547	749
36.	Hissar	96	325		479
37.	Kota	206	254	422	505
38.	Sawai Madhopur	639	1045	519	240

1	2	3	4	5	6
39.	Jaipur	50	160	1088	871
40.	Kanpur	994	1728	1695	1499
41.	Agra	247	1351	1161	1211
42.	Aligarh	73	144	846	521
43.	Lucknow	124	854		910
44.	Moradabad	119	197		458
45.	Bariely	128	517		760
46.	Saharanpur	84	347	320	628
47.	Ambala	95	271		469
48.	Chandigarh	245	400	461	523
49.	Jaito	178	387		804
50.	Jullundhur	142	539		738
51.	Pathonkot	60	392		379
52.	Kotkapura	80	187		249
53.	Bhatinda	82	163	390	455
54.	Patiala	226	262	264	393
55.	Calcutta	2512	9672	2826	2419
56.	Durgapur	2570	5688	914	423
57.	Dhanbad	7650	2181	1196	402
58.	Jalpaiguri	233	332	212	325
59.	Tatanagar	1341	6489	1240	676
60.	Rourkela	1170	1280	721	466
61.	Hirakud	823	711	666	593
62.	Bokaro	946	2939	435	333
63.	Asonsol	2085	1622	468	377
64.	Gauhati	207	446	524	679
65.	Vishakapattnam	1607	180	899	474
66.	Vijayawada	91	449	248	292
67.	Guntur	70	144	416	376
68.	Rajamundri	108	251	618	440
69.	Kakinada	114	413	310	276
70.	Satna	1066	370	769	470
71.	Katni	1538	903	1164	538
72.	Gondia	58	83	475	422
73.	Bhilai	2254	8613	817	501
74.	Raipur	203	195	553	673
75.	Varanasi	16	3135	672	970
76.	Allahabad	166	405	847	860
77.	Patna	600	280	747	790
78.	Gorakhpur	21	202	299	621
79.	Dehri-on-son	236	490	821	412
80.	Madras	2503	4872	1720	1561
81.	Bangalore	278	1227	1237	1083
82.	Hubli-Dharwar	105	562	414	561
83.	Raichur	53	260	183	260

1	2	3	4	5	6
84.	Salem	660	258	1092	619
85.	Erode	65	177	210	508
86.	Coimbatore	234	497	650	710
87.	Mangalore	125	212	276	366
88.	Cochin	196	254	891	673
89.	Trivendrum	14	241	281	288
90.	Tiruchirapalli	190	374	776	654
91.	Madurai	45	284	404	666
92.	Virudhunagar	530	160	674	354

SELECT BIBLIOGRAPHY

Aggarwal Y P (1979) : 'Patterns of railway freight in India : A regional analysis', unpublished M. Phil dissertation of the Centre for the Study of Regional Development, Jawaharlal Nehru University, New Delhi

Aggarwal Y P (1982) : 'Railway freight flows, transport costs and the regional structure of the Indian economy', Ph. D. thesis of the Jawaharlal Nehru University, New Delhi

Aggarwal Y P & Raza Moonis (1981) : 'Railway freight flows and the regional structure of the Indian economy', *The Geographer, No. 3 & 4*

Alampiev P M (1959): *'Economic regionalisation of U.S.S.R.', Economic Literature,* Moscow

Antia F P (1932) : *Inland Transport Cost*

Ashton W D (1966) : The Theory of Traffic Flow, Methuen, London

Assad A A (1980) : 'Models for rail transportation', *Transportation Research,* Vol 14A, No. 3, June

Barker D A (1961) : 'The railway policy in India', *Indian Journal of Economics,* vol. 1, pp. 434-439)

Beckerman W (1956) : 'Distance and the pattern of intra-European trade', *The Review of Economic & Statistics,* vol 38, pp. 31-40

Bedenkova M S (1964) : 'Rational transport — Economic link in the process of development of territorial division of labour in the USSR', *Location of productive Force and Development of Economic Regions,* Moscow

Berry B L J (1959) : 'Recent studies concerning the role of transportation in the space economy', *Annals, Association of American Geographers,* vol. 49, no. 3, pp. 328

Berry B L J (1966) : *Essays on Commodity Flows and the Spatial Structure of the Indian Economy,* Dept. of Geography, Research Paper No. 111, Chicago

Berry B L J and Marble D F eds (1971) : *Spatial Analysis : A Reader in Statistical Geography,* Prentice Hall

Bhat L S and Gidhadhubli R G (1971) : *Economic regions and regional flows, economic and socio-cultural dimensions of regionalisation, Census of India,* Census centenary monograph no. 7, Registrar General of India, New Delhi

Black W R (1972) : 'Inter-regional commodity flows Some experiments with the gravity models', *Journal of Regional Science,* vol. 12, no. 1

Britton J N H (1971) : 'Methodology in flow analysis' *East Lake Geographer,* vol. 7, pp. 22-36

Brown R E (1966) : *Transport and the Integration of South America,* The Brookings Institution, Washington

Burns R E (1969) : 'Transport planning : Selection of analytical tools', *Journal of Transport Economics & Policy,* Sept. pp. 306

Campbell J C (1972) : 'Transportation and its impact in developing countries', *Transport Journal* vol. 2, no. 1

Chakraborty S C (1978) : 'Urban economic base : A review of contemporary Indian exprience', Unpublished paper presented at the Indo-French seminar on urban growth, Jawaharlal Nehru University, New Delhi

Chakraborty S C (1980) : 'The functions of the Indian railroad system : An enquiry into the possible areas of research' *Transactions Institute of Indian Geographers,* vol. 2, no. 1

Chapman A S (1954) : 'The functional pattern of Freight traffic in Turkey', *Ann Arbour*

Chapman Keith (1919); *People and Process,* Arnold Heinemann, London

Chenery H B and Clark P G (1959) : *Inter-Industry Economics,* Wiley, New York

Chisholm M (1959) : 'Economics of scale in road goods transport of farm mills collection in England and Wales' Oxford Economic Papers, vol. 2, pp. 282-92

Chisholm M (1971) : Freight transport costs, industrial location and regional development in Chisholm M and Manners G (ed.) *Spatial Policy Problems of British Economy,* Cambridge University Press, Cambridge

Chisholm M and Manners G eds (1971) : *Spatial Policy Problems of the British Economy,* Cambridge University Press

Chisholm Michael and O'Sullivan Patrics (1973) : *Freight Flows and Spatial Aspects of the British Economy.* Cambridge University Press, Cambridge

Chojnicki E (1961) : 'The structure of economic regions in Poland analysed by commodity Flows, *Geographia Polonica,* vol. 1, pp. 213-30

Chojnicki Z and Czyz T (1970) : 'Structural changes of the economic regions in Poland : A study by factor analysis of commodity flows', *Geographia Polonica,* vol. 25, pp. 31-47

Christopher Brook and Alan Hay (1974) : *The Macro Approach—The Analysis of Regional Change,* The Open University Press

Christaller W (1932) : *Die Raumlicha Ordung Der Wirtschaft,* Jena G. Fisher

Currie A W (1959) : *Economics of Canadian Transportation,* 2nd ed., University of Toronto Press

Curry L (1972) : 'A spatial analysis of gravity flows', *Regional Studies,* vol. 6, pp. 131-147

Dalvi, M Q et. al. (1979) : 'Operational transport policy planning model for India. Some methodoiogical issues and tentative results', working paper No. 9, *UNDP Transport Policy Planning Project,* Planning Commission, New Delhi

Duncan O P et al. (1960) : *Metropolis and the Region,* John Hopkins Press

Dutta Mondira (1979) : 'Metropolis and hinterland : A spatial analysis of commodity flows in India,' Unpublished M. Phil. dissertation of the Jawaharlal Nehru University, New Delhi.

Easton J A (1957) : *An Economic Analysis of Phillipine Domestic Transportation,* vol. 2, commodity flows and passenger movement, Stanford Research Centre

Easton J A (1970) : Transportation of freight in the year 2000, Developing urban detroit area research Project and Detroit Edition C.

Eisen E E (1934) : 'The structure of the Rhine traffic', *Economic Geography, V. 10*

Eisen E E (1968): The freight transport system of Columbia, *in Stockes C J (ed) Transportation and Economic Development in Latin America,* New York,

Fogal R W (1964) : *Railroads and American Economic Growth : Essays in Economic History,* Baltimore

Freemar D B (1973) : *International Trade, Migration and Capital Flows : A Quantitative Analysis of Spatial Economic Inter-action,* research paper no. 146, Department of Geography, University of Chicago, Chicago.

Friedman J (1966) : *Regional Development and Policy : A Case Study of Venezuela,* Cambridge, Mass.

Friedmann John and Alonso William eds (1964) *Regional Development and Planning,* MIT Press, Cambridge

Fueton Maurice and Hoch Clurton (1959) : 'Transportation factors affecting location decisions', *Economic Geography,* vol. xxxv, January, pp. 51-59

Garrison W L (1960, a) : 'Connectivity of the inter state highway system', *Papers and Proceedings of Regional Science Association,* no. 6, pp. 121-37

Garrison W L (1960, b) : 'Spatial structure of the economy', *Annals of the Association of American Geographers,* v. xliv, pp. 232-239 and 471-482 : vol. 1, pp. 357-373

Garrison W L (1962) : Intra and inter-urban Networks, in Pitts, T A (ed.) *Urban Systems and Economic Development,* University of Oregon, School of Business Administration, pp. 27-38

Garrison W L and Marble D F (1962) : *The Structure of Transportation Networks,* U S Army transportation, Command Technical Report No. 62-11

Garrison W L and Marble D F (1964) : Factor analysis study of the connectivity of a transportation network, *Papers and Proceedings of the Regional Science Association,* vol. 12, pp. 211-38.

Gary Frown ed (1965) : *Transport Investment and Economic Development,* The Brookings Institure

Gauthier H L (1966) : 'Highways development and urban growth in Seo-Paulo : A nework analysis', North-west University, Ph. D. dissertation

Gauthier H L (1968) : 'Transportation and the growth of the Sao Paulo economy', *Journal of Regional Science, no. 1, pp. 77-79*

Gauthier H L (1973) : 'Transportation and the growth of the sao-Paulo economy' in Hoyle B S (ed) *Transport and Devleopment,* Macmillan

Ghosh A (1965) : *Efficiency in Location and Interz-regional Flows : The Indian Cement Industry during Five Year Plans,* North Holland

Ghosh S C (1911) : *Indian Railway and Indian Trade*

Ghosh S C (1918) : *A Monograph on Indian Railway Rates*

Golledge R S (1963): *'A geographical analysis of new castle's rail freight traffic',* *Economic Geography,* vol. 31, pp. 60-73

Gordon Ian R (1976) : Gravity demand functions, accessibility and regional trade, *Regional Studies,* v. 10, pp. 25-37

Gould P R and Smith R H T (1961) : 'Methods in commodity flows analysis,' *Australian Geographer,* vol. 8, p. 73

Government of India, Central Statistical Organisation, *National Income Statistics*

Government of India, Department of Commercial Intelligence and Statistics : *Account Relating the Inland (Rail-River Borne) Trade in India,* Calcutta

Government of India, *Regional Transport Survey Reports,* Joint Technical Group, Planning Commission, New Delhi

Government of India, Lok Sabha Secretariat, (1975) : *Ninth Report of Railway Convention Committee-(1973) : Social Burdens on Indian Railway,* New Delhi

Government of India, Ministry of Railways, (1948) *Indian Railway Enquiry Committee-1947,* New Delhi

Government of India, Ministry of Railways, (1958) *The Railway Freight Structure Enquiry Committee, 1955-57,* New Delhi

Government of India, Ministry of Railways, (1961) *Preliminary Report of the Committee on Transport Policy and Coordination,* New Delhi

Government of India, Ministry of Railways, (1978) : *Report of the Expert Group on the Capital Structure of Indian Railways,* New Delhi

Government of India, Ministry of Railways, (1979) *Report of the High Level Committee on Social Burdens on Indian Railways,* New Delhi

Government of India, Ministry of Railways, *Statistical Aid to Railway Operations,* Technical Paper No. 330

Government of India, Ministry of Railways, *Annual Report & Accounts* (for various years)

Government of India, Ministry of Railways, (1980) *Report of the Rail Traffic Enquiry Committee* (1977-1980), New Delhi

Government of India, Planning Commission, (1966) : *Final Report of Committee on Transport Policy and Co-ordination,* New Delhi

Government of India, Planning Commission, (1980) : *Report of the National Transport Policy Committee,* New Delhi

Government of India, Central Statistical Organisation, *Economic Surveys* for various years

Greenhut M L (1959) : 'Space & economic theory', *Papers & Proceedings of the Regional Science Association,* vol. v, pp. 267-280

Hagget P (1959) : *Locational Analysis in Human Geography,* Edward Arnold Publishers, London, pp. 61-152

Hagget P *et al.* (1977) : *Locational Models,* Edward Arnold, London

Hampton P and Rayner A C (1977) : 'The use of multivariate methods in economics with reference to regional analysis, *Regional Science and Urban Economics,* vol. 7, pp. 267

Harris C D (1954) : The geography of manufacturing, *American Geography Inventory & Prospect,* edited by James P E and Jones S B, Syracuse University Press, Syracuse

Harris C D (1954) : 'The market as a factor in the location of industry in the United States', *Annals of Association of American Geographers,* vol. xliv, December, pp. 315-348

Hashim S R (1966) : 'The pattern of inter-regional commodity flows, India (1950-51 to 1959-60) and a derivation of comodity flows,' unpublished Ph. D. dissertation of the University of Poona

Hashim S R (1970) : 'Inter-regional lingakes and economic regionalization', *Indian Journal of Regional Science,* vol. ii, pp. 11-20

Hashim S R (1977) : 'Inter-regional linkages and the changes in the pattern of commodity flows in India : 1950-51 to 1959-60,' *The Indian Economic Journal,* no. 2

Haughton B (1955) : *Indian Railway Network*

Hazlewood Arthur (1964) : *Rail and Road in East Africa : Transport Co-ordination in Under Developed Countries,* Monograhp of the Institute of Economic and Statistics, University of Oxford, England

Holsman A J (1975) : 'Inter-state interaction patterns in Australian economy', *Australian Geographical Studies,* vol. 18

Hoover E M (1948) : *The Location of Economic Activity,* McGraw Hill, New York

Hoyle B S (ed.) : *Transport and Development.* Mc Millan, London

Hunter Holland (1968) : *Soviet Transport Experience : Its Lessons for other Countries* The Brooking Institution Transportation Research Pragramme, Washington D C

Hurst M E (ed.) : (1974) : *Transportation Geography : Comments and Readings,* McGraw Hill

Indian Railway Conference Association (1976) :*Goods Tariff, No. 35-Part I & II,* IRCA, New Delhi

Irwin L H (1975) : Transportation for developing countries : *An Annotated Bibliography,* Cornell University, New York

Isard W (1953) : 'Regional commodity balance and inter-regional commodity flows', *The American Economic Review,* vol. xliii, no. 2, May, p. 167

Isard W (1954) : 'Location theory and trade theory : Short-run analysis', *Quarterly Journal of Economic.* vol. lxviii.

Isard W and Merton J Peak (1954) : 'Location theory and international and inter-regional trade theory' *Quarterly Journal of Economic* vol. lxviii, p. 97

Israd Walter (1956) : *Location and Space Economy,* MIT Press, Cambridge, pp. 1-9

Israd Walter (1960) : *Methods of Regional Analysis : An Introduction to Regional Science,* MIT Press, Cambridge

Jean Weelbrook (1966) 'The growth propelled export models of international trade : Empirical basis and dynamic stability', unpublished research paper, University Libre de Bruzelles and MIT, p. 5-16

Johnson J J (1963) *The Economic of Indian Rail Transport*, Bombay, Allied

Johnston R J (1966) : 'An index of accessibility and its use in the study of bus services and settlement patterns', *Tidscrift Voor Economische on Sociale Geographic*, vol. 37, pp. 33-38

Joseph De Salvo (1973) . *Perspectives on Regional Transportation Planning*, Lexington Books Lexington

Kakar K L (1968) : *Transport Costs—Rail and Road*

Kansny K J (1963) : *Structure of Transportation Networks : Relationship Between Network Geomatry and Regional Characteristics*, University of Chicago, Deptt. of Geography Research Paper No. 84, University of Chicago Press

Kar N R (1963) : 'Economic character of metropolitan sphere of influence of Calcutta', *Geographical Review of India*, vol. xxl, no. 2

Khan Shah Alam (1973) : Study of highway inpact and its effect in developing countries, Masters Thesis, Cornall University, Cornell

Khurana Indu (1979) : Economic Base and Freight Characteristics : A study of the Indian urban system, Unpublished M.Phil Dessertation of the Jawaharlal Nehru University, New Delhi

Kistanev V V (1965) : 'Complex development specialisation of the economic regions, *Ekonomics*, Moscos

Konig Benes (1936) : *Theoric Der Endlichen and Unendlichen Grapher*, Leipzing

Kumar A (1977) : 'Transport Connectivity and the Regional Structure of Indian Economy—A Spatial Analysis, Unpublished M.Phil Dissertation, CSRD, Jawaharlal Nahru University, New Delhi

Kusch H H (1937) : 'Structure of the eibe river traffic', *Economic Geography*, vol. 13, pp. 53-67

Lananne Leon (1963) : An essay on the theory of railway system based on observation of facts and the basic laws governing population distribution in *Compnes Reudus Des Saunces* de l Academic Des Sciences, lvii, p. 206

Lefebber Louis (1958) : *Allocation in Space*, North Holland, Amsterdam

Lefebar L & Chaudhary Dutta (1971) : *Regional Development Experiece in South and South East Asia*, Mouton, Paris

Lewis D E (1978) : 'Regional trade flows of manufactured products', *The Annals of Regional Science*, vol. 12, November, no. 2

Longbrake D E (1964) : 'The regional and inter-regional relations of the port of Madras'. unpublished Masters dissertation, Department of Geography, University of Chicago

Losch A (1940) : *Raumlicha Ordung Der Wrtschraft* Jena G. Fisher

Lowry I S (1965) : 'A short course in model design'. *Journal of the American Institute of Planners*, vol. xxxi, no. 2, pp. 158-65

Maotjamo B P (1974) : 'A method to rationlize fare and freight rate differences : Within and between regions', *Indian Journal of Regional Science*, vol. 6, no. 2

Mayer H M (1945) : 'Emerging developments in intercity transportation', *The Annals of the Americal Academy of Political and Social Science*, Nov. pp. 52-66

Mayer H M (1954) : 'Accessibility as a measure of the extent of urban modality in the Chicago region', *Abstract, Annals Association of the American Geographers*, vol. 44, pp. 226-27

Mayer H M (1970) : 'Making a living in cities : The urban economic base', *A Geography of Urban Place : Selected Reading* ed. Putnam R J Taylor P J and Ketele P G Methuen, pp. 125-42

Mehta N B (1972) : *Indian Railways — Rates and Reguations*

Meyer John R (1963) : 'Regional economics : A survey', *American Economic Review*, Vol. LII, March 1963, pp. 47-48

Meyer J R (ed.) : (1971) : *Techniques of Transport Planning* The Brooking Institution Transportation Research Programme, Washington D C

Mitsuhashi Setsuko (1970) : 'Japanese commodity flows', Selected Papers. Vol. II, 'Economic Geography, 21st

International Geographical Conference, India, 1968. National committe for Geography, Calcutta. pp. 177

Modak S K and Pat Kar V N (1979) : A Macro-model for optimization of inter-modal mix in freight transport, *Indian Journal of Regional Science*, Vol. XI, No. 1

Mridula Krishna (1980) : *Economics of Transport : A Trend Report in Survey of Research in Economics, Vol. VI, Infrastructure*, Indian Council of Social Science Research, New Delhi

Munshi Sunil (1975) : 'Railway network growth in eastern India : 1854-1910', Occassional paper No. 3, Centre for Studies in Social Sciences, Calcutta (mimeo)

Munshi S K (1980) : *Geography of Transportation in Eastern India under the British Raj*, Mongraph No. 1 Centre for Studies in Social Sciences, Calcutta

Myrdal G (1957) : *Economic Theory of Under-Development*, Duckworth

National council of Applied Economic Research (1962) : *Economic Atlas of Madras State*, NCAER, New Delhi

National council of Applied Economic research (1963) : *Transport Requirements of Iron & Steel belt*, NCAER, New Delhi

NCAER (1972) : 'Market towns and spatial development', National Council of Applied Economic Research, New Delhi

Nelson H J (1955) : A service classification of American Cities, *Economic Geography*, Vol. 31, No. 3, July, p. 189

Olsson G (1965) : *Distance and Human Interaction A Review and Bibliography*, Regional Science Institute

Olsson R (1964) : 'Commodity flows and regional inter-dependence,' *Papers and Proceedings Regional Science Association*, Vol. 12, pp. 225-30

Order A (1965) : 'The transhipment problems', *Management Science*, Vol. 2, pp. 276-85

Owen W (1965) : Transport and economic development, *American Economic Review*, Vol. 49, p. 179

Owen W (1968) : *Distance and Development : Transport and Communication in India*, The Brookings Institution

Pal M N (1975) : Regional disparities in the levels of development in India, *Indian Journal of Regional Science*, Vol. 7, No. 1

Patton D (1956) : 'The Traffic pattern on American Inland waterways', *Economic Geography*, No. 132, pp. 29-37

Perle E D (1964) : *The Demand for Transportation : Regional and Commodity Studies in the U S*, Unversity of Chicago, Deptt. of Geography, Research Paper No. 95

Pitfield D E (1978) : The volume of internal and external trade : Is Britain a closed economy, *Regional Studies*, Vol. 12, 1978, pp. 665-682

Potts R B and Oliver R M (1972) : *Flows in Transport Network*, Academic Press

Pred A (1964) : 'Toward a typology of manufacturing flows', *Geographical Review*, Vol. 54, pp. 65-84

Probst A F (1962) : 'Location of industry under Socialism (Theoratical Eassavs)', *Ekonomizat*, Moscow

Rail India Technical and Economic Services Limited (1978) : *Inception Report : Study on Medel Cost, Traffic Flows and Transport Network*, New Delhi

Rail India Technical and Economic Services Limited (1979) : *Interim Report on Commodity Flows, Volume I*, New Delhi

Ramachandran, H (1973) : 'Transport in Tamil Nadu — network and connectivity analysis', Unpunlished M Phil. dissertation, CSRD, J N U, New Delhi

Ramachandran, H (1977) : Transportation and Urban Attributes in the Coimbatore Region — A Case Study of an Interacting System, Unpublished Ph.-D, dissertation, CSRD, J N U, New Delhi

Ramachandran N (1975) : Commodity Flows and the Spatial Organisation of the Indian Economy — A Case Study of Punjab, Unpublished M Phil. dissertation, CSRD, J N U, New Delhi

Ramachandran N (1979) : Commodity Flows and the Regional Organisation of the Indian Economy, Ph. D. dissertation, Jawaharlal Nehru University, New Delhi

Rao C L (1949) : 'On the distance between two populations' *Sankhya.* Vol. IX, pp. 246-48

Rao MA (1975) : *Indian Railways Series : India—The Land and People,* National Book Trust

Ray D M (1965) : *Market Potential and Economic Shadow : A Quantitative Analysis of Industrial Location in Southern Ontaric,* Research Paper No. 101, Department of Geography, University of Chicago, Chicago

Raza Moonis AggarwalY P (1980, a) : Distance decay and Railways freight flows in India : A preliminary enquiry', *Indian Journal of Regional Science,* Vol. XII, No. 1

Razo Moonis Aggarwal Y P (1980, b) : Metropoles and the Spatial Organization of the Indian Economy : A Case Study of Under-development', Paper presented at the International Conference on Planning and Management of Metropolitan Regions : Nagoya, Japan, October, 1980

Raza Moonts & Aggarwal Y P (1981) : 'Commodity flows and levels of development in India : A districtwise analysis' in L R Singh (ed), *New Prespectives in Geography,* Thinker's Library, Allahabad, pp. 47

Raza Moonis Aggarwal Y P and Khurana Indu (1980) : 'economic base and commdity flows : A case study of the Indian urban system'. *The National Geographical Journal of India,* Vol. 25, Parts 3 & 4, Sept-Dec. pp. 157-173

Raza Moonis, Habeeb Atiya Kundu Amitabh and Aggarwal Yash Pal (1981) : *Urbanization and National Development : Some Aspects of the Indian Experience,* United Nations, Centre for Regional Development, Nagoya, Japan

Raza Moonis & Aggarwal Y P (1983) : Urbanization in a fragmented world : some Aspects of international inequities, *Urban India,* Vol. 3 No.2

Reed W E (1967) : *Areal interaction in India : Commodity flows of the Bihar Bengal Industrial Area,* Dept. of Geography, Research Paper No. 110, University of Chicago

Reed W E (1970) : 'Indirect connectivity of hierarchies of urban dominance', *Annals, Association of the American Geographers,* Vol. 60. pp. 770-85

Rimmer, P J (1970) : *Freight Forwarding in Australia,* Dept. of Human Geography, HG/4 Research School of pacific Studies, Australian National University, Canberra

Rosenbluth G (1957) : *Concentration of Canadian Manufacturing Industries,* National Bureau of Economic Research, Princeton University Press, Princeton

Saxena H M (1975) : *Geography of Transport and Market Centres — A Case Study of Hadaoti Plateau,* S Chand and Co. New Delhi

Sdasyuk G (1968) : *'Transport and formation of economic regions in India' in Sengupta P and Sdasyuk G, Economic Regionalsation of India-Problems and Prospects,* Census of India — 1961, Monograph Series. Vol. 1, No.8

Shah K T (1923) : *Trade, Tariffs & Transport in India,* National Book Depot, Bombay

Shimbel A (1953) : 'Structural parameters of communication networks, *Bulletin of Mathematical Bio-physics.* No. 15, pp. 501-507

Singh J (1966) : 'A Precpective on the pattern and problems of coal transport in India', *National Geographical Journal of India* Vol. 12, No. 2, p. 96

Singh J (1970) : 'Transport network, traffic flow and locasian of industries in the Iron and Steel Belt of India, *Selected Paper Vol. II Economic Geography 21st International Geographical Congress,*

Singh V L and B K Misra (1976) : 'The beta and gamma indices of graph theroretic measures of comparing transport network in the districts of Orissa in retation to composite development indicators', *Research Bulletin No. 3,* Eastern Geographical Society, Utkal University. Bhubaneswar

Smith R H T (1963) : 'Railway commodity movements between new South Wales and Victoria — The 1960 Pre-Scandinavion Situation', *Australian Geographer* Vol. 9, pp. 88-96

Smith R H T (1970, a) : 'Concepts and methods in commodity flow analysis', *Economic Geography,* Vol. 46, pp. 404-76

Smith R H T (1970, b) : Inter-regional trade as a component of National unity' in Chatterjee, S P (ed). *Proceeding of the 21st IGU Conference,* National Comittee for Geography. Calcutta

Smith R H T & Gould P R (1961) : Methods in commodity flow studies. *Australian Geographer,* Vol. VIII, p. 73-77.

Smith R H T and Hay A M (1969) : 'A theory of spatial structure of internal trade in under-developed countries', *Geographical Analysis,* Vol. 1, 1969, pp. 121-36

Spiegalgias S (1960) : 'Some aspects of state to state commodity flows in the U S', *Journal of Regional Science,* Vol. 2. pp. 71-80

Steed G P F (1968) : 'Commodity flows and inter-industry linkages of Northern Irelands' Manufacturing Industries'. *Tijdscrift Voor Economische on Social Geographie,* Vol. 59, pp. 245-59

Susuki Keisuke (1971) : 'Observations on the stability of the inter-regional flow of goods' *Journal of Regional Science.* Vol. 11, No. 2

Taafle (1962) : 'Transportation and regional specialization : The example of Soviet Central Asia', *Annals of Association of American Geographers,* Vol. 52, pp. 80-98

Taaffe R N (1970) : *Rail Transportation and Economic Development of South Central Asia,* Research Paper No. 64. University of Chicago, Dept. of Geography, Chicago

Taaffe E J Gauthier H L Jr (1973) : *Geography of Transportation,* Foundations of Economic Geography Series, Printice Hall, Inc

Tewari A K (1972) : 'Connectivity of transport network', *Analytical Geography,* pp. 88-96

Tewari C P (1921) : *The Indian Railway : Their Historical Economical and Administrative Aspects.*

Tewari R D (1937) : *Railway Rates in India*

Tewari R D (1941) : *Railways in Modern India,* New Book Co.

Thompson J M (1974) : *Modern Transport Economics,* Penguin Modern Economics Texts, Middlex, England

Thorner D (1955) : 'The pattern of railway development in India', *Far Eastern Quarterly,* Vol. 14, p. 201

Ullman E L (1954) : 'Geography as spatial interaction', Annals of the *Association of American Geographers,* No. 44

Ullman E L (1956) : The role of transportation and the bases of Interaction, in *Man's role in Changing the face of Earth,* Thomas william L ed. university of Chicago Press, Chicago pp. 862-880

Ullman E L (1957) : *American Commodity Flows, A Geographical Interpretation of Rail & Water Traffic Based on Principles of Spatial Interchange,* University of Washington Press

Ullman E L (1967) : *Urban Goods Movement Demand,* Columbus Ohio : Battelle Memorial Institute.

Ullmam E L (1970) : 'The urban movement of Goods', *Proceedings of the 3rd Technology Assessment Review,* Washington, D C Organisation for Economic Co-operation and Development

United Nations Industrial development organisation (1971) : *Industrial Location and Regional Development,* Proceedings of International Seminar, Minsk, August 1968, United National, New York

U S Congress Senate (1973) : Committee on agriculture and forestry, *The Immovable Feast* Washington D C U S Government Printing Office, pp. 134

Watch W F (1974): *The Domestic Air Transporiation New work of the United States,* Research Paper No. 154, Department of Geography, University of Chicago, Chicago

Wallace I (1974): 'The relationship between freight transport organisation and industrial linkage in Britain', *The Institure of British Geographical Transaction,* No. 62, July 1974, pp. 25

Wallace W H (1958): 'Railroad traffic densities and densities and patterns', *Annals Association of American Geographers,* No 48, pp. 352-32

Wallace W F (1963): 'Freight traffic functions of Anglo American railroads', *Annals, Association of American Geographers,* Vol. 53, 1963. pp. 312-32

Walters A A (1968): *Integration of Freight Transport,* London, the Institute of Urban Affairs

Webb M (1972): *Transporting Goods by Roads, Policies, Techniques and Distribution Efficiency,* London School of Economics, London

Williams E S Jr (1962): *Freight Transportation in the Soviet Union* N J Princeton University Press, pp. 122

Wilson A G (1967): 'A statisical theory of spatial distribution models, *Transportation Research,* Vol. 1, pp. 253-69

Wilson A G (1970): 'Inter-regional commodity flows Entropy maimizing appoaches', *Geographical Analysis,* Vol. 2, pp. 255-82

Wiseman Robert (1976): Interpretation of factored flow data : A comparison of two traffic systems : *The Professional Geographer,* Vol. XXVIII, No. 2

INDEX